The Philosophy of Virginia Woolf

ALSO AVAILABLE FROM BLOOMSBURY

Modernist Lives, Claire Battershill
A Poetic Philosophy of Language, Philip Mills

The Philosophy of Virginia Woolf

Moments of Becoming

Thomas Nail

BLOOMSBURY ACADEMIC
LONDON • NEW YORK • OXFORD • NEW DELHI • SYDNEY

BLOOMSBURY ACADEMIC
Bloomsbury Publishing Plc
50 Bedford Square, London, WC1B 3DP, UK
1385 Broadway, New York, NY 10018, USA
29 Earlsfort Terrace, Dublin 2, Ireland

BLOOMSBURY, BLOOMSBURY ACADEMIC and the Diana logo are
trademarks of Bloomsbury Publishing Plc

First published in Great Britain 2025

Copyright © Thomas Nail, 2025

Thomas Nail has asserted his right under the Copyright,
Designs and Patents Act, 1988, to be identified as Author of this work.

For legal purposes the Acknowledgments on p. xvi constitute
an extension of this copyright page.

Cover design: Ben Anslow
Cover image: Blue Acrylic Pour Color Liquid marble abstract surfaces Design.
(© zodar / AdobeStock)

All rights reserved. No part of this publication may be reproduced or transmitted
in any form or by any means, electronic or mechanical, including photocopying,
recording, or any information storage or retrieval system, without prior
permission in writing from the publishers.

Bloomsbury Publishing Plc does not have any control over, or responsibility for,
any third-party websites referred to or in this book. All internet addresses given
in this book were correct at the time of going to press. The author and publisher
regret any inconvenience caused if addresses have changed or sites have
ceased to exist, but can accept no responsibility for any such changes.

A catalogue record for this book is available from the British Library.

A catalog record for this book is available from the Library of Congress.

ISBN: HB: 978-1-3505-2606-8
 PB: 978-1-3505-2605-1
 ePDF: 978-1-3505-2607-5
 eBook: 978-1-3505-2608-2

Typeset by Integra Software Services Pvt. Ltd.
Printed and bound in Great Britain

To find out more about our authors and books visit www.bloomsbury.com
and sign up for our newsletters.

For Jared Nieft

Contents

Preface ix
Acknowledgments xvi
Works by Virginia Woolf xvii

Introduction 1

Part One A Theory of Moments 11

1 Woolf's Process Materialism 13

2 Let Us Trace the Patterns 25

Part Two Moments of Being 45

Brief Moments 47

    Moment 0: The Trance into Which Movement Had Thrown Them 47

Individual Moments 65

    Moment 1: Neither This nor That 65

    Moment 2: Connected by Millions of Fibers 72

    Moment 3: The Death of the Soul 78

    Moment 4: Time Split Its Husk; Poured Its Riches over Him 89

    Moment 5: The Knotted Roots of Infinite Ages 97

    Moment 6: She Felt Herself Everywhere 106

    Moment 7: The Lake of Being 115

Moment 8: The Fluidity of Life 124

Moment 9: There Is No Stability in This World 136

Non-Human Moments 149

Moment 10: Part I, A Glimpse Only 149

Moment 10: Part II, Stars Flashing in Their Hearts 162

Extended Moments 173

Moment 11: Part I, Hail! Natural Desire! 173

Moment 11: Part II, The Beauty of Movement 182

Moment 12: Everything Was Partly Something Else 197

Collective Moments 207

Moment 13: The World Wavered 207

Moment 14: "The Moment: Summer's Night" 214

Moment 15: Now the Current Flows 222

Conclusion: Moments of Being Political 235

Appendix 245
Notes 247
Index 270

Preface

Imagine that you are on a walk one day and your senses suddenly widen so that your whole body feels like a highly sensitive spiderweb that can pick up and respond to every tiny vibration around you. Your five senses, emotions, and thoughts are all amplified from their average volume level of 5 to their maximum of 10. The space around you that seemed empty is now completely saturated with innumerable tiny perceptions. You feel as if all your pores have opened up, and your body has become a vessel floating in a stream of tiny vibrations that together form waves and patterns of rippling sensation previously invisible to you. All your senses become magnified and begin to mix and mingle to the point that you can see birds' sounds echoing through the trees and smell the color of the sky.

Imagine that in this stream of saturated feeling, everything begins to lose its sharp edges, including your thoughts. You see that each singular feature of the world is deeply woven into the others around you in clearly iterated but irregular patterns. Instead of isolated objects in empty space, you can now see that things connect through long chains of tiny contiguous relationships, each nested and playing off the others. You feel your body is the world itself folded up and iterated in a unique way. When this shift first begins to take hold you feel a tinge of fear that some impersonal force may be dissolving you, but if you let the force continue it brings immense joy.

Imagine that you could hold your attention long enough on a flower bud to watch it bloom in time-lapse. Imagine finally that your saturated perception of these tiny vibrations becomes broader and broader until it encompasses your city, your country, the Earth, and the cosmos. Each smaller space is nested into larger ones. Each singularity is imbricated and iterated through others in fractal patterns like tree branches. You also feel time begin to dilate. As singular sensations multiply, the present starts to expand like a drop of water gathering in a cloud, larger and larger until it reaches the size of a year, then a decade, then a century, and then the duration of the universe. The world changes before your eyes, but no chronological time seems to pass. It is as if you are living in an eternal present filled with sensual ecstasy.[1] All things feel interrelated.

This is what Virginia Woolf called a "moment of being."

As a philosopher reading Virginia Woolf, these are the moments I find most striking and philosophical. When I read Woolf I follow her lovely linear narrative for about thirty to fifty pages, but then suddenly the world of the novel begins to waver and ripple like the surface of a pool. The character's senses start to widen and become synesthetic.[2] Space and time begin to dilate. The characters catch a glimpse of some profoundly different and interpenetrating reality below the surface of things. Then, just as suddenly as they come, the moments pass, and the narrative resumes sometimes as if nothing had happened. Woolf's characters reach no particular epiphany in these moments.[3] The moments are beautiful, luminous, but ephemeral.

These sudden and fleeting moments have always been my favorite parts of her novels. Over the years, I found myself returning to them again and again. I wanted to recapture the feeling of their profound strangeness and joy. And over time, I started to build a collection of my favorite and most sustained moments of being in her novels so that whenever I wanted to recapture those feelings, I could pick up her books and read a few moments in a row like fireworks. The effect was striking. I could immediately feel my thoughts in these moments, as many readers probably do, working very differently than before I picked up the book. After a while, I started to feel like these little moments were like doses of some beautiful and mysterious tonic or medicine.

I wrote this book because these moments captured my imagination, and I wanted to understand the philosophy behind them. I want to present here some of their common features, what they tell us about the nature of reality, and their consequences for a number of traditional philosophical questions.

The first feature I noticed in my research of these moments was the striking use of fluid dynamic images that accompany them. In these moments, solid objects dissolve, and the world begins to *flow*. They seem to be re-activating the etymological heart of the word "moment," from the Latin word *momentum*, thus becoming "movements of being." For instance, Woolf describes moments of being with fluid images such as mists, clouds, fogs, halos, wind, waves, ripples, streams, floods, currents, pools, tides, and whirling eddies. Woolf's moments of being contain some of the highest concentrations of fluid dynamic imagery in all her writing. This was my first clue that Woolf's moments of being were working as unique philosophical descriptions about the patterned and processual nature of reality.

The second feature I discovered was how the moments from her novels matched up with her autobiographical description of moments of being. There are two aspects that Woolf attributes to her own experience of these "moments."

Early in her life, she says they felt more frightening, impersonal, like enemies attacking her. Later, however, she discovered that if she tried to understand them and write about them, they revealed "hidden patterns" in reality and the greatest joy she had ever known. I noticed that the characters in her novels had similar experiences that could be terrifying and ecstatic at the same time when they saw these patterns in moments of being.

I also noticed that not all moments of being were the same across her texts. They all shared some core features, but Woolf also experimented with them over time. For instance, in her early novels *The Voyage Out* and *Night and Day*, she described only brief moments. Then, starting with *Mrs. Dalloway,* the moments of being got longer and more developed around single individuals. In *To the Lighthouse*, Woolf then expanded a moment of being to a large block of time which included non-human agencies. Then, in *Orlando*, she combined individual and historical moments into a new and even more sustained transpersonal moment. In *Mrs. Dalloway*, the short piece "The Moment: Summer's Night," and *The Waves*, Woolf also experimented with the idea of a collective moment of being shared by several people at once. To get a quick view of this, I created an Appendix to this book, where I put a reference graph showing the length and type of all these moments.

The subtitle of this book, *Moments of Becoming,* refers to Woolf's phrase "moments of being," which she used in her autobiography to describe the most significant experiences in her life. There, she says that these moments defined her "*philosophy*" and made her an artist. When I first read her unfinished autobiography, "Sketches of the Past," I was struck by her description of these moments and felt an immediate resonance with my favorite passages from her novels.[4] If Woolf says she has "a philosophy," what is it?

However, Woolf only used the precise term "moments of being" about her personal experiences, so many scholars have treated moments of being as strictly biographical.[5] Nevertheless, I could not help but notice that the same terms she used to describe her own moments, such as "shock," "vision," "blow," and "moment," also appear throughout her novels in such moments for her characters. Perhaps her characters were also having moments of being. This resonance prompted me to dig deeper into these moments and their precursors and see how Woolf adapted them in her novels. I was also curious to know why she called these moments her "philosophy." What kinds of philosophical insights come from these moments? This is the line of questioning I have tried to trace for the reader in the first two chapters of this book.

The phrase "moments of *becoming*" is my way of emphasizing the fluid and transformative nature of Woolf's moments of being. I use the word "becoming" in this book's title because I want to highlight a key feature of Woolf's philosophical method: *movement*.[6] In all the moments of being I explore in this book, it is *movement* (of traffic, urban crowds, seasons, water, sound, wind, etc.) that initiates the *shock* of a moment of being. Motion is crucial. After the first shock of a movement, the whole world begins to flow together. In her autobiography Woolf explicitly said that moments of being were more than internal states. They were glimpses into the *reality* behind the cotton wool of daily things. This and its philosophical consequences are what I want to look at in this book.

What is a moment of being? When I first started studying these moments, I only had a vague feeling that all these significant passages had *something* in common, but I was not sure *precisely* what that was. As I slowly worked through them one after the other, I began to see the "pattern behind the cotton wool," as Woolf says (MB, 72). All her moments of being involved *processes of interrelated movement* between:

- Subject and object
- Movement and stability
- Space and time
- The senses (synesthesia)
- Life and death

Moments of being reveal reality as in flux, motion, and becoming, and characterize Woolf's "philosophy" as one of movement. Or at least this is the argument I want to make in this book.

Moments of being share some features with altered states of consciousness, including mania, hypnotic states, dream states, meditation, psychedelic states, and mystical experiences.[7] Many scholars believe Woolf was what we now call "manic depressive." She had hallucinations, took psychotropic/hypnotic sedatives (chloral hydrate), and spent more time than most in various dream states on bed rest.[8]

There is no doubt in my mind that the frequency and duration of her altered states of consciousness played an influential part in her moments of being.[9] Among other things, they helped shape her unique perspective on reality. The moments she describes in her novels also shed light on her illness and her altered states of consciousness.

However, Woolf's altered states of being were neither unmediated revelations of divine truth nor irrelevant delusions to be dismissed as pathological "illness." Instead, I argue in this book, they tell a particular philosophical story about the world that we can study and make use of without uncritically favoring it or unfairly discriminating against it *merely because* a "madwoman wrote it." Woolf's writing continues to shed rare light on one of the most mysterious and exciting features of reality: what we might call "the material unconscious." For this reason, among others, it is worth taking her work seriously and *philosophically*.

Who is this book for? I wrote this book for anyone who wants to learn more about Woolf's philosophy and her moments of being. It is not intended as a book of literary criticism or Woolf scholarship. It does not offer *literary* close readings that show how various elements such as syntax, sentence structure, metaphor, irony, juxtaposition, and formal structures relate to one another in a written composition. It does not compare and contrast Woolf with other post-war literary modernists, or look at her use of modernist techniques such as the use of irony, avant-garde modification of the Victorian realist novel, or cross-medial engagements with painting and music, and it does not treat her deep training in the history of literature. Nor does this book seek to draw significantly on Woolf's biography or her historical context to show how her work relates to the First World War. There are volumes of excellent scholarship on these important issues already.

My questions and methods are different. My question is: "What is Woolf's philosophy?" My method is to locate the *one concept* she explicitly said defined her philosophy, her "moments of being," and describe in detail how its key philosophical characteristic of "kinetic interrelation" works. I treat her moments as philosophical descriptions of the *process-nature* of knowledge, beauty, consciousness, and reality. In other words, I am a philosopher reading literature *as philosophy*, not using literature as an example or illustration of a philosopher's concept. I could have written this book as an intellectual history or an author study that charted Woolf's relation to the philosophers of her time. But I chose to restrict my discussion of this issue to a short review of the books and essays that have already done this. Instead, what makes this book's method distinctly philosophical is that I have decided to read Woolf as professional philosophers read other philosophers: as having her *own* rich and original philosophical understanding of the world worthy of study.

There is currently no consensus among scholars about what a moment of being looks like in Woolf's novels or why she calls this her "philosophy." Nor has anyone tried to trace the development of Woolf's moments of being across all her novels to establish a philosophical idea at work in them. As far as I know, this is the first book to attempt to answer these questions and trace the development of these moments in her work into a unique philosophical idea and method.

In my view, Woolf's work is not merely an example or illustration of Deleuze's or someone else's philosophy.[10] There are certainly connections between Woolf's thought and the tradition of what philosophers call "process philosophy," but I believe Woolf also makes her own original contribution to it.[11] My central argument in this book is that Woolf was a process philosopher of motion and that she manifested this philosophy in her moments of being.

Yet, Woolf also says that writing about her moments of being was therapeutic and brought her the greatest joy she has ever known. I think this is also how she would want us to read these moments. In addition to their philosophical insight, I hope they also bring great pleasure to the reader as they have to me. I have thus written this book as a kind of *philosophical amplification* of Woolf's work. I hope it can deepen and extend our appreciation of Woolf's moments to see them together like this.

This book is a trip or travel guide to these moments, not a substitute for them. The book's goal is to amplify the philosophical effects of the original medicine, not explain them away. I hope my expositions and elaborations of Woolf's moments of being will be part of a thoughtful set and setting for their philosophical enjoyment. I hope this book will show readers the patterns hidden across Woolf's moments of being.

Moments of being are events that the conscious mind can glimpse only with extraordinary effort and mostly seem "strange." Yet, we rarely forget them. Woolf's moments help provoke a broader range of perception than is usually available to us in daily life. Woolf's philosophy is thus less a systematic philosophy in the style of the Cambridge philosophers around her at the time than a description of the pre-philosophical material conditions of philosophy itself. In other words, moments of being are not moments of transcendence outside the world, but rather less filtered perceptions of it than we normally have. If reading these moments collected in this book begins to feel like a hallucination, this is normal.[12] Its effects are working.

I have curated these moments because I was interested in how they work directly on our bodies and brains in the world. I was less interested in their literary structure or how they compared to things other philosophers said than how these moments entrain the reader's senses to a world in motion. Perhaps next time you are riding a train, watching traffic flow by, or looking out a window at a tree, or walking along a busy urban sidewalk, you will feel yourself like *Mrs. Dalloway* melting into the stream of the world or cutting through it like a knife.

Or, maybe, like Bernard from *The Waves,* you will find yourself looking more closely at all the micro-movements and sensations of the world that you typically ignore. Perhaps you will forget for a while where you are going, what time it is, and who you are. You may find yourself living and breathing in the ecstasy of an expanded geological time scale.

The famous Chilean-French film director Alejandro Jodorowsky once said in an interview that he wanted his films to change human perception just like LSD did. "I wanted to make a film that would give the people who took LSD at the time the hallucinations that you get with that drug, but without hallucinating."[13] Among other things, I have a similar hope for this book. By assembling and intensifying some of Woolf's most sustained moments of being, I hope the reader will become more capable of the "shocks" Woolf felt and considered a "philosophy."

Acknowledgments

In the publication of this book, I am grateful for the feedback of the anonymous reviewers of this book who provided encouragement and constructive criticism. I thank the Bloomsbury Press staff who helped edit this book, and in particular Liza Thompson, for her unflagging support for this project.

Many thanks especially to my colleague Jared Nieft who read early drafts of this manuscript and taught it to his students, whose enthusiasm, in turn, motivated me through many revisions of this manuscript over the years. I also thank my research assistant Jacob Tucker for his help in researching, editing, and proofing versions of this book. He also helped assemble the Appendix of this book.

Although I began this book based on a love of Woolf's moments of being, I completed it for my peers and students who found inspiration in these moments as well. For the past several years I have taught an upper-division philosophy seminar called "Great Thinkers: Virginia Woolf," and through it I have learned much from my students and colleagues at the University of Denver. It has been a great joy. The University of Denver also provided financial support for this book's index.

Works by Virginia Woolf

BA   *Between the Acts* (New York: Harcourt, 1941).

CR1 *The Common Reader* (New York: Harcourt, 1925).

CR2 *The Second Common Reader* (New York: Harcourt, 1932).

CSF *The Complete Shorter Fiction of Virginia Woolf* (New York: Harcourt, 1985).

D1–5 *The Diary of Virginia Woolf* (New York: Harcourt, 1977, 1978, 1980, 1982, 1984).

E1–6 *The Essays of Virginia Woolf* (New York: Harcourt, 1986, 1987, 1988, 1994, 2010, 2011).

F   *Flush: A Biography* (New York: Harcourt, 1933).

L1–6 *The Letters of Virginia Woolf* (New York: Harcourt, 1975, 1976, 1977, 1978, 1979, 1980).

JR   *Jacob's Room* (New York: Harcourt, 1922).

MB   *Moments of Being* (New York: Harcourt, 1976).

MD   *Mrs. Dalloway* (New York: Harcourt, 1925).

ND   *Night and Day* (New York: Harcourt, 1920).

O   *Orlando: A Biography* (New York: Harcourt, 1928).

PA   *A Passionate Apprentice* (New York: Harcourt, 1990).

RO   *A Room of One's Own* (New York: Harcourt, 1929).

TG   *Three Guineas* (New York: Harcourt, 1938).

TL   *To the Lighthouse* (New York: Harcourt, 1927).

VO   *The Voyage Out* (New York: Harcourt, 1920).

W   *The Waves* (New York: Harcourt, 1931).

Y   *The Years* (New York: Harcourt, 1939).

Introduction

There is no philosophic error so enormous as to count as philosophers only the philosophers.[1]
—PAUL VALÉRY

Toward the end of her life, Virginia Woolf declared for the first time that she had a "philosophy,"—the "constant idea" that "makes her a writer." This is the same idea which gave her "the strongest pleasure known to [her]."

> Behind the cotton wool is hidden a pattern that we—I mean all human beings are connected with this; that the whole world is a work of art; that we are parts of the work of art. Hamlet or a Beethoven quartet is the truth about this vast mass that we call the world. But there is no Shakespeare, there is no Beethoven; certainly and emphatically there is no God; we are the words; we are the music; we are the thing itself. And I see this when I have a shock.

She called these shocks "exceptional moments" or "moments of being" (MB, 72).

This book's thesis is that these moments are the key to understanding Woolf's unique philosophical contribution. In her description of these moments, Woolf gives us a description of a world in motion and process, where all of nature and matter flow, ripple, quiver, and interconnect. In these moments, the division between humans and nature dissolves into flows and metastable patterns. In these moments, matter is dynamic, and what originally appeared fixed is perceived as woven, porous, and fluid. This dynamism is why I also call them *"moments of becoming."*

This is the first and only book-length study of Woolf's moments of being.[2] It has two main theses or contributions. First, it offers a precise definition of these moments and traces Woolf's experimentation with different types of moments throughout her writing. Second, it argues that Woolf developed a unique kind of process philosophy of motion through these moments: this is the constant idea of her philosophy. In this introductory chapter, I want to situate and clarify these two contributions before moving on to a closer description of how her moments of being work philosophically.

Moments of Being

Two years before her death, Virginia Woolf wrote an unfinished autobiography titled "A Sketch of the Past" (1939–40). Jeanne Schulkind edited and posthumously published the text and several other autobiographical writings in 1976 as *Moments of Being*. In it, Woolf revealed that her "central idea" or "philosophy" (MB, 72) and what "has remained interesting" (MB, 78) in her life and writing were the "moments of being" that "made her a writer" (MB, 72).

Ever since the book's publication, scholars have puzzled over Woolf's mysterious remarks about the nature of these moments in her life and how she might have expressed them in her writings. Forty-five years later, there is still no explicit consensus on the meaning of these moments and no book-length systematic account of how these moments evolved through her work and composed a unique *philosophical* view, as she claimed they did. This is what I want to do in this book.

The existing literature on Woolf's moments has done well to identify several aspects of these moments. However, the study of these moments of being has so far been fragmentary. Scholars have tended to focus on one aspect of a moment and a couple of texts at most. This makes sense for article or chapter-length works but means that we are still missing a synthetic account of how moments of being work across Woolf's texts and what they have to do with her *philosophy* more generally. The scholarship on Woolf and philosophy has not foregrounded the study of her moments of being and has tended instead to compare her work to traditionally recognized philosophers.

In this chapter, I want to present and build on the existing insights about moments of being from Woolf scholars before moving on to closer readings of these moments and their philosophical importance.

Interrelation

In my view, a moment of being is a deep awareness of material and kinetic *interrelation* of some kind. I do not mean "interrelation" as a connection between two discrete things but rather as an ongoing process from which relatively distinct things emerge as related. For instance, flower petals are not related by first being separate and then being added together into a patterned calyx. Rather, the petals all grew together from the same bud in a particular way. Interrelation is thus a process of *becoming* not sticking together discrete beings. An eddy of water is interrelated with a stream because its vortex pattern is not fundamentally different than the water itself.

I find that there are at least five critical aspects of interrelation that Woolf highlights in her writings and that scholars have variously identified as defining her moments of being. The first is the *interrelation between subject and object*. For Woolf, moments of being are not merely interior psychological states that arrest time or transcend the "present detached from all other temporalities," as Naomi Toth writes.[3] "Such experiences cannot be restricted to the personal sphere, nor to a reified consciousness, but rather connect the subject of a 'shock' to a pattern that is at once impersonal and intimately experienced."[4] Thus, moments of being are neither strictly subjective states nor pure visions of objective reality. They are visions where we become aware that there is no ontological division between subject and object at all. In her moments, Woolf presents an image of the world "as a pulsating field of mind and matter in which everything is interconnected," as Michelle Pridmore-Brown explains.[5] The world is interconnected and interrelational, even though we mostly live as if it is not. As Becky Tipper writes, "These moments are centrally about a shift in perception. They have in common a sense of sudden connection or empathy and a dissolution of conventional boundaries between things (in these instances, between people, apple trees, flowers, and the earth)."[6]

The second aspect of moments of being is the *interrelation between life and death*. "They seem to entail an awakening to the enormity of life and death, to the sadness and vastness of the world, and to the infinite, inexplicable interrelations between its parts," as Tipper continues.[7] In Woolf's fiction, moments of being tend to arise when characters confront death in some way. For example, in *Mrs. Dalloway*, Peter Walsh sees an ambulance drive by and is suddenly "struck" with a moment. In *The Voyage Out*, Rachel is very ill and begins to think about life and death. Rachel says:

> And life, what was that? It was only a light passing over the surface and vanishing, as in time she would vanish … Her dissolution became so complete that she could not raise her finger any more, and sat perfectly still, listening and looking always at the same spot. It became stranger and stranger. She was overcome with awe that things should exist at all.
>
> (VO, 125)

Life is non-living matter carried out by other means and dissolves back into the non-living.

The third aspect of Woolf's moments is the *interrelation between the senses*. Woolf's moments frequently entail an amplification of sensation and synesthesia. In her book on Woolf and Heidegger, for instance, Emma Simone calls moments of being "a sudden heightened awareness and openness to the world."[8] We tend to isolate and limit our senses in daily life. We often privilege some above others, such as sight and sound above taste and smell. We also tend to treat thought as distinct from sensation and as capable of judging the senses. For Woolf, however, thinking is an interrelated sense like the others. Synesthesia is the concurrence and interrelation of the senses in which one might smell a color or feel a sound. "It is this synesthetic quality that Woolf remained interested in exploring in her fiction and essays throughout her life,"[9] writes Adriana Varga. When *Moments of Being* was first published, this was the primary conclusion of one of its first reviewers, Louise DeSalvo. "With utmost clarity, she explains what I have intuited, guessed at and groped for half a life-time: that synaesthesia is the central and synecdochic structural principle of all her work .... no one will ever be able to look at or listen to Woolf's work in the same old way again."[10]

The fourth feature of Woolf's moments is their *interrelation between movement and stability*. The problem of reconciling *process* and *solidity* haunted Woolf her whole life. She wrote:

> And now is life very solid or very shifting? I am haunted by the two contradictions. This has gone on forever; goes down to the bottom of the world—this *moment* I stand on. Also it is transitory, flying, diaphanous shall pass like a cloud on the waves. Perhaps it may be that though we change; one flying after another, so quick, so quick, yet we are somehow successive, and continuous.
>
> (WD, 138)[11]

Woolf presents a unique solution to this apparent contradiction in her moments of being by thinking of things as *metastable patterns*. Clouds and waves are relatively stable discrete things made of shifting flows. They maintain their relative solidity by continually iterating a similar pattern. Each cloud and wave is continuous with others as a comparable concentration of water vapor that successively flies one after another. Clouds are not separate from the sky, and waves are not separate from the ocean. Yet, they appear relatively discrete until they dissipate back into their milieu.

Woolf's moments of being are metastable events. They are like momentary crystallizations of ordered motion. The world is neither a discontinuous nor a continuous substance, but an indeterminate metastable process. Her "constant idea" was that kinetic *patterns* form the world into apparently discrete cotton wool objects. These objects fly like successive clouds or waves in the continual flux of nature (MB, 72). For instance, a wave is such a pattern. It is curled and folded up into a relatively stable moving object but is also a continuously changing fluid process at the same time. It is "somehow successive and continuous." As Meg Jensen writes in her excellent article on Woolf's moments of being, "For Woolf, this 'pattern' is a paradigm of connection, of universal meaning and purpose normally unseen or unnoticed in everyday life. ... Her works highlight what she termed 'moments of being,' in which the 'cotton wool' is lifted, and repetitive, wordless rhythms are revealed."[12]

The fifth aspect of her moments is an *interrelation between time and space*. In Woolf's moments, past, present, and future feel like interpenetrating regions of an ongoing material process. Moments of being help us understand, as Emma Simone writes, "the essential connectedness and interpenetration of the past, present, and future. Such a perspective is in marked contrast to the traditional discourse of historicism, which is founded upon an understanding of time as a series of homogeneous and successive 'nows', as reflected in 'clock-time.'"[13] In moments of being, Woolf's characters "come to realise that each moment includes not only the here and now, but also that which has been, as well as what is yet to come."[14] Simone writes that moments of being form "web-like strands from which not only the self and Other come to be inherently connected, but so too the past, present and future."[15] For example, as Orlando sits under a tree he thinks: "What is love? What friendship? What truth? but directly he came to think about them, his whole past, which seemed to him of extreme length and variety, rushed into the falling second, swelled it a dozen times its natural size, coloured it all the tints of the rainbow and filled it with all the odds and ends in the universe" (O, 99).

In moments of being, space also dilates to geological proportions and we feel ourselves like "ants" (W, 262) or "cows" (VO, 127) in the wider world of non-human processes.[16] As Louise Westling observes, Woolf "increasingly placed human ambitions and systems of meaning against the backdrop of enormous geological forces and vast reaches of time. Increasingly she sought to portray the non-human ... world within which we are tiny and only momentary presences."[17] "Thus Woolf explored the nonhuman and the porous, the metamorphic boundaries between forms and species, and our deep enmeshment within this dynamic, shifting real."[18] "From a height it looks as though the whole land were flowing,"[19] Woolf wrote about the English Downs.

In summary, different Woolf scholars have tended to focus on *particular* dimensions of interrelation in particular moments of being. In this book, I want to bring them all together and track them as they develop over time into her philosophy.

One outcome of this method is that by tracking these moments across her oeuvre, we can see a pattern. Specifically, moments of being in Woolf's early and late novels are briefer and contain fewer aspects of interrelation. In her middle novels (1925–31), however, she expanded how long the moments last and how many elements of interrelation she incorporated into them. In her early and late works, moments of being also tend to occur briefly in individual people. But in the middle novels, they are extended to non-human times and spaces and eventually become collective moments that include several people. I will discuss the details of this development in Part II.

Next, we look at Woolf philosophically. If Woolf says her moments of being define her "*philosophy*," how should we understand this?

Woolf and Philosophy

Many scholars have written on Virginia Woolf and philosophy.[20] The studies so far fall into three approaches. Let's look at each and consider a fourth possible way.

The first approach to Woolf and philosophy is to make a close study of the direct and indirect philosophical *influences* on Woolf. For instance, Ann Banfield has written a book-length study of the influence of the English philosophers Bertrand Russell and G.E. Moore on Woolf's thinking.[21] Banfield argues strongly that "contrary to a common assumption, Woolf adopted not Henri Bergson's philosophy but G. E. Moore and Bertrand Russell's realism."[22] For Banfield, Woolf's thought can be entirely circumscribed by the ideas of these philosophers, plus the English painter Roger Fry and writer Katherine Mansfield. Other scholars have also argued for the direct influence of the English process philosopher Alfred North Whitehead,[23] G.E. Moore,[24] Bertrand Russell,[25] and the Scottish philosopher David Hume on Woolf's philosophy.[26]

There is no doubt that Woolf had direct and indirect philosophical influences at various points. However, not all her philosophical influences came from philosophers or from the so-called "Cambridge apostles," which included Russell, Moore, Fry, and all the men of the old Bloomsbury group with whom Woolf was friends with, except Clive Bell.[27] For instance, in *Moments of Being*, Woolf cites her mother as her truest "obsession" from age thirteen to forty-four and that "the influence on me of the Cambridge Apostles" was much less "definite" and less "capable of description" (MB, 80). The only concrete evidence we have of direct influence by the Cambridge philosophers on Woolf is that she heard one of Russell's public lectures and read Moore's book *Principia Ethica* (1903).[28] By 1920, though, Woolf explicitly repudiated Moore and the Apostles' early influence on her work. "I don't see altogether why he [Moore] was the dominator & dictator of youth. Perhaps Cambridge is too much of a cave" (D2, 49). While he was not an Apostle, Woolf also wrote that "I have never read Bergson" (L5, 92).

As Banfield describes well, Whitehead, Russell, and Moore were logical formalists who believed that being was entirely discontinuous and discrete, while Bergson thought it was a continuous flux. Whitehead's processes were discrete and *without movement* and required God, while Bergson's processes were vitalistic.[29] Woolf was aware of both these ideas but I believe she chose her own unique path, which I will try to outline in this book.

The second and most common approach to studying Woolf and philosophy is reading her work *alongside* or *among* philosophers with similar ideas. Many scholars have drawn on European philosophers who wrote during Woolf's life, intimating that their views were "in the air." There are articles and chapters that connect Woolf's thought to the French philosophers Henri Bergson[30] and Maurice Merleau-Ponty,[31] and the German philosophers Walter Benjamin,[32] Martin Heidegger,[33] Friedrich Nietzsche,[34] and Edmund Husserl.[35] This remains an attractive approach with much merit as long as we do not use these studies to reduce Woolf to these philosophies. We must be careful not to use canonical philosophers to validate Woolf's philosophy as if she were incapable of having her own philosophical perspective and could only be used as a literary example to demonstrate or parallel the philosophies of others.

A third approach is to reject Woolf as a philosopher entirely. Only a few scholars take this position. For example, Michael Lackey's argument is not so much that the influence and intellectual history approaches to Woolf and philosophy are wrong but that "Woolf, while influenced by philosophy early in her career (1904–1919), had a radical change of heart around the year 1920, which led to her direct and focused assault on philosophy in the mid to late 1920s."[36] Lackey cites as evidence Woolf's diary entry against Moore and the Apostles mentioned above and another diary entry where Woolf writes that "I don't want 'a philosophy' in the least" (D4, 126). Lackey also argues, accurately, that other modernist authors tended to reject the grand narratives of philosophical metaphysics. He thus concludes that "to have an intimate understanding of Woolf and her work, we must banish philosophy and the philosopher."[37] Erwin Steinberg similarly cites Woolf's paucity of explicit citations of philosophers and critical comments about them as evidence that "in her novels, Woolf does not espouse, adhere to, instantiate, or even reflect the ideas of any particular philosopher or philosophy."[38] Steinberg even claims that in *To the Lighthouse*, Woolf modeled the pitiful philosopher Mr. Ramsey on Woolf's philosopher father Leslie Stephens and G.E. Moore.

There are merits to each of these approaches, but I would like to propose a different one here. I want to read Woolf as a philosopher *in her own right*. I share the worry with Rohini Shukla that "reducing her writings to literary articulations of what other philosophers have said, as has been the popular trend, denies her any philosophical merit in her own right."[39] I agree with Lackey and Steinberg's anti-philosophical intuitions, but only if we define philosophy narrowly as "metaphysics." But not all philosophy is metaphysics. Woolf and many other modern philosophers and artists increasingly rejected traditional metaphysical philosophies, but this led to a transformation of philosophy rather than its abandonment in the twentieth century. Oddly, Steinberg cites Woolf's claim to have "a philosophy" grounded in moments of being but then he dismisses this evidence because it lacks the language and references associated with traditional philosophical methods. But this is only valid if one defines philosophy as "the act of citing philosophers." Thus, Lackey and Steinberg fail to see that Woolf was trying to change the definition and practice of philosophy itself.

I believe Woolf was right to reject idealism, metaphysics, and the anthropocentrism of the philosophers of her time, but this does not make her non-philosophical.[40] Quite the opposite. Great philosophers create something new. Some philosophers may view the rejection of the subject-object division as fundamentally non-philosophical. In my view, however, Woolf was so far ahead of her time that her philosophy of moments of being only recently makes sense as part of a general change in philosophy today called "new materialism."[41] Even now, I find that Woolf's philosophy pushes beyond new materialism in certain ways.

However, some difficulties are facing any study of Woolf's philosophical method. First of all, Woolf is explicit that her "philosophy" "will not bear arguing about; it is irrational … reality comes rushing in like a flood" (MB, 122). Woolf even described the sensuous feeling of her philosophy of becoming as intuition and instinct: "this intuition of mine—it is so instinctive that it seems given to me, not made by me" (MB 72). Following the first quote in this chapter, we are led to conclude that there is no Woolf; the whole world is a work of art. "We are the words; we are the thing itself." With this simple statement, Woolf did what few in the history of philosophy have ever dared to do. She overturned the division between the for-itself and the in-itself at the center of the Euro-Western tradition. In this book, I would like to show the dramatic consequences of this overturning in her moments of being.

What can we make of such a philosophy of irrational feeling such that the author herself does not take credit for deducing through reason?[42] This idea flies in the face of what is often considered "philosophy" by professional philosophers. Indeed, this is why A. O. Frank in his book on Woolf's philosophy rejects the so-called "misguided pseudo-philosophical" interpretations of Woolf that focus on her "philosophy of the exquisite sensation" and not "the more solid stuff of [rational] thought" that Frank prefers.[43] However, unlike Frank, suppose we want to take Woolf seriously when she says that moments of being *are her philosophy*? In that case, we have to give up the notion that we are writing or reading *about* some fixed set of rational propositions in her work.

How then do Woolf's moments of being work as a distinctly philosophical method? Based on her autobiography I propose we think about three aspects of their operation. First, Woolf says the moment of being is a "rapturous" "revelation" of processes of "ordered" interrelation that *cannot be represented in words*. The moment of being is the "irrational" and ineffable "rushing in of reality" that feels very "unreal" (MB, 72).[44] Second, *after* the moment passes, Woolf says she tries to write about it and make it feel more "real by putting it into words. It is only by putting it into words that I make it whole." Woolf says that this is what "makes her a writer" (MB, 73). "I seem to be discovering what belongs to what; making a scene come right; making a character come together" (MB, 72). Therefore, we may surmise that art and literature come after moments of beings as ways of working through and weaving together, but not representing, what the moment revealed.

Third, then, philosophy comes after moments of being.

> From this I reach what I might call a philosophy; at any rate it is a constant idea of mine; that behind the cotton wool is hidden a pattern; that we—I mean all human beings—are connected with this; that the whole world is a work of art; that we are parts of the work of art … we are the words; we are the music; we are the thing itself. And I see this when I have a shock.
>
> (MB, 72)

In other words, Woolf's philosophy has at least one concept called "moments of being," which is her name for what is ultimately unnamable, unknowable, and yet entirely real and material. In short, she has a moment, tries to integrate it into reality with art, and then tries to conceptualize the event by calling it a "moment of being."

Her concept "moments of being" contains two other sub-concepts: the "cotton wool" of daily instrumental activity and the processual "patterns" that weave everything together. For Woolf, reality and nature are ultimately processes that generate patterns that she calls "works of art." In this way, Woolf is saying that she makes art in response to her moments of being just as nature makes art/itself as the product of its deeper patterning process. Moments of being reveal that nature is processes that weave patterns, which appear to us as simple "things" (cotton wool).

Her point about nature being a work of art of which we are its words and music is what makes Woolf's claim *decisively philosophical* and not just psychological or literary. She is claiming here that moments of being are the events that give her insights into *the nature of reality*. These insights are not limited to her mind, childhood memories, or her literary arts. The qualities of her art and even the concepts of her philosophy are to some degree attempts to name and make sense of her ontological vision of reality "as interrelated processes." Thus, the passages above are the core textual basis that allows us to read Woolf as a *philosopher in her own right* and not merely as an example of someone else's philosophy.

These quotes from her autobiography are direct evidence that Woolf had a distinct vision of reality and a distinct performative-process theory of knowledge since "we are the thing itself." These are ontological and epistemological claims she says are borne out and evidenced in her writing. These visions of reality, Woolf says, "made me a writer." Unfortunately, Woolf did not live long enough after making these philosophical claims to demonstrate how they applied to her novels in detail, but that is what I would like to begin in this book. More specifically, I want to show that her philosophy of interrelation is expressed in her moments of being in terms of movement, matter, fluidity, and metastable patterns.

Conclusion

This chapter introduced the reader to Woolf's moments of being and how scholars have received them and treated her philosophically. I also tried to make clear here the aim of this book as a whole. I wrote the book because I wanted to show that Woolf's moments of being articulate various aspects of her philosophical claim that nature is processual patterns of *interrelation*. Building on Woolf scholars' various observations, which I think are generally correct, I want to argue that the philosophical concept of interrelation accurately synthesizes moments of being and is consistent with what Woolf says about her philosophy in her autobiography.

I also tried to make clear in this chapter exactly which of Woolf's statements I find strictly philosophical and what kind of philosophical method I am using in this book. Instead of a literary study, author study, influence study, intellectual history, or anti-philosophical reading, I want to read Woolf as a philosopher in her own right and in her own words. Woolf's ontological claim that nature is interrelated "hidden patterns" and that her philosophical concept of moments of being describes this interrelation are the textual starting points of this book.

PART ONE
A Theory of Moments

Chapter 1
Woolf's Process Materialism

*Philosophy is imperceptible. It is never in the writings of philosophers—
it can be felt in all human works having little or nothing to do
with philosophy and it evaporates as soon as an author wants to
philosophize.*[1]

—PAUL VALÉRY

In this chapter, I want to look more closely at Woolf's philosophy of interrelation. *What* exactly is becoming interrelated in her moments of being? My argument is that Woolf's philosophical description of interrelation is of *real material processes*. I call this her "process materialism," although this is not a term she used. To show why I think the term is fitting nonetheless, I focus here on Woolf's discussion of materialism, naturalism, and realism and its similarity to what is today called "new materialism."

Materialism

In "Modern Fiction," Woolf famously denounced the earlier Edwardian writers Arnold Bennet, H.G. Wells, and John Glastonbury for being "materialists" who were "concerned not with the spirit but with the body" (E4, 158). However, this does not mean that Woolf rejected materialism tout court. She only rejected reductive and mechanical materialism which was based on solid, static, and exhaustive descriptions of the world. "If we fasten, then, one label on all these books, on which is one word materialists, we mean by it that they write of unimportant things; that they spend immense skill and immense industry making the trivial and the transitory appear the true and enduring" (E4, 159). Here, Woolf did not criticize materialism per se but a particular interpretation of matter as passive and trivial. For Woolf, *materiality* was *too important* to treat in a discrete, mechanical, and surface way.[2]

Thus, later in the same essay, Woolf offered her alternative definition of matter. She wrote that life is

> an incessant shower of innumerable atoms; and as they fall, as they shape themselves into the life of Monday or Tuesday, the accent falls differently from

of old; the moment of importance came not here but there. ... Is it not the task of the novelist to convey this varying, this unknown and uncircumscribed spirit, whatever aberration or complexity it may display?

(E4, 160)

For Woolf, matter is something that flows, falls, and swerves aberrantly. She deliberately combines the images of aberrant matter with uncircumscribed spirit, thus changing the meaning of matter and spirit simultaneously. She also uses a similar mixture of contrasting images of "gravity" and "rainbow" throughout her work to describe her materialism, as Derek Ryan has argued convincingly.[3] Ryan argues that "Woolf's writing is not so much concerned with a 'materiality [...] which blots out the light' of being, as it is with illuminating materiality as precisely the possibility of being: the becoming of the material world."[4]

What is so beautiful about Woolf's essay "Modern Fiction" is that she describes matter as a process of becoming or interrelation that is "varying," "complex," and "aberrant." Her description of the fall and aberrant swerve or "accent" of atoms, whose flowing shapes make up the world, comes from her reading of the Roman poet Lucretius. The key idea of his poem *De Rerum Natura* was that the *material nature* of things is *not* reducible to visible *things*. For Lucretius, nature was *material processes* that fall, fold, and weave into *things* like threads into a fabric. Lucretius argued that matter was a continually and indeterminately swerving process without any fixed substance. He wrote that matter is "constantly swerving" (*declinare solerent*) in "indeterminate times and indeterminate spaces" (*Incerto tempore, incertisque loci*).[5] Matter, for Lucretius, was not deterministic or merely passive but also creative.

Woolf read and translated parts of Lucretius' poem several times throughout her life. It seems likely that she has his unique idea of the swerve in mind here. Following her inspiration from Lucretius' indeterminate process materialism, Woolf also rejected crude empirical materialism of the merely external or merely internal world "centered in a self which never embraces or creates what is outside itself and beyond" (E4, 162).

Woolf wrote that "Fiction is like a spider's web" and "these webs are not spun in mid-air by incorporeal creatures, but are the work of suffering human beings, and are attached to grossly material things, like health and money and the houses we live in" (RO, 42). Woolf here repeats the image of matter as flows of threads that weave together reality and art, just as Lucretius described.[6] Fiction is not an empirical representation of spiritual minds and inner selves. For Woolf and Lucretius, the fall and swerve of matter are always in motion and irreducible to either discrete particles or spiritual forces. Fiction, for Woolf, is such a material process.

Just as Woolf encouraged us to see Mrs. Brown as "a dancing light, an illumination gilding up the wall and out of the window" (E3, 387), Rachel Vinrace, in *The Voyage Out*, asks her lover, "'Does it ever seem to you, Terence, that the world is composed entirely of vast blocks of matter, and that we're nothing but patches of light'—she looked at the soft spots of sun wavering over the carpet and up the wall—'like that?'" (VO, 292). Matter, as Woolf knew from quantum physics, is not solid or static but fluid, luminous, and indeterminately swerving.[7] Woolf's unique version of materialism also influenced her original interpretations of naturalism,[8] and realism.[9]

Woolf and New Materialism

For Woolf, matter is what is interrelated in moments of being. Woolf's theory of materialism takes inspiration from Lucretius' idea of indeterminate processes and is a precursor to what contemporary philosophers call "new materialism." I am not alone in coming to this conclusion.[10] There is a rapidly growing body of writing that has recognized how Woolf's materialism is similar to new materialism.

What is new materialism? Philosophers started using the term "new materialism" around 2008[11] as part of a project to bring the *agency* of matter to the forefront of feminist theory and philosophy in general.[12] These theorists argued that the degradation of matter was at the heart of the hierarchical chain of being and underpinned our hierarchal dualisms and structures of domination. Men are over women; humans are over non-humans; life is over death; white is over non-white because everything is over matter.[13] Feminist new materialism aims to topple this hierarchical tower and offer a *non-anthropocentric philosophical realism*.

Materiality, however, is also a contested category in feminist theory. It is historically associated with biological determinism, naturalistic essentialism, and the subordination of women, people of color, animals, and nature. Thus, many feminists have responded to the degraded status of matter, historically associated with women's bodies, by emphasizing the power of human culture, discourse, language, and social structures to shape and construct nature and gender. If gender is not natural, then it can escape subordination through culture. The conceptual distinction between biological sex and cultural gender did vital work to liberate women and others from the shackles of so-called biological destiny in the 1960s.

However, some feminists now feel that we may have been too quick to abandon philosophical realism and the agency of non-human matter in favor of linguistic constructivism.[14] Matter does not have to be understood deterministically. This feeling seems especially true in the historical context of climate change, where materiality shapes social construction quite profoundly.

To describe new materialism as radically "new," however, would not be accurate. There are several precursors to new materialism in the Western tradition of which Woolf is only one.[15] New materialism also has similarities with some pre-Western and non-Western philosophies.[16] The promise of new materialism is not so much, in my opinion, its "newness" for European philosophers, but its discovery of similar ideas among marginalized philosophies and thinkers before, inside, and outside the Euro-Western tradition.

The term "new materialism" has been around for more than a decade. Nevertheless, "we" Europeans are still at the beginning of this project in terms of locating its shared historical and geographical milieu.[17] Elsewhere I have tried to make a case for at least two other new materialist figures *avant la lettre* inside the Western tradition: Lucretius and Karl Marx.

Why does Virginia Woolf belong to this list of historical "new" materialists? The broadest answer is that her philosophy of interrelation expressed in her moments of being is non-anthropocentric, realist, and treats matter as creative. However, my aim here is not to demonstrate how Woolf's writing exemplifies the theories of new materialist philosophers. Derek Ryan has already written a lovely book on this.[18] Rather, I want to show how Woolf reached these and other important philosophical conclusions using her own method prior to and independent of the advent of new materialism.

By my count, Woolf is without contest the single-most cited historical feminist by feminist new materialists.[19] Indeed, there are already four essays and one book published with the thesis that Virginia Woolf was new materialist avant la lettre.[20] I am greatly encouraged to find such a commonly agreed-upon historical precursor to contemporary feminist new materialism.

Nonetheless, as I have said, this is not that kind of book. I am not trying to show how Woolf's writing is an example of or consistent with Deleuze's philosophy. Nor is this book a review essay or sustained engagement with the state of Woolf studies or philosophers comparing Woolf to other philosophers. There are already good literature reviews on these topics.[21] I have read the existing literature, discussed it briefly in the introduction to this book, and would like to take a different path.

More specifically, I add to the thesis that Woolf held a non-anthropocentric philosophical realism by showing that hers was a distinctly *kinetic* or *process materialism* reached *through moments of being*. I want to read Woolf as a philosopher in her own right, in her own words, and with her own unique methods and conclusions. Specifically, her method of revelation through moments of being is quite distinct from the methods of many new materialist philosophers. This is significant. Even though I may agree with the comparisons scholars have made of Woolf to Karen Barad, for instance, this is not the substance of this book.

I am arguing here specifically that Woolf's entire philosophy, *regardless of who we compare it with*, stems from a single concept: her moments of being. Moments of being, in Woolf's own autobiographical statement, are the source of her deepest ontological and epistemological commitments. They are what motivate her as a writer, she says. Indeed, I believe philosophers have something to learn from Woolf as more than an illustration of canonical ideas. I have personally learned a lot from Woolf and have let her thought transform my own. More specifically, and uniquely, my argument is that, after carefully reading as many of Woolf's moments as I could find, the description of reality common to all of them is that we live in a material and interrelated world of patterned processes. Even more precisely, and distinct from other readings, I argue here that Woolf was a philosopher of movement.

What is the philosophy of movement? The philosophy of movement is the idea that reality is nothing but indeterminate material processes.[22] One of my motivations for writing this book is that I have been trying for a decade to trace the history of philosophers who held this relatively rare belief in Euro-Western history. In my research, I have been surprised to find that although many philosophers discussed motion, very few treat it as ontologically primary. Western philosophers have tended to define the movement of matter as moved by something else: space, god, forms, vital forces, or time.[23] So far, I have only been able to show that three thinkers *fully* endorsed the idea that there is only indeterminate matter in motion, without any higher metaphysical explanation: Lucretius, Marx, and Woolf. This has been a surprising outcome since none of these three were not my first intuitions. It has been an unusual and rewarding journey.

In other words, I am not arbitrarily reading Woolf as a philosopher of movement because I read everyone that way. Most Western philosophers and even most new materialists are not philosophers of movement.[24] I have been searching Western history according to some relatively unique philosophical criteria and wanted to write about Woolf, in part, because she is one of the rare few who fulfill them. In other words, I am not pretending to be a naive reader who has no motivations and interests prior to reading Woolf. Everyone comes with something. I am being forthcoming with some of my own motivations that I think are significant for the broader history of philosophy.

Naturalism

Woolf's philosophy of interrelation is also a kind of naturalism insofar as she defines her moments of being as the interrelation between humans and the natural world. "We—I mean all human beings—are connected with this [pattern]; that the whole world is a work of art; that we are parts of the work of art ... we are the thing itself. And I see this when I have a shock" (MB, 72). For Woolf, "there is no God," only processes of natural-cultural creation of which humans are part. In moments of being, humans become aware that they are "part of the nature of things" (TL, 188).

The phrase "the nature of things" is from Lucretius' naturalist poem *On The Nature of Things*. Several scholars have appropriately discussed the Lucretian naturalism of Woolf's work.[25] For Lucretius, nature is nothing other than matter in motion indeterminately swerving. There are no gods, no masters, and no hierarchies built into nature. There are no heaven, hell, no immaterial souls, no limits to the cosmos, nor anything immaterial or metaphysical in the world. There are only woven patterns of matter tending toward dissolution and recombination through metastable forms we call "things."

This is one of the most radical materialist and naturalist ideas in the Western tradition. Most historical readers of Lucretius have tended to supplement Lucretius' vision by adding God, the soul, freedom, vitalism, or other metaphysical figures that explain away the indeterminate swerve of matter.[26] However, Woolf was one of the very few who held to naturalism in its most radical and indeterminate form, first proposed by Lucretius.

Young Virginia learned of Lucretius and naturalism from her father, Leslie Stephen, who despised idealism, and her brother Thoby, who was a die-hard naturalist. All three, later including Leonard Woolf, read Lucretius carefully and took annotations in their copies of *De Rerum Natura*, which reside in the Woolf library.[27] I have read Woolf's annotations of this book with great interest.

Virginia also grew up as a naturalist, collecting insects, plants, mushrooms, and sea creatures with her siblings. Her parents encouraged their children's interest in astronomy and other natural sciences. As an adult, Woolf worked with the Bloomsbury group of writers and artists in London, who also loved Lucretius and shared her interest in philosophical naturalism.[28] Indeed, the third book published by Roger Fry's Omega Workshops Press was a selected translation of Lucretius' *De Rerum Natura* in 1917, of which Woolf owned a copy.[29] The biography of the Stephens' naturalism and Woolf's regular intimate contact with nature and naturalism has now been documented wonderfully and at length by Christina Alt.[30]

Woolf's naturalism had significant consequences for her work, as many have shown.[31] Notably, the French philosopher Simone de Beauvoir was one of the first to identify naturalism as a crucial aspect of Woolf's thought. In *The Second Sex* (1949), Beauvoir wrote that "very rare are those who approach nature in its inhuman freedom, who try to decipher its foreign meanings and lose themselves in order to unite with this other presence: hardly any women venture down these roads Rousseau invented, except for Emily Brontë, Virginia Woolf, and sometimes Mary Webb."[32] To "an even greater extent we can count on the fingers of one hand the women who have traversed the given in search of its secret dimension: Emily Brontë explored death, Virginia Woolf life, and Katherine Mansfield sometimes—not very often—daily contingence and suffering."[33]

While other modernist writers such as Yeats, Pound, Eliot, and Lawrence were all proudly anti-science, even rejecting Einstein's theory of relativity,[34] Woolf remained critical but open-minded to the new physics.[35] She read popular accounts of Einstein's, Bohr's, and Heisenberg's discoveries in the 1930s written by James Jeans and Arthur Eddington and kept up an interest in physics for the rest of her life.[36] In 1910 Ernest Rutherford showed that the atom was not a solid, static, and discrete thing but was porous—composed of small sub-atomic particles swirling around. As Eddington put it, "all that we regard as most solid" turned out to be "tiny specks floating in void."[37]

Woolf first discovered the materialist-naturalist idea of porosity in Lucretius' theory of "pores" (*foramina*) in her early twenties and then again in quantum physics. She alluded to the porosity of matter in her novel, *The Years* when she says that "Things seemed to have lost their skins; to be freed from some surface hardness; even the chair with gilt claws, at which she was looking, seemed porous" (Y, 287). "Even the little red brick villas on the high roads had become porous, incandescent with light" (Y, 306).

Woolf also uses numerous naturalistic descriptions in her novels. In *Orlando*, she writes of Orlando's becoming-nature: "It was odd, she thought, how if one was alone, one leant to inanimate things; trees, streams, flowers; felt they expressed one; felt they became one; felt they knew one, in a sense were one" (O, 63). In *To the Lighthouse* the narrator asks, "What power could now prevent the fertility, the insensibility of nature?" (TL, 138). This perhaps referred to the generative and non-empirical nature of matter in Lucretius and the new quantum physics. Woolf loved to describe natural metastable patterns such as waves, eddies, clouds, and pools beneath the cotton wool. Or, at least, this is what I want to show in the central moments of this book.

Woolf studied non-human nature and its agency quite carefully, and her writing shows this. She writes:

> The lemon-coloured leaves on the elm trees, the round apples glowing red in the orchard and the rustle of the leaves make me pause to think how many other than human forces affect us. While I am writing this, the light changes; an apple becomes a vivid green. I respond—how? And then the little owl [makes] a chattering noise. Another response.
>
> (MB, 114)

Perhaps authors would write differently, Woolf suggests, if they too studied nature more carefully. "Sufficient attention has scarcely been paid to this aspect of literature, which, it cannot be denied, has its importance. Our brilliant young men might do worse, when in search of a subject, than devote a year or two to cows in literature, snow in literature, the daisy in Chaucer and in Coventry Patmore" (E4, 192). Thomas Hardy, Woolf writes, was "a minute and skilled observer of nature; the rain, he knows, falls differently as it falls upon roots or arable; he knows that the wind sounds differently as it passes through the branches of different trees. But he is aware, in a larger sense of Nature as a force" (E5, 562).

For Woolf, we must remember that naturalism did not mean determinism, hierarchy, reductionism, essentialism, or discrete objects. Quite the opposite. For Woolf, nature was an indeterminate process of aberrant swerving that weaves together metastable patterns. On the surface, these look like cotton-wool objects, but in moments of being, we feel nature is not merely passive but interrelated, porous, and responsive. This kind of naturalism is also very much related to her different understanding of realism.

Realism

I also argue in this book that Woolf's moments of being are not merely interior subjective states of mind. They are *real* states of material interrelation. Just as Woolf distinguished between *passive* and *indeterminate* materialisms, she also distinguished between two kinds of realism.[38] The first kind of realism is what we might call an *empirical realism* that Woolf associates with the simple description of unimportant psychological or physical details. This empirical realism is the realism of the Edwardians, Dorothy Richardson, and others that Woolf often criticized for their trivial materialism. This first type of realism remains entirely at the surface level of things and does not penetrate below the cotton wool of solid objects to the patterns beneath.

The second kind of realism is what we might call a *kinetic realism* that Woolf associated with the moving patterns beneath but *immanent to* the cotton wool of things. These are what her moments of being reveal. "It is realism of the right, of the poetic kind" (E2, 120–1). This second kind of realism is processual and in motion. In her diary, Woolf describes "a consciousness of what I call 'reality': a thing I see before me; something abstract; but residing in the downs or sky; beside which nothing matters; in which I shall rest and continue to exist. Reality I call it. And I fancy sometimes this is the most necessary thing to me: that which I seek" (D3, 196).

Reality occurs *through* sensation, *through* the downs and sky, *through* her life but is "abstract" in the sense that it is not a discrete thing or substance. Reality is a process of interrelation felt in moments of being. "'People are somnambulists—the material is not the real—only the visible, the real being invisible optically'" (Quoting Hardy's notebook, E4, 571). Reality is not things, but what "floods" in *through* the cracks in things; through our "sealed vessels afloat on what it is convenient to call reality" (MB, 122).

For Woolf, reality is always *on the move*. It is not a subjective state as it was for idealists or an objective state of affairs, as it was for Moore and Russell.[39] "We are the thing itself," Woolf wrote (MB, 72). "Whether we call it life or spirit, truth or reality, this, the essential thing, has moved off, or on, and refuses to be contained any longer in such ill-fitting vestments as we provide" (E4, 160). As Mark Hussey writes in his book *The Singing of the Real World: The Philosophy of Virginia Woolf's Fiction,* reality, for Woolf, is "an abstract 'gap' in actual life that cannot be directly referred to in language, but is certainly a potential experience of human being."[40] No empirical sensation or aesthetic representation can capture fluid reality, but this is *not* because reality is missing, transcendent, or metaphysical. Reality is not representable because it is a process, a flow, a wave, a kinetic pattern. As such, no static snapshot, photo, word, form, or color will ever stop it. One never steps into the same river twice; one never *contains* reality in art or science. Instead, one has to join the process to become part of the process of reality. Woolf, it seems to me, held a kind of performative realism.

This kinetic reality is not radically other than empirical reality but rather exists immanently within and *through* it, *traversing* and *iterating* it. Realism is more than "human beings ... in their relation to each other but in relation to *reality*" (RO 149). In her book on Woolf's realism, Pam Morris correctly connects Woolf's materialism, naturalism, and realism to Lucretius' poem. Woolf's realism, she says, is part of her "anti-idealism, [and] her insistence upon the materiality of body and mind" just as it was for Lucretius.[41] "Her intense sense of connection to the larger universe evokes that of another determinedly anti-religious poetic sceptic: Lucretius."[42] In my view, this is because Lucretius and Woolf both came to this truth in moments of being or ecstatic vision where the feeling of interrelation was central. "Woolf's Lucretius-scale ambition to present a wholly materialist account of the universe" where matter swerves indeterminately is at the heart of her realism.[43]

Thus Woolf does not reject realism but rather locates a "true reality" beneath the surface of empirical realism. While earlier scholars tended to either read Woolf as rejecting empirical realism,[44] or affirming it,[45] more recent scholarship, which this book builds on, has argued that Woolf's realism is of an entirely different sort.[46] My contribution to this rethinking of Woolf's realism is to think of it in terms of *processes* and *movement*.

But process reality is an odd kind of "truth" that is not a fixed objective truth. Reality is a metastable state. "We want to be rid of realism," Woolf writes, "to penetrate without its help into the regions beneath it" (WW, 191). Woolf thus rejects empirical realism or "actualism," as Pam Morris calls it,[47] in favor of going even deeper beneath it. Beneath the cotton wool of real objects are the deeper real patterns and processes that sustain those objects. For example, in *The Waves*, as Percival enters the room, "The light falls upon real objects now" (W, 127) since the reality of the interrelational processes that compose the scene is finally tied together in the moment of being. This is the reality of metastable events and not of discrete objects.

In a letter to David Garnett, Woolf asks, "But how far can one convey character without [empirical] realism? That is my problem—one of them at least. You're quite right that I can't do the realism, though I admire those who can"

(L2, 571). As Woolf's kinetic realism increased, her novels became less about character and plot [empirical realism] and more about the transversal process and diffractive patterns found in moments of being. Having these two different definitions of realism, Woolf can say that Arnold Bennett "depresses me with his very astute realism" [empirical realism] and that Miss Viola Meynell "depresses me with her lack of realism" [kinetic realism] (L2, 81). This contrast is also explicit in her description of photographs as offering something "more real, or real with a different reality from that which we perceive in daily life" (L2: 496). This is an explicit contrast between perceptual empirical realism and the different "more real" reality of Woolf's kinetic realism.[48]

Woolf highlights a similar kind of realism in her biography on Roger Fry. "The aesthetic emotion seems to him [Fry] of supreme importance. But why?—he cannot say." Quoting Fry, Woolf writes:

> "One can only say that those who experience it feel it to have a peculiar quality of' 'reality', which makes it a matter of infinite importance in their lives. Any attempt I might make to explain this would probably land me in the depths of mysticism. On the edge of that gulf I stop." But if he [Fry] stops it is in the attitude of one who looks forward. We are always left with the sense of something to come.

"But if reason must stop short, beyond reason lies reality," Woolf says (RF, 229).

However, Woolf was able to move beyond Fry's "edge" of aesthetic emotion without falling into the depths of mysticism by defining her moments of being by material interrelation without transcendence. Instead of the Scylla and Charybdis of representation and mysticism, Woolf chose to develop a kinetic realism or mystical materialism of the processes, "design, rhythm, and texture" of these moving patterns traversing moments of being (RF, 240).[49]

Conclusion

In this chapter, I wanted to give a more definite and philosophical meaning to the idea of interrelation that defines Woolf's moments of being. In moments of being, we *sense* the interrelation of the world. We feel we are the thing itself. Reality floods in, and we see the moving material processes whose patterns support the metastable world of cotton wool objects of daily life around us. Woolf's experience of moments of being profoundly shaped her understanding of matter, nature, and reality. For her, matter, nature, and reality were not static states but indeterminate, swerving processes that continually elude our attempts to freeze them into words and even concepts. This is why I call it a kind of "process" or "kinetic" materialism. Reality cannot be captured rationally or even artistically, not because it is beyond nature, but because it is always moving and changing immanent to nature. "Beyond reason lies reality" because reason cannot wholly capture the process of the moving patterns beneath the cotton wool.

Now that I have introduced the broad philosophical idea of material interrelation, I would like to begin a more in-depth definition and discussion of Woolf's moments of being and how they express this philosophy. I hope this broad discussion in the next chapter will help prepare the reader for a close study of these moments in Part II of this book.

Chapter 2
Let Us Trace the Patterns

We are not the stuff that abides, but patterns that perpetuate themselves.

—NORBERT WIENER

Woolf offers us a rare and beautiful glimpse into a world in motion. Through her vision, we see below the surface of solid objects, which float like corks in the fluid medium of what she calls "reality." We feel the world, and our bodies become waves, curled up, iterated, and diffracted across the luminous shore of existence.

This book takes the reader on a deep dive into Woolf's moments of being to discover the kinetic philosophy they contain. Before we begin our journey into these watery realms of waves, pools, fogs, and bubbles, it will help get a handle on how these moments work. What are the ideas and techniques that guided her exploration of these moments? Once we understand her broader vision and aims, we can see how these moments emerge and develop throughout her work.

What is a moment of being? This chapter looks at three aspects of Woolf's moments and their connection to her process philosophy of interrelation. (1) Woolf's descriptions of moments of being all describe nature as a fluid *process* where solid objects are only metastable folds, bubbles, or congelations. (2) These processes are only occasionally revealed to us in sudden shocks or *moments* of becoming. (3) In these moments, we see below the apparent solidity and stasis of things and discover the kinetic *patterns* and orders that immanently support them.

This chapter unpacks the philosophy of movement at work in these three aspects of Woolf's moments of being.

Nature Is Process

For Woolf, everything flows—including the author. Woolf even described herself and her philosophy in fluid terms. "I see myself as a fish in a stream; deflected; held in place" (MB, 80). She is not a generic flux but a particular metastable formation in a flow. Woolf is a process or flow whose movement with and against a moving current gives the appearance of stability.

She says she "fancies [herself] afloat, [in an element] which is all the time responding to things we have no words for—exposed to some invisible ray" (MB, 115). The world and her body are continually changing with one another in a fluid medium of imperceptible patterns. We lack words to describe this world adequately because it is not a thing but a process. Written language runs up against the limits of representation because of the fluid nature of reality. How can a static word or idea possibly capture a fluid process? The challenge of writing, for Woolf, is how to say the unsayable process. How can we *become* part of the process *through* writing and not represent the process *with* writing?

It is unfortunate that early interpreters of Woolf described her as a "naïve, untutored modernist, obsessed by interior, subjective, and mystical experience."[1] This is an outrageous misinterpretation. By contrast, Woolf is quite clear that what made Tolstoy "the greatest of all novelists," in her opinion, was that he proceeded, "as we are accustomed to proceed, not from the inside outwards, but from the outside inwards" (E4, 187–8).[2] Elsewhere, Woolf explicitly rejected the private interiority of psychology: "The psychological novelist has been too prone to limit psychology to the psychology of personal intercourse," she says (E4, 435). Despite her typical reception as a "stream of consciousness" modernist, Woolf never explicitly identified herself as such because of its fixation and limitation on individual consciousness.

It is not just consciousness that is streaming for Woolf; *everything* is streaming. In her diary, Woolf wrote that her idea for *The Waves* was to write it as "some continuous stream, not solely of human thought, but of the ship, the night, all flowing together" (D3, 139). She called it an "abstract mystical eyeless book" and imagined its form as a metastable pattern like a wave.

> Suppose I could run all the scenes together more? By rhythm, chiefly. So as to avoid those cuts; so as to make the blood run like a torrent from end to end—I don't want the waste that the breaks give; I want to avoid chapters; that indeed is my achievement, if any here: a saturated, unchopped, completeness; changes of scene, of mood, of person, done without spilling a drop."
>
> (D3, 343)

Instead of chapters, the book has waves and tides that ebb and flow. She describes them as "currents" producing degrees of "intensity" (D3, 229).

For Woolf, mind and nature cannot be separated or isolated. They flow together thoroughly. As she says, "We are the words; we are the music; we are the thing itself" (MB, 72). Woolf places no ontological division between the interior and exterior, human and nature, but instead describes them as folds or eddies in the current of broader processes. "'I is only a convenient term for somebody who has no real being," she writes (RO, 4). The notion of an interior "I" that *is* or *knows* separate from nature is a metaphysical abstraction.

For Woolf, "real beings" are fundamentally relational and kinetic. They are waves or whirlpools caught up in a real world, not interior spirits or minds. This fluid dynamism is what Woolf loved about the novels of Dostoevsky. "The novels of Dostoevsky are seething whirlpools, gyrating sandstorms, waterspouts which hiss and boil and suck us in. They are composed purely and wholly of the stuff of the soul. Against our wills, we are drawn in, whirled round, blinded, suffocated, and at the same time filled with a giddy rapture" (E4, 186).

In her own work, Woolf tried to describe a relational world of motion, "a world where each part depends upon the other, the serene, impersonal, and indestructible world of art" (E6, 121). Woolf's world of art is not one of interior monologues but impersonal processes and transformations. She wanted to "achieve a symmetry by means of infinite discords, showing all the traces of the mind's passage through the world" (PA, 393). Word and mind are not static or distinct but pass through one another and leave traces of their transformation. Instead of logical or ontological negation or contradiction, Woolf was interested in what she called "discordant harmonies" (BA, 175).

The world is not substances chopped up into discrete pre-ordered universal forms. "Life is not a series of gig lamps symmetrically arranged; life is a luminous halo, a semi-transparent envelope surrounding us from the beginning of consciousness to the end" (E4, 160). Gig lamps, or car headlights, appear discrete and isolated in the dark with nothing between them. Woolf similarly rejected the idea put forward by the Cambridge philosopher Alfred North Whitehead, Bertrand Russell, and G.E. Moore that reality was like a cinemascope of frozen discrete pictures in time. Woolf flips this idea on its head by implying that the solid lights are relatively intense condensations or metastable states of luminous halos spreading out into the world.

Life is a luminous halo precisely because "human beings [are] not always in relation to each other but in relation to reality" (RO, 114). They are regions of nature. Consciousness is not made from the inside out but from the outside inward. It is nature folded up, and thus, "there is always about them a little blur of unconsciousness, that halo of freshness and margin of the unexpressed which often produce the most profound sense of satisfaction" (E4, 510).

When Woolf writes characters in this way, something incredible happens. Take the hypothetical character of Mrs. Brown. She will begin to

> react to her surroundings ... her solidity disappears; her features crumble; the house in which she has lived so long (and a very substantial house it was) topples to the ground. She becomes a will-o'-the-wisp, a dancing light, an illumination gilding up the wall and out of the window, lighting now in freakish

malice upon the nose of an archbishop, now in sudden splendor upon the mahogany of the wardrobe ... the most ordinary she invests with beauty. She changes the shape, shifts the accent, of every scene in which she plays.

(E3, 387)

Mrs. Brown resists all attempts to make her solid, discrete, and fully knowable precisely because she becomes fluid, relational, and *in process*.

In *To the Lighthouse*, Lily feels the moments in which "life, from being made up of little separate incidents which one lived one by one, be[comes] curled and whole like a wave" (TL, 47). In *Mrs. Dalloway*, Woolf says that "there are tides in the body" (MD, 113). The tides are indeterminate processes, "neither this nor that" but becoming through ordered patterns and diffracting on the shore. "It was Yes, No. Yes, yes, yes, the tide rushed out embracing. No, no, no, it contracted" (BA, 215). Clarissa, riding a bus on Shaftesbury Avenue, claims to have "felt herself everywhere; not 'here, here, here'; and she tapped the back of the seat; but everywhere" (MD, 152). She is not made of discrete solid objects but "laid out like a mist [...] spread ever so far, her life, herself" (MD, 9). If the world is patterns, then, as Bernard says in *The Waves*, "There is no stability in this world .... To speak of knowledge is futile. All is experiment and adventure. We are for ever mixing ourselves with unknown quantities. What is to come? I know not" (W, 118).

Knowledge of the fixed states of static objects is impossible because as the waves collide and diffract, they change the water's entire surface. The wave is not only what appears on the surface. Its being extends deeper and more extensively to the whole of the ocean. As Mrs. Dalloway says, "Our apparitions, the part of us which appears, are so momentary compared with the other, the unseen part of us, which spreads wide" (MD, 153). "Beneath it is all dark, it is all spreading, it is unfathomably deep; but now and again we rise to the surface and that is what you see us by" (TL, 62). In *Mrs. Dalloway*, Septimus similarly sees the trees "connected by millions of fibres with his own body" (MD, 22).

In short, nature is a process but also hides this process through the metastable formations of apparently solid objects. This is the cotton wool. Only in certain *moments* do we sense how these flows "flood" or "saturate" a situation in the spreading processes that compose it and ourselves.

Moments of Becoming

In Woolf's moments of being, the reality of flux and movement comes flooding in as "shocks" or "blows." They are not events that can be consciously induced or planned but are "sudden surprises" that occur "in a great, apparently involuntary, rush" of "rapture" and "ecstasy" (MB, 81).

I receive these sudden shocks, they are now always welcome; after the first surprise, I always feel instantly that they are particularly valuable. And so I go on to suppose that the shock-receiving capacity is what makes me a writer. I hazard the explanation that a shock is at once in my case followed by the desire to explain it. I feel that I have had a blow; but it is not, as I thought as a child, simply a blow from an enemy hidden behind the cotton wool of daily life; it is or will become a revelation of some order; it is a token of some real thing behind appearances; and I make it real by putting it into words. It is only by putting it into words that I make it whole; this wholeness means that it has lost its power to hurt me; it gives me, perhaps because by doing so I take away the pain, a great delight to put the severed parts together. Perhaps this is the strongest pleasure known to me. It is the rapture I get when in writing I seem to be discovering what belongs to what; making a scene come right; making a character come together. From this I reach what I might call a philosophy.

(MB, 72)

Writing helps weave things together into a whole. Woolf's moments of being are not moments of inner genius, transcendence, or divine revelation. They are involuntary, yet they also provoke a response. As a writer, Woolf says she has to have a "shock-receiving" capacity. Yet, she also has to respond to it by putting the parts together. The moment is only real or revelatory because Woolf makes it real. But she can only put it into words and make it real because the moment happened to her.

The idea that culture and nature are two aspects of the same indeterminate flow and flux of nature is a radical one. Writing, for Woolf, is not a representation but an immanent pleasure of ordering words. Nature orders itself in the same way. Writing is not *about* nature but is a performative expression *of* nature. Moments of being are not discrete points in time but open performative processes developed into artworks. They are nature's way of extending its pattern of motion by other means: through culture.

However, since Woolf's moments are processes, they cannot be captured by any static image. "That is what is indescribable, that is what makes all images too static, for no sooner has one said this was so; than it was past and altered" (MB, 79). Aesthetic images cannot represent the flow of images in the world but only add to them.

Most of daily life is what Woolf calls the "cotton-wool of non-being." This is the fragmented world of everyday discrete objects and separate people. Now and then, a moment rushes in like a flood. Woolf's writing aims to describe moments of being and non-being as well as the transition back and forth between them. There is no dualism between being and non-being. One is not superior to the other. They are two sides of the same surface of a pool of water. Moments of non-being are not false appearances, but only partial and limited regions, like the tip of icebergs. "Often when I have been writing one of my so-called novels I have been baffled by this same problem; that is, how to describe what I call in my private shorthand—'non-being.' Although it was a good day the goodness was embedded in a kind of nondescript cotton wool. This is always so" (MB, 70). Most of our days, for Woolf, are lived in the cotton wool that Bernard describes in *The Waves*:

> Call the waiter. Pay the bill. We must pull ourselves up out of our chairs. We must find our coats. We must go. Must, must, must—detestable word. Once more, I who had thought myself immune, who had said, 'Now I am rid of all that.' find that the wave has tumbled me over, head over heels, scattering my possessions, leaving me to collect, to assemble, to heap together, summon my forces, rise and confront the enemy.
>
> (W, 293)

Bernard's moment of being has taken him up in a wave and dispersed him. After dinner ends, he falls back into the world of cotton wool necessities. Woolf's novels move back and forth between the surface of solid cotton-wool objects and the depths of the kinetic whirlpools that sustain them.

> This confirms me in my instinctive notion: (it will not bear arguing about; it is irrational) the sensation that we are sealed vessels afloat on what it is convenient to call reality; and at some moments, the sealing matter cracks; in floods reality; that is, these scenes—for why do they survive undamaged year after year unless they are made of something comparatively permanent? Is this liability to scenes the origin of my writing impulse?
>
> (MB, 122)

The world flows and folds up into sealed vessels. It is neither pure flow nor fully discrete. In Woolf's moments of being, she sees the vessels begin to crack. What appeared to be sealed containers of subject and object become metastable bubbles made of watery processes. "Like a plant in a pot, it begins to crack the earthenware. Often I feel the different aspects of life bursting the mind asunder" (D2, 304).

Growing up, Woolf felt these moments of becoming on many occasions. Her earliest memories of these moments became the basis for the moments that emerge throughout her fiction. Her first memory was of hearing waves crashing on the beach.

> It is the most important of all my memories. If life has a base that it stands upon, if it is a bowl that one fills and fills and fills—then my bowl without a doubt stands upon this memory. It is of lying half asleep, half awake, in bed in

the nursery at St Ives. It is of hearing the waves breaking, one, two, one, two, and sending a splash of water over the beach; and then breaking, one, two, one, two, behind a yellow blind. It is of hearing the blind draw its little acorn across the floor as the wind blew the blind out. It is of lying and hearing this splash and seeing this light, and feeling, it is almost impossible that I should be here; of feeling the purest ecstasy I can conceive.

(MB, 64–5)

This memory is the sensuous basis upon which her entire life is continuously filled and overflowed with ecstasy. It is also a material pattern and rhythm connected to all her moments of being.

In another one of her earliest experiences of these moments, Woolf sees a flower and suddenly sees its relational processes at work. "'That is the whole,' I said. I was looking at a plant with a spread of leaves; and it seemed suddenly plain that the flower itself was a part of the earth; that a ring enclosed what was the flower; and that was the real flower; part earth; part flower" (MB, 71). She sees that the flower is not discrete and separate from the earth but is a regional expression of the whole of nature. The flower is the Cosmos and Earth carried out by vegetal means.

Another moment happens when she is on a walk at night and feels the becoming of the mountains, clouds, sky, moon, earth, and herself as "the thing in itself achieved." At this moment, being, knowing, and feeling unite in a single event.

Then (as I was walking through Russell Square last night) I see the mountains in the sky: the great clouds; and the moon which is risen over Persia; I have a great and astonishing sense of something there, which is 'it'. It is not exactly beauty that I mean. It is that the thing is in itself enough; satisfactory; achieved. A sense of my own strangeness, walking on the earth is there too: of the infinite oddity of the human position; trotting along Russell Square with the moon up there and those mountain clouds. Who am I, what am I, and so on: these questions are always floating about in me: and then I bump against some exact fact—a letter, a person, and come to them again with a great sense of freshness. And so it goes on.

(WD, 85)

However, moments of being that "burst the mind asunder" can also feel overwhelming and terrifying. Woolf gives three examples. "There was the moment of the puddle in the path; when for no reason I could discover, everything suddenly became unreal; I was suspended; I could not step across the puddle; I tried to touch something … the whole world became unreal" (MB, 78).

> The next thing I remember is being in the garden at night and walking on the path by the apple tree. It seemed to me that the apple tree was connected with the horror of Mr, Valpy's suicide. I could not pass it. I stood there looking at the grey-green creases of the bark—it was a moonlit night—in a trance of horror. I seemed to be dragged down, hopelessly, into some pit of absolute despair from which I could not escape. My body seemed paralysed.
>
> (MB, 71)

In both these moments, the reality of nature and death came rushing in so suddenly that young Virginia could not make sense of her self's dissolution into nature. It made her feel taken over into some more comprehensive natural process, which she was powerless to change.

Her third moment of being overwhelmed was fighting with her brother.

> I was fighting with Thoby on the lawn. We were pommelling each other with our fists. Just as I raised my fist to hit him, I felt: why hurt another person? I dropped my hand instantly, and stood there, and let him beat me. I remember the feeling. It was a feeling of hopeless sadness. It was as if I became aware of something terrible; and of my own powerlessness. I slunk off alone, feeling horribly depressed.
>
> (MB, 71)

Nature can be violent, and one cannot always stop humans' senseless violence against one another. Again, Virginia felt the powerlessness that can come with a moment of being if one thinks about themselves in the broader processes of nature and history.

The potential for despair is a crucial aspect of moments of being. The difference between "despair" and "satisfaction," Woolf writes, "arose from the fact that I was quite unable to deal with the pain of discovering that people hurt each other; that a man I had seen had killed himself. The sense of horror held me powerless" (MB, 72). However, as she got older, Virginia learned to see that both kinds of moments taught her something about the broader interconnection of natural processes with her self. Toward the end of her life, Woolf believed that "as one gets older one has a greater power" to explain these moments. Thus, the argument of this book is that her explanation of these moments is her philosophy of movement. "They are now always welcome; after the first surprise, I always feel instantly that they are particularly valuable" (MB, 72).

Moments of being are not always joyful, and Woolf explored this idea in her novels as well. In *Mrs. Dalloway*, Septimus has moments that "terrified him" and "rooted [him] to the pavement" (MD, 15). In *The Waves*, Neville thinks of "death among the apple trees" and is "unable to lift [his] foot" (W, 24). Rhoda, thinking about being consumed by a thunderstorm, says, "I came to the puddle. I could not cross it. Identity failed me. We are nothing, I said, and fell. I was blown like a feather" (W, 64). This is what Woolf discovered beneath the surface of the sealed vessels and cotton wool.

The Epiphany Tradition

Woolf was not the first one to describe these kinds of moments. Woolf's moments of being are part of the deep and diverse epiphany tradition stretching back to Minoan Crete and Homeric Greece, at least.[3] The word "epiphany" comes from the ancient Greek word ἐπιφάνεια, *epiphanea*, "manifestation, striking appearance" and is an experience of a sudden and striking realization or vision. In the age-old battle between philosophy and poetry, Woolf sides with poetry.

Woolf read and wrote explicitly about the ancient epiphanic tradition in her Greek and Latin notebooks. She took extensive notes on Greek drama and poetry that dealt with epiphany and the "Bacchic rites at Delphi"—in Euripides' *Bacchae, Ion,* and in Homer (GLN, 123).[4] The explicit connection between these ancient moments of being and her own comes out in her description of Septimus' moment in *Mrs. Dalloway*.

> A sparrow perched on the railing opposite chirped Septimus, Septimus, four or five times over and went on, drawing its notes out, to sing freshly and piercingly in Greek words how there is no crime and, joined by another sparrow, they sang in voices prolonged and piercing in Greek words, from trees in the meadow of life beyond a river where the dead walk, how there is no death.
>
> (MD, 24–5)

Epiphany comes to Septimus through a bird's song as it did for so many Greek and Roman poets. The meadow of life and the river of the dead refer to the oldest and most sacred religious ritual of the ancient world: the Eleusinian mysteries. The myth of the cycle of life and death goes back to the Minoans and the Homeric Hymn to Demeter. Demeter's daughter Persephone gathers flowers in a meadow when she is suddenly abducted by Hades and taken across a river to the underworld. Demeter, the grain goddess, halts all growth in protest, and eventually, the gods allow Persephone to return for the six summer months of the year.

The Eleusinian mystery was an annual reenactment of this myth at the Greek city of Eleusis. Initiates walked fourteen miles from Athens to Eleusis, crossed over the river Rheitoi, and drank a mystery potion spiked with psychedelic ergot.[5] They experienced moments of profound vision that they said made them unafraid of death. Almost every eligible person in the surrounding area participated in these rituals at some point in their life. Greeks and Romans practiced the mysteries of Eleusis for over two thousand years, and its epiphanic rites had an enormous impact on ancient culture. Woolf read about these rituals in the British anthropologist Jane Harrison, who explicitly connected them with modern art and aesthetic moments of vision.[6]

Woolf's interest in ancient poetic epiphany is most striking in her annotated copy of the Roman poet Lucretius' *De Rerum Natura*. Woolf did not annotate and translate the whole or even most of *De Rerum Natura*. Instead, she focused primarily on very particular moments in the text. Specifically, she focused on Lucretius' three epiphanies or moments of vision: (1) His divine vision of Venus (1.1–30); (2) His Bacchic vision at Delphi (1.921–30);[7] and (3) His rapturous vision of nature in motion (3.28–30).[8]

The single most frequent word translated in Woolf's copy of *De Rerum Natura* is the word "shock" (associated with the sudden shock of her moments of vision). The next most frequent word she translates is "whirl" from the Latin word *raptum*, meaning rapture.[9] The connection between shocks, rapture, and metastable whirl patterns was important for Woolf's writing. Among her very few annotations in book three, she chose to translate the most dramatic and explicit moment of epiphany in all of Lucretius: "*divina voluptas percipit atque horror*" (3.28–30) as the "thrilling awe of rapture."[10]

Lucretius, unlike Epicurus, explicitly embraced the poetic and dramatic tradition of Greek moments of vision. Woolf understood and loved this.[11] The phrase "*divina voluptas percipit atque horror*" literally means "desire of divine rapturous vision." Woolf then connected this translation directly to Septimus' vision when she writes that "The earth *thrilled* beneath him" (MD, 68).[12]

Woolf also explicitly studied these moments of vision in several modern authors who took up this long epiphany tradition from the ancients before she did. She explicitly describes Thomas Hardy's aesthetic "moments of vision" (E2, xiv), Walter Pater's aesthetic "susceptibilities,"[13] Joseph Conrad's "moments of vision" (E2, 142),[14] and Roger Fry's theory of "aesthetic emotion" (RF, 229) as the most significant aspects of their work.[15] Thus, the ancient and modern epiphany traditions had an enormous impact on Woolf's understanding of her moments of being.[16]

The origin of Woolf's moments has been attributed and sometimes reduced to her mental illness,[17] drug use,[18] Eastern-influenced "natural mysticism,"[19] or various combinations of the writers, poets, painters, and philosophers she read. Indeed, all of these and the epiphany tradition had their influence, but they do not explain Woolf's moments.

They only raise the more primary question of why she felt so compelled and interested in exploring such moments in the first place.

In her autobiography, Woolf had the chance to explain the source of her artistic motivation by any one of these if she wanted to, but she did not. Instead, she revealed that from a very early age, she had had these "moments" *before* her major episodes of mental illness, drug use, interest in natural mysticism, or having read Harrison, Harvey, Conrad, Pater, Fry, or anyone else. Thus, her personal experience of these moments cannot be *explained by* these or any other external factors but rather *explains* her interest in them as possible descriptions, allies, or ways of thinking and developing her own theory about these moments.

Although it is tempting to explain the source of Woolf's moments by recourse to her vast range of historical influences,[20] it is also crucial to take her explanation, vocabulary, and claim to an original philosophy seriously as *irreducible* to the sum of her influences. In this book, I argue that although Woolf's work takes place within this epiphanic tradition, she describes them with a unique process philosophy of movement.

Woolf's description of reality beneath the cotton wool is her process philosophy. This fluid reality is what others were all circling in their own way. Woolf was interested in illness, drugs,[21] physics, mystical experience, and aesthetic visions *because* she was trying to develop her own philosophy and literature of these states (MB, 72). She was subject to altered states of consciousness and her canon of influences, but she also developed her own unique philosophy to understand them. Or at least this is what I would like to argue in this book.

One danger of explaining Woolf's moments fully by something or someone else is that it trivializes her moments and ignores her unique philosophy. For example, if we treat her visions as *mere* mental illness symptoms and drug use, they are explained away as "false" visions. But this is not what Woolf believed. Woolf believed that her moments of vision were glimpses of reality made up of affective movements and processes that typically go unnoticed. She knew that others also experienced these moments but came to her own conclusions about reality from them (MB, 73).

While Woolf was writing, quantum physics was also describing a world of processes and indeterminate fluctuations deeper than the world of solid objects and atoms.[22] Woolf felt this in her own way in her moments of being. Mystical, religious, aesthetic, and psychedelic experiences often include amplified sensations of the world that people often describe in terms of indeterminate processes. For Woolf, moments of being were not things to be explained, but *explanations of* reality.

For Woolf, moments of being are not deformed visions of reality but floods of sensation that are typically limited by what Aldous Huxley called the "reducing valve" of consciousness.[23] When Woolf heard people describe visions of God, the soul, or minds independent of reality, she was interested and more open-minded than her father or husband (who were hard-nosed empiricists). She was interested in understanding the sensuous structure of the patterns she and others saw in these moments.

Reality has many patterns, but we typically only see the ones we are in the habit of seeing. There is no God, no immortal soul, no transcendence, or unchanging Platonic forms beneath the cotton wool for Woolf. Patterns are shifting processes that traverse us. The discovery and description of these patterns are what I am calling Woolf's process philosophy of movement.

Kinetic Patterns

In this way, Woolf discovered moving patterns beneath the surface of appearances in her moments of being.[24] These patterns are singular but also iterative continuations of larger natural patterns. "Behind the cotton wool is hidden a pattern; that we; I mean all human beings; are connected with this; that the whole world is a work of art; that we are parts of that work of art" (MB, 72). Below the apparent discreteness of things, Woolf saw the world as a patterned work of art in which we are a part.

As Woolf says, this pattern is not a question of *beauty*, but of *being* (WD, 85). Aesthetic patterns are real patterns in being not merely subjective states of appreciation. Patterns are what weave together all the qualities that make up sensuous reality. Woolf's belief in the unity of nature and art is why Woolf says that "'The proper stuff of fiction' does not exist; everything is the proper stuff of fiction" (E4, 164).

In her moments of being, Woolf describes "a revelation of some order," "some real thing behind appearances." The appearance of discrete things is like "little corks that mark a sunken net" (MB, 116) of something "immeasurable; a net whose fibres pass imperceptibly beneath the world" (W, 214). The "real thing" is not a discrete object but rather an expansive and entangled pattern weaving the world together. These patterns or nets, Woolf says, are the "invisible" "backgrounds," or "scaffolding," "behind" but still *immanent to* the world (MB, 73). They are the processes that sustain metastable appearances—upon which the corks of people and objects float. These background patterns "prove that one's life is not confined to one's body and what one says and does; one is living all the time in relation to certain background rods or conceptions. Mine is that there is a pattern hid behind the cotton wool" (MB, 73).

The patterns beneath the cotton wool are not substances or visible things, nor are they unchanging metaphysical forms. The patterns are invisible, but not because they are beyond reality. They are invisible because they *are reality* itself, as a web or net of changing relations often obscured when we treat them as objects of our instrumental actions. Kinetic *processes* are neither empirical nor metaphysical. Their in-between status is why they often elude our experience and why moments of vision are needed to reveal them.

The most common patterns that Woolf describes in her moments of being are branching patterns (webs, weaving, vegetal growth) and fluid dynamic patterns (eddies, vortices, waves, ripples, clouds) of water and air. These are the patterns

I will highlight in Part II. These two kinds of patterns are also significant because they are fractal patterns. A fractal is a pattern that iterates across scales of magnification like dendritic patterns of tree growth repeat in branches, twigs, and leaf veins. Patterns at a smaller scale are recursions or iterations of those at larger scales, differentially repeating. The swirling fluid dynamic patterns of eddies, waves, and clouds, for example, also occur across several scales of magnification from rivers, oceans, to spiral galaxies.

Scientists have shown that these kinds of fractal patterns have physical and psychological effects on us that confirm many of Woolf's intuitions. People not only tend to find fractal patterns more beautiful and interesting than non-fractal ones, but fractals also tend to reduce stress and encourage mind-wandering, imagination, and pareidolia.[25] This is one of the reasons we tend to see faces and animal shapes in fractal surfaces, such as clouds, tree tops, and rocky mountain sides, as Lucretius was one of the first to describe.[26] The movements of our eyes when we look at these things and the default frequency range of our brain activity are also fractal.[27] Thus, Woolf intuited correctly that there are indeed hidden patterns that connect us to nature as a work of art. Much of the natural world is fractal as is much of our body and when we experience the world the process is also uniquely fractal.[28]

Virginia Woolf did not use the term "fractal," which was invented in the 1970s by Benoit Mandelbrot.[29] However, just like the archaic Greek concept of *poikilos*[30] and Gerard Manley Hopkins' idea of "inscape,"[31] probably inspired by the idea of Greek *poikilos*,[32] Woolf was similarly struck by the fractal patterns that can trigger moments of awe, imagination, and experiences of interconnection. It was probably no coincidence that Hopkins, a great lover of fractals, was Woolf's favorite poet.[33]

Indeed, scientists recently analyzed sentence length variability in Woolf's novel *The Waves* and discovered that the sentences exhibited a self-similar or fractal distribution in which groups of sentence variation lengths mirrored the total variations of the whole book.[34] Her novel has a specific fractal ratio of a few long sentences, more medium length ones, and many shorter ones. Just as large waves crash into a thousand smaller ones on the shoreline, Woolf's novel uses sentence length in the same way. Out of the 113 novels the researchers analyzed with this method, they found *The Waves* to be the second most fractal in sentence length variation. The most fractal novel in the study was another stream of consciousness book, *Finnegans Wake* by James Joyce.

Let Us Trace the Pattern

Woolf described the kinetic nature of these patterns similarly in her essay "Modern Fiction."

Look within and life, it seems, is very far from being 'like this'. Examine for a moment an ordinary mind on an ordinary day. The mind receives a myriad impressions—trivial, fantastic, evanescent, or engraved with the sharpness of steel. From all sides they come, an incessant shower of innumerable atoms; and as they fall, as they shape themselves into the life of Monday or Tuesday, the accent falls differently from of old; the moment of importance came not here but there.

(E4, 160)

Life does not occur as a series of accurate empirical descriptions but articulates innumerable material kinetic processes whose iterative movements produce and sustain the forms of life and interrelated reality itself. Depending on the fall, relations, and curvature of matter, daily empirical life is assembled even though the falling matter itself is *not something empirical*.

This is a fascinating interpretation of Lucretius—whom Woolf, her Latin tutor, her husband, her father, brother, and many in her Bloomsbury cohort all read quite closely and discussed.[35] For Lucretius, matters (*materies*) were not empirical or metaphysical but were kinetic processes, continually falling, swerving, and flowing into various metastable patterns or figures. The discrete things, or *rerum*, we see with our eyes are only the surface shape of a deeper pattern produced by continually folded and woven threads of matter.[36] Woolf's description of reality above is nearly identical to Lucretius' in his poem *De Rerum Natura*.[37]

Life is not a series of gig lamps symmetrically arranged; life is a luminous halo, a semi-transparent envelope surrounding us from the beginning of consciousness to the end. Is it not the task of the novelist to convey this varying, this unknown and uncircumscribed spirit, whatever aberration or complexity it may display, with as little mixture of the alien and external as possible?

(E4, 160)

Life is not a series of discretely ordered static atoms, like the "gig lamps" or headlights that adorned carriages on the street, but the swerving aberrations and complex relationality of moving flows of matter that shimmer and traverse us like a luminous halo. This semi-transparent envelope or membrane of vibrating matter is what Lucretius called *simulacra*. Simulacra are the flows of matter that radiate from within all things—like photon waves flying around and colliding in midair. The diffraction patterns of all these flows make up sensuous reality— according to Lucretius.[38] We see discrete things, but these things are the product of more primary kinetic diffraction patterns of swerving matters.

Woolf, drawing on Lucretius, thus gives the novelist the same task Lucretius gave to the poet-philosopher: the description of these unknown kinetic patterns.

Let us record the atoms as they fall upon the mind in the order in which they fall, let us trace the pattern, however disconnected and incoherent in appearance, which each sight or incident scores upon the consciousness. Let us not take it for granted that life exists more fully in what is commonly thought big than in what is commonly thought small.

(E4, 161)

For Woolf, modern fiction aims to trace these material-kinetic patterns or processes behind the cotton wool of daily life. Here is an incredible proposal. Woolf is essentially telling us that the challenge of art is not to describe or represent the empirical substances and objects of the world but to describe the real, imperceptible, but entirely material processes and patterns that produce them. As she says in "A Sketch of the Past," the description of them is performatively part of what they are: "I make it real by putting it into words." Life exists in these small, invisible, background processes, perhaps more fully than it does in the macroscopic world of people and things.

Woolf reiterates this Lucretian idea of kinetic patterns of falling matter in various places throughout her work. In connection to her attraction to her lover Vita Sackville-West she says: "As a body hers is perfection. So many rare & curious objects hit one's brain like pellets which perhaps unfold later" (D2, 306). Love makes Woolf receptive to the fall, flow, fold, and patterns of matter emanating from Vita. Staring out of a window one morning in London, Woolf watches "a single leaf detach itself from the plane tree at the end of the street, and somehow it was like a signal falling, a signal pointing to a force in things which one had overlooked" (RO, 96). Falling matter points to the deeper web of kinetic patterns beneath the apparent fixity of the tree.

In another beautiful scene, Woolf describes a woman who looks at some flowers "through a pattern of falling words." The woman starts to become like the flower swaying back and forth like a stalk in the wind: "She stood letting the words fall over her, swaying the top part of her body slowly backwards and forwards, looking at the flowers" (SF, 93).

Aesthetic Materialism

Woolf also adopted the study of aesthetic patterns from the nineteenth-century Lucretian materialist philosopher and English author Walter Pater—whom Woolf read carefully. Pater was the older brother of Woolf's Latin tutor, Clara Pater. Woolf sometimes even found herself frustrated by Pater's influence, feeling that she had "inherited modernism rather than created it herself."[39] Pater was an aesthetic materialist who saw reality as a constant state of flux. He described solidity as merely an illusion created by language almost precisely the way Woolf described it later.

Pater writes: "That clear, perpetual outline of face and limb is but an image of ours, under which we group them—a design in a web, the actual threads of which pass out beyond it."[40] Discrete things and forms are merely metastable kinetic patterns woven from threads of material processes that stretch out like nets into the rest of the world. Pater's view of aesthetics anticipates Woof's in his description of the self as fluid and susceptible to sensation with a "constantly renewed mobility of character."[41] For Pater, aesthetic experience was like "a well-executed piece of music; [to] that 'perpetual motion' in things, according itself to a kind of cadence or harmony."[42] "That continual change, to be discovered by the attentive understanding where common opinion found fixed objects, was but the indicator of a subtler but all-pervading motion."[43] For Pater, art aimed to make the body "susceptible" to these sensuous but non-empirical patterns of motion.

Plot and Pattern

Woolf not only had this "susceptibility," but attained and cultivated it *through* the act of writing. The act of describing the patterns was part of the patterns themselves.[44] "What then has remained interesting? Again those moments of being" (MB, 78). Woolf developed the study and description of the patterns she saw in her moments into its own art form. "And in its lava I still find most of the things I write about. It shoots out of one everything shaped, final, not in mere driblets, as sanity does" (L4, 180). She describes her moments of manic being as flows of lava that congeal into discrete solid objects of everyday experience.

Therefore, Woolf's description of these moments and the patterns beneath them are punctuated exceptions to the cotton wool of daily life. Nonetheless, their shock is a fundamental organizing feature of her work. The cotton wool of discrete people and things she describes in her writing are only the corks of a sunken invisible net of the material processes and relations that traverse and constitute them. Just as life is mostly cotton wool punctuated by aesthetic moments of becoming, where one discovers the net, so are Woolf's novels. Her writing takes us down into these moments and brings us back like the diving kingfisher in Orlando. *The Waves* is perhaps her most daring attempt to sustain these moments and their diffractive patterns through virtually the entire book.

Woolf increasingly began structuring her work less by the plot and symbolic meaning in her middle novels than by the iteration of specific kinetic patterns or images like waves, pools, clouds, bubbles, fog, and others. For example, when asked by Roger Fry about the meaning of the lighthouse in her novel *To the Lighthouse*, Woolf emphatically rejected the idea that the image had any *meaning*: "I meant nothing by the lighthouse. One has to have a central line down the middle of the book to hold the design together" (L3, 385). Fry thought works of art based on "associated ideas" were inferior to those based on "design" and "systems of formal relationship," and this affected Woolf's writing.[45]

Especially in Woolf's mature fiction, Susan Roe argues, "pattern is introduced, not simply as a way of organizing or plotting material, but fundamentally, organically, and intrinsically."[46] Certain iterated images take over the function of structuring the novel's form.[47] For Woolf, the lighthouse is not a symbol, representation, metaphor, or referential meaning. When James finally reaches the lighthouse, it is "as if he were saying, 'there is no God'" (TL, 241).

Instead of relying on metaphor, Woolf says she increasingly writes with color, texture, shape, and pattern.

> If I were a painter I should paint these first impressions in pale yellow, silver, and green. There was the pale yellow blind; the green sea; and the silver of the passion flowers. I should make a picture that was globular; semi-transparent. I should make a picture of curved petals; of shells; of things that were semi-transparent; I should make curved shapes, showing the light through, but not giving a clear outline. Everything would be large and dim; and what was seen would at the same time be heard; sounds would come through this petal or leaf-sounds indistinguishable from sights.
>
> (MB, 66)

Instead of representing reality or even sketching it impressionistically, Woolf invents a different philosophy. She describes its kinetic and synesthetic patterns of curvature and luminosity. By the time she writes *The Waves*, however, she seems to feel that even color and texture are insufficient to describe a world without a self. "But how to describe a world seen without a self? There are no words. Blue, red—even they distract, even they hide with thickness instead of letting the light through. How describe or say anything in articulate words again?—save that it fades, save that it undergoes gradual transformation" (W, 192).

This is why, in Part II of this book, I do not read Woolf's use of patterns as metaphorical in the sense Aristotle understood metaphor as "giving the thing a name that belongs to something else." What is at stake in this decision? I worry that when Woolf talks about moving patterns, readers interpret the patterns as not *really* being about movement but about something immaterial, ideal, or static. For example, when Woolf says that "there are tides in the body," I worry that readers do not think there are actually moving fluids ebbing and flowing in the body that have their evolutionary origins in the sea. If one reads "tides" as a metaphor for "psychological impulses," then one trades a material and kinetic pattern of waves for an idealist category of thought or psychological preference and loses the pattern. This is why in Part II I try to stick closely to the direct materiality and kinetic aspects of her use of patterns without treating them as names for what belong to something else.

The Secret Life of Words

How can we describe a moment of being that we cannot represent? If words are not representations of events, then what do they *do*? Woolf has a brilliant answer to this. She treats words as processes and agents of motions that work *through* us. For Woolf, words have a performative material ecology.

> They hang together, in sentences, in paragraphs, sometimes for whole pages at a time. They hate being useful; they hate making money; they hate being lectured about in public. In short, they hate anything that stamps them with one meaning or confines them to one attitude, for it is their nature to change … and it is because of this complexity that they survive.
>
> (E6, 97)

Words have kinetic agency "flashing this way, then that … because the truth they try to catch is many-sided, and they convey it by being themselves many-sided," and mobile (E6, 97). They live "much as humans live, by ranging hither and thither, by falling in love, and mating together" (E6, 96). Words do not represent but *act*. "Most emphatically," they are most active and mobile when there is *silence*. They "like us to pause; to become unconscious" so that a rhythm or pattern can develop.

> Now this is very profound, what rhythm is, and goes far deeper than words. A sight, an emotion, creates this wave in the mind, long before it makes words to fit it; and in writing (such is my present belief) one has to recapture this, and set this working (which has nothing apparently to do with words) and then, as it breaks and tumbles in the mind, it makes words to fit it.
>
> (L3, 247)

The world senses itself, and the mind is a continuation of this sensation. The patterns of the world are continued as waves and produce non-representational and non-linguistic patterns in our bodies. Moving sensations gather in our body in a wave pattern. In the silence of matter, our brains and bodies shiver and vibrate in diffractive relations until finally the wave breaks and crashes on the shoreline and makes words. These words then take on an agency and mobility of their own in our bodies and the world and feedback into the kinesthetic process of sensation to produce new waves. Words do not represent sensation but "fit it" like diffracting waves in an iterative feedback loop.

Modernist writers often used an "automatic" or "involuntary" writing method but confined it narrowly to their minds. Woolf, by contrast, saw, as Lucretius did,[48] that the stream of thought was in flux alongside all the other senses and the rest of the world. This is precisely why the patterns in Woolf's mind take on the world's material patterns that fit it, like bubbles. Woolf says she wrote *To the Lighthouse*

> in a great, apparently involuntary, rush. One thing burst into another. Blowing bubbles out of a pipe gives the feeling of the rapid crowd of ideas and scenes which blew out of my mind, so that my lips seemed syllabling of their own accord as I walked. What blew the bubbles? Why then? I have no notion. But I wrote the book very quickly.
>
> (MB, 81)

Involuntary rhythm is the ordered pattern and feedback of sensations and words. "And so pausing and so flickering, she attained a dancing rhythmical movement, as if the pauses were one part of the rhythm and the strokes another, and all were related" (TL, 158). Form does not exist before motion. Woolf was not a Platonist. Form is always and fundamentally something iterated in kinetic patterns—as is evident in her invocation of Lucretius' materialist theory of form.

Conclusion

In this chapter, I have introduced Woolf's moments of being and tried to show how they work to express her philosophy of movement and interrelation. This chapter argues that Woolf thought of nature as a fluid process wherein solid objects are only metastable folds, bubbles, or congelations. Although we mostly experience the world of cotton-wool people and things, we sometimes catch a glimpse of these processes in moments of being. During these moments, we see below the apparent solidity and stasis of things and discover the kinetic *patterns* that immanently support them.

In Part II of this book, I want to turn to look at how these moments evolved in her work and expressed a philosophy of movement and interrelation.

PART TWO

Moments of Being

Brief Moments

Moment 0: The Trance into Which Movement Had Thrown Them

Part II of this book is a philosophical study of Virginia Woolf's moments of being. I have three aims for this study. At the broadest level, I want to show how her philosophical *idea* of interrelation is expressed concretely in various moments of being. More specifically, I want to show how she describes the world of *movement* and *flow* beneath the world of relatively stable cotton-wool objects in these moments. The patterns of motion Woolf describes do not transcend the world of objects but are like waves in water.

I also want to show that not all Woolf's moments of being work the same. Woolf experimented with several different kinds of moments of being in her writing. Her first attempts at describing moments of being were brief experiences of interrelation limited to a few sentences or less than a page. These moments typically describe only one or two aspects of interrelation.

These brief moments began in her first novel *The Voyage Out* (1915), and continued through her later writings. I call them "brief moments" because beginning with *Mrs. Dalloway* (1925), Woolf started weaving these brief moments into longer blocks of text several pages long and articulating numerous philosophical aspects of interrelation. I call these second kinds of moments "individual moments" because they always happen to specific individuals. After Woolf developed these individual moments, she used them in her later works as well.

But this was not the end of her experimentation with moments of being. In *To the Lighthouse* (1927), she described a vastly extended moment not attributed to any specific human individual. The moment is called "time passes" and lasts for twenty pages. It weaves together years of natural and human events interweaving the local and the global. I call it a "non-human" moment of being.

In her next book *Orlando* (1928), Woolf built on this idea and wrote a fictional biography of a character who lives the interrelation of past, present, and future; nature and culture; male and female, across hundreds of years. In addition to her earlier moments, Woolf expanded the individual moment of being to an incredible thirty-four pages at the end of the book. This is what I call an "expanded" moment of being.

After this, Woolf wanted to push the envelope and write something completely new that broke with the novel's form more generally. Woolf did not intend *The Waves* (1931) to be a novel but an "abstract play-poem" without chapters or divisions. Instead of abrupt shocks between the cotton wool of daily life and luminous moments of being, Woolf wanted to write a book with "currents" and degrees of intensity. Like the form of a wave, the book hits its peak of intensity near the middle. At this point in the book, Woolf invents a new collective moment of being shared by six characters at a farewell dinner for their friend Percival. Together, the six characters share several aspects of interrelation throughout their dinner. While preparing *The Waves*, Woolf also experimented with a short essay called "The Moment: Summer's Night." She described a very similar lengthy collective moment in which four people experience a moment of being together as the sun sets.

I have, therefore, organized Part II of this book into five sections, each of which provides a *philosophical* close reading of one of these kinds of moments. There is no strictly linear progression of new types of moments of being in Woolf's work, but there is a tendency to develop and expand them, reaching a peak between 1924 and 1931. I have included an Appendix with a graph of these moments organized by kind and length. Eventually, her discovery of the collective moment of being in her later work raises questions of their social and political possibility. This is the subject of the conclusion of this book.

My method in Part II is a philosophical, not a literary one. Let me clarify. As a novelist, Woolf's writing exemplifies many of the literary techniques/devices associated with modernist literature. The literary techniques she employs aid the reader not only in understanding but even experiencing the "kinetic interrelatedness" of life. These literary techniques, their history, and their relation to Woolf's biography and geography are the focus of literary scholars trained to study the qualities of textual art.

However, in addition to these literary techniques, Woolf also says she had at least one guiding *philosophical concept* throughout her work, "moments of being." A philosophical concept is a technique for emphasizing and understanding an aspect of reality. For example, Woolf's concept of moments of being distinguishes between the "cotton wool" of how things appear in daily instrumental life and the "patterns beneath the cotton wool" that her characters experience in moments of being that flow and weave that reality together. At first glance things in the world seem discrete and separate from us, but in moments of being Woolf's characters sense their full entanglement and kinetic interrelation with reality. In my view, Woolf is correct to call this a properly "philosophical idea" since it concerns her fundamental orientation to *reality* and conceptually structures all the specific moments of being she described in her writing.

As readers and scholars, we can shift our attention more toward the singular literary features of each moment she describes or we can shift it more toward the broader philosophical features of these moments. In other words, we can treat moments of being as literary techniques that relate to the qualities within the novel or Woolf's novels more generally. However, we can also treat a moment of being, as Woolf did in her autobiography, as a philosophical *concept*, that is, as a broad description or claim about the *nature of reality beyond the borders of the novel*. This second perspective is what I am mainly interested in with this book.

Of course, concepts and qualities are never separate from one another in the world. But scholars can, and often do, choose to study one dimension at a time. This can give readers an added sense of the depth and range of a work. Literary approaches can dive deep into the biographical, historical, narrative, and stylistic context of a work's qualities. Philosophers can dig into the conceptual assumptions, distinctions, and implications for our understanding of reality and knowledge. Both approaches contribute to a richer, varied, and vibrant understanding of a work of art.

For example, as a philosopher, I treat and read the *concept* of "material interrelation" in Woolf's moments as a broad, not abstract, feature common to reality and knowing. My close-readings are *philosophical* in the sense that I try to show how reality, knowing, and sensation *outside the novel* fit with Woolf's descriptions inside the novel. This is different from a literary study that emphasizes a specific novel, author, or character study. With a philosophical method we gain an emphasis on the non-textual world of material interrelation even if we may lose a degree of emphasis on the singular qualities of *textual* "interrelation," such as inter-textual connections, tones, allusions, and devices. It is not an either/or situation, of course, but one of degree. My reading of Woolf's moments is not completely decontextualized and I have tried to stay very close to Woolf's words and images in the selected passages, but I am not attempting anything like a close *literary* analysis in this book.

Instead, I am offering a different *methodological* perspective on Woolf *as a philosopher*. My argument is not that the *only* insights to be gained from reading Woolf's moments of being pertain to her process materialist philosophy. Rather, I am arguing that this is one important thing, among others, active in her work. It is the primary *focus* of this book and my training as a philosopher to show this, just as literary scholars may equally focus on the non-philosophical dimensions of these moments without discussing philosophy. In short, this book is my contribution to reading Woolf *as a philosopher*, and should be read with that particular focus in mind.

*

I want to begin this effort by looking at some of the briefer moments of being scattered throughout Woolf's work. These moments may only be a few lines long, but they have similar philosophical implications as the more extended moments, only briefer. They describe, in short, a world of moving patterns beneath the cotton wool of solid objects. Since *Mrs. Dalloway*, *To the Lighthouse*, *Orlando*, and *The Waves* have much longer and in-depth moments of being, I want to look at those in more detail in this book's later sections. These four novels also contain brief moments of being that I have chosen not to include here for the sake of space and redundancy. My argument here about the brief moments I highlight in this chapter is that they initiate and imply various aspects of ontological interrelation, although in a much shorter form.

In this chapter, I have collected and will compare Woolf's use of what I call "brief moments of being" in *The Voyage Out*, *Night and Day*, and *The Years*. These novels are not any less successful because they "bookend" the four middle novels or have less sustained moments. Indeed, these novels allow us to trace an interesting wave-pattern in Woolf's writing career. Woolf's use of moments of being rises in the early works, reaching an intensive peak in the middle works, and then tapers off in the later novels like an ocean tide coming in and breaking on the shore. The reader can see this pattern most clearly in the Appendix to this book.

It is worth noting too that *Jacob's Room* and *Between the Acts* are interesting novels in part because they show how moments of being can fail to manifest. *Jacob's Room* mentions the idea of synesthesia, and *Between the Acts* invokes deep history a couple of times but, based on Woolf's definition of a moment of being, I do not find any moments of being in these novels. I discuss this more below as I treat the novels in order.

For the sake of space, however, I cannot discuss all the brief moments of being throughout all Woolf's fiction, which includes her short stories. I also do not have space here to give full chronological expositions of the moments I highlight below. This is beyond the scope of my concerns. My purpose here is primarily to establish the existence of brief moments of being outside of Woolf's four middle novels and show how they articulate Woolf's philosophical vision of what I am calling her process-relational materialism.

The Voyage Out

In Woolf's first novel, the young Rachel Vinrace travels to South America on her father's ship and experiences several brief moments of being during her trip. The first comes during a massive storm at sea that shakes the boat violently. The sudden gripping movement initiates a brief moment of being where Rachel feels how small she is on the ocean. Space dilates, and she feels the deep material turbulence of the world, then things settle again. Woolf writes:

> Choked by the wind their spirits rose with a rush, for on the skirts of all the grey tumult was a misty spot of gold. Instantly the world dropped into shape;

they were no longer atoms flying in the void, but people riding a triumphant ship on the back of the sea. Wind and space were banished; the world floated like an apple in a tub, and the mind of men, which had been unmoored also, once more attached itself to the old beliefs.

(VO, 72)

In this moment, Rachel describes reality in Lucretian terms of swerving atoms in the void. She feels, as Woolf describes, that nature is fundamentally turbulent and unstable but formed into metastable patterns of motion. The "shape of the world," Woolf writes, emerges from a "drop" of falling matter. Here, in Woolf's philosophy, form does not pre-exist its turbulent figuration. The world floats on a turbulent sea like an apple just as people ride triumphantly on their boats.

Furthermore, the "minds of men" and their knowledge, for Woolf, are interrelated with this deep, fluid dynamic process. We humans are not outside the world objectively observing it but tossed on its seas and embedded in it. In a storm our minds become unmoored. Our imaginations run wild and possibilities multiply. As the storm settles, we settle back into our old beliefs and patterns of action, Woolf says. Moments of being, we could say, are like existential storms where everything swerves and interrelates but afterward sets us back down like a boat on the ocean. In these few short sentences, Woolf manages to paint an intricate picture of the interrelation between movement, stability, and human knowledge.

Once Rachel arrives in South America, she meets a group of people who take a trip into the hills to picnic together. A young man named Hewet, who helped organize the picnic, pauses at a stream and says something similar to Rachel's experience of the storm at sea.

He wondered why on earth he had asked these people, and what one really expected to get from bunching human beings together in a crowd. "Cows," he reflected, "draw together in a field; ships in a calm; and we're just the same when we've nothing else to do. But why do we do it?—is it to prevent ourselves from seeing to the bottom of things" (he stopped by a stream and began stirring it with his walking-stick and clouding the water with mud), "making cities and mountains and whole universes out of nothing, or do we really love each other, or do we, on the other hand, live in a state of perpetual uncertainty, knowing nothing, leaping from moment to moment as from world to world?—which is, on the whole, the view I incline to."

(VO, 127)

Hewet stirs up the mud in the stream like a storm at sea to show the tumult below stable things. From this turbulent state of swerving matter, as Lucretius described, metastable patterns emerge. Nature, for Hewet and Woolf, is fundamentally indeterminate and uncertain, leaping, and swerving from moment to moment. Human knowledge and belief try to build from this turbulence but continually face the fundamental indeterminacy of matter.

The next moment of being in *The Voyage Out* happens to Rachel when she is walking in the woods one day. This moment is similar to Woolf's own moment of being, which she described in her autobiography, where she sees an apple tree and cannot pass it (MB, 71). Rachel is wandering through the woods while vividly and freely thinking of the previous night's events. The events are "surging around in her head" like a "tumultuous background," Woolf writes. In her state of mental and physical turbulence, Rachel suddenly sees a tree.

> So she might have walked until she had lost all knowledge of her way, had it not been for the interruption of a tree, which, although it did not grow across her path, stopped her as effectively as if the branches had struck her in the face. It was an ordinary tree, but to her it appeared so strange that it might have been the only tree in the world. Dark was the trunk in the middle, and the branches sprang here and there, leaving jagged intervals of light between them as distinctly as if it had but that second risen from the ground. Having seen a sight that would last her for a lifetime, and for a life-time would preserve that second, the tree once more sank into the ordinary ranks of trees, and she was able to seat herself in its shade and to pick the red flowers with the thin green leaves which were growing beneath it. She laid them side by side, flower to flower and stalk to stalk, caressing them for, walking alone, flowers and even pebbles in the earth had their own life and disposition, and brought back the feelings of a child to whom they were companions.
>
> (VO, 174)

In this moment, time and space dilate around the tree for Rachel. Something about the tree, and its jagged patterns of light feel so meaningful that Rachel will remember it for a lifetime, even if that lifetime, for her, will end prematurely in illness. In other words, this particular space and time dilates out to Rachel's entire childhood, to her death, and even occasions her feeling that flowers and rocks are animate friends as they were to her in childhood. This brief moment of being occasioned by the fractal tree allows Rachel to experience matter's animacy.

Later in the novel, Rachel feels again this moment when Woolf writes that "her mind was as the landscape outside when dark beneath clouds and straitly lashed by wind and hail." "With a joy and colour in its events that was unknown before; they had a significance like that which she had seen in the tree: the nights were black bars separating her from the days; she would have liked to run both nights and days into one long continuity of sensation" (VO, 223).

What is common to these two brief moments is that they begin with turbulent movement and draw from it a more profound feeling of interrelation in time and space. Rachel runs her sensations of time and space together in these moments. She "seemed to see and hear a little of everything, much as a river feels the twigs that fall into it and sees the sky above" (VO, 260). In other words, her heightened sensations run together to create rich fluid dynamic synesthesia.

Toward the end of the book, Rachel has a final moment of being when her "thoughts wandered" thinking about the dance she had attended previously.

> She felt herself amazingly secure as she sat in her arm-chair, and able to review not only the night of the dance, but the entire past, tenderly and humorously, as if she had been turning in a fog for a long time, and could now see exactly where she had turned. For the methods by which she had reached her present position, seemed to her very strange, and the strangest thing about them was that she had not known where they were leading her. That was the strange thing, that one did not know where one was going, or what one wanted, and followed blindly, suffering so much in secret, always unprepared and amazed and knowing nothing; but one thing led to another and by degrees something had formed itself out of nothing, and so one reached at last this calm, this quiet, this certainty, and it was this process that people called living. Perhaps, then, every one really knew as she knew now where they were going; and things formed themselves into a pattern not only for her, but for them, and in that pattern lay satisfaction and meaning.
>
> (VO, 314)

Rachel calmly feels the meaning of her life form out of swerving uncertainty of things, just like her ship after the storm and the stream of water Hewet stirred it with this walking stick. From her initial state of non-knowledge in the dissipated fog of the cotton wool, she sees a hidden pattern emerge. The meaning of life, she thinks, is not about the knowledge of universal forms or laws, but is an emergent pattern of which we are part. We find ourselves always already in it. Woolf's key philosophical insight here is that the material processes of how things emerge are also the shape of their meaning. What we call meaning emerges from and as the uncertain material patterns. This is an important idea I will return to throughout this book: that meaning is, for Woolf, an emergent material pattern of motion. Once Rachel sees the pattern she feels she can accept anything that comes to her without being perplexed by the form in which it appeared (VO, 314–315).

Just like her moment with the tree, Rachel says this moment in her chair will stay with her for a lifetime.

> Why should this insight ever again desert her? The world was in truth so large, so hospitable, and after all it was so simple. "Love," St. John had said, "that seems to explain it all." Yes, but it was not the love of man for woman, of

Terence for Rachel. Although they sat so close together, they had ceased to be little separate bodies; they had ceased to struggle and desire one another. There seemed to be peace between them. It might be love, but it was not the love of man for woman.

(VO, 315)

Sitting in her chair after dancing, Rachel feels that her body is not separate from the world but rather a pattern in a larger pattern, like a wave in the ocean. Individual love is only an instance of a more massive inter-relational love of all things woven into one another. The broader philosophical conclusion is that the individual struggle of the subject for or against objects is only a local instance of a more extensive process that also weaves together Rachel and Terrence.

Therefore, Rachel says, "Does it ever seem to you, Terence, that the world is composed entirely of vast blocks of matter and that we're nothing but patches of light—" she looked at the soft spots of sun wavering over the carpet and up the wall—"like that?" (VO, 292–3). Rachel's idea is consistent with Woolf's understanding of quantum physics.[1] The world is made of indeterminate matter like photons shimmering up the wall. Just as the position and momentum of a photon are impossible to simultaneously determine, so Rachel feels that her own body is made of such indeterminate material fluctuations. These fluctuations form the unpredictable patterns our Monday or Tuesday.

Night and Day

Woolf's second novel, *Night and Day*, is filled with many brief moments of being as it follows and contrasts four central characters' daily lives and their romantic engagements. I would like to highlight below some of the philosophical implications of a few brief moments of being that emerge in the novel but then quickly dissolve.

In the first moment, one of the novel's main characters, Mary Datchet is wandering down a busy street without destination when she "half holds" a vision of great importance but only ends up mumbling out little fragments of speech.

Strange thoughts are bred in passing through crowded streets should the passenger, by chance, have no exact destination in front of him, much as the mind shapes all kinds of forms, solutions, images when listening inattentively to music. From an acute consciousness of herself as an individual, Mary passed to a conception of the scheme of things in which, as a human being, she must have her share. She half held a vision; the vision shaped and dwindled.

(ND, 259)

Like all of Woolf's moments of being, Mary's vision begins in motion. The turbulence of the street traffic has a material effect on Mary's thoughts. As her body wanders without destination so does her mind: a well-described psychological phenomenon.[2] Her consciousness is not independent from her body or from the world around her but woven into it. As her body and mind wander inattentively, she enters an altered state of consciousness and begins to have a vision of some larger process.

After this moment on the street, Mary feels she cannot fully communicate her vision in language, or she will lose it. This is similar to Woolf's own explicit statements about not being able to represent her philosophical ontology seen in moments of being. Mary also feels the interrelation between life and death and sees the whole meaning of things laid out in the material wave patterns of people walking in the street. Again we can see the philosophical idea of material kinetic patterns as meaning at work. Woolf writes:

> But if she talked to any one, the conception might escape her. Her vision seemed to lay out the lines of her life until death in a way which satisfied her sense of harmony. It only needed a persistent effort of thought, stimulated in this strange way by the crowd and the noise, to climb the crest of existence and see it all laid out once and for ever. Already her suffering as an individual was left behind her. Of this process, which was to her so full of effort, which comprised infinitely swift and full passages of thought, leading from one crest to another, as she shaped her conception of life in this world, only two articulate words escaped her, muttered beneath her breath—"Not happiness—not happiness." She sat down on a seat opposite the statue of one of London's heroes upon the Embankment, and spoke the words aloud. To her they represented the rare flower or splinter of rock brought down by a climber in proof that he has stood for a moment, at least, upon the highest peak of the mountain. She had been up there and seen the world spread to the horizon.
>
> (ND, 260)

In this moment, Mary feels herself to be ascending the wave pattern of reality. She sees the whole pattern laid out in front of her as if standing on a mountain and looking down to see the bigger picture of how things move together. Except she is also part of this pattern. Strangely, the noise and movement of the crowd amplify her moment instead of distracting from it. This effect is similar to what scientists call "stochastic resonance," where background noise will amplify a signal instead of drowning it out.

For Woolf, Mary's words are not representations but souvenirs. Then, like a wave she washes up on the shores of the nearby Embankment and utters her words out loud. The philosophical structure of this moment is that Mary saw the world temporally and spatially dilated and saw herself interrelated with the whole of life and death. Nature, in Woolf's philosophy, is not about happiness or anything else in particular. It is a patterning process of experimentation making and dissolving forms on the luminous shores of existence. Woolf writes:

> Her soliloquy crystalized itself into little fragmentary phrases emerging suddenly from the turbulence of her thought, particularly when she had to exert herself in any way, either to move, to count money, or to choose a turning. "To know the truth—to accept without bitterness"—those, perhaps, were the most articulate of her utterances, for no one could have made head or tail of the queer gibberish murmured in front of the statue of Francis, Duke of Bedford.
>
> (ND, 261)

In Mary's moment of being, language is material and performative. It is her *act* of murmuring that brings her to the truth of reality without bitterness, not what the words *mean*. In this passage, Woolf suggests that words are crystallizations of turbulent movements and not meanings that stand alone in our minds. Sounds play through our bodies and come out like waves crashing on the shoreline of our lips. Nature does not tend toward happiness but toward vast patterns of motion within which Mary finds herself interwoven.

Another of Woolf's main characters in *Night and Day* is Katharine Hilbery, a friend of Mary's. Katherine also has a moment of being while walking on the busy streets of London. Similar to Mary, the tumult of movement brings Katharine to see the larger and indifferent patterns of motion at work in reality. Woolf writes:

> She stood fascinated at the corner. The deep roar filled her ears; the changing tumult had the inexpressible fascination of varied life pouring ceaselessly with a purpose which, as she looked, seemed to her, somehow, the normal purpose for which life was framed; its complete indifference to the individuals, whom it swallowed up and rolled onwards, filled her with at least a temporary exaltation. The blend of daylight and of lamplight made her an invisible spectator, just as it gave the people who passed her a semi-transparent quality, and left the faces pale ivory ovals in which the eyes alone were dark. They tended the enormous rush of the current—the great flow, the deep stream, the unquenchable tide. She stood unobserved and absorbed, glorying openly in the rapture that had run subterraneously all day. Suddenly she was clutched, unwilling, from the outside, by the recollection of her purpose in coming there. She had come to find Ralph Denham.
>
> (ND, 439)

In this brief moment of being, Katharine sees the interrelation of humans and nature as they flow ceaselessly like rolling waves. This vision brings her an exaltation characteristic of Woolf's moments of being and a joy of being part of a larger spreading diffusion of nature. For a moment, Katharine becomes part of the "eternally moving pattern of human life" (ND, 82) and feels her self dissolve in the evening light like Rachel Vinrace imaged herself as light moving up a wall. Woolf describes the natural light of the sun mixing with artificial lamp light suggesting that this natural-cultural mix is what makes Katharine invisible. In the flow, people appear to lose their discreteness and individuality, becoming semi-transparent opalescent envelopes of flux.

Katharine feels that reality, as Woolf believed, is fundamentally processual. It is a deep river current that sweeps up human bodies, traffic, and all matter and spreads it out like the veins of a river delta. The flow and spread of matter in the universe is an unquenchable tide and the city is an ocean of currents sweeping in and out. In her moment of being, Katharine becomes part of his anonymous surge of material interrelation and cosmic entropy. Philosophically speaking, Woolf reveals in this passage that the division between "for itself" and "in-itself," culture and nature, is a superficial abstraction.

Below the cotton wool of discrete things and people, Katharine discovers an underground flow of deep currents and patterns: a process reality. Katharine feels this dissolution and interrelation as a glorious rapture uncut by the pang of discrete cotton wool bodies.

"Suddenly," though, just as quickly as the moment began, it ends when she is torn "unwilling" by "purpose" to search for her friend Ralph. Instrumental rationality, as we will see in later moments as well, pops the moment of being like a bubble and Katharine is back in the cotton wool.

Jacob's Room

By Woolf's definition of a moment of being, Jacob's room does not have any, even brief, moments of being. The novel certainly casts doubt on the cotton wool of daily life as the only reality, but unlike her other novels, Woolf leaves the reader to fill in the patterns surging beneath. Thomas Caramagno describes the novel perfectly in his book *The Flight of the Mind*.

> *Jacob's Room* leaves us in a transitional space where we have suspended analysis but have not yet perceived the hidden order that comes when analysis and global empathy find each other. The Jacob we seek exists somewhere between the text and the reader—and between the left hemisphere and the right. That neither Jacob nor the reader achieves a moment of being does

not make this an unsuccessful novel. It is, rather, an appropriate precursor to *Mrs. Dalloway* and *To the Lighthouse*, both of which also create this space between objectivity and subjectivity but, in addition, fill the void.[3]

In agreement with Caramagno on this, I want to move on to look at a few more brief moments of being in *The Years* and *Between the Acts*.

The Years

In Woolf's second to last novel, *The Years* (1937), she traces the Pargiter family's history from the 1880s to the present-day of the mid-1930s. The novel develops many important themes in Woolf's work, which I do not have space to touch on here. Instead, my focus again will be on the *philosophical* implications of Woolf's use of brief moments of being in this novel similar to those in *The Voyage Out* and *Night and Day*.

The first brief moment I want to look at in *The Years* is similar to the one experienced by Mary Datchet and Katherine Hilbery in *Night and Day*. Here, Woolf describes again the way that turbulent street traffic can provoke a moment of expansive ontological vision. Eleanor, the eldest daughter of Colonel Abel Pargiter in her early twenties, is walking along a major thoroughfare in central London called the Strand when she suddenly feels a "shock."

> The uproar, the confusion, the space of the Strand came upon her with a shock of relief. She felt herself expand. It was still daylight here; a rush, a stir, a turmoil of variegated life came racing towards her. It was as if something had broken loose—in her, in the world. She seemed, after her concentration, to be dissipated, tossed about. She wandered along the Strand, looking with pleasure at the racing street.
>
> (Y, 110)

The turmoil of motion makes her feel that something has broken loose in her and the world at the same time because she and the world become one interwoven reality. Both break down, loosen up, and weave together. Just as Rachel Vinrace felt similarly while tossed in a storm at sea, Eleanor feels it on the Strand. To Eleanor, the dissipation is even pleasant, because it loosens her from her self. The world is not attacking her because the world is also loosened as well.

Later in *The Years,* Sally, the mid-twenties daughter of Colonel Abel Pargiter's brother Sir Digby Pargiter, has a brief moment of being while lying in bed after reading the Greek play, "Antigone." Sally hears the rush of traffic, distant but constant from her bedroom. The sound of motion makes it impossible to sleep or read, and so Sally begins to think of a book she had been reading earlier. The author of the book claimed that the "world was nothing but thought." In a beautiful critique of idealism, Sally tries to become pure thought but instead involuntarily becomes a tree dappled in sunlight.

> Well, since it was impossible to read and impossible to sleep, she would let herself be thought. It was easier to act things than to think them. Legs, body, hands, the whole of her must be laid out passively to take part in this universal process of thinking which the man said was the world living. She stretched herself out. Where did thought begin? In the feet? she asked. There they were, jutting out under the single sheet. They seemed separated, very far away. She closed her eyes. Then against her will something in her hardened. It was impossible to act thought. She became something; a root; lying sunk in the earth; veins seemed to thread the cold mass; the tree put forth branches; the branches had leaves. "—the sun shines through the leaves," she said, waggling her finger. She opened her eyes in order to verify the sun on the leaves and saw the actual tree standing out there in the garden. Far from being dappled with sunlight, it had no leaves at all. She felt for a moment as if she had been contradicted. For the tree was black, dead black.
>
> (Y, 132–3)

What is philosophical about this moment of being, in my view, is that it is involuntary and evokes a feeling of interrelation between thought, matter, humanity, and nature. For Sally, thinking is an act performed with the body. The world is not pure thought, but thought is a bodily expression of natural neuronal growth like the dendritic veins and leaves of a tree in the sunlight. Thought is the growth and flowering of the body and mind. It is a wholly material activity.

Sally tries to become pure thought by *performing* it with our body, beginning with her feet. The feet, in particular, are the inverse of the head. They are appendages of motion. The feet move the body and brain, and hence motion here becomes the source of thought for Sally. The feet are the *roots* of the body.

Against Sally's will, her body hardens like a tree and begins to sprout. She feels the material patterns of woven and threaded veins that compose her body like the veins of tree leaves and branches. The philosophical implication here is that thought is not a mere effect of the will but rather an organic expression of material growth and dissipation. Just as trees dissipate heat and water vapor, so the body dissipates heat and grows thoughts.

The body with its veins and arteries follows the same fractal patterns as trees. Sally waggles her fingers like leaves in the dappled sunlight. When she opens her eyes, she sees the world of discrete objects, the cotton wool above the dendritic patterns that support them. She sees the winter tree. Thus ends suddenly Sally's brief moment of being and her philosophical insight into the material interrelation of reality.

Around the middle of *The Years*, Woolf writes another beautiful brief moment of being. Kitty Malone, a cousin of the Pargiter family, goes for a walk on a beautiful morning in the countryside. Toward the end of her walk, Kitty comes to a hill overlooking the countryside. She looks around her and feels space and time dilate and interrelate.

> Suddenly she saw the sky between two striped tree trunks extraordinarily blue. She came out on the top. The wind ceased; the country spread wide all round her. Her body seemed to shrink; her eyes to widen. She threw herself on the ground, and looked over the billowing land that went rising and falling, away and away, until somewhere far off it reached the sea. Uncultivated, uninhabited, existing by itself, for itself, without towns or houses it looked from this height. Dark wedges of shadow, bright breadths of light lay side by side. Then, as she watched, light moved and dark moved; light and shadow went traveling over the hills and over the valleys. A deep murmur sang in her ears—the land itself, singing to itself, a chorus, alone. She lay there listening. She was happy, completely. Time had ceased.
>
> (Y, 277–8)

In this moment, Kitty's senses widen and heighten, and she feels small in the face of nature. She feels she is an interrelated part of the earth's natural process that stretches to the sea and exists for itself. Light and dark move and alternate like days running together in time. She hears a deep and ancient murmur of the earth singing to itself in a chorus. The world, as Woolf wrote elsewhere, is a "work of art" of which we are part. Kitty lays her body out on the ground to dissolve into the chorus of reality and the woven work of art that is nature-culture. Philosophically, here, we see again the themes of spacetime dilation and the interrelation of nature-culture. Kitty becomes the "thing herself," that she is. Her brief moment also, as with many others, brings her great ecstasy. Linear time ceases for Kitty and becomes only the movement of matter changing and spreading out in the cosmos. There is no background time that remains the same as the world changes and moves. The whole of nature changes continually such that there is no single line of time. Kitty's moment ends abruptly at the end of the chapter.

Finally, toward the end of *The Years,* and in contrast to Kitty's moment alone in the countryside, Woolf describes a moment of being among other people in the city. Woolf does not romanticize nature as the only thing that can occasion a moment of being. A moment of being can occur almost anywhere, as we will see throughout this book. For example, Woolf tells how Eleanor Pargiter's niece,

Peggy, in her late thirties at the time, was playing the game "exquisite corpse" at a party and started to laugh involuntarily. Peggy's laughter was so intense that it caused her to envision a state of being completely interrelated with all things. However, like Mary from *Night and Day*, Peggy cannot communicate this feeling in words.

> But her laughter had had some strange effect on her. It had relaxed her, enlarged her. She felt, or rather she saw, not a place, but a state of being, in which there was real laughter, real happiness, and this fractured world was whole; whole, vast, and free. But how could she say it? "Look here …" she began. She wanted to express something that she felt to be very important; about a world in which people were whole, in which people were free … But they were laughing; she was serious. "Look here …" she began again.
>
> (Y, 390)

Peggy's moment of being is not occasioned by any event in particular but rather occurs *involuntarily*, as Woolf echos in her autobiography, by her own laughter. Somehow the physical act of laughing draws her in to the source of "real laughter," which is a whole world woven together. It's philosophically interesting that she feels that the world *itself* is free. It is not humans that are free and the world mechanical, but for Peggy, that the world is free and, as part of the world, humans participate in this freedom. But the moment is brief and Peggy is unable to say anything about it to anyone else. As usual, this is how the brief moment ends.

Between the Acts

Let's turn now to consider Woolf's final, and posthumously, unfinished novel, *Between the Acts* (1941). The novel is about a woman, Miss La Trobe, who puts on a play about English history, and the audience who watch the play. Miss La Trobe directs the play in a small village in England, just before the outbreak of the Second World War. *Between the Acts* is filled with many hints of beauty and interrelation but technically, I would say, no moments of being.

This novel was motivated by Woolf's idea of writing collective moments of being, but ultimately she felt *Between the Acts* was not able to pull it off. For instance, she conceived of the work as "a centre: all literature discussed … but 'I' rejected: 'We' substituted … we all life, all art, all waifs and strays—a rambling capricious but somehow unified whole—the present state of my mind? And English country … facts and notes" (D5, 135). Woolf's idea was that "We act different parts but are the same."

Unfortunately, after she completed *Between the Acts* Woolf wrote, "I've just read my so called novel over; and I really don't think it does. Its much too slight and sketchy ... its too silly and trivial. I didn't realise how bad it was till I read it over" (D6, 482; 486). In the novel, this is also Miss La Trobe's assessment of her play. "Hadn't she, for twenty-five minutes, made them see? A vision imparted was relief from agony ... for one moment ... for one moment." As her audience wanders away, she feels "she hadn't made them see. It was a failure, another damned failure!" (BA, 98).

In her essay on moments of being in Woolf's fiction, Nicole L. Urquhart argues convincingly that

> Miss La Trobe, like Lily Briscoe, tries to capture and share her vision. Her play can be seen as an attempt to present a moment of being to the audience ... Her assessment is correct. Throughout the play the audience is frequently distracted and contentious. As an artist, she cannot hold them in her grasp. Miss La Trobe fails to impart a vision, in part, because her play is not very good. The play is derivative and her language never soars. As a result, a moment of intense awareness never comes.[4]

In the novel, the audience of Miss La Trobe's play even explicitly rejects her moment of vision.

> Look! Out they come, from the bushes-the riff-raff. Children? Imps-elves-demons. Holding what? Tin cans? Bedroom candlesticks? Old jars? My dear, that's the cheval glass from the Rectory! And the mirror that I lent her. My mother's. Cracked. What's the notion? Anything that's bright enough to reflect, presumably, ourselves? Ourselves! Ourselves! Out they leapt, jerked, skipped. Flashing, dazzling, dancing, jumping. Now old Bart ... he was caught. Now Manresa. Here a nose ... There a skirt ... Then trousers only ... Now perhaps a face .... Ourselves? But that's cruel. To snap us as we are, before we've had time to assume ... And only, too, in parts .... That's what's so distorting and upsetting and utterly unfair.
>
> (BA, 183–4)

Miss La Trobe's artistic vision is too fragmented and distorted to produce the collective moment achieved in *The Waves*. In *The Waves*, the group was smaller and grew up together. In *Between the Acts*, the group is much larger and perhaps too heterogeneous to sustain a moment of being. What remains interesting philosophically for me in *Between the Acts* is that Woolf tried to expand her moment of vision to a broader social level through art, even if it did not succeed. This was the final direction of her work before she died and remains an open question today: how can we create a socially collective moment of being? Thus, I consider this question more closely in the conclusion of this book.

Conclusion

In this chapter, I hope I have given the reader a sense of how Woolf's descriptions of brief moments of being work and some of their philosophical implications. For Woolf, a moment of being might be extraordinarily brief and even poorly communicated but is still just as profound and meaningful. For instance, Rachel's brief moment will last her whole life even though her life will be short and her moment ends almost immediately. Mary mumbles queer gibberish, and everyone laughs at Peggy's attempt to communicate it. These are real philosophical challenges to sustaining and describing moments of being that Woolf is getting at in these novels. How can brief moments of being be drawn out, illuminated, and shared?

In this chapter, I tried to show that each of these brief moments describes some aspect of Woolf's constant philosophical idea of interrelation. Beneath the cotton wool of stable things is a turbulent world of motion that cannot be rationally known but rather felt as an integrated pattern. Storms, wind, street traffic, and rivers all tend to put Woolf's characters into a "trance into which movement among moving things had thrown [them]" (ND, 94). This is in part because vortical and dendritic patterns are nearly universal fractal patterns in nature and tend to suggest a deeply patterned interrelation across scales of time and space. A key thesis of this book is that these are the kinds of patterns beneath the cotton wool Woof refers to in her autobiography. Nature, for Woolf, is a process that cannot be frozen and known objectively. When Woolf's characters see dramatic processes at work, they often feel nature itself is a similarly patterned process that they are part of.

All the brief, prematurely ended, and even failed (in the case of *Jacob's Room* and *Between the Acts*) moments of being I discussed in this chapter raise a critical question: how does one keep these moments going and how deep can Woolf's characters go before resurfacing? What do they find when they can prolong these moments? These are the questions I want to answer in the next section of this book on "individual" moments of being in Woolf's four middle novels.

Individual Moments

Moment 1: Neither This nor That

Beginning in the 1920s, Woolf began experimenting with moments of being and trying to develop them more than she had in her early novels. She held onto the idea that a moment of being is something that happens to a single person. She also used many of the same themes of water, trees, traffic, and turbulence to initiate her character's trances and entrainments into the movement of things. In addition to prolonging these moments, however, she also made them more frequent in her middle novels. *Mrs. Dalloway*, in particular, has a lot of moments of being compared to the novels discussed in the last chapter (see Appendix).

Philosophically, Woolf's individual moments in her middle novels are also more intense. The extra length of the moments also allowed Woolf to develop several aspects of interrelation during the same moment. In these moments, the characters see nature, culture, past, future, the senses, and other aspects of reality as emergent features of an interrelated fluid reality. This is what I want to show in the following sections of this book.

In this particular section, I want to showcase several individual moments of being and show how they work. What starts them, how long they last, and what brings them to an end? How intense and varied is the philosophical idea of interrelation that Woolf said defined her moments? In the sections that follow, I look at individual moments from *Mrs. Dalloway*, *To the Lighthouse*, *Orlando*, and *The Waves* to place together their shared and divergent philosophical features. These are rich moments with more going on than one can cover in a single book. However, again, my approach is to look at them from a largely philosophical perspective to see how Woolf's ontological statement from her autobiography is expressed through these moments.

I begin with *Mrs. Dalloway*, published in 1925, and then move forward with the other novels chronologically. Individual moments are longer than the brief moments I discussed in the previous section, but not nearly as long as the moments I discuss in some later novels. Specifically, individual moments are about 400–1,800 words long compared to brief moments of the last section, which were about 40–200 words.

*

Mrs. Dalloway is a story about a day in the life of Clarissa Dalloway, an aristocratic woman in post-First World War England. Over the course of one day, three individual characters experience moments of being that expose them to a vision of interrelated reality beneath the cotton wool of solid objects. Each of their moments is initiated by movement and expresses several aspects of philosophical interrelation consistent with Woolf's ontological claims from her autobiography. Although Woolf describes here a single person involuntarily experiencing individual moments, these moments are not merely psychological. They are profoundly ecological and atmospheric. I also aim to show here how individual moments in *Mrs. Dalloway* support her ontological claims about the nature of reality.

The first moment of being in *Mrs Dalloway* happens to Clarissa on her walk through London's streets to get flowers for her party. Clarissa Dalloway stops at the gates of St. James Park and stands for a moment watching the omnibuses circulate through Piccadilly square.

Suddenly, the shocking sight of vast masses of people, buses, and taxis moving along the crowded street fills her with an overwhelming sensation of movement and mobility. She begins to feel her movement is entrained in this much more expansive flow of urban, natural, and cosmic movements. She feels it is odd to feel one's self as a process nested within other processes. Since a process cannot be stopped long enough to know it as a discrete or static thing, Clarissa feels a strange epistemological indeterminacy about the nature of things. Her feeling of interrelation in this moment is not the same as a feeling of simple unity with the world. Woolf does not say that Clarissa feels "one with the world" but that she "slices through the world" as a process among processes. In short, Clarissa's being in motion is not a *state* of being. While in motion, she can never be fully present or identical to herself. This is what Clarissa begins to feel from the traffic of Piccadilly, just as Mary and Katharine felt it in *Night and Day*.

She Felt Very Young; at the Same Time Unspeakably Aged

In Clarissa's moment of being at St. James Park, it is not just Clarissa's consciousness that is streaming; it is the real material world. She suddenly feels that she is a process and as a process is neither one determinate thing nor another. She is continually changing and *indeterminate*. "She would not say of any one in the world now that they were this or were that" (MD, 8). Why not? Because processes are not this or that. They are continual transformations.

Not only is Piccadilly in constant motion but so is everything in the world. Everything flows together and is interrelated. Since we are all entangled, no one can be this or that because they are continually becoming something else. In Clarissa's moment, space dilates to encompass the world as a whole. She suddenly realizes it's not just her but everyone and everything else in the world that is also "neither this nor that."

Clarissa also feels time dilating. "She felt very young; at the same time unspeakably aged" (MD, 8). Compared to the cosmos, Clarissa is young. She is only a drop of dew recently formed in the world. However, she is also made of cosmic debris, gas from ancient burned-out stars, dinosaurs, and other people she has never met. In this sense, perhaps, she is unspeakably aged. Clarissa cannot separate herself from the material and historical processes that have wound their way through the universe to become her. The deep material past does not disappear but is interrelated and enfolded in the present. In this sense, too, she is neither this nor that. She is the folded-up intersection of innumerable movements.

She Sliced Like a Knife through Everything

Woolf writes that as Clarissa walked down the street "She sliced like a knife through everything; at the same time was outside, looking on" (MD, 8). What does this mean philosophically? If Woolf believes that we are the thing itself, then we are not in the world as actors are on a stage. We are in the world as waves in water. Insofar as Clarissa is a process within processes she moves through the world as the world moves through her simultaneously. She is neither fully interior nor exterior to the world but rather acts as a portion of the world folded up inside itself and moving through itself.

As the people and taxi cabs ebb and flow all around her, Clarissa feels as if she is afloat on a vast swaying ocean. "She had a perpetual sense, as she watched the taxi cabs, of being out, out, far out to sea and alone; she always had the feeling that it was very, very dangerous to live even one day" (MD, 8).

What is so dangerous about this feeling of being a wave at sea? It feels dangerous because far out on the ocean, everything is flux and flow without any solid land or any visibly discrete beings or fixed points of reference. As Woolf writes in *Orlando*, "Our most daily movements are like the passage of a ship on an unknown sea, and the sailors at the masthead ask, pointing their glasses to the horizon: Is there land or is there none? to which, if we are prophets, we make answer 'Yes'; if we are truthful we say 'No'" (O, 78).

Ontological indeterminacy is dangerous because we can never be entirely certain about what will happen. Our lives are experiments in an uncertain world and so it is possible to become lost alone at sea in the flux of things. This is part of the dark side to Woolf's moments of being. The same moment that occasions rapture may occasion terror. When one realizes that one converges with nature, and that nature is indeterminate flux, one may experience a feeling of smallness as if in an ocean entirely swept away.

Woolf also writes about her moments of being, "The sense of horror held me powerless ... Many of these exceptional moments brought with them a peculiar horror and a physical collapse; they seemed dominant; myself passive" (MB, 72). On the other hand, when she can describe the moment as part of a more extensive process or ordered *pattern*, it can be transformed into a rapturous "discovery." The attempt to name her moments and discover their patterns, Woolf says, is what gives her a philosophy, including the concepts of moments of being/non-being, and makes her a writer of literary art.

She Knew Nothing

Because of their irrational and involuntary nature, Woolf is insistent that moments of being do not require any technical knowledge or special conditions. For example, In *Mrs Dalloway*, Clarissa is not an intellectual or an academic. She is merely capable of receiving a shock and widening her senses to feel her entanglement with the world.

> Not that she thought herself clever, or much out of the ordinary. How she had got through life on the few twigs of knowledge Fraulein Daniels gave them she could not think. She knew nothing; no language, no history; she scarcely read a book now, except memoirs in bed; and yet to her it was absolutely absorbing; all this; the cabs passing; and she would not say of Peter, she would not say of herself, I am this, I am that.
>
> (MD, 8)

For Woolf, moments of becoming are not intellectual or rational deductions *about* the nature of reality. Moments of being are not propositional, even if one can make propositions or art about them afterward. Moments of being do not arise through contemplation, communication, or reason. For Woolf, we are nature sensing itself, and so require no special knowledge or propositions to performatively know what we are. In other words, if in Woolf's philosophy, there is no ontological rift between thinking and being, then there is no barrier to knowing the world as there is for those in the post-Kantian tradition who accept such a division.

Laid Out Like a Mist

To have a moment of being Clarissa requires only her capacity to receive sensuous shocks from the world and be absorbed by a flow of movement, such as taxi cabs. Her philosophical conclusion from this experience, Woolf writes, is that everything is interrelated in patterns of ebb and flow.

> Did it matter then, she asked herself, walking towards Bond Street, did it matter that she must inevitably cease completely; all this must go on without her; did she resent it; or did it not become consoling to believe that death ended absolutely? but that somehow in the streets of London, on the ebb and flow of things, here, there, she survived, Peter survived, lived in each other, she being part, she was positive, of the trees at home; of the house there, ugly, rambling all to bits and pieces as it was; part of people she had never met; being laid out like a mist between the people she knew best, who lifted her on their branches as she had seen the trees lift the mist, but it spread ever so far, her life, herself.
>
> (MD, 9)

If all of nature consists of flows like those in Piccadilly, what is the meaning or order to it all? Why are things as they are? For Clarissa, and Woolf, there is no transcendent meaning to the world. There are no forms that shape the world in advance. There are only emergent patterns and rhythms that ebb and flow. To live, for Clarissa, is to ebb and flow with the rest of the world and make patterns like the shape of traffic in London.

Clarissa thus answers the philosophical question, "Does the world have meaning?" in a profoundly original way. The world does not *have* meaning. The world *is* meaningful because it is ordered and patterned by the movement of matter. The world structures itself through meaningful ebbs and flows, rhythms, and tides. Things survive and mean something only in and through their relations with these deep patterns.

In the passage above, Clarissa thinks to herself that she survives and lives *through* her interrelations: Peter, trees, her house, and all her material conditions. There is no isolatable or isolated Clarissa, only a region or network of flows running through her like a terminal, intersection, or conjunction. She imagines herself like a mist evaporated and held in place by trees. Just as trees produce mists, fog, and clouds by evaporating water through their bodies, so individual people and things emerge and condense from broader material processes that carry them on their tide.

This is a very process materialist way to think about things. Clarissa feels she would not exist without the trees whose breath she breathes, whose weather she moves through, and whose bodies she lives in as a house. Her body and thoughts are part of the metabolic process of the city where people live *through* one another.

Invisible, Unseen; Unknown

As Clarissa continues to walk through the traffic of Piccadilly and up Bond Street, she suddenly realizes that everything and everyone emerges from a vast material ecology of interrelated processes. Seemingly discrete things such as a taxi are really moving processes rising and falling within larger historical patterns. She feels that the discreteness of things disappears to some degree in the process. Woolf writes:

> She had the oddest sense of being herself invisible, unseen; unknown; there being no more marrying, no more having of children now, but only this astonishing and rather solemn progress with the rest of them, up Bond Street, this, being Mrs. Dalloway; not even Clarissa any more; this being Mrs. Richard Dalloway.
>
> (MD, 10)

The name "Clarissa" tries to capture the vast network of processes that make her up. But there is no stable or self-identical Clarissa separate from all the ebbs and flows that support her and carry her on in the world. In this scene, Woolf articulates her idea that a discrete autonomous person is an abstraction. The names "Clarissa," "Mrs. Dalloway," or "Mrs. Richard Dalloway" cannot capture the constantly changing processes that make up what she is. And so, in this sense, Woolf says, Clarissa feels "unseen" and "unknown" to herself.

The philosophical implication here is that reality, as a process, is not stable or discrete enough to see all at once or know entirely. What one is and can know is inseparable from all the processes that weave one together. "That clear, perpetual outline of a face and limb is but an image of ours, under which we group them—a design in a web, the actual threads of which pass out beyond it," as Walter Pater wrote in his conclusion to *The Renaissance*.[1]

Or, as Woolf wrote about one of her own moments in her autobiography, "I was looking at a plant with a spread of leaves; and it seemed suddenly plain that the flower itself was a part of the earth; that a ring enclosed what was the flower; and that was the real flower; part earth; part flower" (MB, 71). The real flower is the flower as an expression of the Earth as an interrelated process. Similarly, the *real* Clarissa is the relational material process of the innumerable matters (trees, people, barns, flowers) that flow through her and leave their iterated patterns in the outline of her body.

Elsewhere, in one of her short stories about a walker, Woolf describes this feeling of interrelated movement with the world. "The walker's thoughts and emotions were largely made up of these outside influences. Walking thoughts were half sky; if you could submit them to chemical analysis you would find that they had some grains of colour in them, some gallons or quarts or pints of air attached to them. This at once made them airier, more impersonal" (CSF, 206). For Woolf, the walker's thoughts are not isolated abstract ideas in their heads. Thinking and walking are material processes that incorporate the world around them. In this sense, our thoughts are ways that the world expresses or thinks itself through us. Hence, Woolf says, our thoughts are part sky. This statement sounds fanciful, but oxygen fuels our bodies and neurons. Without it, our brains would die. The sky is also part of the deep evolutionary and material history of our brain. If we took away the sky, there would be no brain.

Clarissa thinks all this as she walks up Bond Street in the early morning. She passes a fabric shop, a fishmonger, and pauses to look through a glove shop window. "That is all," she said, "That is all" (MD, 11). What is there to say about a world of interrelated patterns of moving unpredictable, unseen, unspeakable, and unknowable? Clarissa's moment of being is ineffable and in the end all she can say is, "that is all ... that is all." Appropriately, Woolf ends Clarissa's moment of being with these words.

Moment 2: Connected by Millions of Fibers

Ten pages after Clarissa has her moment of being walking up Bond Street, Woolf describes another character's moment of being as he walks through Regent's Park. The character is Septimus Warren Smith, a shell-shocked First World War veteran living in London with his Italian wife Lucrezia. At this moment, I want to look at some of the philosophical implications of Septimus' experience of synaesthesia for a materialist theory of language.

As Septimus walks through the park with his wife, they see an airplane skywriting letters in the air, and Septimus experiences a profound significance and beauty.

> So, thought Septimus, looking up, they are signaling to me. Not indeed in actual words; that is, he could not read the language yet; but it was plain enough; this beauty, this exquisite beauty, and tears filled his eyes as he looked at the smoke words languishing and melting in the sky and bestowing upon him in their inexhaustible charity and laughing goodness one shape after another of unimaginable beauty and signaling their intention to provide him, for nothing, for ever, for looking merely, with beauty, more beauty! Tears ran down his cheeks.
>
> (MD, 21–2)

One of the interesting ideas in this moment is that Septimus sees the letters, not as symbolic representations but beautiful performances that are meaningful *in themselves* without referring to anything else. Instead of thinking about what the letters refer to, their shape and texture work *directly* on Septimus' brain. This is philosophically interesting because typically, we think of shapes and patterns as fundamentally meaningless unless humans bestow them with arbitrary meaning or use them to refer to other things.

In this passage, Woolf introduces the idea that shapes and patterns are material performances in their own right with meaning. Patterns are a kind of visual language without a dictionary of set meanings. This is in part what Woolf means by "patterns beneath the cotton wool." These patterns are the language of reality that can make us feel and think even if we do not know what they refer to semiotically.

Woolf describes here a materialist theory of language where meaning and beauty are communicated to Septimus directly through his body. In other words, we can see here how Woolf reverses the anthropocentric bias about language. Instead of humans bestowing meaning upon nature through language, letters in the sky bestow non-referential meaning upon Septimus with inexhaustible generosity.

Instead of experiencing language as a symbol that stands in for a missing idea or a "real" thing, Septimus sees the letters as the real material things that they are. He feels what raw shapes do to a body. A major philosophical implication here is that, for Woolf, material reality lacks nothing. Humans are not cut off from nature doomed to wonder what the world is "really" like or what it "really" means. Instead, the smoky matter of the letters in the sky offers Septimus an excess of beauty and meaning without him "knowing the language." In Septimus' moment of being, matter and meaning are joined together and he experiences meaning as an incredible gift that the world is sharing with him.

Her Voice Sent Running Up into His Brain Waves of Sound

As Septimus and his wife stand in Regent's Park looking up at the smoke letters in the sky, a nearby nursemaid with a baby also sees the letters in the sky and says them out loud in a low voice right behind Septimus. When Septimus hears them, he does not think of them as sounds that represent letters in the alphabet but rather as noises that reverberate through his whole body. The sound is a material vibration that produces an incredible synesthetic experience in Septimus. Septimus *feels* the woman's *sound* as a touch inside his body.

> "K ... R ..." said the nursemaid, and Septimus heard her say "Kay Arr" close to his ear, deeply, softly, like a mellow organ, but with a roughness in her voice like a grasshopper's, which rasped his spine deliciously and sent running up into his brain waves of sound which, concussing, broke. A marvellous discovery indeed—that the human voice in certain atmospheric conditions (for one must be scientific, above all scientific) can quicken trees into life!
>
> (MD, 22)

In this moment, Septimus experiences what scientists call auditory-tactile synesthesia. Indeed, Woolf gives here one of the earliest recorded descriptions of this phenomenon that scientists now call "autonomous sensory meridian response" (ASMR). ASMR is a euphoric tingling sensation that typically begins on the scalp and moves down the back of the neck and upper spine when one hears certain sounds like soft whispering close to the ear or certain scratching noises.[2] Slow-paced low-pitched tiny sounds tend to be the most effective triggers[3] of ASMR, although some people are more susceptible to this phenomenon than others.

In other words, Septimus feels the materiality of the sound as it stimulates and moves directly through his nervous system.[4] His body continues the sound wave by other means. This is philosophically important because it expresses a unique dimension of Woolf's concept of material interrelation in moments of being. The world is continually weaving through our bodies and minds such that in a moment of being we can feel how sounds or noises penetrate and resonate inside us.[5] We do not try to understand their representation or symbolic meaning and instead directly feel their material meaning as they affect us.

Sound is a material process that works on us and through us below the level of representation. Typically, we tend to ignore the sounds and feelings of words in our bodies and mouths because they distract from what the word or sound is supposed to symbolize. Yet, in moments of being and close listening, one becomes hypersensitive to the material and performative aspects of language. Philosophically, this reveals the normally hidden patterns and affects beneath the cotton wool of referential thought and language.

ASMR is a beautiful example of how "non-musical" sounds of everyday life and nature can have euphoric physical effects if we stopped to feel each tingle running through our bodies. Woolf calls it the wave-like materiality of words (L3, 247). In *Mrs. Dalloway*, Septimus' ASMR experience also triggers a broader synesthesia and feeling of interrelation with the trees around him. Septimus feels his body and brain respond to the micro-movements of the trees.

By observing closely the moving patterns woven through nature, he feels beauty and joy as he sees the trees rising and falling like waves directly coordinated to the sounds of someone speaking nearby.

These sounds begin to act directly on his brain like waves rising and crashing. They induce an "excitement of the elm trees rising and falling, rising and falling with all their leaves alight and the colour thinning and thickening from blue to the green of a hollow wave, like plumes on horses' heads, feathers on ladies', so proudly they rose and fell, so superbly, would have sent him mad" (MD, 22). Without the filter of normal consciousness to separate him from the world, Septimus can no longer distinguish his own feelings, sensations, and thoughts from the rest of the world. This is not because he is hallucinating but that human brains only function "normally" when they limit the range of their sensations and ignore many of the typically imperceptible sensations and bodily responses that affect them. We do not stop to study and feel every breeze or color or cloud. If we did, we would never make it to our destination on time. Septimus feels he may go "mad" because European civilization defines "normal" as being much more cut off from the full range of environmental synesthesia. Thus his "madness" is feeling everything without individuated ego. Frequencies of light and sound travel through our bodies and modulate our nervous system, but to function instrumentally we have to ignore most of it. And our bodies and brains have evolved to do just that and to process the micro-movements and affects around us unconsciously. The result is a diminished capacity for ecological awareness and sensation but a heightened ability for abstraction and instrumental rationality.

> They beckoned; leaves were alive; trees were alive. And the leaves being connected by millions of fibres with his own body, there on the seat, fanned it up and down; when the branch stretched he, too, made that statement. The sparrows fluttering, rising, and falling in jagged fountains were part of the pattern; the white and blue, barred with black branches. Sounds made harmonies with premeditation; the spaces between them were as significant as the sounds. A child cried. Rightly far away a horn sounded. All taken together meant the birth of a new religion.
>
> (MD, 22–3)

Here, Woolf is describing a version of what scientists call "mirror-touch synesthesia." When someone with mirror-touch synesthesia sees someone else touch their face, they feel the touch in their own face. In her description of Septimus' moment of being, Woolf describes something similar here but with trees. As the trees move like waves in the wind, Septimus feels their movement in his body. The movement of birds and fountains as well as the sounds and silences around the park create patterns of sensation directly in his body without representing anything. Septimus can feel the movements of the world happening in his own body.

Scientists have only very recently confirmed that this is also what happens neurologically to everyone—only unconsciously. We have neurons in our brains scientists call "mirror neurons" that fire when we see someone or even something move. Our brains register the movement in the same neurons that would have been active as if we had performed the actions ourselves.[6] This has important philosophical consequences. It means that the world not only happens outside us but inside us, even if we are unaware of it. There is no sharp division between us and nature. Woolf's genius was that she understood and described this experience so beautifully before scientists had considered it a possibility.

Woolf described a similar experience in, *To the Lighthouse*. "It was odd, she thought, how if one was alone, one leant to inanimate things; trees, streams, flowers; felt they expressed one; felt they became one; felt they knew one, in a sense were one" (TL, 63). The double experience of expressing nature and having nature express one's self is philosophically crucial to Woolf's moments of being. When our mirror neurons fire the world is not represented in cognition but felt directly in the body synesthetically. The world's movements become our feelings and then we immediately find them out in the world as expressions of ourselves. We do not know the trees and streams around us as external objects but as dimensions of ourselves. They know us as we know ourselves.

Septimus is not giving a "metaphysical" account of his experience. He is not seeing a transcendent world beyond this one but rather richly varied patterns immanent to this world. Ironically, Septimus declares, "for one must be scientific" (MD, 22). However, his descriptions sound less scientific than psychedelic. But on the other hand, his experience is in some ways more scientifically perceptive and accurate than most people's because of how closely he feels the microscopic changes of the world. It is as if Septimus, "had a microscope stuck to [his] eye" as Woolf says of Orlando (O, 320). Septimus can feel the rays of light connecting the trees to his eyes and nervous system. He feels all the tiny changes of their scintillation. As he watches the rays of light move, his own body and nervous system change subtly in response to the trees' changes in light and color. This is an accurate scientific fact and yet most of us ignore these kinds of minute affects. Yet, Septimus feels directly how the fractal patterned movements and orders of nature like leaves blowing in the wind and sparrows diving structure and order our world of micro-affective sensations.

Something similar happens when he listens to a range of various sounds in the urban landscape.[7] He hears baby cry, street traffic, a car horn and together discovers their hidden pattern or frequency range filled with meaning and interest. Septimus experiences a sonic pareidolia. As he watches a sparrow move erratically in the air its fractal hunting pattern synchronizes with the urban sounds to create a beautiful synesthetic composition. These are how the patterns beneath the cotton wool work for Septimus.

Additionally, insofar as Septimus feels himself woven into this mass of interconnected patterns he feels it means the birth of "a new religion." Woolf's suggestion here is perhaps that moments of being and the interconnecting patterns of the world are the basis of many religious experiences. However, for Septimus, it is an immanent religion of nature, not of a transcendent deity. Septimus' moment of being is an altered state of consciousness whose effects overlap with mystical, religious, trance-like, psychedelic, and manic states. In these states, people become aware of the more typically unconscious connections and affects which are normally filtered out. While some may interpret this as "other worldly," or "religious," Woolf treats it as a fully material and natural experience neither fully scientific nor fully religious at the same time.

Unfortunately, when religious or mystical experiences do not align with historically dominant narratives about reality, science, or religion, they are treated as "hallucinations" or mental illness. In the Euro-Western tradition specifically, the material world is not typically understood as meaningful on its own. Only humans grant meaning to the world. This is not the case for the experience Woolf describes here or for many non-Western religious traditions where art and religion are understood to be fully continuous with the natural world. This profound feeling of being continuous with the world is perhaps at the very foundations of religion, spirituality, philosophy, and human meaning.[8]

Septimus is right that this would be the rebirth of a "new" religion relative to his European context where nature lacks meaning. Septimus' vision would not be the birth of a new *transcendent* religion but the birth of an *immanent* religion, a *materialist mysticism* without god or transcendence.[9] In such a religion, everything is saturated with sacred and singular meaning if only we would listen more carefully. Septimus' moment of being ends with this final idea of an unnamed and un-described "new religion—." Meanwhile, in the same park, another one of Woolf's characters has a vision in a dream of a sacred mother goddess in the tree branches.

Moment 3: The Death of the Soul

The next moment of being in *Mrs. Dalloway* happens to Peter Walsh, an old friend of Clarissa's, who has just come back to London after being in India for many years. Peter goes for a wandering walk through the streets of London one day. As he is walking through Regent's Park, he starts to feel drowsy. He sits down on a bench, falls asleep, and has a vision, after which he concludes, "the death of the soul."

This moment of being is interesting because it is the only moment, by my count, that occurs while dreaming. The occurrence of moments of being during illness, madness, and dreams makes it explicit that Woolf's moments of being are related to altered states of consciousness. However, although they are related to brain states, moments of being are not reducible to them. In Woolf's descriptions, as we see below, moments reveal how deeply interconnected one's brain state is with atmospheric aspects of the natural environment, urban traffic, sounds, weather patterns, and tree shapes.

Peter's dream is a moment where the reality of the dream state blends beautifully with the world such that we can easily see how the interior of his mental life is interrelated to the outside. Reality folds itself up and plays out in dreams.

What Odd Shapes They Take

As Peter's body wanders through the streets of London so does his mind. He sees Regent's Park and remembers his childhood when he used to walk there. Thinking of his childhood makes him think of Clarissa because women "live more in the past" than men, Peter thinks. Then he recalls the long straight walk of the park, and a little house in the park, and then a statue there.

Peter's free associating about childhood and women leads him to a park bench where he sees a woman and a baby.

> He looked for an empty seat. He did not want to be bothered (feeling a little drowsy as he did) by people asking him the time. An elderly grey nurse, with a baby asleep in its perambulator—that was the best he could do for himself; sit down at the far end of the seat by that nurse.
>
> (MD, 56)

He then sits down and begins to think of Clarissa's child, Elizabeth, and the relationship between mother and daughter. He lights a cigar, sees an hourglass in the smoke, and begins to dream about walking down a long path in a forest, a mother figure, and a house at the end.

> The rich benignant cigar smoke eddied coolly down his throat; he puffed it out again in rings which breasted the air bravely for a moment; blue, circular—I shall try and get a word alone with Elizabeth tonight, he thought—then began to wobble into hour-glass shapes and taper away; odd shapes they take, he thought.
>
> (MD, 56)

Here, Woolf interleaves third-person narrative with Peter's first-person thoughts showing the interrelation between our conscious awareness and the material patterns of the world. Our thoughts are not separate from the world, but limited regions of awareness woven into the world. Our first-person thoughts weave tiny areas within third-person processes.

Peter forms his turbulent cigar smoke into an eddy and then into metastable rings just as the turbulent world of matter forms itself into Peter's body and metastable mind. The rings then deform into an hourglass shape before falling apart. The rings "dissolve in the air" like the "leaden circles" of the Big Ben clock tower that chimes throughout the novel and the skywriting that Septimus sees (MD, 4, 48, 94, 186).

Peter's cigar smoke, among other things, dramatizes the processual nature of matter whose forms emerge from turbulence and then dissolve over time. He blows his rings bravely but time dissolves them and they sink into entropy as do our attempts to measure time with clock bells. Our written words, clock bells, and smoke rings do not capture or measure reality but weave into it for a while before dissipating. One day, London will be grass and the city itself will have been a metastable moment in earth's deep history. The smoke of cannons and rifles in war dissolves in the air as human empires rise and fall through history (Figure 2.3.1).

Peter's cigar smoke mixes with his breath and dissolves just as Peter's body and mind will dissolve back into nature. Indeed, the English word "soul" comes from the archaic Greek word *psukhḗ* meaning "breath." In this way, Peter's dissolving cigar rings foreshadow his first words after waking from his dream, "Lord, Lord, the death of the soul." But this is an odd expression. For Plato and the Christian tradition, souls are supposed to be indestructible because they are immaterial. Here, however, Woolf dramatizes a philosophy of the *material* soul made of breath and illuminated/dissipated as cigar smoke. All things, even souls, dissolve.

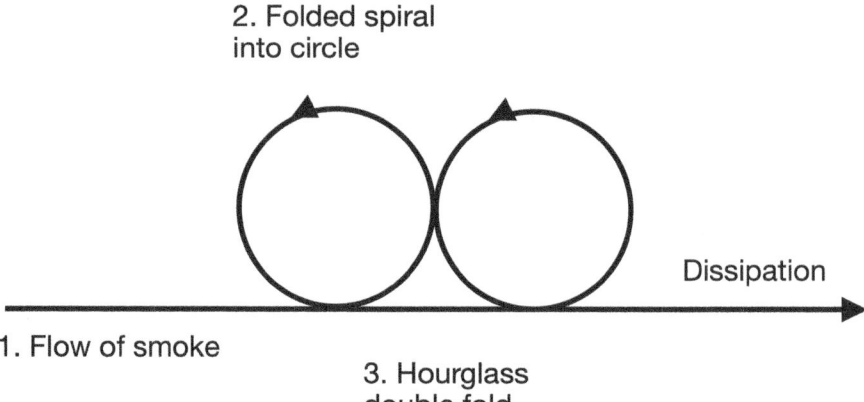

Figure 2.3.1 Peter's cigar smoke performs the process-oriented nature of things. His smoke, like the energy of the cosmos, flows and cycles through interlocking metastable cycles before ultimately dissipating. Peter's smoke is a microcosm of the process-universe.

Down He Sank into the Plumes

If the soul is material, what becomes of it after death? Lucretius described the process in the same kinetic terms as Woolf—it leaves the body like smoke.[10] When Peter's cigar smoke dissolves over time, like all forms in nature, he falls asleep as if he were dying.

> Suddenly he closed his eyes, raised his hand with an effort, and threw away the heavy end of his cigar. A great brush swept smooth across his mind, sweeping across it moving branches, children's voices, the shuffle of feet, and people passing, and humming traffic, rising and falling traffic. Down, down he sank into the plumes and feathers of sleep, sank, and was muffled over.
> (MD, 56)

All the movements around him (moving branches, waves of sound, moving people, and moving cars) do not disappear but flow smoothly and evenly across his mind as if a brush were sweeping them all together into his unconscious. Peter sinks into the fluid pattern of muffled feathers. Depth, sleep, and death all share a similar pattern of decreasing conscious activity.[11] The plumes of feathers are related to the smoke plumes whose "disordered" state is similar to the disordered state of our brains that require sleep.[12]

The grey nurse resumed her knitting as Peter Walsh, on the hot seat beside her, began snoring. In her grey dress, moving her hands indefatigably yet quietly, she seemed like the champion of the rights of sleepers, like one of those spectral presences which rise in twilight in woods made of sky and branches.

(MD, 56)

The nurse is the color of twilight. She is gray like the interrelation of dark and light, night and day, and a champion of sleepers, those traveling *between* defined states of consciousness. She watches over the transition between the daily cotton wool of consciousness of discrete things to the "unreal reality" of processes and flows. Instead of the hourglass, she is the moving weaver like the Greek fates who portioned out the thread of a mortal life, woven into a textile, and cut it when it was time to die.[13] Past, present, and future weave together on the bench in the figures of the young baby, mid-life Peter (in his fifties), and the elderly gray nurse.

Here we also have a more material and kinetic theory of time. Time is not an abstract chronological sequence but rather a name we use to describe the movement of the universe as it spreads out from hot to cold. The world is woven together and so we feel time pass more or less quickly depending on how we are woven into it.[14] Matter does not move *in* time but weaves a temporal world.[15] The nurse who watches over Peter is a weaving champion of motion, transition, and becoming. She is the weaver and unweaver of time just like the fates.

In this passage, Woolf also gives us a fascinating theory of what we might call the "material unconscious." That is, that our unconscious mind is not purely interior or immaterial but rather like a fold in the world itself. For example, all the things Peter sees in the world before he falls asleep continue to play out in his dream in mythological form. Woolf may be suggesting here that mythology and religious experience have their origins in the material patterns of the world. In some way not fully known to us, our stories are iterations of the world itself working its patterns through us and our dreams.

What is the material basis of a goddess figure if not an expression of the experience of something like tree branch silhouettes at dusk and the feeling that the forest supports and nurtures us like a nurse or mother through the night? Perhaps some of the first human experiences of the gods were ones of pareidolia, seeing meaningful patterns in natural images. Like faces in the hillside, or voices in a babbling spring, the gods have always been material patterns with their own kind of agency to act on and through us. They are not just *social* or *psychological* constructs.

Lucretius proposed a similar materialist theory of the unconscious and dreams. He writes:

and in whatever things we have been engaged in before and on which our mind has been more intent, in dreams we often seem to engage in the same things.[16]

Dreams, for Lucretius and Woolf, do not disclose idealist *a priori* archetypes of the mind, universal forms, or human society. Neither are they unmediated access to truth or transcendent revelation. Dreams are entirely sensuous processes that merely continue the flow and circulation of matter by other means through us as we sleep. The gray-colored nurse merges with the moving branches, the color of twilight, and the sky to produce Peter's dream.

The Solitary Traveler

Peter, who had been walking alone in Regent's Park and wanted to sit alone, now becomes the "solitary traveler" in his dream.

> The solitary traveller, haunter of lanes, disturber of ferns, and devastator of great hemlock plants, looking up, suddenly sees the giant figure at the end of the ride.
>
> By conviction an atheist perhaps, he is taken by surprise with moments of extraordinary exaltation. Nothing exists outside us except a state of mind, he thinks; a desire for solace, for relief, for something outside these miserable pigmies, these feeble, these ugly, these craven men and women. But if he can conceive of her, then in some sort she exists, he thinks.
>
> (MD, 56–7)

He now embodies all the imperceptible motions that were there but unseen in the world of waking life. In the world of flow and process, he travels and moves through the lanes and rides through the streets whose traffic washes over him as he falls asleep.

Peter experiences a "moment of extraordinary exaltation," or what Woolf calls a moment of being. This moment is not about religious transcendence, God, revelation, or salvation. Peter, like Lucretius, is an atheist. But what then is this feeling of being interwoven with the world? What do dream images tell us about the philosophy of interconnection?

Just as Mrs. Dalloway becomes a mist between tree branches, Peter sees a sensuous pattern or figure. The pattern, made by silhouetted tree branches in the evening, is a powerful image because it is not strictly a thing, nor is it anything transcendent. It is a kinetic pattern, gestalt, or pareidolia made by moving branches from the perspective of a moving traveler. It is a kind of constellation composed of Peter's desire for solitude from the masses of people asking the time and running around *doing* things.

This constellation is the material reality of his dream. He continues his solitary walk through London by other means. His brain continues to iterate the patterns he has seen from waking life in his sleep. This continuation is not his merely interior imagination, although for a moment, he, like Sally in *The Years*, tries out the idea of idealism and solipsism. However, his vision of a woman in the branches means that something outside him must be real in some sense. His dream is entirely continuous but not identical to the exterior world. It is produced by and through the world. His dream world emerges like a mist or pattern from within the material world. This pattern is now carried along *in* his body as he sleeps.

Indeed, sleep is not just a mirror or an internal reflection of the exterior. It is an *enfoldment* of nature itself and thus exposes an affective reality circulating beneath the surface of things. Beneath any solipsistic mind is the real world in which the doubting mind is only a fold. In short, Woolf offers a material interpretation of dreams where dreams are not merely representations of an external world but folds of the world itself.

Such Are the Visions

In her moments of becoming, Woolf often feels that the world becomes "unreal." She must make the moments real by describing them afterward. In his dream, Peter has a moment of exaltation, but he also feels he is actively shaping it like a lucid dream to make it "real." Peter "endows" the leaves in the breeze with generosity, wisdom, and absolution, just as numerous groups of people have for millennia in the oral and oracular traditions.[17]

> Advancing down the path with his eyes upon sky and branches he rapidly endows them with womanhood; sees with amazement how grave they become; how majestically, as the breeze stirs them, they dispense with a dark flutter of the leaves charity, comprehension, absolution, and then, flinging themselves suddenly aloft, confound the piety of their aspect with a wild carouse.
>
> (MD, 57)

But what does it mean to endow a vision? If humans are "the thing itself," then it is nature that endows itself through humans. In this sense, charity is not an arbitrary social construct. Trees generously give 99 percent of all their energy back to the Earth through evaporation. They give us their breath and bodies. In a sense, perhaps, this is part of their wisdom or comprehension. The comprehension they share with us is their realization that to survive on this planet together it is best to share as much of their energy as they can with others. The water from their evaporation becomes clouds and weather. Their canopy becomes a home for animals and insects. What they *know* is what they *do*. The forgiveness of the trees is their continued generosity in the face of constant ecological destruction by humans. Trees do not judge humans and in that sense offer a kind of absolution.

Peter's dream is not a divine vision of God but a sensual and pareidolic image of matter's agency. The leaves of the tree suddenly fly up in the breeze in a turbulent carouse because nature is not pious, but "muddled" and "mixed," as Orlando says (O, 77–9). Nature is not one thing or several things but the pied process of transformation itself. Nature gives everything that God does in the moment of exhalation but without transcendence, unity, or judgment.

> Such are the visions which proffer great cornucopias full of fruit to the solitary traveller, or murmur in his ear like sirens lolloping away on the green sea waves or are dashed in his face like bunches of roses, or rise to the surface like pale faces which fishermen flounder through floods to embrace.
>
> (MD, 57)

The basis of Peter's moment of exaltation and vision is Woolf's radical naturalism, which was likely inspired in part by Lucretius and Jane Harrison's study of ancient religion. It is a vision of natural excess and knowledge of moving processes. The cornucopia is not only Demeter's woven horn-shaped basket filled with food. It is also an ancient basket or *calathus* for holding weaving materials connected to wisdom and art, or what the Greeks called *metis*.[18]

Peter's moment summons an image of Penelope, the weaver, and Odysseus, the solitary traveler. The sirens offer all the wisdom of the world to Odysseus with their beautiful song. Their song is so beautiful and full of meaning that it seduces the listener to keep listening until they die. In this way, Woolf summons Homer's image to show the connection between beauty, wisdom, and death. The wisdom of the siren's song is that beauty unravels the self into the world. Wisdom is the death of the self and eventually the death of the body. This, too, is similar to Woolf's moments of being in which one's ego is dissolved into the world. Peter's moment of being is beautiful but also leads him toward the death of the soul.

The pale faces in the water that Peter sees are images of Narcissus, beauty, and art.

Here Woolf draws again on another myth whose material basis is the way that flowers (the narcissus) and beauty more generally can pull us in deeper and deeper toward moments of being and ego death. To the degree that our bodies and minds iterate the same patterns of the cosmos, we become continuous with processes larger than ourselves. They may not always do so, but they can also occasion, as they did for Woolf a moment of being in which a single flower is "the whole." Woolf writes, "I was looking at a plant with a spread of leaves; and it seemed suddenly plain that the flower itself was a part of the earth; that a ring enclosed what was the flower; and that was the real flower; part earth; part flower" (MB, 71).

Woolf casts the weaving nursemaid as the modern goddess of sleepers and of moments of vision. Historically, nurses brought humans into the world as midwives and often saw them out of the world if the mother or baby died in childbirth. So the gray nursemaid sits in Regent's Park as the material basis of the myths of goddesses watching over those on their way between life and death; waking and sleeping. Odysseus, the solitary traveler, was the only mortal to visit the underworld and return. He was also the only mortal to hear the siren's song and live. Thus, Woolf here connects Peter's dream to the journey between life and death and to ecstatic moments of vision between conscious and non-conscious states.

Myriads of Things Merged in One Thing

In these moments of kinetic becoming, the myriad of things in nature align and form a meaningful pattern or figure. In this case, Peter sees the image of the sky through silhouette branches at twilight. The pattern is not *a priori* or divine but is emergent from the complex milieu of Peter's nap in the park. Peter's vision takes on a shape continuous with nature, just like waves are emergent forms continuous with the sea, which produces kinetic wave-forms that are distinct from but do not transcend the sea.

> Such are the visions which ceaselessly float up, pace beside, put their faces in front of, the actual thing; often overpowering the solitary traveller and taking away from him the sense of the earth, the wish to return, and giving him for substitute a general peace, as if (so he thinks as he advances down the forest ride) all this fever of living were simplicity itself; and myriads of things merged in one thing; and this figure, made of sky and branches as it is, had risen from the troubled sea (he is elderly, past fifty now) as a shape might be sucked up out of the waves to shower down from her magnificent hands compassion, comprehension, absolution.
>
> (MD, 57)

Peter's visions draw him deeper and deeper toward images of interconnection to the point that he almost forgets himself or his ego and the wish to return to the world of waking life. He sees the patterns of the world increasingly weaving together into a wave that holds everything together. The world of things dissolves into threads and is woven into waves from which it is no longer possible to tell who or where one is.

Moments of being, for Woolf, are not above the earth or only in the mind but are *in the world*. They draw on the senses to proffer peaceful images of a complex and turbulent world. They reveal a pattern immanent to, not beyond, the cotton wool. In moments we know that we are the interrelated "thing itself" (MB, 72).

> So, he thinks, may I never go back to the lamplight; to the sitting-room; never finish my book; never knock out my pipe; never ring for Mrs. Turner to clear away; rather let me walk straight on to this great figure, who will, with a toss of her head, mount me on her streamers and let me blow to nothingness with the rest.
>
> (MD, 57–8)

After seeing this profound emergent figure saturated with the meaning of the "whole" (MB, 72), the ordinary world of things appears fragmented and shallow compared to this deeper pattern beneath them. The "myriads of things merged in one thing" (MD, 57), which was not a thing but a metastable figure like a waveform emerging from the sea or like the natural fractal imbrications of the dendritic tree branches. He imagines becoming one with these flows in her tresses and blown to nothingness with the rest of nature—headed entropically toward dissipation. Peter's cigar smoke, his material soul, the wisdom of the ancients, and the trees' expenditure are all images of nature's energetic dissipation toward death.

> Such are the visions. The solitary traveller is soon beyond the wood; and there, coming to the door with shaded eyes, possibly to look for his return, with hands raised, with white apron blowing, is an elderly woman who seems (so powerful is this infirmity) to seek, over a desert, a lost son; to search for a rider destroyed; to be the figure of the mother whose sons have been killed in the battles of the world. So, as the solitary traveller advances down the village street where the women stand knitting and the men dig in the garden, the evening seems ominous; the figures still; as if some august fate, known to them, awaited without fear, were about to sweep them into complete annihilation.
>
> (MD, 58)

When the traveler passes through the wood and is beyond the vision, he finds a mother: an iteration of the forest mother. The living mother looks into the forest as if looking into the mythopoetic past. Instead of the misty tree weaver in the forest, Peter finds domestic knitters and diggers waiting for the moment when death will take them as well.

In short, Woolf gives us a dream-image in which the material flow of nature sweeps all things away. But there is, as Lucretius says, no reason to fear death.[19] This is the lesson of the trees and the sirens. Nature is generosity and expenditure without judgment or morality. In essence, nature will sweep us all up into its flux. We will all be unwoven.

Among Ordinary Things

In his dream, Peter returns to the world of "ordinary things," which are stabilized versions of larger natural processes.

> Indoors among ordinary things, the cupboard, the table, the window-sill with its geraniums, suddenly the outline of the landlady, bending to remove the cloth, becomes soft with light, an adorable emblem which only the recollection of cold human contacts forbids us to embrace. She takes the marmalade; she shuts it in the cupboard.
>
> (MD, 58)

A profound reality or larger vision now coexists immanently with the cupboard, the table, and marmalade. They all appear strange in the context of the streaming whole of nature.

> There is nothing more to-night, sir?
> But to whom does the solitary traveller make reply?
>
> (MD, 58)

Who does Peter reply to? This is the fundamental question of the moment of being. Is it nature, death, and flux or the landlady and her marmalade, or something else entirely? The answer is fundamentally indeterminate because it is "neither this nor that." The marmalade too is woven from the flux.

> So the elderly nurse knitted over the sleeping baby in Regent's Park. So Peter Walsh snored. He woke with extreme suddenness, saying to himself, "The death of the soul."

"Lord, Lord!" he said to himself out loud, stretching and opening his eyes. "The death of the soul."

(MD, 58)

Peter's dream-vision of radical naturalism means not only that the landlady and the table are indeterminate—neither this nor that—but so is the material soul itself—his soul. One lives through the dissipative and kinetic streaming of this vast figure of nature. The material soul is always dying and dissipating like the ring of cigar smoke or the form of a wave. In this way, Peter's moment of being shows him not only his interconnection with nature but also how the movement of matter forms the patterns of reality itself. His moment ends when he awakes. Not long after he awakes in Regent's Park, Woolf writes another moment of being with Septimus in the same park.

Moment 4: Time Split Its Husk; Poured Its Riches over Him

After Peter wakes up from his dream, Septimus has another moment of being in Regent's Park. In this moment, Septimus also experiences wisdom, generosity, and absolution through patterns in the trees.

Septimus' moment begins when he sits on a bench in Regent's Park. Cars and people stream by him. Suddenly, the Earth begins to quiver. It starts to share with him a profound revelation about the nature of truth and beauty.

> The supreme secret must be told to the Cabinet; first that trees are alive; next there is no crime; next love, universal love, he muttered, gasping, trembling, painfully drawing out these profound truths which needed, so deep were they, so difficult, an immense effort to speak out, but the world was entirely changed by them for ever.
>
> (MD, 67)

One may recall that wisdom, generosity (love), and absolution (no crime) are the same three truths Peter Walsh was offered by a tree in his dream on another park bench. But what is the philosophical truth of the trees that Woolf keeps figuring in moments of being? Perhaps the idea is that there is no judgment or morality in nature. If there are only branching spreading tree-like patterns of energy in the universe, there is no God to judge us and no absolute moral hierarchy, and we are free to live together as we please. We are even free to change our mind about how we want to live together. Trees do not tell us exactly how to live, but as a fundamental ontological pattern they at least replace the metaphysical great chain of being that has so burdened philosophy.

Another wisdom of trees is generosity. Trees release 99 percent of the energy they take in from sunlight and the earth through transpiration. Their waste makes our weather. Their bodies make our homes. Their fruits fill our stomachs. Perhaps their generosity is a lesson for how ecosystems and cultural systems should share if they want to survive.

These three truths of wisdom, generosity, and absolution are hard for Septimus to speak or represent in speech. How can Septimus communicate the truths which were not spoken to him in the first place? The tree communicates not with words but with its being and actions. For the same reason, Peter does not know how to respond to them after his forest vision. It is also a key feature of Woolf's moments of being that words and communication are incapable of representing them.

How then is "the world entirely changed," for Septimus, by the utterance of these truths? If, as Woolf says elsewhere, "we are the thing itself" (MB, 72), then truth has a performative dimension. Truth is like the sounds that travel up Septimus' spine. Speech acts are actions that do something in the world. They are nothing but their effects.

The Flesh Was Melted Off the World

Septimus' brain is the product of millions of years of evolution that has made it incredibly sensitive to the environment's smallest changes.

> But what was the scientific explanation (for one must be scientific above all things)? Why could he see through bodies, see into the future, when dogs will become men? It was the heat wave presumably, operating upon a brain made sensitive by eons of evolution. Scientifically speaking, the flesh was melted off the world. His body was macerated until only the nerve fibres were left. It was spread like a veil upon a rock.
>
> (MD, 68)

The human nervous system has more neurons for its size than any other animal. The waves of heat, swaying of branches, and the sounds of the park all act directly on his nervous system. While most people ignore the vast majority of these sensations, Septimus, in this moment, becomes ultra-sensitive to them. He feels all the microscopic movements and the full network of relations that compose him. His senses widen, expand, and feel the world at their maximum capacity without the filter of his normal consciousness.

Septimus says the flesh is melted off the world because he sees things as no longer separated from one another by their surfaces. He sees and feels the kinetic waves flowing through everything. He feels the earth rippling and quivering as his own body. His thoughts and feelings are not subjective mental states but directly connected to atmospheric and material processes. This experience is not a hallucination even if it is ironic that the war-traumatized "mad man," Septimus, is the one who is being the most "scientific" about the situation of ecological, evolutionary, and natural interconnection. Although his descriptions would hardly be recognized as scientific during his time, invisible interconnects are not entirely unscientific by modern standards.

Next, Septimus' body is shaken and macerated by vibrations until his nerve fibers spread out like a veil. Septimus had felt earlier that nature "beckoned; leaves were alive; trees were alive. And the leaves being connected by millions of fibres with his own body, there on the seat, fanned it up and down; when the branch stretched he, too, made that statement" (MD, 22). This "veil of fibers" is another recurring kinetic and fractal pattern in Woolf's moments of being. It connects the "veil" of the event on Bond Street and the dove-gray image of the tree on the motorcar (MD, 14) to the "misty trees" that Mrs. Dalloway becomes (MD, 9) and to the knitting gray twilight figure in the trees in Peter's dream (MD, 56). Woolf also draws a connection here between the material kinetic pattern of the dendritic "fibers" of the trees and the dendritic fibers of the human nervous system.

Septimus can see through bodies, just as Mrs. Dalloway cut through the world like a knife and became an "invisible, unseen" "mist" (MD, 11). Septimus sees the subtle movements, patterns, and webs of relationships that compose reality. However, "invisible" does not mean unreal but rather the unseen *process* that composes "ordinary things" (MD, 58) rendered visible in a moment of being.

The Earth Thrilled beneath Him

Septimus feels his body spread out into a web of relations with the world. He feels that flowers grow through this flesh. From this point, he can see all the knotwork of patterns that compose him.

> He lay back in his chair, exhausted but upheld. He lay resting, waiting, before he again interpreted, with effort, with agony, to mankind. He lay very high, on the back of the world. The earth thrilled beneath him. Red flowers grew through his flesh; their stiff leaves rustled by his head.
>
> (MD, 68)

Most of us feel that the earth is a stable or static place that we walk on top of. But in his moment of being, Septimus feels the earth thrill and quiver beneath him. The earth is not static but continually shifting and metamorphosing. He does not feel that the flowers are out there in the world but inside him as his body and mind respond to them.

The philosophical point here for Woolf's realism is that reality is in motion. Processes do not happen inside or outside but through the world. However, since we are largely in the habit of filtering out all these tiny movements and imagining that things are not in motion, the experience of movement feels unreal and hallucinogenic when we read it. Woolf gave a lovely example of this kinetic reality in her early journals:

> As we drove along through lanes deeply cut in the chalk, I kept likening the downs to the long curved waves of the sea. It is as though the land here, all molten once, and rolling in vast billows had solidified while the waves were still swollen & on the point of breaking. From a height it looks as though the

whole land were flowing. Man, too, has done nothing to change the shape of these breakers. He has planted them to a certain extent, but has mostly left their grass untouched for his flocks. You see a thatched shed or so on the down side where the shepherd lives, but no other human house. The villages have all sunk into the hollows between the waves; & the result is a peculiar smoothness & bareness of outline. This is the bare bone of the earth.

(PA, 192)

Here, Woolf sees that the stable earth is really similar to an ocean whose waves of dirt and rock are relatively solid. Water and earth look very different to us, but only because their movement is relative to our own. At every scale of reality, matter flows and curves into wave-like patterns. These are the hidden fractal patterns that Woolf sees in her moments of being that thread everything together. Humans, for Woolf, are not separate from these patterns which occur across scales. Humans make their homes in the waves of the earth.

Similarly, Septimus feels the earth thrilling and flowing beneath him. He feels red flowers and leaves growing up through his flesh as the flowers and leaves excite his nervous system, and amplify his senses. In his moment of being, Septimus feels his body as a geological ripple in the flow of the earth. When he is dead the flowers and leaves will feed on his body and grow through his flesh. Septimus feels time rush by as nature weaves in and out through his body.

Music Should Be Visible

High on his wave, Septimus then begins to hear the sounds around him as they diffract with one another in the air and form synesthetic patterns. Woolf writes:

> Music began clanging against the rocks up here. It is a motor horn down in the street, he muttered; but up here it cannoned from rock to rock, divided, met in shocks of sound which rose in smooth columns (that music should be visible was a discovery) and became an anthem, an anthem twined round now by a shepherd boy's piping (That's an old man playing a penny whistle by the public-house, he muttered) which, as the boy stood still came bubbling from his pipe, and then, as he climbed higher, made its exquisite plaint while the traffic passed beneath. This boy's elegy is played among the traffic, thought Septimus. Now he withdraws up into the snows, and roses hang about him—the thick red roses which grow on my bedroom wall, he reminded himself. The music stopped.

(MD, 68)

In this moment, Septimus feels "shocks of sound" not as background city noise but as waves, visible columns, and kinetic forms diffracting into a mobile "anthem" played among the traffic. What others experience as unrelated "noise," Septimus hears as a hidden pattern and harmony of a meaningful anthem. The sounds he hears occur alongside visible motions and he thinks of shapes simultaneously that feel part of the sounds. His moment of being is, therefore, also one of synesthesia.

> But he himself remained high on his rock, like a drowned sailor on a rock. I leant over the edge of the boat and fell down, he thought. I went under the sea. I have been dead, and yet am now alive, but let me rest still; he begged (he was talking to himself again—it was awful, awful!); and as, before waking, the voices of birds and the sound of wheels chime and chatter in a queer harmony, grow louder and louder and the sleeper feels himself drawing to the shores of life, so he felt himself drawing towards life, the sun growing hotter, cries sounding louder, something tremendous about to happen.
>
> (MD, 68–9)

This passage is full of the crucial fluid dynamic images that Woolf uses to describe moments of being. Septimus falls beneath the waves and into the undifferentiated ocean of flux. Below the surface of diffracting ripples, waves, and sensible forms, is death. Life, for Septimus, is only a moment, a crest, a little island, or rock. Being dead is like sleeping. As he awakes from his dreams, he comes to the shores of life where things are brighter, hotter, and louder.

This fluid dynamic drama is similar to how the Roman poet Lucretius described the birth of Venus and Epicurus' revolt against religion. Venus, Lucretius says, brings everything from the ocean onto the shores of light and life.[20] Indeed, Woolf's copy of *De Rerum Natura* has copious notes about Venus, creation, beauty, and truth written in the margins of this opening birth scene on the beach. Lucretius also says that Epicurus was the first to "open his eyes" against the darkness of religion in which the "fear of death" acted like a "weight" on him.[21] Woolf writes that Septimus "had only to open his eyes; but a weight was on them; a fear" (MD, 69). In other words, Woolf seems to have borrowed some of her fluid dynamic language from Lucretius' account of the dialectic between the darken submerged fear of death and the feeling of being like a crest of a wave brought to life and light by love.

Beauty Was Everywhere

As Septimus opens his eyes, he sees the park bathed in light and feels as if he was reborn into the world. Septimus continues to see the hidden fractal patterns in the movement of tree branches, leaves, dappled light patterns, and the hunting and evading patterns of birds and flies.[22] Each pattern is beautiful on its own but shares its fractal dimension with the others tied together in the fractal eye movement patterns of the viewer.

Long streamers of sunlight fawned at his feet. The trees waved, brandished. We welcome, the world seemed to say; we accept; we create. Beauty, the world seemed to say. And as if to prove it (scientifically) wherever he looked at the houses, at the railings, at the antelopes stretching over the palings, beauty sprang instantly. To watch a leaf quivering in the rush of air was an exquisite joy. Up in the sky swallows swooping, swerving, flinging themselves in and out, round and round, yet always with perfect control as if elastics held them; and the flies rising and falling; and the sun spotting now this leaf, now that, in mockery, dazzling it with soft gold in pure good temper; and now and again some chime (it might be a motor horn) tinkling divinely on the grass stalks—all of this, calm and reasonable as it was, made out of ordinary things as it was, was the truth now; beauty, that was the truth now. Beauty was everywhere.

(MD, 69)

The light streams, the trees wave, the antelopes stretch, beauty springs, leaves quiver, air rushes, swallows swerve, and sounds tinkle on grass stalks. Septimus' senses have become so widened he sees all these singular movements interwoven together in an open and tessellated gestalt. He hears the sound from a horn diffracting off each blade of grass.

This is philosophically important because it demonstrates how moments of being do not reveal a transcendent reality beyond the world, but rather emerge within it. What Woolf calls "reality" is the coordinated fractal patterns of motion in daily events that we often ignore. The truth and beauty of this world are not an abstract idea but an immanent and singular pattern of motion that we feel ourselves woven into in moments of being. The unpredictable swerve of the swallow is also perhaps a reference to Lucretius' theory of the swerve of matter,[23] and his self-identification as a swerving swallow.[24] In book three, Lucretius calls himself a swallow right before he goes into an ecstatic rapture when he thinks of the interconnection of nature. Indeed, these are also passages Woolf translated in her copy of *De Rerum Natura*.

In other words, Septimus solves the philosophical tension in Peter's dream between the immanent flux of the tree goddess and the "ordinary things" he finds in the old woman's cupboard (MD, 58). How can ordinary things be woven from indeterminably swerving motions? How can truth and beauty be immanent to ordinary things but also invisible to us most of the time? Why don't we see and feel everything in its full interconnection? As Septimus's moment of being shows, moments of being are altered states of consciousness not conducive to instrumental daily action. Occasionally, they are even terrifying.

For instance, to get to this vision of patterned beauty, Septimus feels like he is dying. The cost of gaining the world is losing his limited sense of self. Once he is reborn in and as the world he sees that "ordinary things" are stabilized patterns of indeterminate flux. The trees welcome and accept him without judgment because he is one of them. The branching veins of his body have the same fractal pattern as the tree.

Beauty is *everywhere,* but can also be filtered out by our habits of perception, habits of shaping our environment, and our state of consciousness. Human knowledge and sensation are not something other than nature, but "the thing itself," as Woolf says. The whole of nature is a work of art without sin, separation, or transcendence of any kind. Septimus undergoes both sides of the moment of becoming: the impersonal horror of nature and death as well as the exquisite joy created by the discovery that a flower (the rose) *is* also the whole interconnected thrilling Earth beneath us.

An Ode to Time

Septimus' moment ends as Peter's moment began, with time. Peter sat on the park bench to avoid people asking him the time. Septimus' moment ends when his wife Rezia tells him "it is time." Septimus' experience of fluid and fractal dynamism of the natural world ends when Rezia tries to capture or measure it in time. Time, for Septimus, in his moment, is merely a discrete measurement or *husk* composed of a more primary fluid process of motion.

> "It is time," said Rezia.
> The word "time" split its husk; poured its riches over him; and from his lips fell like shells, like shavings from a plane, without his making them, hard, white, imperishable words, and flew to attach themselves to their places in an ode to Time; an immortal ode to Time. He Sang.
> (MD, 69–70)

For Septimus, the word "time" is like the husk of a seed that tries to capture the immeasurable and unspeakable fluidity of living reality. Time, as Lucretius believed, was just a measure of matter in motion. Nothing more. When Rezia says the word, "time," the discrete husk of the word cannot handle the movement as it pours out. The word "time" fails to capture what time is as a process of motion. But the sound of someone saying the word time is filled with sonic, haptic, and sensuous richness. For Woolf, words and measured units of time are like shells washed up from a "vast multitudinous sea" (D4, 126; E6, 95). Each attempt to capture process and motion in a word or idea is only a piece of the process, like a shell or a wood shaving from a plane. This is the meaning of Woolf's recurring concept of hard white things such as bone, shell, or rocks washed up by the ocean.

Words are not representations but are rather bits and pieces of processes washed ashore. Each word is an addition, another shell on the beach, a piece of the ocean. They are not representations *of* anything. When words fly into motion together, they resonate and sing in a "queer harmony" (MD, 68) or "discordant harmonies" (BA, 175). As a process, reality is timeless because it is never the same twice. Each change in the world changes the whole of nature. The habit of coordinating the motions of clock hands has to be sung into existence along with everything else. In this sense, every ordinary object is a little refrain helping to keep time as everything changes.[25]

Septimus' moment ends when time is marked and yet reality continues on beneath his threshold of consciousness awareness. In Woolf's next moment of being, this escaped flow of time returns to Peter as he leaves the park and becomes geological. This is what we will look at next.

Moment 5: The Knotted Roots of Infinite Ages

After Septimus' moment of being ends, Peter Walsh gets up from his bench in Regent's Park where he fell asleep and begins to think about life and death. As Peter walks by Septimus in Regent's Park, his attention is arrested by a woman's song on the street. The bewitching song triggers the "astonishing accesses of emotion" and another moment of being for Peter (MD, 80).

The Supreme Flavor to Existence

Right before Peter hears the song, he was walking and thinking about his susceptibility to passion and emotion. Peter observes that although his feelings have remained as intense as ever, age has allowed him to savor much more than youth. Indeed, this is exactly what Woolf says about her own moments of being in her autobiography. She learned to appreciate what they taught her and she became less terrified of them.

> The compensation of growing old, Peter Walsh thought, coming out of Regent's Park, and holding his hat in hand, was simply this; that the passions remain as strong as ever, but one has gained—at last—the power which adds the supreme flavour to existence, the power of taking hold of experience, of turning it round, slowly, in the light. Life itself, every moment of it, every drop of it, here, this instant, now, in the sun, in Regents Park, was enough. Too much indeed. A whole lifetime was too short to bring out, now that one had acquired the power, the full flavour; to extract every ounce of pleasure, every shade of meaning; which both were so much more solid than they used to be, so much less personal.
>
> (MD, 79)

This is a wonderful passage that illuminates Woolf's philosophical relationship to her moments. Moments of being, for Woolf, become less personal, more meaningful, and interconnected as one ages. The enjoyment of the moment comes when one discovers that nature's impersonal processes are not alien to one another or to us. As we age, we see more how each thing fits together and iterates the others. One is more able to feel, see, and taste the synesthetic constellation that one is. "'I'," as Woolf says, "is only a convenient term for somebody who has no real being" (RO, 4). Nature no longer appears as foreign to the ego but as immanent to it—saturating it. This is the philosophical basis of the enjoyment of moments of being. Far from lacking meaning, nature, for Woolf, is saturated with meaning.

The Aesthetics of Saturation

The term "saturation" is interesting, and Woolf uses it and similar words often in her description of moments of being. In moments of being, Woolf says things are "enough," "achieved," "accomplished" (TL, 113), or "saturated." She writes that "It is that the thing is in itself enough; satisfactory; achieved" (WD, 85); "The ecstasy burst in her eyes and waves of pure delight raced over the floor of her mind, and she felt, It is enough! It is enough!" (TL, 56–7). Indeed, she says of her writing method that "The poets succeeding by simplifying: practically everything is left out. I want to put practically everything in; yet to saturate" (D3, 210).

> The idea has come to me that what I want now to do is to saturate every atom. I mean to eliminate all waste, deadness, superfluity: to give the moment whole; whatever it includes. Say that the moment is a combination of thought; sensation; the voice of the sea. Waste, deadness, come from the inclusion of things that don't belong to the moment; this appalling narrative business of the [empirical] realist: getting on from lunch to dinner: it is false, unreal, merely conventional.
>
> (D3, 209)

What is the philosophical significance of Woolf's interest in saturation? The basic idea is that nature is enough without any form of transcendence. Nature does not need a creator. Nature does not need human beings to know it or give it meaning because it is already meaningful to itself. Humans do not add anything to nature nor take anything away from it. They modify and mutate it. They can feel its saturation in moments of being. Nature has no goal or objective given in advance of its own unfolding. Thus, it is always "achieved." Moments of being feel this immanent achievement.

Human sensation is not faulty or deficient. Our senses are not out to trick us. Rather, the problem is that we are capable of so much sensation that it overwhelms us. So we limit and filter sensations to protect ourselves. Furthermore, sensation is naturally synesthetic because the senses work together. Yet, synesthesia is not a pathological or clinical condition. Rather, a consequence of habitually limiting our range of sensation and attention is that we also feel that we are missing something. We feel that our senses are deceptive and that synesthesia is an anomaly. But the senses are not wrong, they are just partial and limited. Yet, they can be opened in moments of being.

Woolf's literary method of saturation does not add discrete, separate sensations to one another to produce an empirical description of "the whole." For her, real saturation occurs in the hidden patterns and diffractive processes between sensations. Each pattern of sensation becomes a fractal iteration of the others. The flight pattern of a sparrow has a similarly fractal pattern as Septimus' eye movements as he watches trees move in the wind. In reality, as opposed to what Woolf calls traditional "realist narrative," thoughts, feelings, and sensations are all mixed together in shifting patterns. In other words, Woolf's saturation is a kind of literary synesthesia.

But, for Woolf, the world is also a work of art. The natural world is pure saturation. If human experience and reality are ultimately synesthetic, for Woolf, it is because she believes nature is saturated as both art and artist. Humans, being part of nature, are born into this saturated and entangled reality. Nature does not isolate its sensations. It mutates and coordinates them together and with one another. Woolf's method of literary and philosophical saturation is to widen our senses through moments of being.

Things do not move in nature, as if nature were a spatial container. Rather, all of nature moves and changes simultaneously. The "whole" of nature is not a single solid state. Just as we would destroy a Beethoven sonata by treating it as a frozen whole, so our understanding of reality is misguided if we think of it as something static or determinate. Freezing the process kills it. There are no parts or whole in a Beethoven sonata. One cannot listen to a "whole" piece of music simultaneously. Music requires motion and cannot be "a" whole or totality.

For Woolf, nature weaves its artworks through saturation. Energy is neither created nor destroyed, only rearranged and rewoven. In this sense, the past is never truly gone. Deep history and deep space saturate each present moment. The deep web of ecological, geological, and cosmic processes is all here now. This is why a single lifetime, as Peter says, would not be enough to enjoy even a drop of sensation.

An Ancient Spring Spouting from the Earth

Peter crosses the street. In doing so, he also crosses over to an altered state of consciousness. He hears a barely audible inhuman sound and suddenly feels the saturation of his moment in deep time.

> A sound interrupted him; a frail quivering sound, a voice bubbling up without direction, vigour, beginning or end, running weakly and shrilly and with an absence of all human meaning into

ee um fah um so foo swee too eem oo —

the voice of no age or sex, the voice of an ancient spring spouting from the earth; which issued, just opposite Regent's Park Tube station from a tall quivering shape, like a funnel, like a rusty pump, like a wind-beaten tree forever barren of leaves which lets the wind run up and down its branches singing

ee um fah um so foo swee too eem oo

and rocks and creaks and moans in the eternal breeze.

(MD, 80–1)

Just as Mrs. Dalloway and Septimus were interrupted by sounds (motorcars and horns), Peter is interrupted by the singer. The sounds of moving water and wind through trees are important here because they share a fractal frequency pattern. Scientists call these sonic patterns "pink noise," because when the visible light spectrum contains redder (low-frequency high power) waves inversely proportional to blue (high-frequency lower power) waves, the light appears pink like the fading light of a sunset. When sonic frequencies have the same inverse distribution it is called "pink noise."[26] The sound of waves crashing, rain falling, water trickling and bubbling in a creek bed, and wind blowing through trees shares a similar or "fractal" noise spectrum. The spectrum is called "fractal" because slower frequencies are a precise fraction of the next faster one. So there are proportionally less higher frequencies mixed into pink noise than lower ones. This is important because studies of pink noise show that it tends to make people feel more relaxed and creative. They also tend to find pink sounds to be more aesthetically pleasing and help people sleep better while listening to them.[27] This is perhaps because humans have evolved in close proximity to the sounds of waves, rain, wind, and the calming pink of the sunset before bed time.

This is important because Peter is sensitive enough in his moment of being to perceive the relationship of fractal patterns across seemingly different things. The human singing voice, like most bird song, has a fractal frequency distribution that connects it to the pink noise of bubbling water and wind in trees. The pattern of playful pink noise traverses time and space and is shared across scales of reality.

The bubbling spring and the tree-pump also share a common spatial-spreading pattern. They push water out of the earth and into the air, forming the breeze that carries the sound to Peter's ear like a phonograph horn. The woman sings like the bubbles and the wind in the trees. There is also a material and historical reason why the three sounds are connected. These sounds were some of the most common sources of ancient oracles. Fractal shapes and sounds tend to produce experiences of pareidolia, or seeing images or visions like faces in natural patterns.[28] For instance, the ancient Greeks built the oracle of Delphi on top of the Neolithic priestess Telphusa's oracular spring, whose bubbling she would interpret for visitors. Similarly, the oldest Greek oracle of Dodona was an oak tree that spoke words of wisdom in the wind.

The common kinetic pattern in many oracles is one in which matter flows up and out of the deep earth into the air. The woman singing the song is not just a symbol of an ancient tradition. She is still doing it, though today, few listen. Similarly, the tree pumps water out of the ground, amplifying it like a funnel. It makes foggy mists, veils, or clouds in which we see visions, faces, and animals. As Peter walks through this scene, the halo of the "wider circumference of the moment" (E6, 510) envelopes him.

Spatially, the woman's body is performatively doing what the tree is doing. Her limbs and branching nervous system are like the branches and capillaries of a tree pumping and funneling vibrations and fluids that diffract with the wind. Woolf's description of Peter's moment highlights the fact that sound is not just something we hear inside our head. It is a real material pressure wave that travels on the breeze and diffracts off surfaces. Sound effects and palpates the entire world, not just our eardrums. Its physical origins seems apparent but the environment diffracts what and how we hear.

As Peter walks, he hears the words of the song not as representations but as affective patterns (*ee um fah um so*), including "flavors" (MD, 79) and "shapes" (funnel, pump, tree). In his moment of being, language is stripped of its abstract and symbolic function and revealed to be part of a material kinesthetic atmosphere. Words become patterned sounds and rhythms sharing qualities with non-human sounds.

What we call "the meaning of words" is the way a sound in the world affects our body and brain. Over time we make physiological associations with certain sounds. Woolf's brilliant description of this process highlights the affective and material power of the singer's words as sonic bodies. Woolf writes elsewhere, "The words ... now hit the mind with a wad, then exploded like a scent suffusing the whole dome of the mind with its incense, flavour" (E6, 510). Thus, Woolf understands words as material processes with a life of their own. Each has its own unique synesthetic network of connections including smells, tastes, between the world and the play of the receiver's body.

Woolf also describes words as "arrows" (E6, 510). They fly and physically hit the world with real impact that stirs all the senses, not just the "mind" or "ears." Since we do not see sounds, Woolf says they are like smells or tastes that affect us. They are a flavor of the world around us. So it is with the "*ee um fah um so*" of the tube singer's song. Stripped of its representational meaning, the song reveals its inhuman materiality and encourages the free play of association and imagination.

The Geology of Music

Another important dimension of sound is its resonance with the past. This is what Woolf highlights in Peter's moment of being at the tube station. What is sound made of? It is a pressure wave in the air that vibrates our bones. At every stage, it is made of molecules and atoms that the Earth has been moving around for millions of years before they arrived in our ear. The frequencies that humans make are not unique to them, but are borrowed from the earth. When humans sing, it is with the pieces of sound and song made of the same stuff of the Earth. The common fractal frequencies of song, wind, and water suggest to Peter something common that makes them interrelated aspects of the same natural process. Woolf writes:

> Through all ages—when the pavement was grass, when it was swamp, through the age of tusk and mammoth, through the age of silent sunrise, the battered woman-for she wore a skirt—with her right hand exposed, her left clutching at her side, stood singing of love—love which has lasted a million years, she sang, love which prevails, and millions of years ago, her lover, who had been dead these centuries, had walked, she crooned, with her in May; but in the course of ages, long as summer days, and flaming, she remembered, with nothing but red asters, he had gone; death's enormous sickle had swept those tremendous hills, and when at last she laid her hoary and immensely aged head on the earth, now become a mere cinder of ice, she implored the Gods to lay by her side a bunch of purple heather, there on her high burial place which the last rays of the last sun caressed; for then the pageant of the universe would be over.
>
> (MD, 81)

The same drama of life and death, love and loss, has been playing out on earth for millions of years. Human love and life are only one iteration of this drama, not something radically different. Peter imagines when London was grass and swamp just as passers-by did when the motor car broke down on Bond Street. Woolf's point here is material. We are all made of that same stuff recycled. "There were rhododendrons in the Strand; and mammoths in Piccadilly" (BA, 30), she writes. Springs and trees sang the songs of the Earth before humans lived to hear them. Now in London, some humans sing them too for a while. Eventually, the springs and trees will sing them alone after humans are gone.

The planet sings one continuous song with different singers carrying it on at different times like a pageant: the universe's pageant. "One becomes aware that we are spectators and also passive participants in a pageant" as Woolf says (E6, 510).

For Woolf, the woman's song is one iteration of an ancient song of life and death. Love brings matter together in the spring and summer (May), bringing in crops and life. Then death tears them apart with his harvest sickle in winter.[29] So the seasons cycle and iterate one after another in distinct and enormous patterns of motion. These patterns are, in turn, part of even larger patterns in the cosmos. One day, the last cycle will come, and the Earth will die, and the cosmos will become cold. Woolf's vision of the death of the universe here follows the science of thermodynamics of her time, which in turn followed Lucretius' vision of a dying material universe.

In this passage, Woolf is able to turn a single sound stripped of its representational meaning into a full dilation of geological and cosmic time. For Woolf, the immortality of the soul, God, and universal knowledge are delusions. There is only a dying natural world. A pageant that will end with the death of the world. Human language is one iteration of a cosmic song of love and death.

Nietzsche shared a similar sentiment:

> In some remote corner of the universe, poured out and glittering in innumerable solar systems, there once was a star on which clever animals invented knowledge. That was the highest and most mendacious minute of "world history"—yet only a minute. After nature had drawn a few breaths the star grew cold, and the clever animals had to die.[30]

Woolf has no aspirations of absolute knowledge. All will perish in "the last rays of the last sun." Woolf, instead, describes moments of being in which we saturate space and time to reveal a common kinetic pattern across millions of years.

> As the ancient song bubbled up opposite Regent's Park Tube station still the earth seemed green and flowery; still, though it issued from so rude a mouth, a mere hole in the earth, muddy too, matted with root fibres and tangled grasses, still the old bubbling burbling song, soaking through the knotted roots of infinite ages, and skeletons and treasure, streamed away in rivulets over the pavement and all along the Marylebone Road, and down towards Euston, fertilising, leaving a damp stain.
>
> (MD, 81)

Material history is indeed knotted roots. The distribution of dark matter in the universe follows the same fractal branching pattern as tree roots because all matter is doing the same thing: iteratively spreading out. Everywhere the cosmos moves from hot to cold. A stream of water and a stream of song from a woman's mouth are contributing to this project in their own way. The forms of things all change as matter is continually recycled and spread out. Every blade of grass, tree root, river, and human song sings this cosmic refrain. Nature reproduces similar fractal patterns across millions of years, and this woman's song is just one incarnation or expression of this pattern. Fractal entropy is the pattern that lies beneath the cotton wool.

The Hydrology of Time

For Woolf, the past is not chronologically before the present but materially hidden *within* the present as an immanent depth. One of her most striking discussions on the theory of time comes from her autobiography. She writes:

> The past only comes back when the present runs so smoothly that it is like the sliding surface of a deep river. Then one sees through the surface to the depths. In those moments I find one of my greatest satisfactions, not that I am thinking of the past; but that it is then that I am living most fully in the present. For the present when backed by the past is a thousand times deeper than the present when it presses so close that you can feel nothing else.
>
> (MB, 98)

In Woolf's moments of being, she experiences the past as immanently folded up *in the present*. Moments of being are not just about the interrelation of patterned processes around us. They include the interrelation of the past inside and saturating the present.

Woolf's image of time as a river also has an ecological dimension. If time is a river whose surface is the present and whose depth is the past, then time is not linear but rather an emergent product of the whole river's moving transformation. There is no objective past state of the river to contrast the present since the entire surface (and depth) of the river is continually different. In Woolf's theory of time, there is no prior river "state" that we can point to and say the current river is Time 2 after Time 1. There is no "common time" because there is no fixed *a priori* ecological background we could call nature that remains the same through its changes.

In short, Woolf adds to the ancient Greek philosopher Heraclitus' belief that one could not step into the same river twice, the correlate, that we cannot be the same "we" who steps into the non-same river even once. River and human both continually change. Nature is not merely flux, but like a river, creates eddies of stability. It has its moments of clear and muddy water.

Time, for Woolf, is not a series of discrete states happening on a static background but a name we give to a continuously changing whole in constant flux. The river's movement is primary, and in rare moments of being, one discovers this. Woolf's moments are therefore not discrete slices of time. Each moment contains the deep history of the cosmos. When the river's surface is smooth, as it is in her moments of being, one can see straight to the bottom.

This is why Woolf writes that the woman's song burbles up through millions of years. The rippled opaque surface of the river is the cotton wool of daily life, and the clear, calm surface is the moment of being that reveals the deep kinetic patterns of order running through deep time immanent to the present. In this way, Woolf's moments of being are glimpses of the entire cosmos unfolding itself in a fully saturated present.

In such a vision as this, the old woman on the street "no longer saw brown eyes, black whiskers or sunburnt face but only a looming shape, a shadow shape, to which, with the bird-like freshness of the very aged she still twittered, 'give me your hand and let me press it gently'" (MD, 82). As millions of years race by, the woman sees only shadowy shapes in motion. She is profoundly old and yet fresh, like Clarissa, a songbird.

> And the passing generations—the pavement was crowded with bustling middle-class people—vanished, like leaves, to be trodden under, to be soaked and steeped and made mould of by that eternal spring.
>
> (MD, 82)

In millions of years, everyone on that street will be turned to dust and composted back into the Earth. The woman's song puts everything in its broader geological context of decay, rebirth, and process, '"and if someone should see, what matter they?" Woolf writes. Anyone glaring at the woman's poverty is but leaf mold for future generations. They are mud, dirt, roots, and grass. This is the stuff that composes nature. The song or material process of death and rebirth continues. For those who listen, it reveals the truth and reality of the *deep present*.

All this is streaming through Peter's mind and body as he gives the woman a coin and gets in his taxi. Peter's moment of being ends quickly when he is ready to get on with his affairs in the world. He shuts the door of his taxi and the moment ends.

Let's look at one final moment of being in *Mrs. Dalloway*. It is a strange and beautiful moment toward the end of the book that fittingly links together the moments of Septimus, Peter, and Clarissa.

Moment 6: She Felt Herself Everywhere

The last individual moment of being in *Mrs. Dalloway* happens to Peter Walsh as he walks down the street and hears an ambulance. Although the moment is happening to Peter, Woolf connects it to Septimus, whose ambulance it may be, and Clarissa whose philosophy Peter is recalling in his moment. In the novel, Septimus has just committed suicide, and after a sudden paragraph break, Woolf begins writing about Peter walking past the British Museum.

In Peter's moment, the sudden rush of the moving ambulance throws him into a moment of becoming. He feels that everything around him starts to flow together. Life, death, space, time, and sensation all converge.

> Swiftly, cleanly the ambulance sped to the hospital, having picked up instantly, humanely, some poor devil; someone hit on the head, struck down by disease, knocked over perhaps a minute or so ago at one of these crossings, as might happen to oneself. That was civilisation.
>
> (MD, 151)

The passing ambulance has a similar effect on Peter as the motorcar on Bond Street had on nearby walkers. It prompts thoughts of death and deep history. The fact that it may have been Septimus' death that triggered this moment for Peter reminds us of Clarissa's philosophical idea that everyone "lived in each other," and were "part of people [they] had never met" (MD, 9).

Peter imagines that the man in the ambulance was struck down at a crosswalk just like the one Peter crossed when he began to hear the woman's ancient song in Regent's Park and he thought of death. Peter thus imagines the crosswalk as a kind of river of death like Acheron or Styx. Indeed, the crosswalk was a frequent site of death in London just as bodies of water were in the ancient world. "It is dangerous to live even one day," as Mrs. Dalloway says.

What Is Civilization?

The passing ambulance makes Peter, who lived for many years as an expat in India, think of London from a broader perspective of space and time. It makes him think about civilization as a historical phenomenon. London, as a major city of civilization, is constantly dealing with dead bodies. Administrators must manage the living and dead bodies alike.

Civilization, Peter thinks, is the "communal spirit" (MD, 151) when people move aside to let the ambulance pass in honor of saving an anonymous life. The feeling of shared anonymous life and anonymous death is strikingly impersonal and yet at the heart of major cities like London.

Accidents, injury, and disease flourish and have always thrived in cities. With massive social circulation comes collision. Indeed, crosswalk deaths are built-in aspects of roadways. In an odd way, civilization is both poison and remedy at the same sweeping us all along and exposing us to an impersonal life and death among the flows of traffic. Peter thinks on:

> Perhaps it was morbid; or was it not touching rather, the respect which they showed this ambulance with its victim inside—busy men hurrying home yet instantly bethinking them as it passed of some wife; or presumably how easily it might have been them there, stretched on a shelf with a doctor and a nurse. … Ah, but thinking became morbid, sentimental, directly one began conjuring up doctors, dead bodies; a little glow of pleasure, a sort of lust too over the visual impression warned one not to go on with that sort of thing any more—fatal to art, fatal to friendship. True.
>
> (MD, 151)

The event of anonymous death is both morbid and touching. It is profoundly impersonal and intensely personal at the same time. Many other people are anonymous to Peter just as he is anonymous to them. They live anonymously together in the city. There is something powerful about a social order that can allow total strangers to live together in huge numbers but also a shocking amount of structural and impersonal death.

Peter even feels a bit of lust over the idea of such paradoxical extremes of cruelty and generosity to strangers. What could be crueler than perpetuating a structural death machine like civilization? But what could be more generous than the act of saving the lives of total strangers? These are the thoughts that begin Peter's moment of being: "the efficiency" (MD, 151) of the circulation of anonymous life and death.

Aesthetic Susceptibility

But Peter quickly feels that to dwell too long on these impersonal processes is detrimental to art and friendship, which flourish under the *singular* and *personal*. Art and friendship require us to attend to the detailed patterns and orders that emerge from nature and within civilization.

And yet, thought Peter Walsh, as the ambulance turned the corner though the light high bell could be heard down the next street and still farther as it crossed the Tottenham Court Road, chiming constantly, it is the privilege of loneliness; in privacy one may do as one chooses. One might weep if no one saw. It had been his undoing—this susceptibility.

(MD, 151)

Strangers can sometimes feel free to let their senses expand and their minds wander because no one is there to judge or direct them otherwise. Clarissa, too, "had a perpetual sense, as she watched the taxi cabs, of being out, out, far out to sea and alone" (MD, 8). In this moment, Peter sees his "susceptibility" to the world, just as Woolf did, as a precondition for receiving shocks or moments of vision (E5, 140). Woolf describes it as "open[ing] a space in the mind to the shock of experience. What had been insensitive before felt" (E5, 616).

Woolf offers no guidebook or instructions about how to have a moment of being. Many situations seem to occasion them while others do not, but there is no set of rules. Each is singular. All Woolf says is that one can try to "open a space in the mind," to new sensations and see. Perhaps, Woolf suggests, it might take repeated unfelt shocks to prepare the way. She says, "perhaps—repeated shocks, each unfelt at the time, suddenly loosening the fabric breaking something away. Only this image suggests collapse and disintegration, whereas the process I have in mind is just the opposite. It is not destructive whatever it may be, one might say that it was rather of a creative character" (E3, 152).

Peter's (and Woolf's) susceptibility to these shocks is a source of horror about cosmic impersonality and the conditions for aesthetic creativity. The shocks reveal a fuller reality of the moving patterns that weave things together, but they also help "loosen the fabric" of the world to make something new. "And so I go on to suppose that the shock-receiving capacity is what makes me a writer," Woolf says (MB, 72). Woolf writes that Peter's shock-receiving capacity is his undoing in society but allows him to feel ecstasy, beauty, and sensuous saturation in every drop of reality. Socially, Peter cries or laughs out of tune with the expectations of others. This awkwardly disappoints expectations but opens him to a wider range of feelings.

I have that in me, he thought standing by the pillar-box, which could now dissolve in tears. Why, Heaven knows. Beauty of some sort probably, and the weight of the day, which beginning with that visit to Clarissa had exhausted him with its heat, its intensity, and the drip, drip, of one impression after another down into that cellar where they stood, deep, dark, and no one would ever know.

(MD, 152)

Peter's explanation for why he is crying at the pillar-box is philosophically interesting because it is not causal. Something different is happening. It is not one thing which causes him to feel a certain way but a web of associations. Instead of behaviorism, symbolism, pathology, or metaphor, Peter simply lists the affects that compose his singular moment of becoming. There is a degree of beauty, some weight, some heat, a degree of intensity, and his talk with Clarissa. Emotion, in Woolf's description, is not something that happens inside us; it is something that the world does *through us*. A feeling is an expression of an entire atmosphere or ecology at work under the cotton wool of conscious perception and attention. A feeling bubbles up like an eddy swirls into existence in a river and then dissipates. Millions of tiny affects working together produce an unexpected and untraceable novelty.

Peter also describes his sensations as drips falling into the dark pool of the body and mind. This is an interesting theory of emotions. Once a drop of water enters a pool, it becomes the pool. The pool is affected by each drop but the effects of the drops cannot be traced through the pool as discrete individuals. In other words, each singular sensation or experience changes the whole such that there is no stable background to compare the "cause" of our feelings. Here, Woolf uses fluid-dynamic images to treat emotions as continual transformations.

The Atmosphere of Affect

Woolf has a similarly fascinating theory of sensation. We typically think of sensation as empirical and tied directly to solid discrete objects. We *have* feelings *about* things, people, or situations. But Woolf, through Peter, describes a much more atmospheric process.

By "affect," I mean a qualitative change that occurs above or below the normal level of our perception. An affect can be a subtle temperature change in a room, a pattern formed by a nearby leaf moving in the breeze, or a very quiet sound, or a something small or hidden in daily life that we were too busy to hear, see, hear, or smell. Affects below the relative level of our perception play a non-trivial role in our sense of reality. If they disappeared, the world would not hold together. And yet, we cannot sense them all or we would never get anything done. A trillion tiny processes that seem individually trivial on their own occur all around us but we typically only notice them when they break or go missing. What we think of as important is made of a trillion "unimportant" affects.

Affects are often atmospherically responsible for our feeling that everything is good, bad, or unsafe, even if we cannot say exactly why or how. However, in certain moments, we can sense the "whole" atmosphere of these little affective processes working through us. This happens to Peter as he walks past a mailbox near the British Museum.

> Partly for that reason, its secrecy, complete and inviolable, he had found life like an unknown garden, full of turns and corners, surprising, yes; really it took one's breath away, these moments; there coming to him by the pillar-box opposite the British Museum one of them, a moment, in which things came together; this ambulance; and life and death. It was as if he were sucked up to some very high roof by that rush of emotion and the rest of him, like a white shell-sprinkled beach, left bare.
>
> (MD, 152)

Peter's moment of being is powerful in part because it is so secretive. However, moments are not secretive or mysterious because they transcend nature. Rather, moments are woven from immanent but relatively unseen affects in this world. The web of affects is secretive like the weather or an atmosphere. It's everywhere but nowhere in particular and its causes are so distributed that no one knows where a single gust of wind came from. For instance, we feel that it is "warm" outside. Yet, the precise variables that make up this singular and unique warmth (season, time of day, clothing, hydration, colors, and shapes of objects nearby, etc.) are so numerous that they work at a "secretive" affective level that boggles the mind. We sense only habitually privileged bits here and there of a vast webwork of material flows.

In a moment of being, though, there is a gestalt switch and the parts disappear to reveal an interwoven tapestry of millions of tiny shifting changes. This is what happened when Peter stopped looking at individual tree branches and saw the pattern they made together against the evening sky as the weaving goddess.

Our sensations and emotions are *in the world* like a rain shower or a halo in fog. We do not have feelings about things but rather *through* things. Emotions in moments of being are atmospheric. They rise, fall, and dissipate like clouds. Feeling is not a mental state but a place continuous with geography. Beneath the cotton wool are real affective patterns that weave us into the world.

Kinesthetic Perception

Peter experiences "a moment, in which things came together; this ambulance; and life and death. It was as if he were sucked up to some very high roof by that rush of emotion and the rest of him, like a white shell-sprinkled beach, left bare" (MD, 152). Synesthesia is not the *delusion* that sounds cause sights. It is the coordination of sensations in motion together: the ambulance, life, death, the memory of Clarissa, and the dissolving pillar box.

What we might call "kinesthesia" is the whole moving and changing gestalt pattern of sensation. Gestalt vision, as I think it applies to Woolf's moments of being, is not when one "fills in gaps in visual perception with the mind." This is an anti-realist and anthropocentric understanding. Woolf's moments of being are much more like gestalts in the sense that they reveal the hidden processes and patterns of movement that shape reality.[31] Humans are not the only ones with a perspective or orientation to the world. The world has many singular orientations to itself, none of which are "more true" than the others.

This is the sense in which Peter gets sucked upward to see the whole shifting pattern of reality. Simultaneously, he is also able to see how the relatively discrete objects and people around him and including him emerge and persist as distinct. The world of determinate objects is like shells that emerge from the ocean tide and return. The flux of reality is like the ocean whose ebbs and tides produce and weave the cotton-wool things of the world.

Process Epistemology

Peter's moment of being weaves together sensations, emotions, and memories that lead him back to thoughts of Clarissa. In his moment of susceptibility, he remembers that Clarissa had similar moments of being. Indeed, he recalls that Clarissa even proposed a whole theory about these moments of susceptibility sitting atop a bus as she and Peter rode down Shaftesbury Avenue. Peter then recalls this theory in his moment of being,

> But she said, sitting on the bus going up Shaftesbury Avenue, she felt herself everywhere; not "here, here, here"; and she tapped the back of the seat; but everywhere. She waved her hand, going up Shaftesbury Avenue. She was all that. So that to know her, or any one, one must seek out the people who completed them; even the places. Odd affinities she had with people she had never spoken to, some woman in the street, some man behind a counter—even trees, or barns. It ended in a transcendental theory which, with her horror of death, allowed her to believe, or say that she believed (for all her skepticism), that since our apparitions, the part of us which appears, are so momentary compared with the other, the unseen part of us, which spreads wide, the unseen might survive, be recovered somehow attached to this person or that, or even haunting certain places after death ... perhaps—perhaps.
>
> (MD, 152–3)

Clarissa's theory has some interesting resonances with Woolf's philosophy of moments of being. First, it is worth noting that Clarissa has this moment of philosophical clarity while she is in motion on top of a bus riding down a busy street. *In motion,* she begins to feel herself everywhere and asks an important question about the nature of knowledge. How do we come to know things? Her answer is that we do not know other people or things at all as discrete entities. They are, like the rest of nature, processes in relation. How can one possibly *know* or have any *fixed* knowledge of a process that is continually changing? What then is knowledge without essences? What if there is no*thing* to know at all, but only patterns that are woven and unwoven beneath the cotton wool of discrete things?

In short, Clarissa's theory rejects the idea that reality is made of anything discrete or static. Even touching her seat, she says she is not "here." She is a webwork of relational affects. Each singular moment of her being is woven into the whole of Shaftesbury Avenue as she waves her hand. To know someone, for Clarissa, is to know their atmosphere of singular changing relations.

For Clarissa, people, trees, and barns are not things but patterns woven from one another. People are made of places not only because the places mean something to them psychologically. Rather, the vast majority of connections are unknown to us. We do not see how we breathe in the water vapor from trees and how they breathe in ours. People are geographically, geologically, and materially aspects or dimensions of the same movement. We are not just influenced by the weather and plants, we breathe them and eat them. They become us and when we die we become them. We are the thing itself. We are the stuff of the world. Crucially, Clarissa does not say she is "like" everything or, "thinks about" everything but instead says that she *is* everything. She is a realist. She cannot unentangle her being from the world because they are regions of the same unfolding process.

Clarissa's theory of knowledge is one that occurs through movement. If we are not separate from nature, if we are "the thing in itself," then our thoughts and actions are the thoughts and actions of some region of nature. All our actions and perceptions are, in a sense, performatively true aspects of nature. We can be surprised by it, of course. For instance, just because a stick looks bent in water does not mean that nature or our senses are deceptive. It just means we saw something novel that we did not expect. But there is nothing "false" in nature, in the same way humans distinguish between "true" and "false."

The Transcendental Materiality of the Soul

Another consequence of Clarissa's philosophy is that the soul is entirely material, immanent, and distributed in the world. If who we are is spread out "here, here, here" all down Shaftesbury Avenue, then the soul is a *mixture* of human and non-human elements (people, places, trees, barns, etc.). If the soul is spread out, immanent, and fully material *throughout* the world, according to Clarissa, then it cannot be immortal. It has to change *with* the world. This is an interesting way to think about death. Clarissa says:

> The part of us which appears, are so momentary compared with the other, the unseen part of us, which spreads wide, the unseen might survive, be recovered somehow attached to this person or that, or even haunting certain places after death.
>
> (MD, 153)

For Clarissa, the discrete part of us that appears at the limits of our flesh is small compared to the spreading mist of relations that support it. In her theory, who we are does not transcend the world. We are not merely unaware of our psychological unconscious, but are unaware of our "material unconscious." Our physical being is spread out through all the relatively imperceptible affects and material relations that compose us. Therefore, if our life spreads out in this way, Clarissa reasons, then so does our death. Our energy and our web of affects are not destroyed but transformed when our particular body breaks down in the ground. So, although there is no God or immortal soul for Clarissa, there is still a sense in which the unseen portions of our being "survive" in the places, people, and things that made us up in the first place.

Clarissa's theory also gives a new materialist meaning to the term "haunting." We tend to think of ghosts as immaterial entities. But Clarissa uses the term to describe the persistence of unseen people, places, and things that shaped us after our visible portion is in the ground. Just as those processes shaped us, we shape them back. So when we die they continue on changing having been altered by us somehow. Haunting, for Clarissa, is the action and performance of all the affects of daily life that we do not pay attention to or see. Yet, the world is supported by them.

Woolf often writes of mists, veils, or clouds to describe precisely this atmospheric material reality. In Clarissa's theory, there is no ontological dualism between life and death, seen and unseen. Instead, the seen is only a small portion, as the tip of an iceberg, of the unseen. The unseen is not invisible in principle, but only relative to the specific form of visible presence we are in the habit of seeing or can see at our scale.

For Clarissa, the soul is not immaterial but affective, relational, and spread out. That is why we cannot hold it in our hand or see it all at once. Peter calls Clarissa's theory of the soul "mysterious" (MD, 153), for this reason. But mysticism does not need to be transcendent. Indeed, Clarissa's theory is a kind of materialist mysticism.

After remembering Clarissa's theory, Peter reflects on its application to his moment of being. "A sharp, acute, uncomfortable grain—the actual meeting;

horribly painful as often as not; yet in absence, in the most unlikely places, it would flower out, open, shed its scent, let you touch, taste, look about you, get the whole feel of it and understanding, after years of lying lost" (MD, 153).

His meeting earlier in the day with Clarissa was short and uncomfortable but afterward its effects saturated his whole day. In her non-fiction writing, Woolf describes a similar process by which affects spread out in the world. She says that the flow of matter is "engraved with the sharpness of steel" (E4, 160) like "so many rare & curious objects hit[ting] one's brain like pellets which perhaps may unfold later" (D2, 313; D3, 287; D2, 306). Woolf's description of Peter's moment and her writing elsewhere suggest that sensations are less like representations of the world outside us and more like arrows that enter into us and transform us. When the arrows of sensation hit us, they set off a synesthetic relay of smell, touch, taste, and sight, giving one a sense of their range of associations and connections. Or, at least to the degree we are sensitive enough to them.

Peter's last moment of being in *Mrs. Dalloway* ends as a response to his first moment of being: "the death of the soul." Peter ultimately concludes that Clarissa's materialist and affective theory of the soul ultimately "works to an extent." Peter's moment of being lasts as long as he continues to walk down the street. Once he reaches his hotel, however, it stops.

This chapter concludes our close look at individual moments of being in *Mrs. Dalloway*. In the next few chapters, let's look at how these individual moments are enlarged even further and ultimately extended to the non-human world in Woolf's next novel, *To the Lighthouse*.

Moment 7: The Lake of Being

After extending her brief moments of being from her earlier novels into longer individual moments in *Mrs. Dalloway*, Woolf further built on this technique in her next book, *To the Lighthouse* (1927). Here, Woolf continued to expand the length of her individual moments of being, as I show below. She also described an incredible non-human moment of being. Before then, I want to look at two individual human moments of being in *To the Lighthouse*.

To the Lighthouse tells the story of the English Ramsay family and their summer visits to the Isle of Skye in Scotland between 1910 and 1920. *To the Lighthouse* is one of Woolf's most personal and deeply philosophical novels.

The first individual moment of being I want to focus on happens to a character named Mrs. Ramsey, the mother of the Ramsay family. At the end of a busy day at their beach house, Mrs. Ramsey is finally free to sit alone and relax in silence. Her children are asleep and her husband is busy in the other room. She sits in her favorite chair and begins knitting. Suddenly, as she is knitting, she begins to feel things come together in a moment of being. Woolf writes:

> She could be herself, by herself. And that was what now she often felt the need of—to think; well, not even to think. To be silent; to be alone. All the being and the doing, expansive, glittering, vocal, evaporated; and one shrunk, with a sense of solemnity, to being oneself, a wedge-shaped core of darkness, something invisible to others. Although she continued to knit, and sat upright, it was thus that she felt herself; and this self having shed its attachments was free for the strangest adventures. When life sank down for a moment, the range of experience seemed limitless.
>
> (TL, 62)

Just like Peter Walsh, solitude seems to facilitate Mrs. Ramsey's moment of being. In this moment, she does not need to be there for others or even herself. Mrs. Ramsey does not take this time to contemplate the nature of being or such metaphysical abstractions as occupy her husband in the other room. Rather, she is free to "be" silent, to "be" alone. She is free to become something else. In this moment, all the cotton wool of daily life "evaporates" like a mist or fog. Mrs. Ramsey sinks below the surface of glittering and expansive waves of everyday sensation and into a core of darkness where other unperceived affects spread out.

A Moment of One's Own

Mrs. Ramsey is, like the gray nurse in *Mrs. Dalloway*, a weaver. As she knits out a rhythm in the twilight, she begins to feel her attachments shedding away. The moment is so significant she sits up to feel it like a strange freedom. Her solitude is not an egocentric interiority like her husband, the philosopher Mr. Ramsey, who is tortured by insecurity. Mrs. Ramsey finds herself not as an identity but as a wedge of spreading darkness, unseen.

For Mrs. Ramsey, freedom is not in the "I" but through the distribution of spreading affects, imperceptible sensations, and material rhythmic processes that weave the "I" together. This is a strange idea of freedom in the Western tradition because it is not the freedom of the isolated ego. In this scene, Woolf also gives us a striking description of the gendered nature of subjectivity. In the patriarchal culture of Woolf's time, most men did not believe that women could do art, science, or have meaningful, transformative experiences. Women were limited to making pudding and knitting. As Woolf writes in *A Room of One's Own*:

> Women are supposed to be very calm generally: but women feel just as men feel; they need exercise for their faculties and a field for their efforts as much as their brothers do; they suffer from too rigid a restraint, too absolute a stagnation, precisely as men would suffer; and it is narrow-minded in their more privileged fellow-creatures to say that they ought to confine themselves to making puddings and knitting stockings, to playing on the piano and embroidering bags.
>
> (RO, 69)

Yet, with Mrs. Ramsey, Woolf changes the narrative entirely. In her moment of being, Mrs. Ramsey is temporarily free to feel, imagine, and explore her senses—finding them deep and spreading wide. At one level, Mrs. Ramsey makes pudding and knits. However, it is in the utterly ordinary acts of making dinner and knitting that two of the most profound aesthetic visions happen in *To the Lighthouse*. In *A Room of One's Own*, Woolf laments the fact that we know almost nothing of women's lives before the eighteenth century. Yet, they felt, thought, and undoubtedly experienced profound moments of imagination that have gone unrecorded. For instance, Mrs. Dalloway was not educated or smart, but these are not prerequisites for sensuous revelation or moments of being.

When the cotton wool of the day sinks away, Mrs. Ramsey sees and feels the subtle patterns of the self and the world woven together in the twilight. The short amount of time between the cotton wool of the day and the inky black of night is the time when shadows reveal their secret patterns, and the inanimate world becomes increasingly prominent—as human activity recedes into its houses to rest. Twilight was also the time of day in Peter's dream on the park bench.

Weaving the Self

Just as Peter and Clarissa in *Mrs. Dalloway* feel that no one knows anyone, Mrs. Ramsey feels that the depth and wide distribution of our becoming dwarf the appearance of what we say and do. Mrs. Ramsey thinks:

And to everybody there was always this sense of unlimited resources, she supposed; one after another, she, Lily, Augustus Carmichael, must feel, our apparitions, the things you know us by, are simply childish. Beneath it is all dark, it is all spreading, it is unfathomably deep; but now and again we rise to the surface and that is what you see us by. Her horizon seemed to her limitless.

(TL, 62)

For Mrs. Ramsey, the world of discrete "things" is ridiculously simplistic. Beneath the surface of sensation and visibility, there is a vast world of relations, connections, processes, and currents just as the horizon of the sea hides limitless creatures. As one approaches the limits of a horizon, the horizon is pushed forward such that one never reaches it. So it is with the spreading web of relations beneath all of us. The closer we look at the nature of things the farther the horizon goes.

Here, Woolf paints a picture of reality as the depth in the ocean or a horizon on the earth. Freedom, for Mrs. Ramsey, is movement in these indeterminate and limitless spaces. Mrs. Ramsey thinks to herself, "This core of darkness could go anywhere, for no one saw it. They could not stop it, she thought, exulting" (TL, 62). Mrs Ramsey can imagine places she has never been and feel the stroke of the light across the room. In her moment of being, Mrs. Ramsey's self is distributed and mobile rather than destroyed. Her self becomes "a summoning together, a resting on a platform of stability" (TL, 63). In other words, Woolf describes the state of consciousness in a moment of being as like a metastable whirlpool. She is a stability in motion. More specifically, Mrs. Ramsey's weaving facilitates her mind-wandering state where heterogeneous thoughts and associations play without fear of contradiction or the crucible of reason. Mrs. Ramsey thinks to herself:

Not as oneself did one find rest ever, in her experience (she accomplished here something dexterous with her needles) but as a wedge of darkness. Losing personality, one lost the fret, the hurry, the stir; and there rose to her lips always some exclamation of triumph over life when things came together in this peace, this rest, this eternity.

(TL, 63)

Mrs. Ramsey's mobile stability is also a kind of rest from herself. At the moment of this realization, Mrs. Ramsey does something exceptionally dexterous with her needles that links her to the long history of women's knowledge. The goddesses, Leto, Rhea, Athena, and the mortals Penelope and Helen of Troy were all great weavers or users of what the Greeks called *metis*. *Metis* was a kind of contextual wisdom that happens through making. For the ancient Greeks, *metis* was a form of dexterous swerving that twists to evade stasis and entrapment. Metis was how Odysseus escaped from the cave of the cyclops and how Penelope's endless weaving and unweaving of her father's death shroud helped her avoid remarrying, and how Rhea escaped from the patriarchy of Cronus' rule. Weaving was not only a craft; for the Greeks, it was an iteration of what nature was doing more broadly.[32] To weave is to know the universe from the inside.

Indeed, weaving helps Mrs. Ramsey evade herself, which seems to rarely let her rest. Only in her evasion of self through weaving is she able to lose her anxiety in the world of discrete things and instrumental activity. Then, finally, things can come together in new ways. This is precisely what Woolf herself did to escape her self and her depression: she knitted. Early in 1912, she reported to Leonard Woolf before they were married, and shortly after, when she had been in a rest home for her illness, that "knitting is the saving of life" (L1, 491).

We Are the Light

Soon Mrs. Ramsey begins weaving in a certain rhythm that becomes entrained and coordinated with her thoughts and the patterned stroke of the light from the lighthouse so that she feels the whole structure of motion all around her as integrated into a grand counterpoint of woven processes. Woolf writes:

> [A]nd pausing there she looked out to meet that stroke of the Lighthouse, the long steady stroke, the last of the three, which was her stroke, for watching them in this mood always at this hour one could not help attaching oneself to one thing especially of the things one saw; and this thing, the long steady stroke, was her stroke. Often she found herself sitting and looking, sitting and looking, with her work in her hands until she became the thing she looked at—that light, for example.
>
> (TL, 63)

Just as Mrs. Ramsey's weaving attaches string to string, the light from the lighthouse attaches thought to thought and movement to movement. Together they weave a whole ordered pattern beneath the cotton wool of things. Mrs. Ramsey sits and looks and feels all the world's imperceptible rhythms until her being fully entrains itself with them. With her knitting in her hand, she becomes the light-weaving-twilight-silence.

As she sits, little phrases bubble up to her as if not from herself. Specifically, she finds herself saying, "We are in the hands of the Lord."

But instantly she was annoyed with herself for saying that. Who had said it? Not she; she had been trapped into saying something she did not mean. She looked up over her knitting and met the third stroke and it seemed to her like her own eyes meeting her own eyes, searching as she alone could search into her mind and her heart, purifying out of existence that lie, any lie.

(TL, 63)

Mrs. Ramsey, like Woolf, is an atheist. As Woolf says, "Emphatically, there is no God; we are the words; we are the music; we are the thing itself" (MB, 72). For Mrs. Ramsey, we are the same light that we see. We are the same woven stuff of the world. When we look at the world, it looks back at us. This is what Woolf's favorite poet Gerard Hopkins called the "instress" of things, when "What you look hard at seems to look hard at you."[33]

Moments of being are often interpreted as religious, but this is not what Mrs. Ramsey or Woolf has in mind. Moments of being may be ineffable, but for Woolf this does not mean they need to be transcendent. The real world, for Woolf, can still be mysterious, novel, and ineffable without God.

Another of Woolf's favorite poets, Lucretius, gives a similar description of his philosophical method. He says he wants to "hold a clear light up to your mind" to shatter the fear and darkness "not by the rays of the sun" but by "the external appearance and inner conditions of nature" [*naturae species ratioque*].[34] In other words, Lucretius' materialist philosophy aims not to shine the divine transcendent light of reason upon the world but to expose the inner light of nature's hidden patterns.

In Mrs. Ramsey's moment of being she becomes the thing itself. The third beam of light is not out of this world but radically in this world. It is illuminating and searching her, purifying her of any scrap of transcendent belief with its immanent materiality. For Mrs. Ramsey, transcendence in all its forms is a *lie*. The metaphysical speculations of the philosophers are lies. Mrs. Ramsey's body, made of photons, is saturated with the photons of the light beam. Together, they mix and diffract into a beautiful luminous array spread out over the room, neither purely subject nor object.

Mrs. Ramsey is not merely "representing" the world of inanimate things in her mind. She is not merely "like" them. Mrs. Ramsey *becomes* the inanimate world. She is them. Scholars sometimes call Woolf's realism "magical," but this suggests that there is a reality to which Woolf adds magical elements. Rather, I believe the source of Woolf's realism is that reality is much more "magical" than we think.

This is why Mrs. Ramsey can praise the light without vanity. Nature's ineffable magic is also her own. She is nature.

> She praised herself in praising the light, without vanity, for she was stern, she was searching, she was beautiful like that light. It was odd, she thought, how if one was alone, one leant to inanimate things; trees, streams, flowers;

felt they expressed one; felt they became one; felt they knew one, in a sense were one; felt an irrational tenderness thus (she looked at that long steady light) as for oneself.

(TL, 63–4)

One philosophical consequence of Woolf's view that everything is nature and we are the thing itself is that there is no vanity or hatred. When Mrs. Ramsey is alone, she "leans" to inanimate things. She swerves and bends toward the world like the swerve and curvature of her knitting needles. She is woven and bent into and through the trees, streams, and flowers. What is more, they express her being as she expresses theirs. She feels that the weave and kinetic coordination of the world is held together by a myriad of imperceptible threads and relations.

We "lean" on these woven patterns like spiders on webs. Although, we frequently act "as if" we were autonomous. Like Woolf, Mrs. Ramsey feels that this continually woven balance and mutual "leaning" may be "irrational," insofar as there is no higher reason or power or proposition that fully explains it. It merely is or becomes without reason, beginning, or end.

As Mrs. Ramsey looks in and through the light at herself as herself, she feels an almost ethical tenderness for the inanimate world. However, since she is the world, it is also a tenderness for herself. There are crucial ethical implications of this idea. Ethics, in this view, is not the care of the "other" or the "same" but of a transpersonal milieu of processes. Everything is held up by leaning on everything else.

In this view, there is not a categorical distinction between care for humans and care for nature. As Woolf says in her autobiography, we are all "afloat, [in an element] which is all the time responding to things we have no words for — exposed to some invisible ray" (MB, 115). The challenge of ethics is to modulate this fluid medium together and carefully attend to its ripples and alterations at every scale. No single normative set of rules dreamed up by philosophers will ever be able to tell us how to behave in such a singular and changing matrix.

The Ecological Self

After this feeling of tenderness, Mrs. Ramsey starts to stare into the beam of light, and her needles hang in mid-air. The curve of her knitting matches the curve of her "leaning" to nature. This curve, in turn, matches the curling up of her body and mind into the light. She becomes a curling mist (like Peter's cigar smoke in *Mrs. Dalloway*) spread out like an atmosphere through the world and into the light. Woolf writes:

> There rose, and she looked and looked with her needles suspended, there curled up off the floor of the mind, rose from the lake of one's being, a mist, a bride to meet her lover.
>
> (TL, 64)

First Mrs. Ramsey became trees, streams, flowers, and now she is a lake. Her self becomes the hydrological process. Our bodies evaporate water and heat, condense into mists and clouds, mix with the radiant heat and vapors from other people and things, and form atmospheric circulations. We are the weather. In other words, Woolf is right. Our being is much more like a lake or a mist than a "sealed vessel" (MB, 122). A lake is a site of pooled movement. Our being is not a vessel but a metastable region of liquid continually passing through us.

Our bodies are pools of fluid that pass through, sustain us, and evaporate back into the world only to rain down again.[35] Lakes are bodies of water, and so are we. Water evaporation from lakes, streams, and flowers in the light of the sun is not transcendence. There is no immaterial soul, only warm water vapor: the material and affective soul of Lucretius. In this fascinating theory, Woolf thus gives us a fully immanent and material description of what is historically, mythologically, and philosophically characterized as divine ascension or metaphysical transcendence.

Waves of Pure Delight

Woolf's robust description of Mrs. Ramsey's experience is incredible because of how quickly the stroke of light hits Mrs. Ramsey. The stroke is brief, yet the peace and joy of the stroke seem to encompass all of nature. For Mrs. Ramsey, space and time expand and become indeterminate. The contracted present of spacetime expands to an indeterminate "moment" without discrete measure.

When the moment passes "She returned to her knitting again. … She knitted with firm composure, slightly pursing her lips" (TL, 64). Each stroke and pause of her knitting makes a rhythm that entrains her body and mind with the world.

Woolf describes Mr. Ramsey watching his wife with no idea of the incredible transformation happening to her. Instead, Woolf says, he thinks only of some trivial fact of the biography of the English philosopher David Hume. Far from offering any revelation, Woolf depicts Mr. Ramsey's obsession with academic philosophy as inhibiting him from moments of becoming and ecstatic vision. Mr. Ramsey misses the little singular things of reality that provoke moments of being because of his drive to conceptualize them. In this view, conceptualization is another filter on the mind that only happens after or in addition to the sensuous world.

> Always, Mrs. Ramsay felt, one helped oneself out of solitude reluctantly by laying hold of some little odd or end, some sound, some sight. She listened, but it was all very still; cricket was over; the children were in their baths; there was only the sound of the sea. She stopped knitting; she held the long reddish-brown stocking dangling in her hands a moment.
>
> (TL, 64)

While Mr. Ramsey is thinking of philosophy, Mrs. Ramsey allows the fractal noise of the sea to draw her back into the moment of being. The sea's rhythmic pulse and its waves do not require instrumental action but relax the mind and let it play among the patterns. The pattern is powerful like the siren's song and Mrs. Ramsey stops her knitting again. Her stocking dangles freely, like her, paused before the immensity of nature and the sea.

> She saw the light again. With some irony in her interrogation, for when one woke at all, one's relations changed, she looked at the steady light, the pitiless, the remorseless, which was so much her, yet so little her, which had her at its beck and call (she woke in the night and saw it bent across their bed, stroking the floor), but for all that she thought, watching it with fascination, hypnotised, as if it were stroking with its silver fingers some sealed vessel in her brain whose bursting would flood her with delight, she had known happiness, exquisite happiness, intense happiness, and it silvered the rough waves a little more brightly, as daylight faded, and the blue went out of the sea and it rolled in waves of pure lemon which curved and swelled and broke upon the beach and the ecstasy burst in her eyes and waves of pure delight raced over the floor of her mind and she felt, It is enough! It is enough!
>
> (TL, 64–5)

Another stroke of light from the lighthouse hits Mrs. Ramsey and continues her moment of being. She recalls waking in the middle of night and seeing the same beam of light stroking the floor. Every time the light strokes, it is singular and one's relations have changed completely. Each iteration of light is also a change in the whole world.

Woolf's description of Mrs. Ramsey's experience of light has some interesting philosophical implications. Woolf says the light is "pitiless" and "remorseless" because the light is not a moral agent. When Mrs. Ramsey becomes the light, she also becomes non-moral in a sense. She is neither judged nor judges the world. The light is a continuous transformation that releases Mrs. Ramsey from regret. The light cleanses her of all doubt and lies of transcendence, immortality, and God. In her moment of being, there is nothing outside nature to judge or pity. There is only light and pure transformation. Mrs. Ramsey becomes the light in the sense that she becomes inseparable from the changing relations and patterns that compose her.

Woolf says that the light summons her as a great "involuntary" (MB, 81) force in the middle of the night. The nature of things as they are felt in moments of being is "involuntary" because performative knowledge is not something conceptual or propositional that we can fully solidify. Performative knowledge is a process that we undergo and that involves the world around us. The way into the moment, for Mrs. Ramsey, is not through contemplation but through rhythm, entrainment, and sensation. The rhythm and sensation of the light and sea hypnotize her into an altered state of consciousness. Woolf says that the light breaks open the sealed vessel of the ego's habituated patterns and unleashes a flood of the greatest happiness she has ever known.

Woolf's description of Mrs. Ramsey's moment of being is again similar to how Woolf described her own moments of being in her autobiography. "It is irrational, the sensation that we are sealed vessels afloat on what it is convenient to call reality; and at some moments, the sealing matter cracks; in floods reality" (MB, 122). "It is a great delight. Perhaps this is the strongest pleasure known to me … It is the rapture" (MB, 72).

Like other moments of being, Mrs. Ramsey's happens at twilight or in the middle of night when the light shines in her room creating moving shadows. Although Mrs. Ramsey is sitting in her chair, her moment of being is filled with the movement of waves, lights, and mists. Her eyes, like the eye of the lighthouse, swell with water like the ocean. They produce tears like waves crashing on the ocean, running down her face. The light's stroke illuminates the waves, turning them yellow at the same time as it illuminates her tears making the world shimmer. Delight races over the floor of her mind as light races over the ocean. The outside world of movement is iterated inside her.

In this moment, Woolf describes beautifully how Mrs. Ramsey becomes the thing itself. Woolf describes how affects and hidden patterns in nature traverse Mrs. Ramsey and bring her freedom from judgment and a moment of ecstasy. Nature is "enough" without any transcendence, representation, or god. Woolf ends Mrs. Ramsey's moment of being with a brief paragraph about how Mr. Ramsey resists the temptation to disturb Mrs. Ramsey's moment of being and the section of the book ends.

There are other beautiful moments in *To the Lighthouse*, but let's look at one more with another character, Lily Briscoe, before we move on. In this next moment, Woolf is her most explicit about how moments of being connect to works of art.

Moment 8: The Fluidity of Life

The second moment of being I want to look at from *To the Lighthouse* happens to a character named Lily Briscoe. Lily is a visiting guest at the Ramsay family's summer cottage in the Hebrides, an archipelago off the west coast of Scotland. She is an unmarried painter who struggles throughout the novel with a painting she is working on. Toward the end of the novel, however, she has a breakthough with her painting through a moment of being.

This moment of being is especially interesting because it is perhaps the only one where Woolf elaborates in great detail the connection between moments of being and art-making. Lily's moment is also one of the longest moments of being in Woolf's writing at the time, at about four pages long.

Woolf begins by describing Lily Briscoe standing on the lawn looking at her blank canvas. When she looks away from the canvas at the garden, however, she is suddenly struck by an involuntary feeling. Woolf says Lily's feeling first emerged while she was out on a walk earlier but then suddenly sprang into her mind as she looked at the garden. Lily feels "curiously divided, as if one part of her were drawn out there—it was a still day, hazy; ... the other had fixed itself doggedly, solidly, here on the lawn" (TL, 156). In other words, part of her walk is pulling her mind away to wander and freely associate in the mists. The other part is in front of the canvas to paint as the process unfolds. This is the dynamic that begins Lily's moment of becoming.

The Ecological Imagination

Woolf describes how the misty haze of the weather draws Lily out of herself. Lily begins to remember and imagine freely without trying to paint. The haze of the weather and her walk through the haze are part of what we could call Lily's material or ecological imagination. In wandering with her body in the moving mists, her mind begins to do the same. Woolf writes, "It was an odd road to be walking, this of painting. Out and out one went, further and further, until at last one seemed to be on a narrow plank, perfectly alone, over the sea" (TL, 172).

Lily's walk also triggers an involuntary memory of a pattern in a hedge that begins to bring everything together. Woolf was onto something with this observation about walking and imagination. Recent scientific work shows that walking significantly improves creativity while reducing linear rational thought.[36] Woolf writes that

> something she remembered in the relations of those lines cutting across, slicing down, and in the mass of the hedge with its green cave of blues and

browns, which had stayed in her mind; which had tied a knot in her mind so that at odds and ends of time, involuntarily, as she walked along the Brompton Road, as she brushed her hair, she found herself painting that picture, passing her eye over it, and untying the knot in imagination.

(TL, 157)

Lily saw a pattern of color and line beneath the cotton wool in the hedge that stayed and iterated itself in her brain. Just as Woolf says that words are like arrows that roll up like waves and crash in our brains, Lily feels line and color the same way. Patterns make knots or whirls inside us until they emerge into conscious awareness.

As Lily walked and brushed her hair, the pattern iterated itself inside her. She was entraining her movements and thoughts to the pattern. Philosophically, Lily does not experience the hedge as a discrete object, but rather as a relational pattern of color and line echoing *inside* her. She does not try to represent objects with paint but to feel "the *relations* of those lines" in her body. "It was one's body feeling, not one's mind," Lily says (TL, 178).

Lily's senses become involuntarily amplified and widened to see these singularities. She can dilate her attention wide enough to hold together the whole of the assembly and see that all the tiny singular colorations and lines form an interrelated pattern or rhythm. The colors are not parts in a whole image, but singularities woven, tied, and untied in a fabric that weaves in with her mind and body. In other words, painting the hedge does not happen in her mind, or in her body, or even in the world alone, but in the mixture and iteration of all three in a moving pattern.

Aesthetic Involuntarism

In *Sketches of the Past*, Woolf describes moments of being as happening "in a great, apparently involuntary, rush" (MB, 81). Lily's aim is to experience this rush and then try to highlight a pattern of interconnection within it, using paint. However, before Lily begins painting, Woolf says she starts to subdue all "the impertinences and irrelevances that plucked her attention and made her remember how she was such and such a person, had such and such relations to people, she took her hand and raised her brush. For a moment, it stayed trembling in a painful but exciting ecstasy in the air" (TL, 157). But why? Woolf is implicitly suggesting that the patterns beneath the cotton wool do not resemble and are even obscured by determinate people, relations, and things. Lily is looking for the singular shifting patterns beneath determinate things and thus must subdue her identity.

Even Lily's conscious intention and instrumental action to paint get in the way. In order to see the world, she has to resist all the social relations with other people that threaten to close her into a discrete and definable object. She does not see *things* but rather the whole meshwork of processes weaving the deep green cave of blues and browns.

Right before Lily makes her first brush stroke, she pauses. The painting does not emerge from a pre-given model but has to unfold from each previous stroke. This is why the first stroke is so important. The ecstasy is painful because Lily is exposed to the contingencies of her body, mind, and world as they unfold through paint. Something unexpected will happen when she gives up control. Lily is not representing an image but harnessing it and letting it work through her like knots in a fabric.

> One line placed on the canvas committed her to innumerable risks, to frequent and irrevocable decisions. All that in idea seemed simple became in practice immediately complex; as the waves shape themselves symmetrically from the cliff top, but to the swimmer among them are divided by steep gulfs, and foaming crests.
>
> (TL, 157)

Just as the ocean wave patterns are not visible from the beach, so Woolf's patterns beneath the cotton wool remain mostly invisible in daily life. If one wants to see the patterns, one has to change one's perspective. From the beach, each wave looks relatively discrete from the others, but from the cliff, one can see how they all weave together with one another in a larger process.

> With a curious physical sensation, as if she were urged forward and at the same time must hold herself back, she made her first quick decisive stroke. And so pausing and so flickering, she attained a dancing rhythmical movement, as if the pauses were one part of the rhythm and the strokes another, and all were related; and so, lightly and swiftly pausing, striking, she scored her canvas with brown running nervous lines which had no sooner settled there than they enclosed (she felt it looming out at her) a space.
>
> (TL, 158)

Woolf describes here a rhythmic movement similar to Mrs. Ramsey's knitting that entrains Lily into the moment of being. The movement feels "curious" because it is only partly voluntary. Each stroke is relatively discrete but is woven together with the pauses in a relational pattern. The marks are not Lily's alone but are continuations of the world's marks carried through Lily. The patterns of her brush strokes are not representations of reality but performances or dances of reality itself on the canvas. The painting is only the record of the motions.

Lily's method is not the same as what the surrealists and psychologists call "automatic" writing or automatic art because it is not an expression of the strictly human unconscious. Rather, Woolf describes Lily's painting as influenced just as much by the fog as by her walk and the dance of her arm. For Woolf, the world writes and paints through the human body and mind. Woolf is explicit about this in her autobiography: "that behind the cotton wool is hidden a pattern; that we—I mean all human beings—are connected with this; that the whole world is a work of art; that we are parts of the work of art" (MB, 72).

The human body and its arts are a continuation of the pattern of nature's art. If the world is already a work of art, then our art is not and cannot represent the world. For Woolf, human art is an iteration or continuation of the patterns and processes that are already here. Lily *continues* the dancing rhythm, pausing and flickering, already in the world's imbricated lines and colors. Her strokes and pauses are all related in a single continuous iterative process. The dance of the body is the dance of the world folded back on itself. In short, rhythms and patterns do not represent the world but iterate it.

Undulating Realism

For Woolf, reality is neither this nor that but an indeterminate *process*. It is a shifting pattern we are caught up in unawares. Then, suddenly, in moments of being we see the pattern.

Reality, for Woolf, is not something in contrast to appearances. Reality is something previously unseen that entrains us into the world. Reality undulates, echos, iterates, tessellates, imbricates, but it does not represent anything. As the English anthropologist Gregory Bateson wrote, "My central thesis can now be approached in words: The pattern which connects is a metapattern. It is a pattern of patterns. It is that metapattern which defines the vast generalization that, indeed, it is patterns which connect."[37]

As Woolf demonstrates with Lily's approach to painting, the patterns are not random or deterministic. Unlike mathematical fractals, nature's patterns are not perfectly geometrical or "self-same iterations" that go on to infinity. Real fractal patterns are singular and do not repeat. This is why Lilly cannot merely conceptualize the model of her painting in her mind and reproduce it. She has to entrain her walking, brushing her hair, and thinking to the hedge in order to paint it. Mathematical fractals are to nature's patterns as a crescent shape is to the moon. Mathematical fractals are abstract approximations of the real thing. Woolf writes:

> Down in the hollow of one wave she saw the next wave towering higher and higher above her. For what could be more formidable than that space?

> Here she was again, she thought, stepping back to look at it, drawn out of gossip, out of living, out of community with people into the presence of this formidable ancient enemy of hers—this other thing, this truth, this reality, which suddenly laid hands on her, emerged stark at the back of appearances and commanded her attention.
>
> (TL, 158)

Woolf is describing here a defining feature of fractals: recursive self-similarity. Inside the hollow of a wave pattern is another wave pattern. Each is absolutely singular and yet shares a similar pattern of motion nested in another. As Lily zooms in smaller and smaller, the waves get larger and larger in this vertiginous fractal space without beginning or end. In her moment of being, Lily is drawn involuntarily from the world of discrete things, people, and trivial gossip and placed in the presence of a fractal truth and reality.

Woolf does not describe this as a hallucination, another world, or a transcendence beyond the world. Woolf does not say reality is beyond appearances but rather at the "back" of them like the back of a piece of embroidery reveals the hidden patterns that made the image on the other side possible. Lily's senses are not distorted but intensified and amplified. Earlier in the novel, Lily was too focused on making art or proving that women can paint. She saw only things, peoples, and actions. But those were just the tip of enormous icebergs. Things, as Woolf likes to say, are the thin shiny surface of a deep pond or pool.

For Woolf, reality is fully immanent to appearances like the surface of a pond is continuous with its depth. Our conscious awareness is like a "great reducing valve," that filters perception, as Aldous Huxley said.[38] Or it is, as Bergson wrote in *Matter and Memory*, like a photographic plate that records only a fraction of the reality that passes through it unrecorded.[39] In Lily's moment of being, she can feel a wider range of reality moving through her. A moment of being is not an "out of body experience," but rather a sudden realization of the body's specific continuation of the world. Lily experiences directly what Woolf describes in her autobiography: that our art is a way the world paints itself. Only by letting go of her intention to paint is Lily open to feel the wider relations of her world working through her.

Moments of Nakedness

In Woolf's philosophy, reality is not an objective state of affairs but something we move through as a fluid medium. We are part of the changing thing we are trying to know or to paint. As Woolf says in her autobiography, "I see myself as a fish in a stream; deflected; held in place; but cannot describe the stream" (MB, 80). In other words, Woolf cannot describe the stream of reality because she is that same flowing stream.

Insofar as "stream of consciousness" writers still assumes that human consciousness is distinct from nature, they still wrongly believe that nature can be known from the outside. However, for Woolf, the mind is an ontological region of the same stream as nature. There is no view of nature from outside it. To be is to know the world in a certain way. In her moment of being, Lily explicitly rejects any determinate knowledge of reality.

> Other worshipful objects were content with worship; men, women, God, all let one kneel prostrate; but this form, were it only the shape of a white lamp-shade looming on a wicker table, roused one to perpetual combat, challenged one to a fight in which one was bound to be worsted. Always (it was in her nature, or in her sex, she did not know which) before she exchanged the fluidity of life for the concentration of painting she had a few moments of nakedness when she seemed like an unborn soul, a soul reft of body, hesitating on some windy pinnacle and exposed without protection to all the blasts of doubt.
>
> (TL, 158)

Reality cannot be worshiped because it is not a substance or an object. It is not a man, woman, or God. It is a fluid process that one is continuous with. Transcendent objects can be worshiped because we think they are outside us. But even a real lampshade is impossible to know if it belongs to the immanent world of nature. We cannot know a lampshade as an object separate from us. The challenge for Lily and Woolf is not how to know or represent the lampshade in language, paint, or concepts, but how to feel part of the same world of the lampshade. How does it connect with us here, now, and affect our bodies and minds? This is what "becoming" means for Woolf. Becoming means feeling yourself as the entire sensuous present brimming with singularities. Painting, for Lily, continues the process of the world without trying to instrumentalize it. The challenge of Lily's art of becoming is to make it without making it. How can art be made without forcing it? For Woolf, Lily exemplifies how an artist becomes a relay or crossroads for reality to move through and into a work of art.

Woolf also says that Lily's moment of becoming is a "moment of nakedness." She says it is a full exposure to the world's "winds." What is the philosophical significance of this? When a moment of being amplifies one's senses, one is also left unprotected by one's mental defenses and rationalizations. All one's feelings, thoughts, and sensations can come in and blow through us with all manner of doubts and joys. In moments of becoming, Lily (and Woolf) feels this extreme vulnerability to the world. They become porous with the world and highly susceptible to it. To know, in Woolf's philosophy, is to be receptive to the world one is in. But receptivity is also vulnerability.

Lily wonders if it is in her nature, like Peter's, to be susceptible and porous, or is it in her sex? She does not know. Instead of struggling to become rational agents of universal knowledge like men, Woolf looks to women like Mrs. Ramsey and Lily as historical sites for moments of being. The aim of these moments for women and men is not to become men or women or even humans, as they have been defined. The result of moments of being is to become the singular flow of material processes that make one up.[40]

For example, as Lily's senses are amplified she undergoes a qualitative change of perception. There is not the world "out there" contrasted with her "in here." The movements of the world are like winds that blow through her. As Woolf writes in *The Waves*:

> These attempts to say, "I am this, I am that," which we make, coming together, like separated parts of one body and soul, are false. Something has been left out from fear. Something has been altered, from vanity. We have tried to accentuate differences. From the desire to be separate we have laid stress upon our faults, and what is particular to us. But there is a chain whirling round, round, in a steel-blue circle beneath.
>
> (W, 137)

If we could feel, think, see, taste, hear, touch, and smell every tiny singular sensation that our body could sense, we would feel utterly *saturated* as if floating through a fluid medium in which our bodies were only swirling eddies. Art cannot represent sensation just as the senses cannot represent one another. Rather, art and sensations form a direct relay or system of different affects.[41] Reality is already saturated. Nothing is needed to complete or supplement it. However, since we cannot directly represent this saturated reality, the work of art must try to grab the reader or viewer directly with affects.

Currents of Sensation

Lily, therefore, begins to think about how her work of art will affect others when it is done. This is another difficult problem. There is no one-to-one correlation between the painting and its effects on others or the world. Once the painting is complete, it is part of the world and will affect each person in its own way. Some people may not like it. Lily begins to think about the instrumental effect of her work of art and the judgment of others. What is interesting here is that these thoughts are not meta-thoughts about the painting but are feelings and rhythms that Lily experiences *through the work of art*. There is no outside space of reflection but all thoughts and worries are woven into the act of painting while it is happening.

> Why then did she do it? She looked at the canvas, lightly scored with running lines. It would be hung in the servants' bedrooms. It would be rolled up and stuffed under a sofa. What was the good of doing it then, and she heard some voice saying she couldn't paint, saying she couldn't create, as if she were caught up in one of those habitual currents in which after a certain time experience forms in the mind, so that one repeats words without being aware any longer who originally spoke them.
>
> (TL, 159)

If Lily is open to the forms, habits, and patterns of the world, she is also open to the doubts and judgments of other people in the world. Woolf describes these habits of thinking as currents with their own direction and without clear origin. In a moment of being, one is more susceptible to these currents of doubt as well. Woolf continues:

> Then, as if some juice necessary for the lubrication of her faculties were spontaneously squirted, she began precariously dipping among the blues and umbers, moving her brush hither and thither, but it was now heavier and went slower, as if it had fallen in with some rhythm which was dictated to her (she kept looking at the hedge, at the canvas) by what she saw, so that while her hand quivered with life, this rhythm was strong enough to bear her along with it on its current.
>
> (TL, 159)

The rhythm of the world, the hedge's coloration, and her thoughts of doubt and beauty carry Lily along involuntarily. The rhythms and patterns of the world are directly transmitted into and through her body. Indeed, the voices Lily hears have no isolated origin because they are cultural patterns or habits of instrumentalism and misogyny. Culture, as Woolf describes it here, is not immaterial or symbolic but fully material and kinetic. It is patterned in our bodies like currents in water pushing us along. "What good is art? Women can't paint." Lily also gets caught up in these kinds of habitual currents.

> Certainly she was losing consciousness of outer things. And as she lost consciousness of outer things, and her name and her personality and her appearance, and whether Mr. Carmichael was there or not, her mind kept throwing up from its depths, scenes, and names, and sayings, and memories and ideas, like a fountain spurting over that glaring, hideously difficult white space, while she modeled it with greens and blues.
>
> (TL, 159)

In Lily's moment of being, there is no longer any inside and outside of the reality. There is no "her" painting "nature." It is as if her pores had open so wide that the entire world flowed through, and she lost her name and appearance as distinct from the current of existence flowing through her. Her mind freely wandered among memories, sensations, sayings, and places. In this way, the amplification of her senses is not just an amplification of existing sensations but also an amplification of *the process that connects sensations to one another.* In other words, Lily's moment of being is also one of free association and imagination. Moments of being are also moments of intense mind wandering where thoughts, feelings, and affects seem to emerge from nowhere and mix with another.

The Work of Art and the Meaning of Life

After Lily loses consciousness of outer things, she recalls Mrs. Ramsey's power to

> resolve everything into simplicity and to make angers, irritations fall off like old rags; she brought together this and that and then this, and so made out of that miserable silliness and spite something ... which survived, after all these years complete, so that she dipped into it to re-fashion her memory of [Charles Tansely], and there it stayed in the mind affecting one almost like a work of art.
>
> (TL, 160)

In other words, Lily thinks of Mrs. Ramsey as an artist of existence, memory, thought, and feeling. Lily tries to follow Mrs. Ramsey's lead by dipping into her memories as she dips her brush into paint. She tries to weave the world like a work of art like Mrs. Ramsey did to reveal hidden patterns. Lily continues:

> "Like a work of art" she repeated, looking from her canvas to the drawing-room steps and back again. She must rest for a moment. And, resting, looking from one to the other vaguely, the old question which traversed the sky of the soul perpetually, the vast, the general question which was apt to particularise itself at such moments as these, when she released faculties that had been on the strain, stood over her, paused over her, darkened over her. What is the meaning of life? That was all—a simple question; one that tended to close in on one with years.
>
> (TL, 160)

At this point in her moment, Lily begins to see the whole of nature as a work of art just as Woolf wrote in her autobiography. As Lily increasingly releases her faculties of reason and instrumental action that had previously strained her, her consciousness attention dilates out to include the larger fabric of nature. She sees that the relations of color and line extend out beyond the singularity of the hedge and the canvas indefinitely. This is why the most general philosophical question of meaning becomes particularized with the hedge. Is there a higher purpose or end to all this singular imbricated patterning in nature? Is nature meant for something beyond what it is doing? Woolf's answer to these philosophical questions through Lily is crucial. She writes:

> The great revelation had never come. The great revelation perhaps never did come. Instead there were little daily miracles, illuminations, matches struck unexpectedly in the dark.
>
> (TL, 161)

In Woolf's philosophy, there is no higher transcendent "meaning" beyond nature that would shape it. Nature is not formed in advance. Everything emerges into the light relationally and unexpectedly one moment of being at a time.

This is a fairly radical philosophical position in the West. Nature has no absolute beginning, end, or ultimate aim. It is neither entirely random, deterministic, nor probabilistic. According to Woolf, in this passage, nature proceeds through genuinely novel "miracles" and "unexpected" events, similar to Lucretius' swerve. Matter does not follow mechanistic laws, but weaves itself together by swerving unpredictably.

For Woolf, the ultimate revelation about a fixed nature of things never comes because nature is constantly changing what it is. There are only indeterminate and novel processes unfolding relationally. There is only nature burning itself out in the dark of the cosmos one match at a time.

Therefore, Woolf's moments of being are not epiphanies in the revelatory sense. Woolf's characters discover no "higher" meaning in nature. Indeed, they realize there is nothing to "know" beyond the immanent patterns unfolding all around them. There is no way to fully predict them. In Woolf's onto-epistemology, nature is not a substance that can be known but an ineffable process that the knower is and undergoes in their acts of knowing. The illumination of nature comes not through an external light but an inner or immanent light of unfolding and novel patterns. This is what Lily realizes in her moment of being.

The Aesthetics of Chaos

In Woolf's philosophy, form does not precede matter. Rather, form emerges and dissolves from the flowing chaos of matter. Let's see how this philosophical vision informs her theory of art in Lily's moment of being.

For Lily, the work of art is the artist's attempt to share something stable with others woven from nature's moving patchwork. What can one say or make from a continually moving and changing knot-work of patterns? This is a fundamentally different aesthetic question than most philosophers tend to ask. Most philosophers in the history of aesthetics ask about the forms, laws, judgments, and static structures of art and how humans experience it. These are the kinds of ideas that Lily says one can worship, build icons of, and represent. But, if in Woolf's view, there are only currents, ebbs, pools, and streams of swerving matter, how does one make form from a moving world? Lily recalls again Mrs. Ramsey's way of weaving moments together from chaos:

> Mrs. Ramsay making of the moment something permanent (as in another sphere Lily herself tried to make of the moment something permanent)—this was of the nature of a revelation. In the midst of chaos there was shape; this eternal passing and flowing (she looked at the clouds going and the leaves shaking) was struck into stability. Life stand still here, Mrs. Ramsay said. "Mrs. Ramsay! Mrs. Ramsay!" she repeated. She owed it all to her.
> (TL, 161)

The key philosophical insight here is that stability and form are emergent patterns *of movement and chaos*. Aesthetics, for Woolf, is not about representation or the meaning of life but about weaving metastable patterns from the flow of things. The task is not to stop being from flowing, but to make something stable from the flow, to shape the chaos into something more permanent so others can see it too. This is Woolf's reframing of the traditional aesthetic and ethical questions about form. How can we learn to continue the iterations of chaos in our own way? How can we weave the patterns and miracles of our daily life into regions of livable stability without falling apart? Mrs. Ramsey cultivated this art of weaving the world and Lily adapts it to painting. Lily thinks:

> The faint thought she was thinking of Mrs. Ramsay seemed in consonance with this quiet house; this smoke; this fine early morning air. Faint and unreal, it was amazingly pure and exciting.
> (TL, 161)

Lily feels all the singularities of her specific morning weave together synthetically with her thoughts of Mrs. Ramsey. Here, Woolf describes the fascinating way that the materiality of our thoughts is continuous with the materiality of the atmosphere. Lily's thoughts of Mrs. Ramsey are "faint" just like the faint sounds, faint smoke, and faint early morning air. Everything is thought and felt faintly because the world around is faint.

But the woven singularity of the moment feels "unreal" to Lily, why? Woolf also describes her personal moments of being as "unreal" (MB, 78) "dream"-

like (MB, 69). This is, in part, because moments of being are so *different* from our normal limited range of perception. More precisely, moments of being feel dream-like because their altered state of consciousness is somewhere between waking and dream states. In dream states, our brains are much more freely associative and creative. Things that seem contradictory or impossible in waking life happen easily and without incredulity in dreams. A moment of being, according to Woolf, is dream-like and unreal in the sense that it is more creative, associative, spontaneous, and interconnected than the restricted and discrete divisions of waking life. Woolf's philosophical move here is to say that reality is much more like the dream world than it is like waking life. This is not because waking life is false, but only that it is a limited and constrained vision of the broader world. Moments of being are special because they are like waking or lucid dreams where we are just conscious enough to compare the two states simultaneously. This is why Lily's experience of her moment goes back and forth between conscious intentional efforts to make a painting and moments of complete synesthetic interconnection between herself and "outer things."

This is also why, despite lacking ultimate revelation, Lily feels that "the moment at least seemed extraordinarily fertile" (TL, 172). Moments of being are fertile for Lily, because they are saturated with new sensations and new connections between sensations. Moments of being temporarily relax her typical ways of thinking, seeing, and feeling and make it possible to live and create differently.

Lily's moment of being continues as she paints and remembers people and events from the past, until suddenly, Woolf says, "Against her will she had come to the surface, and found herself half out of the picture, looking, a little dazedly, as if at unreal things, at Mr. Carmichael" (TL, 178). Lily wants to tell her friend Mr. Carmichael all about her moment of being but feels that it is deeply ineffable and instead says nothing to him. As Lily comes to the end of her moment of being she thinks:

> Was there no safety? No learning by heart of the ways of the world? No guide, no shelter, but all was miracle, and leaping from the pinnacle of a tower into the air?
>
> (TL, 180)

For Lily, and Woolf, there is nothing fixed or static in the world. There are no immutable forms or laws of nature that we can learn by heart. There is only the constant "miraculous" swerving of matter as it leaps here and there in relatively stable patterns that are our lives. We can trace the patterns as matter flows and swerves but there is no revelation. There is no divine guide or Mrs. Ramsey to guide us in the correct way to live, make art, or weave a moment. All is experiment. Lily cries out loud for the dead Mrs. Ramsey, but Woolf says, "nothing happened" (TL, 180).

Moment 9: There Is No Stability in This World

The last individual moment of being I want to look at comes from Woolf's most experimental novel, *The Waves* (1931). *The Waves* has many brief moments of being ebbing and flowing in their intensity and duration, but here I want to look at one of the most sustained individual moments.

In *Mrs. Dalloway,* the individual moments of being are comparatively short and distributed among several characters. In *To the Lighthouse,* only two characters have moments of being and the moments are longer. In *The Waves*, though, one long individual moment stands out between the brief moments. One of the novel's main characters, Bernard, rides the train into London, and starts to *become* the movement and *speed* of the world and everyone on the train. He loses his individuality in the crowd. His senses become amplified. Time stretches into the deep past, and space becomes fluid and interrelated. His moment of being almost becomes a collective moment since it involves a shared feeling of commuters riding the train into London. But in the end, it remains focused on Bernard's individual feelings of becoming. Nonetheless, it is an incredible and sustained moment worthy of concluding this section of the book.

Woolf wrote *The Waves* as poetic soliloquies spoken by the book's six main characters. The book spans the lifetime of the characters and their similarities and differences with one another. The character of Bernard is a close observer of people and loves to take notes on them and imagine who they are. In this moment of being, Woolf describes Bernard, an English man in his twenties engaged to be married, riding into London on his way to meet his childhood friends for dinner.

I Am Become Part of This Speed

Bernard races in his train toward London whose gas lamps shimmer "strangely" in the fog. Woolf writes, "The early train from the north is hurled at her like a missile. We draw a curtain as we pass. Blank expectant faces stare at us as we rattle and flash through stations. Men clutch their newspapers a little tighter, as our wind sweeps them, envisaging death. But we roar on" (W, 111).

Here, Woolf beautifully weaves together the thermodynamic processes of rushing wind, ballistic missiles, speeding trains, and the heat death of cosmos. Matter moves from hot to cold everywhere and the train dramatizes this movement. Bernard looks out the window at this dissipating world. Suddenly, the motion and speed throw him into a moment of being. He says:

> Meanwhile as I stand looking from the train window, I feel strangely, persuasively, that because of my great happiness (being engaged to be married), I am become part of this speed, this missile, hurled at the city.
>
> (W, 111)

Like so many other moments of being in Woolf's novels, Bernard's moment begins in mid-movement and looking out a window. The train's swift motion through the vast dark countryside makes him feel relatively small within the world of larger social, technological, and natural processes. Bernard begins to feel like a region of the landscape and of the train body itself. He is also engaged to be married and begins to feel the relaxation of his individuality because of it. He will become part of a couple and eventually a family with children that will outlive him. Bernard's happiness is related to the dissolution or distribution of his self into others through biological reproduction.

In short, Bernard begins to feel enfolded in the broader world of material processes around him. They run through him. Their speed becomes his. Bernard's body becomes a metabolic missile running through a larger world of "majestic animality." Suddenly, the division between nature, culture, and technology crumbles. They are just names we give to one massively interwoven metabolic process. Unlike the other train riders who "fidget" and worry, Woolf says that Bernard is "numbed" and "acquiescent" to this process where "Nothing we can do will avail. Over us all broods a splendid unanimity" (W, 111).

What is the use of worrying, Bernard thinks, when nothing we can do will give us any real advantage over the world? The world flows on through us whether we want it to or not. The world is not ours to dominate and instrumentalize because we are fully immanent within it.

The Community of Desire

Woolf writes that the city-dwelling humans are like "ants" drawn to the breast of a sleeping beast. This is our community of desire. Bernard thinks:

> We are enlarged and solemnised and brushed into uniformity as with the grey wing of some enormous goose (it is a fine, but colourless morning) because we have only one desire—to arrive at the station. I do not want the train to stop with a thud. I do not want the connection which has bound us together sitting opposite each other all night long to be broken. I do not want to feel that hate and rivalry have resumed their sway; and different desires. Our community in the rushing train sitting together with only one wish to arrive at Euston was very welcome.
>
> (W, 111–12)

Woolf describes the train ride like a majestic procession or ceremony that shows the riders their shared community of desire to arrive at Euston station. They are woven and interwoven together with the world like the pattern of feathers in a goose's wing. This is such a beautiful and precise image. It suggests not homogeneity but a holding together of interwoven singularities in a fractal pattern. The train riders are not identical but collectively formed like the imbricated sheaves of tessellated feathers in a goose wing. Everything looks gray from a distance, but closer up, the gray is composed of a vast meshwork of singular gray bodies. Each is distinct but not separate from one another.

The desire of each traveler is a singular dimension of the common desire to move and arrive at Euston. The thud of the train's arrival breaks up this interwoven goose wing of bodies and scatters them into different directions. Ultimately, the range of different directions allows rivalry and conflict to resume. Bernard feels that the moment the desire for arrival is attained; the moment there is a definitive goal; individualization resumes. People "wish to be first through the gate into the lift assert themselves" (W, 112).

> But I do not wish to be first through the gate; to assume the burden of individual life. I, who have been since Monday, when she accepted me, charged in every nerve with a sense of identity, who could not see a toothbrush in a glass without saying, 'My tooth-brush,' now wish to unclasp my hands and let fall my possessions, and merely stand here in the street, taking no part, watching the omnibuses, without desire; without envy; with what would be boundless curiosity about human destiny if there were any longer an edge to my mind. But it has none. I have arrived; am accepted. I ask nothing.
>
> (W, 112)

Bernard loses his individuality but that does not mean he loses his singularity. He becomes like an eddy in the wind, or a feather in a bird's wing. He is singular yet woven into a world in motion. Although Bernard's marriage is individual in a legal sense, its real consequences are collective. It sweeps him up and weaves him in with the other feathers uniquely. Bernard's desire is no longer "his" because his mind no longer has any edges. His movements, thoughts, and feelings have become sensibly continuous with the omnibuses whirling around him. By being accepted into marriage Bernard feels he is accepted by the whole world. The edges of everything have frayed and now show him the misty veil of intertwining relationships. Once he feels fully connected with the world, there is nothing more to desire. Why? Because he has become the desire of the world itself. There is nothing outside him to desire.

The General Impulse

In this moment, Bernard's individuality "drops off," but he does not lose anything. Rather, he gains a continuity with the rest of the world. When Bernard releases the tight grip of his drive for rivalry and self-assertion, he does not stop living. Instead, he becomes attuned and responsive to all the other motions and patterns at work. Becoming means moving and changing in response to as many sensations as one can. Bernard continues:

> Having dropped off satisfied like a child from the breast, I am at liberty now to sink down, deep, into what passes, this omnipresent, general life … One observes curious hesitations at the door of the lift. This way, that way, the other? Then individuality asserts itself. They are off. They are all impelled by some necessity. Some miserable affair of keeping an appointment, of buying a hat, severs these beautiful human beings once so united.
> (W, 112–13)

If the countryside and city are the breasts of civilization, for Woolf, humans are the ones who drink the milk. Our bodies are a continuation of this nourishing flow. Our bodies remake themselves with what they eat and mix with the Earth. Bernard drinks this flow of milk and, like a child of the Earth, relaxes and sinks below the surface of conscious perception. The cotton wool of discrete objects dissolves into "what passes" in the flow and movement of the world.

This is an exemplary statement of Woolf's kinetic realism. At the level of daily perception, there are things and appearances. They are not false but are like a glassy pond—shiny, reflective, visual, and rippling with interest. Beneath this cotton wool of things are the kinetic patterns of "what passes." For Woolf, reality does not mean a set of unchanging objective forms hidden behind appearances. Neither does it mean a naive empiricism where what we see is all there is. Kinetic realism is the reality of what passes as it passes. It is not something we know through propositions, but something we sink down into, drunk on the milk of the world.

In other words, in his moment of being, Bernard's life becomes part of the general movement of reality. Each quiver of a body, each woven color of a trouser, is part of a more general relational pattern playing out below the level of conscious awareness.

Unfortunately, all the walkers, save Bernard, are compelled by some externally imposed necessity like being on time and buying things. In his moment of being, Bernard feels how abstract these things are. Appointments try to fix spacetime into discrete blocks where one must promise the future. Commodity exchange assumes the existence of this same abstract unit of spacetime as if one thing (money) were equal to another (a hat). Commodities also assume the existence of abstract units of time such that we can exchange wages and commodities.

Bernard feels that these philosophical abstractions are what sever these beautiful humans from themselves and the world. These people pretend to bracket or ignore real relations of motion or "passing" and act as if the world were made of a bunch of discrete billiard balls. Bernard responds by saying:

> For myself, I have no aim. I have no ambition. I will let myself be carried on by the general impulse. The surface of my mind slips along like a pale-grey stream reflecting what passes. I cannot remember my past, my nose, or the colour of my eyes, or what my general opinion of myself is.
> (W, 63)

Just like Lily Briscoe, from *To the Lighthouse* (TL, 157), Bernard lets go of himself, his ego, and ambition, and feels carried on by the processes around him. In Woolf's moments of being, her characters are moved by a "general impulse," already at work in the world. It is not just their mind that is caught up in a so-called "stream of consciousness," but their bodies in the stream of the world. Bernard just floats along in the crowd of people.

Philosophically, this scene is a great example of Woolf's fluid dynamic epistemology. Since we are "the thing itself," according to Woolf, the world flows and passes *through* us as us (MB, 72). Woolf describes Bernard's whole body, including his mind, as a fluid medium. Just like a river, Woolf says that Bernard does not represent reality but diffracts it. Bernard cannot remember the past because he is the past folded up in the present.

Beneath the Paving Stones

As he walks through the streets, Woolf writes that Bernard feels the full materiality of the world as if it were a kind of dream where things move *through* him.

> Only in moments of emergency, at a crossing, at a kerb, the wish to preserve my body springs out and seizes me and stops me, here, before this omnibus. We insist, it seems, on living. Then again, indifference descends. The roar of the traffic, the passage of undifferentiated faces, this way and that way, drugs me into dreams; rubs the features from faces. People might walk through me.
> (W, 113)

In this moment, Woolf describes Bernard as only minimally conscious. He is just aware enough of his individuality within the flux of the world to not walk in front of an omnibus. Something in his body and brain kicks in to preserve his life. Other than that, Woolf likens Bernard's moment of being to altered state of consciousness akin to being on drugs or in a dream. Indeed, city sounds and sights can often have a fractal spectrum that may contribute to states of aesthetic reverie, imagination, akin to drug or dream states.[42] For Woolf, so-called natural and artificial sounds can both be iterations of nature. They are works of art. Also, just as Mrs. Dalloway says she cuts through the world like a knife, Bernard feels that people walk *through* him.

Here, Woolf emphasizes not the unity but the singularity of the processes around her characters. For instance, Woolf writes, "We are only lightly covered with buttoned cloth; and beneath these pavements are shells, bones and silence" (W, 113). This is a very materialist conclusion to Bernard's moment in what otherwise could have led to a mystical feeling of transcendence beyond the world. Instead of taking us above the world, Woolf takes us below it into the dirt, shells, and silence of the earth. Bernard does not feel that he is outside space and time but rather deeply and expansively inside it. Humans, Bernard feels, are walking geological layers. In this sense, London is millions of years old and brand new at the same time.

To Embrace the Whole World

A moment of being can be a fragile state. The world is filled with sounds and patterns that can drug one into a dreamy state but also people and things that can pull one out. For example, Woolf writes that Bernard floats along the street like a leaf in a river, but also that he is pricked and plucked by various sensations and feelings as he goes. Many of these sensations threaten to wake him back to consciousness and instrumental individualism. Bernard thinks:

> It is, however, true that my dreaming, my tentative advance like one carried beneath the surface of a stream, is interrupted, torn, pricked and plucked at by sensations, spontaneous and irrelevant, of curiosity, greed, desire, irresponsible as in sleep. No, but I wish to go under; to visit the profound depths; once in a while to exercise my prerogative not always to act, but to explore; to hear vague, ancestral sounds of boughs creaking, of mammoths, to indulge impossible desires to embrace the whole world with the arms of understanding, impossible to those who act.
>
> (W, 113–14)

Bernard wishes to stay underwater, quasi-conscious, in the stream of reality where the world is not sharply divided into discrete objects of desire. As he moves, he does not act but explores and responds to the world of affects. Bernard's "becoming" does not mean that he turns into something else, but rather that he feels himself caught up in and directly responsive to the processes around him. They are always going on, but only in moments of being does he sense them directly.

For instance, Bernard hears a vague noise that reminds him of the fractal sound of wind through ancient trees or the sound of the mammoths of London millions of years ago. Bernard experiences the present as a palimpsest of the past just like Mrs. Dalloway, Septimus, and Peter Walsh did in *Mrs. Dalloway*. The present shares the fractal patterns of the past. The past and present are not strictly identical but they are close enough for Bernard to connect them spontaneously. Urban noises are only tree and mammoth noises in a different medium. These are the fractal patterns that contribute to Bernard's experience of space and time dilation in his moment of being.

Unlike those who act in the limited intentional sense of the word, Bernard can feel and sense the layered fabrics of the world's interrelation around him and through him. What he cannot think in intentional rational thought, namely "the whole world," becomes suddenly possible to feel. Philosophically, this is not because Bernard has a concept of the totality of the world, but because Bernard, like the flower Woolf describes in her autobiography, is an aspect of the whole world. There is nothing that is not the world. Each singular flower is, therefore, for Woolf, also the whole world.

Although Woolf was not aware of it, this is also an important conclusion of contemporary quantum physics. Because our universe exploded from a tiny and energetically connected region, it remains "quantum entangled" or coordinated everywhere as it expands.[43] In his moment of being, Bernard takes a break from instrumental reason and action. Bernard thinks:

> Am I not, as I walk, trembling with strange oscillations and vibrations of sympathy, which, unmoored as I am from a private being, bid me embrace these engrossed flocks; these starers and trippers; these errand-boys and furtive girls who, ignoring their doom, look in at shop-windows? But I am aware of our ephemeral passage.
>
> (W, 114)

This passage is not just Bernard's internal cognitive musings about the world. It is part of Woolf's philosophical description of reality. Bernard's moving body through the world is streaming and trembling with the reverberations of other people's and things' movements and sounds because reality, for Woolf, is relational. Bernard's whole body becomes an instrument vibrating with the sympathetic resonance of the world. His body becomes a relay that shivers, wavers, and oscillates when stimulated by the world.

Bernard's moment of being is not one of philosophical contemplation nor is it a universal insight into reality's absolute ontological structure. His vision is exceptionally singular, local, and passing. His moment of becoming is less a state of mind than a material transformation that is so highly sensitive and responsive to the world that he feels in his body and mind every tiny change and motion in other people and things. Our sensations and cognition are not representations of the world but are profoundly coordinated aspects of the world itself.[44]

"Sympathetic resonance" is a beautiful image of this effect. Sympathetic resonance happens when vibrations from one source start to vibrate another source at the same frequency. For example, if you go to a piano shop and play a note, it will resonate inside the other pianos nearby with the same frequency. For Woolf, the world is like a piano shop where light and sound diffract off one another all around affecting us. This is why Bernard feels such "strange oscillations and vibrations of sympathy." In his moment of being, Bernard realizes this, while other people are looking in shop windows for things to buy. In her autobiography, Woolf described her own moments of being in similar terms. She writes:

> The lemon-coloured leaves on the elm tree; the apples in the orchard; the murmur and rustle of the leaves makes me pause here, and think how many other than human forces are always at work on us. While I write this the light glows; an apple becomes a vivid green; I respond all through me; but how? Then a little owl [chatters] under my window. Again, I respond. Figuratively I could snapshot what I mean by some image; I am a porous vessel afloat on sensation; a sensitive plate exposed to invisible rays. ... I fumble with some vague idea about a third voice; I speak to Leonard; Leonard speaks to me; we both hear a third voice. Instead of labouring all the morning to analyse what I mean, to discover whether I mean anything real, whether I make up or tell the truth when I see myself taking the breath of these voices in my sails and tacking this way and that through daily life as I yield to them, I note only the existence of this influence; suspect it to be of great importance.
>
> (MB, 133)

Other-than-human forces are always moving through us. In Woolf's moments of being, her senses amplify, and she responds to the colors and tiny movements of the leaves "all through her" in sympathetic resonance. Her body and senses react immediately to every micro-movement in the quivering river of sensations that keep her afloat. Woolf describes her body as a porous vessel, just like Bernard's, exposed to all the fluctuations and the normally invisible range of sensations. In addition to the first-person voice that says "I," and the second-person voice that says "you," Woolf thinks about the third-person or non-person voice that says "it" or "they." This is the voice of the green apple, rustling leaves, the hooting owl that speaks through and as the material world. The third voice is the transpersonal affective voice of sound and light.

In Woolf's philosophy, reality is not "out there" in contrast to the "in here" of the human mind. Reality is a material process that moves through things like a wind running through the porous vessels of our bodies. In her moment of being, Woolf does not think of herself as a discrete individual. She is like Bernard, a vessel tacking along like a boat through water and wind. She has some agency but only as much as there is a sensuous current or wind to help her move along. The ebb and flow of daily micro-affects form hidden patterns and currents beneath the cotton wool of discrete people and things.

I Am Not, at This Moment, Myself

Bernard, Woolf writes, does not feel like a discrete raindrop that merely evaporates in the sun but a circulatory process of water moving into and out of soil and trees. This is another materialist image of mystical experience. For Woolf, there is no reason to fear what happens after death because we do not have immortal souls that can be punished. Nor do we merely disappear. As matter, we are recycled into other things. Bernard thinks:

> Hence we are not raindrops, soon dried by the wind; we make gardens blow and forests roar; we come up differently, for ever and ever. This then serves to explain my confidence, my central stability, otherwise so monstrously absurd as I breast the stream of this crowded thoroughfare making always a passage for myself between people's bodies, taking advantage of safe moments to cross. It is not vanity; for I am emptied of ambition; I do not remember my special gifts, or idiosyncrasy, or the marks I bear on my person, eyes, nose or mouth. I am not, at this moment, myself.
>
> (W, 114)

Matter, as Lucretius wrote, is neither created nor destroyed but continually transformed and transmuted. Bernard is not "himself" in the sense that the material and affective processes that constitute him are him also. They are not reducible to his person.

The Sunless Territory of Non-Identity

After walking for some time Bernard's moment of being begins to fade. His drug/dream begins to wear off and he feels the urge to become himself again. Woolf writes that Bernard is suddenly struck by a "persistent smell" that "steals in through some crack in the structure—one's identity" (W, 115). Woolf's philosophical and synesthetic idea that our identities are persistent smells is wonderfully provocative. Bernard thinks:

> I wish then after this somnolence to sparkle, many-faceted under the light of my friends' faces. I have been traversing the sunless territory of non-identity. A strange land. I have heard in my moment of appeasement, in my moment of obliterating satisfaction, the sigh, as it goes in, comes out, of the tide that draws beyond this circle of bright light, this drumming of insensate fury. I have had one moment of enormous peace. This is perhaps happiness. Now I am drawn back by pricking sensations; by curiosity, greed (I am hungry) and the irresistible desire to be myself.
>
> (W, 116)

For Woolf, our identities are not things or even discrete places in our brains but more like smells that pervade, color, or characterize the diverse affects that surround and run through us. The smell touches everything and gives it the scent of "I." We cannot grab hold of it. In a strong breeze, it may even blow away and come back later unexpectedly. Bernard compares his moment of being to a waking dream or sleep walking underwater in the dark. But eventually, Woolf says, a tide comes in and pulls him into the light of the sun where he sparkles like a diamond with many facets. Woolf describes Bernard's return to consciousness like Lucretius describes the birth of Venus on the shores of light.

Just like a tide or wave, Bernard desired to not be himself and was pulled out to sea. Then, like a tide, he was pulled back into and desired to become himself again. This is possible for Woolf philosophically because none of us are either this or that, as Woolf says in *Mrs. Dalloway* and *Orlando*. We are indeterminate because we are not things or substances. We are flows and processes that are never completed and continually changing. A process, by definition, is never the same as itself or fully present to itself because it is continually passing away and becoming something else.

"The sunless territory of non-identity" is a strange land because it is neither a place nor not a place—but a region of *passage*. For Woolf, the sensuous world is a plenum like an ocean breathing in and out of all our bodies like "porous vessels afloat on sensation" or "sensitive plates exposed to invisible rays."

Bernard experiences the return to identity as an increase in frequency. Waking-life is like a rapid drum beat contrasted with the slower rhythms of the oceanic tides. Woolf describes Bernard's body as just one iterated pattern in a world of iterated patterns. The brain and body can move to different rhythms corresponding to different states of mind and mood. Ultimately, Bernard is not happy about something in particular, but happy in *becoming*.

Mixing Ourselves with Unknown Quantities

Hunger brings Bernard slowly out of his moment of being. He has to use some degree of instrumental action to sit down at a restaurant and eat. As he interacts with the Italian waiter, he feels the waiter becoming part of him. The more he attempts to understand and know the waiter, the more he feels in the waiter's position. Woolf says that Bernard "mixes" with the waiter and becomes something new. "I, mixed with an unknown Italian waiter—what am I?," Bernard says.

> There is no stability in this world. Who is to say what meaning there is in anything? Who is to foretell the flight of a word? It is a balloon that sails over tree-tops. To speak of knowledge is futile. All is experiment and adventure. We are for ever mixing ourselves with unknown quantities. What is to come? I know not. But, as I put down my glass I remember; I am engaged to be married. I am to dine with my friends tonight. I am Bernard.
>
> (W, 118)

In this passage, Woolf offers a very fluid dynamic theory of meaning, language, and knowledge. Words do not represent the world but are, like the rest of us, little balloons floating on a windy sea of shifting affects. If we respond to our context and catch a breeze just right we can share some words even but cannot control how they will arrive. Our nervous systems do not duplicate the world but continue like a relay system the world inside us.

This is why, Bernard says, there is no stability in the world. There is nothing static in nature and no position outside it. This means that there is no objective meaning to the world. The meaning of things emerges immanently from within the world. Words are not labels given to objects but sensuous acts in their own terms that do something in the world. They sail over trees like balloons and pop in unique ways. Woolf writes that words converge or "breed" in specific "fertile" ways to form new patterns (W, 117). But if thoughts, words, and things are all singular acts that merely combine into new products, there can be no such thing as genuinely abstract representations or abstract knowledge. For Woolf, there are only performative acts of speaking and understanding that are "experiment and adventure." We hear sounds, think thoughts, and connect sensations. But this is not what philosophers call universal knowledge.

According to Woolf, when we try and "know" something, like Bernard tries to know his waiter, we mix ourselves with something unknown that transforms us. We are changed by the action of knowing and so cannot be neutral knowers of a relational reality. In other words, the object of knowledge contaminates the subject of knowing such that the two change each other. As Woolf writes in *Orlando*, "Everything is partly something else" (O, 323).

For Woolf, the question of knowledge is not "what is true?" but "what can it do?" What will a new mixture between subject and object be able to perform? Can the performance be repeated approximately? There are no absolutes in Woolf's thought but only mixtures and coordinated patterns of mutual and entrained action. What is to come? Knowledge does not predict a generic future but actively shapes and affects the future it predicts by measuring and anticipating it in precise ways.

Woolf's philosophy of mixture follows from the idea that nature is not fundamentally divided into humans and non-humans. Since humans are also nature, they can and must mix with it. If the humans were separate from nature, they could never know it. If they were identical to it, they would already know it. Knowledge, for Woolf, happens only in mixing of things that are related to but not strictly identical to one another, like cream swirling in coffee.

Conclusion

Bernard's moment of being concludes my reading of Woolf's "individual moments" in this book. My aim in this section of the book was not to describe every brief and individual moment of being in all of Woolf's novels but to look at a few diverse moments and use them to illuminate Woolf's larger philosophy. Each moment is unique in its set and setting but also shares some common theoretical features related to Woolf's description of moments of being in her autobiography.

What I am calling "individual" moments of being are longer than the brief moments in her earlier novels by several pages. They also happen only to *individual humans* and are all triggered by motion, use fluid dynamic vocabulary to describe the patterns of reality, and describe several dimensions of ontological *interrelation*.

In the next section of this book, I want to look at one of the most important innovations in Woolf's philosophy of moments of being. Let's turn now to look at a *non-human* moment of being in *To the Lighthouse* called "Time Passes."

Non-Human Moments

Moment 10: Part I, A Glimpse Only

After Woolf worked out a technique for describing longer individual moments of being, she made a giant leap. She tried to describe a moment of being from a non-individual and non-human perspective. In the twenty-page section of *To the Lighthouse* called "Time Passes," Woolf makes clear that moments of being are not merely psychological states. Individual moments of being are periods of amplified sensation of interrelated processes happening in nature. Nature, though, is in a continual moment of being where things are always entangled and interrelated.

Woolf thus describes a moment in which individual humans are not missing, but their lives, deaths, and feelings are tiny regions in larger processes in nature. "Time Passes" is the second-longest moment of being in Woolf's work. In it, she attempts to draw out and expand the moment beyond its merely subjective description through various characters and into an impersonal "third voice." "Time Passes" is a moment of being where space and time dilate, and human lives are carried along like parenthetical corks or ships on the sea of life and death.

The section "Time Passes" is perhaps one of the most memorable in all of Woolf's fiction. Accordingly, this extended moment has a different structure than Woolf's brief or individual moments. Here, motion, widened sensation, interrelation, and spacetime dilation are used directly in the text without being attributed to any particular person. After reading such an incredible description of the world, few readers ever forget it.

The Flood of the Future

"Time Passes" begins with several main characters from *To the Lighthouse*, Mr. Bankes, Andrew, Prue, and Lily Briscoe commenting somewhat cryptically on the *future* and the *darkness* of the night. "Well, we must wait for the future to show," said Mr. Bankes. "It's almost too dark to see," said Prue. "One can hardly tell which is the sea and which is the land," said Lily (TL, 125). The future is coming, and all the characters can do is wait for it to show itself. The moon has sunk, all the lights are out, and they can no longer see the horizon. The future comes darkly and invisibly. Among other things, in "Time Passes," Virginia Woolf offers us a unique materialist philosophy of time. For Woolf, the future is fundamentally dark and unknowable because its arrival does not occur *in linear time* but *through motion*. Or at least this is what I would like to illuminate below.

Woolf begins this moment by describing the connection between time, darkness, and water. Time, as Woolf wrote in her autobiography, is like a river. It does not precede linearly, but ecologically and kinetically. It unfolds unevenly through surface, depth, tides, currents, and eddies. The future, for Woolf, is dark because it is fundamentally unpredictable. The future comes unevenly, like waves on the sea, rain, or flood. Time flows rhythmically through events.

There is no unified self-identical thing called time or space. There are only topological and rhythmic transformations whose origins lie much deeper in the fluctuations of matter.[1] Woolf writes:

> So with the lamps all put out, the moon sunk, and a thin rain drumming on the roof a downpouring of immense darkness began. Nothing, it seemed, could survive the flood, the profusion of darkness which, creeping in at keyholes and crevices, stole round window blinds, came into bedrooms, swallowed up here a jug and basin, there a bowl of red and yellow dahlias, there the sharp edges and firm bulk of a chest of drawers.
> (TL, 126)

The future is dark because it is unknowable and as unknowable it is like the rain of unpredictably swerving matter described by Lucretius.[2] The indeterminacy of the future swallows up the entire house and the sharp edges of the drawers are removed. Woolf writes:

> Not only was furniture confounded; there was scarcely anything left of body or mind by which one could say, "This is he" or "This is she." Sometimes a hand was raised as if to clutch something or ward off something, or somebody groaned, or somebody laughed aloud as if sharing a joke with nothingness.
> (TL, 126)

The impersonal rain of matter creates a *flow* of time. For Woolf, time passes because matter flows—*not the other way round*. In the flow and rain of matter, everything becomes part of a much larger flood. Again, Woolf here articulates indeterminacy as "neither he nor she." "It was all one stream," Woolf says (TL, 113–14). In the dark and rain, everything becomes a region of a much larger movement of nature. The Ramsey family and their guests are swallowed up by the movement of history. Body and mind; female and male, become metastable moments or emergent properties. They are processes, streams, or regions of the rain and flood of matter—not ontological categories that precede the rain. They are flooded.

Instead of people and objects, the dilated flood of matter produces whirls or affects such as "raising or clutching hands." The rain utters non-symbolic sounds like "groans" or "laughs" in the shower's cataract. Gesture and speech thus emerge in and through broader indeterminate kinetic processes. They emerge as motions in the flood and only become coordinated together over time like mind and body, male and female. It is their performance and iteration in the rain of matter that make them what they are.

Time, for Woolf, is a rain or stream of becoming that swallows up and saturates the house. Time is not abstract or given in advance but is as tangible as the rain that fills up bowls and rounds the drawers' sharp edges. In Woolf's philosophy, the passage of time is material and kinetic. Time is the movement and dissipation of matter.

Certain Airs

For Woolf, time passes fluid dynamically, by rain, flood, and air. She writes that "Certain airs, detached from the body of the wind ... crept round corners and ventured indoors. Almost one might imagine them, as they entered the drawing-room questioning and wondering, toying with the flap of hanging wall-paper, asking, would it hang much longer, when would it fall?" (TL, 126). These airs are small non-human agencies of entropy eroding and decomposing things.

Things look all too solid to us through the cotton wool of daily life, but Woolf zooms in on the sub-perceptual airs that constitute the teeth of time. Each little breeze moves a flower, or some wallpaper, or a book just a tiny bit, back and forth, over and over. Over time movement destroys all things. Matter is continually changing and breaking down, and for the most part, we hardly notice, yet this is the materiality of time. "Nothing stirred in the drawing-room or in the dining-room or on the staircase" (TL, 126). Woolf describes a world of motion beneath the level of macroscopic objects. The movement of the airs is guided, just like Lucretius' swerving flows of matter, by

> some random light directing them with its pale footfall upon stair and mat, from some uncovered star, or wandering ship, or the Lighthouse even, the little airs mounted the staircase and nosed round bedroom doors.
> (TL, 126)

Woolf says that the fluctuation of light from stars, ships, or the lighthouse guides the airs upstairs. This is a strange image. Stars, ships, and lighthouses are supposed to guide sailors home from turbulent dark seas at night, but here Woolf describes their pale light as "random." This tells us something interesting about

Woolf's philosophy of time. Time, for Woolf, is not a linear passage, but a material one produced through indeterminate swerving and decay. Time passes because matter swerves and disorders itself. The ship "wanders" like Lucretius' flows of matter. A star *happens* to be uncovered by the wind blowing through the trees. In short, contingency and indeterminacy are at the heart of Woolf's theory of time.

Similarly, Woolf says that the lights "wander" and "slide," while the airs "fumble" and "bend." When they reach the bedrooms, they brush the sleepers' eyes and fingers like feathers and "fold their garments" (TL, 126–7). The airs head back downstairs and "fumble" the rose petals. Then, Woolf says, they "gathered together, all sighed together; all together gave off an aimless gust of lamentation to which some door in the kitchen replied; swung wide; admitted nothing; and slammed to" (TL, 127).

The collective power of the airs in this description is "aimless." Nature has no goal, only contingencies of swerving movements. Time does not head homogeneously to a pre-given end precisely because the indeterminacy of matter guides its passage. Matter gathers in some places more than others and thus produces different regions of spacetime. Some are faster and some are slower.

In some places in the cosmos and on Earth, time passes more or less quickly than others. Time is thus the product of an uneven, wandering, aimless, and fumbling experimentation with patterns of motion and dissipation rates. If time passes depending on how contracted or expanded the movements of matter are, then the more expanded matter is, the more quickly it passes—just as Woolf understood general relativity. Time inside the Ramsey's house passes more rapidly in some places because of the contingencies of certain airs and the differential topology of gravity and entropy.

Time, for Woolf, is not a series of discrete now-points or a homogeneous background field through which things move. Things do not move in or through time. Time is an emergent feature of a world in unpredictable motion. Time "passes" because the world is continually spreading out.[3]

The airs give off an "aimless gust of lamentation" because they *are* the pedetic process of decay, dissipation, and death itself. Their breath is not *like* a song of mourning or weeping but *is* the physical process of aimless dissipation and lamentation itself.

I. Autumn

On the Immanent Causality of a Season

After this moment of turbulent motion and widened microscopic perception, Woolf writes that the nights began to quicken one following another as time and space dilate increasingly.

> But what after all is one night? A short space, especially when the darkness dims so soon, and so soon a bird sings, a cock crows, or a faint green quickens, like a turning leaf, in the hollow of the wave.
>
> (TL, 127)

Woolf writes that one night is only a "short space" because time is spatial, and space is temporal, and both are material. Time passes because matter changes. Light changes, leaves turn in waves, birds sing. These *movements* are what make up one night. The Earth cycles around the sun and turns like a leaf in the hollow of the solar wave. The color green speeds up because color is related to the movement and frequency of light. The speed of green is the speed of how quickly the light returns after night.

Nights follow regularly and iteratively, becoming longer and darker in winter. Colors become slower and shorter as less light touches them. Some nights reveal planets, others do not. Woolf writes:

> The winter holds a pack of them in store and deals them equally, evenly, with indefatigable fingers. They lengthen; they darken. Some of them hold aloft clear planets, plates of brightness.
>
> (TL, 127)

The nights are iterative because they follow one another but are different each time. The Earth is increasingly revealed as one cosmic body among others by the long and dark winter sky. In other words, the seasons reveal not only temporal changes between darker days and colors but also spatial changes in the visibility of the stars.

> The autumn trees, ravaged as they are, take on the flash of tattered flags kindling in the gloom of cool cathedral caves where gold letters on marble pages describe death in battle and how bones bleach and burn far away in Indian sands. The autumn trees gleam in the yellow moonlight, in the light of harvest moons, the light which mellows the energy of labour, and smooths the stubble, and brings the wave lapping blue to the shore.
>
> (TL, 127)

As the leaves begin to change in autumn with the shift of planetary rotation, their colors "red" and "yellow" are shared with the death of human bodies. The death of the leaves and human death are not identical but are iterations of the same cosmic process of decay and dissipation. The leaves turn as *red* as the tattered Union Jack flags hung in British cathedrals. The leaves turn as *gold* as the letters on the marble tombstone of the Tomb of The Unknown Warrior in Westminster Abbey cathedral. The tree's leaves show the fiery color as bright as the cremated bodies of Indian soldiers killed by the British. The tree's limbs are left bare as the bones in the pyre. In these lines, Woolf interrelates scales of time in the seasons, scales of space in British and Indian geographies, and human and natural death.

The rustling and dying leaves of the autumn trees also share the same pattern of motion, oscillation back and forth, as tattered British flags and the flickering funeral flames of Indian soldiers. The colors and motions share a pattern that coordinates humans and nature together in a singular season.

Hence the absurdity, for Woolf, of war, imperialism, colonialism, and racism. In one of the moments of being from her autobiography, Woolf recalls fighting with her brother Thoby. "Just as I raised my fist to hit him, I felt: why hurt another person? I dropped my hand instantly, and stood there, and let him beat me. I remember the feeling. It was a feeling of hopeless sadness" (MB, 71). Death comes for every leaf and life eventually, but why kill others who are part of the same natural processes of the world? Geographical and colonial divisions are arbitrary. For Woolf, human warfare based on the idea of the "natural" superiority of peoples and nations is an absurd misunderstanding of nature. In Woolf's naturalistic philosophy, there is no God and no ideal nation that can justify world war.

As autumn proceeds, the moon rises increasingly toward the center of the sky, bathing all the trees in yellow light. As the moon waxes and becomes full, it turns, like the leaves, a more orange-colored "harvest" moon, the full moon closest to the autumnal equinox. This new bright orange light provides the last burst of night light by which farmers and laborers harvest their final crops. This orange light bathes the stubbled post-harvest land covered in the leftover stems and stalks of the crops. Then the stubbly fields are slowly smoothed out by rain, decay, and the heat of light.

The harvest moon of the autumnal equinox also transforms the earth's oceans' tidal patterns and brings the largest and highest tides of the year. At the equinox, the sun is directly over the equator. If the moon is also at the equator simultaneously, the sun and moon will create the highest of high tides. If the moon is also at perigee (closest to the earth in its orbit), it will produce even higher tides.

Woolf's kinesthetic description of seasonal change here is impressive. She is explicit that the leaves actually "take on" the color of the flags, the golden letters of the British tomb "describe" the cremation of the Indian soldiers, the light of the moon "mellows" the energy of labor, "smooths" the crop stubble, and brings in the tide.

In this small, unassuming passage, we are dealing with a philosophically relational description of reality. If we think of her naturalistic description as a metaphor for human events and war, it keeps nature and culture divided. However, if we want to take Woolf seriously as a "realist," then we must ask what kind of reality she is describing where nature and culture are two aspects of the same process.

For example: In what sense does the light of the moon smooth out the harvested cropland? Moonlight simultaneously shines as work slows down, and it touches the high tides, and the land smooths out in this same light, but is the light the *cause* of the smoothing? Woolf's descriptions challenge us not to try and isolate a single cause of things but to see how they all change simultaneously. In other words, cause, for Woolf, is not mechanical or fully separable from effect. In the passage above Woolf describes a collective transformation of a relational whole.

Philosophically, a realist way to read this passage would be as a kinesthetic description of simultaneously changing patterns of motion. We are not dealing with discrete objects bouncing off one another like billiard balls but rather with a global and regional entanglement of all of nature. Nature changes continually as an open whole without an external or transcendent source of causal action. Instead of causality, analogy, or metaphor, Woolf describes material habits or patterns in nature's performance. Everything moves together in common patterns and habits without any metaphysical notion of causality.

II. Winter

A Glimpse of the Truth

Next, Woolf describes the human attempt to understand this collective transformation. The human feeling of remorse for killing one another and our ambivalence about the apparent necessity to survive by toiling through agriculture give pause to consider the meaning of civilization. In these moments, some people glimpse beneath the cotton wool of daily life and see the bigger picture of entropy, life, and death. Our death and labor are of the Earth and made of the same stuff of the dying and burning leaves. Woolf writes:

> It seemed now as if, touched by human penitence and all its toil, divine goodness had parted the curtain and displayed behind it, single, distinct, the hare erect; the wave falling; the boat rocking, which, did we deserve them, should be ours always. But alas, divine goodness, twitching the cord, draws the curtain; it does not please him; he covers his treasures in a drench of hail, and so breaks them, so confuses them that it seems impossible that their calm should ever return or that we should ever compose from their fragments a perfect whole or read in the littered pieces the clear words of truth. For our penitence deserves a glimpse only; our toil respite only.
>
> (TL, 128)

The "divine goodness" of nature that provides our food and our life occasionally pulls back the cotton wool curtain of discrete "things" and "objects" and reveals behind their "fragments" the "single" and "distinct" "whole" of nature: the "truth." Philosophically, it is important to remember that Woolf does not believe in God or an objective true state of things. So in this passage, Woolf may be playfully adopting the mythological drama of god and curtain in order to draw an analogy with her own description of cotton wool and the hidden patterns beneath.

The hare standing erect in the last autumn moonlight before winter, the falling of the enormous equinox waves, and the rocking boats on them would all be ours together as dimensions of a whole seasonal change if we deserved it. But the "divine goodness" of the harvest season (perhaps the "green man")[4] is not pleased by the *direct* appearance of this truth and he draws the curtain closed again. For Woolf, the curtain's closing visually shatters the direct perception of entanglement in nature into a hail of broken and confused discrete objects on the cotton wool of the curtain.

In Woolf's philosophy of moments of being, we will only be able to see the calm whole of nature in all its becoming and interconnection in glimpses if we are humble toward the material conditions that support and traverse us. We have to see ourselves as aspects of nature and the seasons and not as onlookers of the world. To survive and function in the world of things, we have to deploy a certain degree of instrumental activity. But in rare moments of being, we can have an aesthetic vision as a respite from our toil.

Nature, in Woolf's description above, gives us an immanent glimpse or vision of becoming. The moment is not transcendent but intensifies all the interconnections and sub-perceptual affects at work in the world. The "true" world is the relational changing world. In Woolf's philosophy, nothing can be gleaned from the vision that can *replace* or *represent* the vision. It may be the source of artistic or philosophical inspiration, but the vision itself is just the world as a process-relational world. Again, Woolf's descriptions are not supposed to represent a moment of becoming but to induce one in readers through words.

Next, Woolf says, the hail and confusion increase as winter draws near.

The nights now are full of wind and destruction; the trees plunge and bend and their leaves fly helter skelter until the lawn is plastered with them and they lie packed in gutters and choke rain-pipes and scatter damp paths. Also the sea tosses itself and breaks itself, and should any sleeper fancying that he might find on the beach an answer to his doubts, a sharer of his solitude, throw off his bedclothes and go down by himself to walk on the sand, no image with semblance of serving and divine promptitude comes readily to hand bringing the night to order and making the world reflect the compass of the soul. The hand dwindles in his hand; the voice bellows in his ear. Almost it would appear that it is useless in such confusion to ask the night those questions as to what, and why, and wherefore, which tempt the sleeper from his bed to seek an answer.

(TL, 128)

Woolf says that nature tempts the sleeper to doubt the world of fragmented and seemingly disordered things. This is a very philosophical moment in the text. The sleeper wants to go to the beach and ask nature and the night "what it is" (ontology), "why it is" (cosmology), and "wherefore is it heading" (epistemology). In short, we sleepers are tempted to philosophy by the apparent chaos and disorder of the world. But, for Woolf, the divine night of the future does not give answers to these questions. The walker only feels and hears the night's sea. Philosophy, understood in these terms, for Woolf, is therefore akin to the useless confusion of trying to ask what, why, and wherefore of nature. It is not the kind of philosophy Woolf is proposing with her concept of moments of being.

Nature, in Woolf's thought, is a vast entangled network of processes and thus not a "what." Nature is immanently causal and therefore has no "why." Nature's movements are indeterminate, relational processes and thus have no "wherefore." The whole effort of academic philosophy, for Woolf, is like screaming in the wind on a beach at night. Significantly, in parenthesis at the end of this section, Woolf writes that Mr. Ramsey (the philosopher) reaches out for Mrs. Ramsey one evening only to find she is not there, having died the night before.

Weaving the Veil of Becoming

Now, Woolf says, the stray airs return without resistance since the house is empty of people. The airs brush the boards, nibble the table legs, and tarnish the kitchen supplies. Hanging objects flap. In short, the whole process of entropy and decay that is Woolf's "time" advances.

More importantly, this passage is where the moment of being continues on *without humans*. For Woolf, moments of being are the material processes or patterns behind the cotton wool, *whether humans glimpse them or not*. Therefore, these moments are not reducible to, defined by, or reliant on human experience or perception. Woolf is not an empiricist like her philosopher father. According to Woolf, the world continues to move, pattern, weave, and fold with and without humans perceive it. The moment of being is not an extraordinary world that only humans have access to but rather the world or process that underlies nature.

Woolf, here, writes about nature's moment of being in "Time Passes." The section also discourages attempts to reduce her philosophy to human experience.[5] Woolf is a realist. Without humans, Woolf says, the empty house begins to *form and weave itself* as it always had. Mrs. Ramsey only caught momentary glimpses of these hidden patterns. Human glimpses of becoming are only the tip of an iceberg thrilling beneath their threshold of perception. Woolf's description of the becoming of the beach house makes that explicit.

> Now, day after day, light turned, like a flower reflected in water, its sharp image on the wall opposite. Only the shadows of the trees, flourishing in the wind, made obeisance on the wall, and for a moment darkened the pool in which light reflected itself; or birds, flying, made a soft spot flutter slowly across the bedroom floor.
>
> (TL, 129)

What is a day? It is not an abstract unit of time but the turning of light, as Woolf writes. Each light is singular and irregular. No day is precisely the same length or of the same light because the Earth is slowly moving away from the sun, and the moon slowly away from the Earth. There are no perfect circles or rotations—only irregular ellipses and spirals. These movements are, in turn, entangled with the broader movements of the solar system, our galaxy, and the changing distribution of dark matter in the cosmos.

The philosophical point for Woolf is this. Light shifts across the Earth and shifts across the water that is reflecting a flower. Each ripple in the water shifts the angle of light and shifts the image of the flower. The flower is not a static form or image separate from its diffracting reflections and shadows. It is a moving image continually modulated by the singular shifts of light on it.

The image of the flower, like nature, is a process. It is never identical to itself. In one place, it appears relatively sharp, distinct, and discrete and, in other places, shadowy, rippling, molted with flickering light. The classical interpretation is that the watery reflection is the false appearance of the true, static one, but Woolf has a different analysis here. For her, the inside of the house becomes a dynamic fluid pool of shifting light and shadow. The house always did this, but the human occupants, save Mrs. Ramsey, never saw it.

For Woolf, the house without humans is a kind of "material unconscious." It is all the play of moving patterns of light and sound, texture and touch, that typically fall into the "background" of human instrumental affairs. We walk around and see the sharp images of "things" on the surface, but beneath and around them float a kind of cloth, veil, or shroud of flickering waves of light, sound, and micro-movements that weave everything together. These are the kinds of "hidden" patterns Woolf is talking about beneath the cotton wool.

Without humans around, only the "shadows of the trees, flourishing in the wind," "see" the flower's image on the wall. This is a lovely and philosophically challenging description. How can shadows "see" light flickering on the wall? It certainly broadens our definition of the word "see" to include the micro-physical level at which molecules and atoms touch and respond to one another. We often think of shadows as two dimensional but shadows are actually three dimensional regions. Huge numbers of photons touch and transform the light and heat of things. The trees' shadows also darken the pool where the flower was reflected—changing it as well by cooling it down. Instead of neutral human observers, Woolf describes here a material unconscious made of shimmering pools of light and shadow where each relationship between things changes the open-whole. Light and heat radiate and play with one another in the flickering shadows on the wall.

Woolf also says that trees and birds outside the house move and play inside the house through their shadows. In this way, Woolf describes the house as a möbius strip, a topological shape with one side that appears to have two sides. The inside and outside of the house are only two aspects or regions of the same process. There is no absolute outside or inside of anything. Each inside is the continuation or enfolded region of the outside and vice versa. The flickering patterns of shadows are part of the hidden light patterns behind the cotton wool that make objects visible to us. One of the key philosophical upshots for Woolf in these passages is that form emerges from material processes. She writes:

> So loveliness reigned and stillness, and together made the shape of loveliness itself, a form from which life had parted; solitary like a pool at evening, far distant, seen from a train window, vanishing so quickly that the pool, pale in the evening, is scarcely robbed of its solitude, though once seen. Loveliness and stillness clasped hands in the bedroom, and among the shrouded jugs and sheeted chairs even the prying of the wind, and—the soft nose of the clammy sea airs, rubbing, snuffling, iterating, and reiterating their questions—"Will you fade? Will you perish?"—scarcely disturbed the peace, the indifference, the air of pure integrity, as if the question they asked scarcely needed that they should answer: we remain.
>
> (TL, 129)

In this passage, Woolf describes the interconnected play of light and dark as still but *not static*. Stillness, for Woolf, is active, like a pond, and together with loveliness, shapes a new form of itself without life. Life and vitality are insufficient terms for the kinetic formations of things. Woolf's philosophy is not one of life alone but of the fluid dynamics of the non-living which make life. In the pool, the water is not alive, and yet it is the material conditions of all life. Historically, life emerged from the shape of water pooled up, folded up, woven, and iterated into whirls and patterns. In these whirls, the biomolecules of life first gathered.[6] If life has the form it does, it is precisely related to the material and chemical structure and pattern of water.[7]

In short, without anyone to see it, the forest pool forms itself in Woolf's description. Even when someone glimpses the pool for a moment, it remains solitary and self-organized. Like the non-living movements of the pool, loveliness and stillness *clasp* hands among the woven *shrouds* and *sheets*. Stillness clasps, weaves, and forms itself into patterns.

> Nothing it seemed could break that image, corrupt that innocence, or disturb the swaying mantle of silence which, week after week, in the empty room, wove into the falling cries of birds, ships hooting, the drone and hum of the fields, a dog's bark, a man's shout, and folded them round the house in silence. Once only a board sprang on the landing; once in the middle of the night with a roar, with a rupture, as after centuries of quiescence, a rock rends itself from the mountain and hurtles crashing into the valley, one fold of the shawl loosened and swung to and fro. Then again peace descended; and the shadow wavered; light bent to its own image in adoration on the bedroom wall; and Mrs. McNab, tearing the veil of silence with hands that had stood in the wash-tub, grinding it with boots that had crunched the shingle, came as directed to open all windows, and dust the bedrooms.
>
> (TL, 129–30)

Woolf's use of sonic contrast here is fascinating. Sounds are not woven into the silence, as if silence were a background default for sound, but instead, silence itself is active and positively *woven with sound*. The "silence" thus weaves itself into sound as the shroud, sheets, and cloak are woven and sway in the wind. Sound is an ordered pattern of motion. It is rhythmic waves of pressurized air. Silence is saturated with micro-sonic sounds and hidden patterns that Woolf is pointing to. The house shapes a sonic diffraction zone. Together the silence and stillness form a woven "veil" of relations composed of wavering shadows and bent light.[8] These too are part of the hidden patterns beneath the cotton wool.

In other words, the empty house is not an analogy for the human unconscious. Rather, the human unconscious is structured and conditioned by the material unconscious of the house.[9] Light comes through the windows and adores itself on the wall by reflecting itself. For Woolf, humans are not the only ones capable of self-reflection. There is already a material structure of reflection in nature.[10]

The Puddle and the Stone

Next, Woolf describes a human who seeks answers about the nature of nature and receives the response suddenly by stirring a puddle and looking at a stone. She writes:

> The mystic, the visionary, walking the beach on a fine night, stirring a puddle, looking at a stone, asking themselves "What am I," "What is this?" had suddenly an answer vouchsafed them: (they could not say what it was) so that they were warm in the frost and had comfort in the desert.
>
> (TL, 131)

Woolf was not a religious mystic. However, her moments of being were indeed visions of reality similar to what many call mystical religious experiences. The primary difference is that, for Woolf, moments of being are not visions of anything that transcend nature. Although religious mysticism and Woolf's materialist or kinetic mysticism are both characteristically "ineffable," Woolf's moments are not visions of unity but of sensuous and fluidly woven patterns of singularities.

What is the philosophical source of the ineffability of moments of being for Woolf? If knower and knowledge are not ontologically different from what is known, then knowledge cannot be objective. This was a key finding of quantum physics during Woolf's lifetime. This is also the case for the aesthetic visionary in the passage above. Truth, for Woolf, is immanent with being. By contrast, for the religious mystic, truth is ineffable because it is *beyond* being. Therefore, Woolf's moments of being and religious mystical experiences both eschew representation and propositional truth.

In Woolf's philosophy, the answer to the questions, "what is?" (ontology) and "what am I?" (epistemology) cannot receive a response that can be represented in language because knowledge itself is not representational. There is no being independent of the action or performance of knowing. We can, therefore, call it "onto-epistemological." There is nothing to know *about* the world. There is only the becoming of the world.[11]

For Woolf, the knowledge that the visionary attains is immanent, so she knows it only through performance and enactment. This knowledge does not yield to the propositional form "nature is x"—"I am x." The act of forming a proposition itself *is* already a real act in nature. This immanent way of knowing brings "comfort" to the visionary because they know there is no separation between themselves and the frost or heat.

In this sense, the inside of the house is a pool stilled and stirred by light and sound like the beach puddle. The fluidity of the pool is, in turn, coupled with the solidity of stone. Here again, Woolf gives us the doublet: motion and stillness, fluid and solid, sharp and reflected image. The puddle and the stone are images of becoming and being brought together in the performative act of knowing.

Next, Woolf says, the season changes from Winter to Spring and Summer. These are what we turn to in the second part of this long non-human moment of being.

Moment 10: Part II, Stars Flashing in Their Hearts

III. Spring and Summer

The Materiality of Flesh

Spring arrives, Woolf says, bringing life and death.

> The spring without a leaf to toss, bare and bright like a virgin fierce in her chastity, scornful in her purity, was laid out on fields wide-eyed and watchful and entirely careless of what was done or thought by the beholders. [Prue Ramsay, leaning on her father's arm, was given in marriage. What, people said, could have been more fit- ting? And, they added, how beautiful she looked!]
>
> (TL, 131)

The arrival of the season of fertility coincides with the human drama of Prue's marriage and pregnancy iterating the seasonal alteration of the Earth itself. As the spring days lengthen, the walkers return to the beach in the hope of answers from nature. Woolf writes:

> As summer neared, as the evenings lengthened, there came to the wakeful, the hopeful, walking the beach, stirring the pool, imaginations of the strangest kind—of flesh turned to atoms which drove before the wind, of stars flashing in their hearts, of cliff, sea, cloud, and sky brought purposely together to assemble outwardly the scattered parts of the vision within.
>
> (TL, 131–2)

This is a beautiful and philosophically important passage. The walkers stir the puddle in spring as they had stirred it in fall and winter. However, this time, the whirling and rippling of the pool induce strange imaginations of processes that the walkers do not see directly yet are still physically real. The bodies of walkers are *flows of matter* moved by vast processes across the cosmos.[12] Their bodies are *the same stuff as the world*. Their bodies and minds are pools of accumulated matter rippling and quivering. The hearts of the walkers contain the same atoms that once composed stars. Even the beach itself and its pools are made of and by that same cosmic process.

Earth, sea, clouds, and sky are not the mere background of the walkers' internal contemplations. The material performance of walking, thinking, and feeling is itself a cosmic performance. The walkers are of the earth and its elements simultaneously as they ask questions "about" the world they are. In short, they feel their body as a dimension or iterative fractal aspect of the deeply patterned Cosmos and Earth.

The earth's external assembly into sea, sky, clouds, and cliffs appears to show the walker what the world is, what they are, and what their vision is. All three— subject, object, and visions—for Woolf, are aspects of the same patterned process. If the order of things looks purposeful, it is because the earth existed long before the emergence of human animals and their visions. Once humans emerge, the world appears to mirror the structure of their minds. This is the case, however, because their minds emerged from *the world*. The world looks like it was put together as an external image of our minds because our minds are internalizations of the world. The body and the world are two sides of the same twisted Möbius strip. If the world appears to be flesh to the walkers, it is already because the flesh is the flowing materiality of the world's moving matter.[13]

Pools and Crystals

Woolf continues to describe the walkers on the beach. To do so she iterates the pattern of the "pool" to connect the house, the walkers, and the beach. Conceptually, this lets her show the continuity between nature and culture across scales. Specifically, house, walkers, and beach are iterations of a similar structure that accumulates flows of matter and distributes them into a deep and reflective surface. By absorbing some light and reflecting other light, the house, walkers, and the pool on the beach make their inside continuous with their outside. For example, Woolf says the trees and birds outside the house share their shadows with the inside of the house. The stars and wind outside the walkers share their matter inside the walker's bodies and minds. The pool of water on the beach shares its inner surface reflection with the external sky. The philosophical conclusion here is that Woolf is painting a picture of reality as a möbius strip without an absolute division between interiority and exteriority. She writes:

> In those mirrors, the minds of men, in those pools of uneasy water, in which clouds for ever turn and shadows form, dreams persisted, and it was impossible to resist the strange intimation which every gull, flower, tree, man and woman, and the white earth itself seemed to declare (but if questioned at once to withdraw) that good triumphs, happiness prevails, order rules; or to resist the extraordinary stimulus to range hither and thither in search of some absolute good, some crystal of intensity, remote from the known pleasures and familiar virtues, something alien to the processes of domestic life, single, hard, bright, like a diamond in the sand, which would render the possessor secure.
>
> (TL, 132)

Human minds, for Woolf, are pools of matter that reflect and diffract the world. Clouds of neurons fire together in our brains and produce emergent patterns that we call experience. Our thoughts are shadowing forms. Just as every gull, flower, tree, and person are ordered material patterns so are our thoughts and actions. For Woolf, there is no answer to the question, "what is?" As quickly as we ask the question, something new emerges.

The material patterns of gulls and our thoughts declare that good, happiness, and love prevail, not despite death but *through death*. Through the entropic flow of matter, metastable states emerge, iterate, and reproduce. The dissipation of one order assembles a new order. This is not a romantic "triumph of life,"[14] but the persistence of patterns that we call "good" or "love."

In Woolf's philosophy, the immense joy one feels in a moment of being has its source in the vast implicate order of iterative patterns across scales that cannot be *said* or *thought* in terms of familiar single objects. This is the experience that motivates the walkers to keep walking. They are searching for something concrete to express the continuous transformation of nature. No philosophical concept will do.

Woolf compares the object of their quest instead to an intense crystalline diamond. Why? The diamond is not an analogy or representation of nature. It is organic carbon, like humans, super-concentrated over millions of years into a single, hard, but bright and clear object. The diamond is Woolf's image of order in nature because it is both made of organic carbon, and is not alive. The dendritic and fractal[15] pattern of crystal growth is common to both living and non-living bodies, including minerals, plants, fungi, and animals. Lightning, river deltas, and the dark matter of the cosmos all move dendritically and fractally. If we were to look for a single image to remind us of the vastness of geological time and the fractal patterns common in all of nature but concealed in a single solid object—the crystal diamond is a good one.

Why does Woolf think finding this single, hard, and clear image of the universe "render(s) the possessor secure"? The moment of becoming shows the walker that she *is nature*. Subject and object are not ontologically divided. Death is not destruction but a transformation of energy. If stars flicker in our hearts, then when we die, those atoms and photons from our flickering bodies live on forever and remake the world in a new form. More often than not, religion and philosophy do not overcome the fear of death but increase it by assuming a division between the mind and the world. If the mind is separate from nature, then when it's gone it is a total annihilation.

But, if flows of matter make up our flesh and our hearts are made of stars, then there is no annihilation, only recomposition. If there is no immortal soul, we do not have to worry about being judged by the gods, as Lucretius noted. Woolf's moments of being are, therefore, grounded in a "cosmic naturalism" in which one sees the interrelation of patterns across scales without the fear of punishment after death or total physical annihilation.[16] Woolf continues:

> Moreover, softened and acquiescent, the spring with her bees humming and gnats dancing threw her cloak about her, veiled her eyes, averted her head, and among passing shadows and flights of small rain seemed to have taken upon her a knowledge of the sorrows of mankind. [Prue Ramsay died that summer in some illness connected with childbirth, which was indeed a tragedy, people said, everything, they said, had promised so well.]
>
> (TL, 132)

Here Woolf beautifully weaves the natural drama of the seasons with the human drama of birth, life, and death. From her naturalist philosophical perspective, why should human life follow an entirely different rhythm than the Earth's seasonal cycles? Her account bears a striking resemblance to the Greek naturalist understanding of things. The Greeks described the seasons as a dance between *Horae*, meaning "hours," "moments," "seasons," or "natural portions of time." Woolf's description in "Time Passes" suggests a connection between her "moments of being" and the *hora* of nature.

For the Greeks, as the *Horae* danced they brought fertility to the Earth and moved the stars and constellations. They ordered the world into rhythms without dividing it. Time, in Greek mythology, was performative. It was not abstract or merely chronological. Time or "*chronos*" was first and foremost a *measure* of *hora* a dance, a rhythm, a season, a moment. But the *passage* of time was a real material passage performed by the cosmos, not the change of abstract Cartesian units or Newtonian absolute linear time.

Woolf's description of the spring as female and having a cloak is highly suggestive that she is thinking of the Greek hora, Thallo depicted most famously as covering Venus with a flowery cloak in Botticelli's painting *The Birth of Venus*. In Woolf's description, the *hora* and nature are not moral entities. Spring merely looks away when Prue dies in childbirth. Her view here is consistent with her philosophical naturalism more broadly.

The Mirror Is Broken

Next, Woolf describes the inside of the beach house in more detail. Continuing the image of the pool, she says that the house reverberates light and sound on its surfaces. Gusts of wind, the hum of flies, the tapping of weeds on the windows, and the sunlight on the walls transform the house into a tropical ocean, she says. The sun beams "striped and barred the rooms and filled them with a yellow haze that Mrs. McNab, when she broke in and lurched about, dusting, sweeping, looked like a tropical fish oaring its way through sun-lanced waters" (TL, 133).

Later in the summer, however, the house begins to reverberate with the rhythmic thud of bombs during the First World War. Glasses and tumblers vibrate, teacups crack, and the mirror breaks.

> At that season those who had gone down to pace the beach and ask of the sea and sky what message they reported or what vision they affirmed had to consider among the usual tokens of divine—the sunset on the sea, the pallor of dawn, the moon rising, fishing-boats against the moon, and children making mud pies or pelting each other with handfuls of grass, something out of harmony with this jocundity and this serenity.
>
> (TL, 133)

For Woolf, the beach walkers know nature performatively through watching the sea, sky, and singular patterns of the seasons. Nature is not a concept or a word in a language but a precise kinesthetic coordination of sunset, sea, the color of the dawn, and angle of the moon. The introduction of ashen-gray warships and dark-colored submarines therefore alters the rhythms of things significantly.

> This intrusion into a scene calculated to stir the most sublime reflections and lead to the most comfortable conclusions stayed their pacing. It was difficult blandly to overlook them; to abolish their significance in the landscape; to continue, as one walked by the sea, to marvel how beauty outside mirrored beauty within.
>
> (TL, 134)

In other words, the presence of warfare on Earth alters the Möbius strip of nature. The militarization of the landscape is not only ecological but psychological and physiological, for Woolf. War is a trauma to the earth and a trauma to the onto-epistemology of the sensitive visionaries. War is an attempt to dominate nature and humans. Its performative act of domination and division is then mirrored in the minds of the knowers. For Woolf, this poses the question of the relationship between humans and nature.

> Did Nature supplement what man advanced? Did she complete what he began? With equal complacence she saw his misery, his meanness, and his torture. That dream, of sharing, completing, of finding in solitude on the beach an answer, was then but a reflection in a mirror, and the mirror itself was but the surface glassiness which forms in quiescence when the nobler powers sleep beneath? Impatient, despairing yet loth to go (for beauty offers her lures, has her consolations), to pace the beach was impossible; contemplation was unendurable; the mirror was broken.
>
> (TL, 134)

A key feature of Woolf's philosophy is that physical and psychic landscapes are intimately entangled. One does not know in social, historical, or seasonal isolation. Knowing is always woven from a *horos* or moment. In the same way light bounces off a still pool of water, humans and nature diffract with one another in the act of knowledge.

In this way, the sudden and profound vibrations of the falling bombs shake the mirrored pool so intensely that the surface becomes broken up and indiscernible. War reveals, among other things, that the condition for moments of being and knowing tends to require a certain degree of material peace and safety. Beneath the surface of the pool, there are always turbulent currents that may suddenly rise up and disturb the reflective surface significantly.

For Woolf, nature is fluid dynamic. When mind and world are calm, they can offer sublime beauty but when they are disturbed by misery, meanness, and torture, moments of being feel impossible. When the "nobler powers sleep" below the surface, Woolf says, the pool becomes calm, and the hidden patterns of reality form on its surface. In other words, in Woolf's thinking, our knowledge of nature is not ahistorical in character. It is subject to the fluctuations and vibrations of bombshells and warships. Woolf is keenly aware that in philosophical naturalism, nature is not always beautiful and revealing. War is just as much part of nature as peace.

After the war, Woolf speeds up the passage of time in her description. Instead of seasons passing, years speed by.

IV. Years

The Pedesis of Nature

Specially, Woolf says that time passed by as a "shapeless tumbling." This is yet another interesting observation about the material nature of time in Woolf's thought. This movement of what she calls "shapeless tumbling" is similar to what scientists call "pedesis." Pedesis, from the Greek root -"ped," meaning "foot," is a kind of motion that proceeds through iteration. One step follows after another relatedly but not deterministically. In pedesis, there is no goal and no determined path, but a continual experimentation that is always related to what came before. One can find it in the fractal pattern that lightning makes as it branches and spreads out in the sky. After the war, Woolf says, the turbulence of nature picks up and tumbles shapelessly along by wind and waves.

> Only gigantic chaos streaked with lightning could have been heard tumbling and tossing, as the winds and waves disported themselves like the amorphous bulks of leviathans whose brows are pierced by no light of reason, and mounted one on top of another, and lunged and plunged in the darkness or the daylight (for night and day, month and year ran shapelessly together).
> (TL, 134)

After the disruption of war, nature does not return to its previous stable form. Rather, it tries to begin again to find a new rhythm once more. Forms do not come ready-made, for Woolf, but have to be built from shapeless material experimentation. Like waves falling rhythmically one after another, nature iterates its patterns by mounting them on what came before. There is only mixture and changing rates of metamorphosis.

In Woolf's philosophy of time, there is no pre-determined path for things. Nature does not know in advance which way to go or what forms to make, so it experiments. Time is not a linear passage, but a shapeless running-together of things without reason or direction—only iteration. There are only rhythms of fluid dynamic winds and waters plunging, tumbling, tossing, and disporting here and there like the curving topology of spacetime itself.

The Birth and Death of Form

Over the years, Woolf says, these turbulent patterns of nature increasingly overtake the beach house. The airs that enter are "fumbling." The shawl sways "aimlessly," and the floor is "strewn" with straw. The poppies grow among the dahlias, carnations with cabbages, and artichokes among the roses (TL, 137). These patterns of motion Woolf describes are iterative, tumbling, and mounting just like the kinetic structure of time.

The house decays, but the weeds, mushrooms, and toads flourish inside. Decay, rot, rats, and birds live from the decomposition of the house. They are, in short, the house continued by other means. Just as in all Woolf's individual moments of being, life and death are continuous with one another. But here it is the Ramsey's beach house that undergoes the experience.

The outside of the house (the sand, the moths, toads, swallows, thistles, and mushrooms) becomes the inside. These beings are not just things from outside that have come inside, but they directly transform the matter of the house into themselves. They become the same stuff as the house. For instance, mushrooms literally eat the books and become the books. The swallows build their homes out of the house's scraps. "Life had left" (TL, 137), the house, writes Woolf, and yet the house also became profoundly "fertile" (TL, 138) at the same time. Material fertility and generativity are not the same as vitalism or life.

What is so philosophically innovative in this section of "Time Passes" is that Woolf describes, for the first time, a moment of non-human becoming. The house becomes its surrounding atmosphere filled with water, light, trees, and animals, while the outside folds into the house to become its new interior. After the war, the house does not "return to nature," but rather, mixes into a new nature.

Throughout the house's decomposition, the division between humans and nature increasingly breaks down. Woolf describes the cleaning lady as a tropical fish swimming through light. The drawing-room becomes a nest for swallows.

Nature becomes humanized, and human life becomes naturalized at the same time.

In this way, Woolf iterates the theme of mutual transformation in the *reflective pool*. The mind, house, beach, and time are all pools in Woolf's ontology. Each of these pools stirs, diffracts, and reflects the light of others in a mutual penetration and transformation. Each views itself from the diffracted light of the others. Instead of philosophical essences, Woolf thinks of pools of fluid as simulacra bouncing off and transforming one another.

She asks next, "What power could now prevent the fertility, the insensibility of nature?" (TL, 138). Nature is without reason, causality, or final aim. Then, she says, a threshold in the continuous transformation suddenly approaches. The dawn "trembles," and the whole house could have "sunk and fallen" into a "mound" (TL, 138).

> In the ruined room, picnickers would have lit their kettles; lovers sought shelter there, lying on the bare boards; and the shepherd stored his dinner on the bricks, and the tramp slept with his coat round him to ward off the cold.
> (TL, 138)

The trembling, weight, and fall of the smallest swerving matter, Woolf suggests, might have pushed the house past the point of recovery. The house might have become a site for sex, food, and shelter in an entirely different way. The briars would "grow unequally but lustily over the mound" (TL, 138).

Woolf's image of the house as a mound is the perfect spatial analog to the "shapeless" and "amorphous" movement of time she is describing. A mound or heap is an iterative formation made by processes and not pre-designed. It is the anti-form. One thing mounting on top of another, in Woolf's thought, is how all forms emerge. At some point, the house began as a mound, then it was built into a house, and will return to a grass-covered mound again one day. Perhaps Woolf has in mind the first neolithic mound houses that dot the English countryside. For Woolf, formlessness remains at the heart of form, fertile and pregnant with shapeless movements.

However, if the house "plunged to the depths to lie upon the sands of oblivion," this oblivion would not be nothingness or void. Like the Lucretian swerve and fall of matter, the fall would give birth to new vegetal and animal beings.

> But there was a force working; something not highly conscious; something that leered, something that lurched; something not inspired to go about its work with dignified ritual or solemn chanting.
> (TL, 139)

In other words, for Woolf, the process of rebirth is no less pedetic than that of decay. Nature breaks down and builds back up; life becomes death, and death becomes life using the same patterns. Hence Woolf's turbulent description of how the house cleaners, Mrs. McNab and Mrs. Bast start fixing up the house to be occupied again by its owners.

> Some rusty laborious birth seemed to be taking place, as the women, stooping, rising, groaning, singing, slapped and slammed, upstairs now, now down in the cellars. Oh, they said, the work!
>
> (TL, 139)

The women's bodies curve, bend, and make all kinds of disordered noises. Woolf compares their labor to that of giving birth. The birth of form is made from formless unstable, unequal, trembling, and groaning movements. The workers, as Marx says, are "the material bearers of exchange-value."[17] The cleaning women are the material conditions of domestic reproduction. They bear life and thus carry the forms of value and property in a capitalist society. Form, for Woolf, is always metastable and continually supported by the iterated labor of someone or something else.

The women, Woolf says, "rescued [the house] from the pool of Time" (TL, 139). Here again we can see Woolf's fluid dynamic ontology at work. Time is a pool, for Woolf, because energy comes in and goes out. The house was entropically dissipating energy that was accumulating in a heap, mound, or pool of time. If the house is not supported continuously, it will sink and remerge as something else entirely. For form to persist, it has to be made again and again. Energy has to be put in as labor. So before the house falls entirely into the depths of the pool of time, the women rescue it and reproduce its house-form again. But the new house is not a repetition of the old one but a differential iteration: "Ah, said Mrs. Bast, they'd find it changed" (TL, 140). The flow of energy and time is irreversible and singular.

Toward the end of the day, the workers hear the "discordant harmonies" (BA, 175) around them. Woolf describes the sounds as related, coordinated, but also mysterious and synesthetic.

> Half-heard melody, that intermittent music which the ear half catches but lets fall; a bark, a bleat; irregular, intermittent, yet somehow related; the hum of an insect, the tremor of cut grass, dissevered yet somehow belonging; the jar of a dorbeetle, the squeak of a wheel, loud, low, but mysteriously related; which the ear strains to bring together and is always on the verge of harmonising, but they are never quite heard, never fully harmonised, and at last, in the evening, one after another the sounds die out, and the harmony falters; and silence falls.
>
> (TL, 141)

Here, Woolf offers a philosophically interesting theory of disharmony and sonic forms. In this scene, Woolf describes how a discordant harmony can emerge relationally from heterogeneous micro-perceptions and affects. Here, a sonic form of harmony emerges from a wide range of sonic textures but is never perfectly harmonious. It is similar to how the cleaners repair the house but not perfectly. For Woolf, form is the coordination of various patterns iterating again and again alongside one another without essence or fixity.

Rebirth

After the war is over, peace returns to society, to the beach, to the house, and to the minds of the sleepers. Woolf says that the mirrored pools were stirred, distorted, diffracted, and almost sunk to the bottom. The war nearly destroyed the world. Mrs. Ramsey, Prue, and Andrew Ramsay all died; the house almost fell into darkness, and storms raged on the beach. Now, Woolf writes, the voice of nature returns.

> Through the open window the voice of the beauty of the world came murmuring, too softly to hear exactly what it said ... entreating the sleepers ... if they would not actually come down to the beach itself at least to lift the blind and look out. They would see then night flowing down in purple; his head crowned; his sceptre jewelled; and how in his eyes a child might look. If they still said no ... his voice would sing its song. Gently the waves would break (Lily heard them in her sleep); tenderly the light fell (it seemed to come through her eyelids).
>
> (TL, 142)

After the war, social and natural relationships, like the house's rebirth, have to be reborn. The world becomes a child again with all the beauty, hope, and joy of rebirth. Woolf writes, "The sigh of all the seas breaking in measure round the isles soothed them; the night wrapped them" (TL, 142). The waves' soothing sound and the misty, hazy light of the stars and sun recall Woolf's first memory in her nursery at St. Ives.

> If life has a base that it stands upon, if it is a bowl that one fills and fills and fills-then my bowl without a doubt stands upon this memory. It is of lying half asleep, half awake, in bed in the nursery at St Ives. It is of hearing the waves breaking, one, two, one, two, and sending a splash of water over the beach; and then breaking, one, two, one, two, behind a yellow blind .... of feeling the purest ecstasy I can conceive.
>
> (MB, 64–5)

Similarly, the sleepers, house, and beach in "Time Passes" are all born again in a half-waking hypnogogic ecstasy. The rhythms of existence begin again with the breaking of the waves providing the foundation of a new melody.

The weaving begins again. Woolf describes how bird song is woven synthetically into the whiteness of the dawn. The various noises of "a cart grinding, a dog somewhere barking" begin to be woven into new harmonic forms. The woven veil lifts from Lily Briscoe's eyes and, like the pools, begins "stirring." "Her eyes opened wide. Here she was again, she thought, sitting bolt upright in bed. Awake" (TL, 143).

This long moment of being in "Time Passes" ends after many years. One morning, there is peace after the war, and Lily Briscoe wakes up from a dream. "Time Passes," is an incredible moment of being. It passes through the mind, body, house, and beach as entangled pools of the same process. Space dilates from the white mushrooms growing out of the book to the change of seasons. Time dilates from linear to non-linear shapeless tumbling. The pools of reality ripple, topple, almost sink and become peaceful again. Life dies, decays, and is reborn like waves on the beach.

In her next novel, after *To the Lighthouse*, Woolf expands a moment of being even further and to a single character across hundreds of years. Let's look now more closely at this achievement and its philosophical implications in her novel, *Orlando*.

Extended Moments

Moment 11: Part I, Hail! Natural Desire!

In this section of the book, I want to look at the longest moment of being in Woolf's work. In it, Woolf weaves together every aspect of philosophical interrelation from her other moments. Yet, this long moment in her novel *Orlando* also remains singular. Here, Woolf combined two techniques for writing her moments of being: the extended individual moment and what I called the non-human historical moment. The result was an experimental biography called, *Orlando: A Biography* (1928). In this book, Woolf tells the life story of Orlando, an aristocratic poet based on her friend and lover Vita Sackville-West, who lives over centuries and different geographies and who changes sex from male to female.

In the novel, there are brief moments of being and short individual moments of being. But what is new and especially striking in *Orlando* is that the last thirty pages of the book are one long moment of being that describes Orlando's travel through history and arrival at the present moment. This moment is "individual" insofar as it is happening to a single person, but also vastly longer and more historical like "Time Passes." This long moment of being in *Orlando* is also philosophically important for its incredible ideas of sex, gender, and sexuality.

Since this moment is so long, I have broken it up into three parts. The moment of being begins one spring day, when Orlando puts down a book she is reading about the nineteenth century, pulls up a chair, looks out her window, and concludes that Victorian literature is appallingly decadent. She then begins to stare out the window for a very long time waiting for the world to respond to this conclusion. She then hears music from the street below and is suddenly swept up into a profound wave of thought and becoming. One of the main philosophical ideas developed here is an immanent theory of natural desire.

Tossing on the Waves of Thought

As Orlando stares out the window, Woolf says, the veil of reality draws back to reveal the event of the world's response to her conclusion about the nineteenth century. Suddenly Orlando gives an abrupt start as something begins to take her over. Music begins to play in the street, and she is off on her moment of being. Woolf writes:

> Is nothing, then, going to happen this pale March morning to mitigate, to veil, to cover, to conceal, to shroud this undeniable event whatever it may be? For after giving that sudden, violent start, Orlando—but Heaven be praised, at this very moment there struck up outside one of these frail, reedy, fluty, jerky, old-fashioned barrel-organs which are still sometimes played by Italian organ-grinders in back streets. Let us accept the intervention, humble though it is, as if it were the music of the spheres, and allow it, with all its gasps and groans, to fill this page with sound until the moment comes which it is impossible to deny is coming; which the footman has seen coming and the maid-servant; and the reader will have to see too; for Orlando herself is clearly unable to ignore it any longer—let the barrel-organ sound and transport us on thought, which is no more than a little boat, when music sounds, tossing on the waves; on thought, which is, of all carriers, the most clumsy, the most erratic, over the roof tops and the back gardens where washing is hanging to—what is this place?
>
> (O, 292)

Woolf describes here how the simple sound of an organ-grinder playing in the street begins to "transport" Orlando somewhere completely different and is also somehow a response to her "conclusion" about the nineteenth century. Orlando, like Woolf, opens herself up to a material response from the world in her moment of being. The world responds with a tune that fills the novel's page with sound until "the moment" hits her so hard she cannot deny it. Orlando's thoughts are no longer under her autonomous control but become like a small boat on the waves of a sonic and vibratory world.

Woolf says that the gardens below brim with early blooming bulbs (grape hyacinth, crocus, and almond flower buds) and remind Orlando of the bulbs planted in October. As Orlando looks out the window, she transitions between states of consciousness like a flower blooms. Woolf suggests that the tiny flowers Orlando sees are the visual markers of the deeper bulbs of reality beneath the cotton wool. Woolf writes, "Beneath the delicate, beautiful flower lies the red hairy bulb of reality: the dark dirt of the Earth" (O, 293).

Orlando's thought of this bulb-filled earth starts her "dreaming of more than can rightly be said," and of dreaming of waiting under the oak tree for the kingfisher who "was seen once to cross in the evening from bank to bank" (O, 293). Woolf's invocation is explicit here. The moment Orlando opens herself up to the world's response through the window, music suddenly transports her to an altered state of consciousness akin to dreaming while awake.

Philosophically, Woolf is describing here the way that Orlando's thoughts are natural and psychological at the same time. They follow the rhythms of flowers, bulbs, and street music. In other words, for Woolf, thinking is akin to traveling along the patterns the world carves out. The journey is often involuntary, sudden, perhaps scary, but also illuminating (MB, 72). For Woolf, Orlando's experience shows us, we are frequently only partially in control of these drifts and currents of sound and light.

In her moment of being, Orlando begins to dream while awake. She sits under a tree and waits by the river for a kingfisher bird to cross from side to side while her mind crosses from consciousness to unconsciousness. "Wait! Wait! The kingfisher comes; the kingfisher comes not" (O, 293). Orlando is in-between states of consciousness; between awake and asleep—waiting for reality to show itself behind the veil (TL, 132; O, 292).

Meanwhile ... Natural Desire!

"Meanwhile," Woolf says, in-between states of consciousness, Orlando catches a glimpse of reality through the smoke of her cigarette.

> Behold, meanwhile, the factory chimneys, and their smoke; behold the city clerks flashing by in their outrigger. Behold the old lady taking her dog for a walk and the servant girl wearing her new hat for the first time not at the right angle. Behold them all. Though Heaven has mercifully decreed that the secrets of all hearts are hidden so that we are lured on for ever to suspect something, perhaps, that does not exist; still through our cigarette smoke, we see blaze up and salute the splendid fulfillment of natural desires for a hat, for a boat, for a rat in a ditch; as once one saw blazing-such silly hops and skips the mind takes when it slops like this all over the saucer and the barrel-organ plays-saw blazing a fire in a field against minarets near Constantinople.
>
> (O, 293)

In this altered state of consciousness, Orlando sees the turbulent smoke, the clerks, the old lady, the dog, and the servant girl's hat moving together in the immanent flow of "natural desire." The philosophical question at stake here is the nature of desire. Through Orlando, Woolf offers an interesting theory. Desire, for Woolf, is not only a human want for an external object. Orlando sees through the swirling turbulent plumes of cigarette and factory smoke that human desire is continuous with the immanent movements of nature.

Orlando realizes that the eddies and curls of smoke are not different in kind from the movement of boats down the river or the dog out on a walk. Everywhere the cosmos is spreading out thermodynamically and dissipating energy in its own way.

In Woolf's philosophy, we are not like T.S. Eliot's "Fisher King," who was cursed to have desolate and infertile lands. We are not cut off from our desires, impotent, and dissatisfied with nature. For Woolf, we are the *kingfisher*. We are a bird fluttering back and forth over, below, and above, the river of consciousness. In other words, Woolf offers us a theory of desire and reality radically different than Eliot's.

For Woolf, desire is not a "desire for x" such that the desire is different from what we desire. Desire is not cut off from nature, in Woolf's thought, because "we are the thing itself" (MB, 72). Nature desires *through* us. To be and act is to desire. This broader idea of desire has its roots in the Homeric "Hymn to Aphrodite," and in Lucretius's description of the birth of Venus, which Woolf read and loved. Aphrodite, for the archaic poets and Lucretius, was immanent to gods and humans. She was the desire of nature itself; the golden *ergon,* or "action" of all things.

Woolf says that Orlando "beholds" not only the human desire for a hat but also the smoke plume's desire to rise and swerve in the air. The movement of the boaters, walkers, smoke plumes, and even the decomposing rat are continuations of the natural desire of energetic dissipation. Our universe "desires" to flow, swerve, cycle, and dissipate.

In her moment of becoming, Orlando's mind, for Woolf, becomes a liquid spilling over its cup into the saucer. The plumes of smoke from the factory become the swirling towers of Constantinople in Orlando's pareidolia. Geographies overlap like a folded map. The present mixes with the past. This is not a hallucination. Or if it is, it is a true hallucination that actually tells us something deeply important about the nature of the human mind as a fluctuating, skipping, and spilling-over kind of process. As Woolf writes about her experience on nitrous oxide, "We become aware of something that we could never see in the other world; something that we have been sent in search of" (E6, 451). Orlando is similarly "lured on for ever to suspect something, perhaps, that does not exist."

Although moments of being are psychological, and *Orlando* is literary, Woolf is also making a distinctly *philosophical* statement about the nature of reality here. Nature is desire. The sensuous experience of fractal vortical patterns in her cigarette smoke[1] occasion her experience of pareidolia, seeing towers in the smoke. This prompts her to notice the similarly dissipative energetic patterns between scales and kinds of beings in nature. Ultimately, Orlando concludes that all of nature desires, just as Woolf says in her autobiography that nature is a work of art that makes itself (MB, 72).

Hail! Pleasure of All Sorts!

For Woolf, there is no God, and there is no predetermined higher aim of nature (MB, 72). Nature enjoys and senses itself through the immanent dissipation of energy. Nature pleases itself by increasing its capacity and fluency of energetic dissipation at every scale. It continually seeks out and experiments with the most diverse ways of dissipating its energy. This is what Woolf calls the immanent "divinity" of nature.

> Hail! natural desire! Hail! happiness! divine happiness! and pleasure of all sorts, flowers and wine, though one fades and the other intoxicates; and half-crown tickets out of London on Sundays, and singing in a dark chapel hymns about death, and anything, anything that interrupts and confounds the tapping of typewriters and filing of letters and forging of links and chains, binding the Empire together. Hail even the crude, red bows on shop girls' lips (as if Cupid, very clumsily, dipped his thumb in red ink and scrawled a token in passing). Hail, happiness! kingfisher flashing from bank to bank, and all fulfillment of natural desire, whether it is what the male novelist says it is; or prayer; or denial; hail! in whatever form it comes, and may there be more forms, and stranger. For dark flows the stream—would it were true, as the rhyme hints "like a dream"—but duller and worser than that is our usual lot; without dreams, but alive, smug, fluent, habitual, under trees whose shade of an olive green drowns the blue of the wing of the vanishing bird when he darts of a sudden from bank to bank.
>
> (O, 294–5)

In Woolf's theory of desire, nature pursues all kinds of desires. Like other natural bodies, the human body is one type of technique or experiment to dissipate energy. Plants grow out of the Earth to eat sunlight, transform it into flowering bodies, and dissipate their energy into the air. Humans consume plants, but instead of flowering and growing roots, they develop their ultrasensitive and branching nervous systems.

Humans do this by extending and expanding their capacity for feeling and sensation in art, music, culture, knowledge, travel, language, dancing, and learning. The more their plastic nervous systems grow, the more diverse ways they can dissipate energy. Plants fulfill natural desire through photosynthesis. Humans accomplish it through neurogenesis, making and enjoying art.

Desire, for Woolf, is not necessarily "intentional" or strictly human. It is nothing other than the dissipative movement of matter like smoke from a cigarette. Novelists like T.S. Eliot tell us that life and desire are suffering in the face of a barren Earth. Religions based on renunciation tell us that life is misery, and we must pray for deliverance from nature. Philosophers like Plato tell us that desire is a distraction from real knowledge. But, for Woolf, even when we try to suppress our desires, this too is a desire. The desire to deny desire is still a desire—as Nietzsche said.

Therefore, Orlando does not call for repression but for the expansion of desire. There is no escape from desire in God, Heaven, or consciousness. Orlando acknowledges all desire and even celebrates the innovation of even more and stranger forms not yet imagined. The more diverse and unusual the desires of nature, the more varied and rapid the spread and release of energy into the cosmos. Just as evolution experiments with species, it also experiments with desire and happiness.[2]

In particular, Orlando salutes all the varied forms of desire that interrupt the mechanisms that hold the British Empire together. Woolf's philosophical ethic here is as radical as it is simple. Let all desires flourish that increase the diversity of natural desire while reducing the destruction of others to a minimum. This is consistent with Roger Fry's aesthetic anarchism. Let more and stranger desires increase as long as we are still free to experiment in peace without the tyranny of empire, colonialism, states, and authoritarianism. Political repression is also a form of desire but one that kills off and shrinks the diversity of desire.

Woolf says that natural desire flows like a dark stream. It is like the material unconscious of the world. We know not the source or ends of desire, yet it flows on endlessly generating new desires. Desire is like a dream, for Orlando, in that it is not rational but *relational*. New desires emerge from previous ones without being determined by them. The challenge of Woolf's ethic of desire is how to flow along with this stream and not get caught up in the dull habits and repetitions of empire.

The modern human brain has focused on instrumentality through the subordination of its other desires.[3] The problem now, for Woolf, is that we have got stuck in one state of instrumental rationality and now have trouble going back and forth fluidly between states of consciousness like the kingfisher dives into and crosses the river.

Hail Not! The Splintering of the Whole!

Desire, for Woolf, flows continually through the whole of nature, and everything interweaves through it. The danger, however, is thinking or acting like nature is splintered, torn, and split up into discrete pieces. Nature is not separate pieces, for Woolf, all of being flows, folds, and weaves without any absolute division between anything and anything else. The whole of nature and the cosmos entangles itself such that there are no discrete things or entirely unrelated objects.[4]

In this sense, all perceptions are true performances of nature's real desire. Woolf writes:

> Hail, happiness, then, and after happiness, hail not those dreams which bloat the sharp image as spotted mirrors do the face in a country-inn parlour; dreams which splinter the whole and tear us asunder and wound us and split us apart in the night when we would sleep; but sleep, sleep, so deep that all shapes are ground to dust of infinite softness, water of dimness inscrutable, and there, folded, shrouded, like a mummy, like a moth, prone let us lie on the sand at the bottom of sleep.
>
> (O, 295)

Woolf, via Orlando, wishes us to hail not those images that make the world look spotted and splintered into discrete things here and there. One is, as Woolf said in *Mrs. Dalloway*, neither here nor there but *everywhere* (MD, 152–3). This is why Woolf says the kingfisher and the stream flow "like a dream" that bids us release consciousness and allow the unconscious to dream while awake. This is a true sleep where all discrete forms are ground to a continuous material dust. Woolf again reveals her philosophical description of how form emerges from matter and returns.

In this sleepy awareness of altered consciousness, Orlando sees that forms emerge from soft dust or dark unintelligible material processes. Our unconscious shows us that deep under the surface of the world, things are not cut up and wounded but whole and woven like a fabric. Matter, for Woolf, folds up in layers of veil and shroud-like mummies.

Reality, in Woolf's philosophy, however, is not an objective state that we could see if only we could turn a light on in the depth of the world. Nor is it anything mysteriously withdrawn from the world. Reality is a many-folded textile of patterns beneath the cotton wool of things. In this way, the moth is another beautiful image of Woolf's philosophy of moments of being. People and things are like moths. At a glance, they look like discrete bodies. Yet, upon closer inspection, as Woolf often did with moths in her childhood,[5] one sees that they are intricately and beautifully patterned with unique colorations, lines, and forms so minute one could gaze upon them for a lifetime. When the moth's wings open, they reveal the fractal patterns on the inside. This is perhaps why Woolf originally planned to title her book *The Waves*, *The Moths*.

The patterns of moth wings are also deeply entangled with their environment often appearing like other plants and insects. Moth wing patterns are works of art and natural desire in Woolf's sense because they express their world involuntarily without consciously mimicking or objectifying it. Moments of being let Woolf's characters lay on the bottom of the sandy riverbed of an interconnected world for a while. From these depths they can see the patterns beneath the moth's wings.

Reflowing Like a Tide

But Orlando's moment of becoming, according to Woolf, is not a sleep in which everything goes completely dark. Instead, it is an altered state of lucid unconsciousness brought on by the music of the barrel-organ and the cigarette smoke. In this state, she sees and feels the flow and weave of reality. She can return to consciousness again with this profound knowledge.

> But wait! but wait! we are not going, this time, visiting the blind land. Blue, like a match struck right in the ball of the innermost eye, he flys, burns, bursts the seal of sleep; the kingfisher; so that now floods back refluent like a tide, the red, thick stream of life again; bubbling, dripping; and we rise, and our eyes (for how handy a rhyme is to pass us safe over the awkward transition from death to life) fall on—(here the barrel-organ stops playing abruptly).
>
> (O, 295)

In Orlando's waking dream, the blue kingfisher dives down into the river to catch its prey—traversing the fluid barrier between consciousness and unconsciousness. The kingfisher flies into the water and then bursts back out again with its catch just as Orlando dives down and returns with her score, her knowledge of reality as a woven meshwork of flowing singularities and intricate patterns. Orlando bursts the membrane between waking and sleeping. She lays prone, listening intensely to her expanded sensation of the world, and now like a flood or tide, busts back out of her moment of becoming when the music stops.

Bubbles and drips are perfect material images of mixture and air and water which mark the transition between fluid states. Our bodies and brains are "hyperseas,"[6] as paleontologists Mark and Dianna McMenamin call them. We evolved from water and now carry it with us everywhere we go like a little bit of the sea. The brain is a pool of fluid—of red rushing blood and neurochemicals. Woolf says Orlando rises from her lucid unconscious state like one rises from death to life. Like Odysseus' journey to Hades, Orlando must travel to the world of the dead for knowledge and return to share it in art and action.

When Orlando returns to consciousness, Woolf says, her "eyes fall on ...—" right as the music stops. This is a challenging philosophical aspect of Woolf's moments of being; the transition between the ineffable interconnection of the world and our philosophical and artistic descriptions of it. For Woolf, philosophy and art will never be able to represent moments of being and yet we try anyway. It is as if in the moment of the transition between states of consciousness Orlando's eyes fall on something tangible that might be able to cross over. But right before that, she sees what it is the music stops and it sleeps away like a forgotten but powerful dream.

Suddenly, right as the street music stops, and Orlando seems to be ending her moment of being, she gives birth to a baby and the moment surges on in the novel. Let's look at what happens next and its philosophical implications for Woolf's theory of the self.

Moment 11: Part II, The Beauty of Movement

This next part of Orlando's moment of being takes place many months or years after her son is born. Here, Woolf gives us a fascinating theory of time and subjectivity from her unique process-philosophical perspective. Years after she births her son, Orlando looks out a window again and suddenly feels that all her senses and thoughts are becoming heightened. She is shocked by the feeling that she is in the *present* moment. Suddenly, she jumps into her motorcar. As she drives, things begin to flow and tumble together. Space and time begin to dilate and mix; her subjectivity begins to multiply, swerve, dissipate, and liquify. Even though much time has passed after the first part of her moment of being, Woolf describes the second part as continuous with the first. Let's look now at some of the philosophical implications of Orlando's continued moment of being.

The Amplification of the Senses

Woolf says that Orlando realizes that she is in the present, but this is extremely odd because it assumes that prior to this she must have been living in the past. Orlando's feeling of passing through large amounts of time suggests a strongly expanded sensation of time in her moment of being. Woolf says that Orlando experienced coming into the present as the widening of an "immensely long tunnel in which she seemed to have been traveling for hundreds of years."

> The light poured in; her thoughts became mysteriously tightened and strung up as if a piano tuner had put his key in her back and stretched the nerves very taut; at the same time her hearing quickened; she could hear every whisper and crackle in the room so that the clock ticking on the mantelpiece beat like a hammer. And so for some seconds the light went on becoming brighter and brighter, and she saw everything more and more clearly and the clock ticked louder and louder until there was a terrific explosion right in her ear.
>
> (O, 298)

In Woolf's philosophy of time, the past is not a previous moment like the present, it is a dimension *within the present*. This is why, as Orlando enters the present, Woolf describes it as an amplification of her senses. By attending to all the tiny sounds and lights of the present, Orlando feels more acutely how much of "past" material, such as her nerves, the clock, or light supports her present. Clock, sun, and nerves persist through time but we do not often attend directly to them in our typical experience of the present. In this way, the past emerges as a full intensification of everything that goes into continually supporting the present.

Woolf gives a wonderful description of how our thoughts about the past and future "shelter" us from living fully in the present. But when Orlando arrives in the present, in her moment of being, she realizes how saturated and sensuous it is.

> Orlando leapt as if she had been violently struck on the head … It was the present moment. … No one need wonder that Orlando started, pressed her hand to her heart, and turned pale. For what more terrifying revelation can there be than that it is the present moment? That we survive the shock at all is only possible because the past shelters us on one side, the future on another.
> (O, 298)

For Woolf, our abstract ideas of "past" and "future" often make us less attentive to the present. Our minds often cut the world up into a series of slices in a timeline where the present is an infinitely divisible fleeting moment. However, in Orlando's moment of being, this process is reversed. Everything is sensuously present and undivided. Instead of the present disappearing into the past or future, it becomes everything. Past and future are consumed by the present. Woolf says this is shocking and terrifying to Orlando because in it Orlando feels less individual. If time is not broken up into discrete pieces, then where in time is the self? Orlando's loss of self coincides with her feeling a need for movement and flow in her car.

Life in Motion

And so Orlando's moment of being is amplified by her *movement* as she races through the streets in her car crossing into the present. Woolf writes:

> She ran downstairs, jumped into her motor car, pressed the self-starter and was off. Vast blue blocks of building rose into the air; the red cowls of chimneys were spotted irregularly across the sky; the road shone like silver-headed nails; omnibuses bore down upon her with sculptured white-faced drivers; she noticed sponges, bird-cages, boxes of green American cloth.
> (O, 299)

In short, Orlando's world becomes a blur of motion. Buildings become blue *blocks*; chimneys become *spots* in the sky, and the road becomes a shimmering metallic *surface*. As Orlando races into the present, the world of faces, sponges, birdcages, and cloth appears to emerge from out of the moving flow. Here Woolf gives us a beautiful description of how things emerge from processes. From the flowing torrent of process, blocks of blue emerge, and from patches of color birdcages emerge.

For Woolf, a vast moving process enfolds each object. Woolf says that if Orlando had slowed down to examine these objects, they would overcome her with the depth of their relations and intricate structures. "But she did not allow these sights to sink into her mind even the fraction of an inch as she crossed the narrow plank of the present, lest she should fall into the raging torrent beneath" (O, 299). Again, we see Woolf's favorite image of time as a river at work. The present is a thin surface continuous with the moving turbulence of the past beneath.

> People buzzed and hummed round the plate-glass windows within which one could see a glow of red, a blaze of yellow, as if they were bees, Orlando thought—but her thought that they were bees was violently snipped off and she saw, regaining perspective with one flick of her eye, that they were bodies.
>
> (O, 299)

In her moment of being, Orlando sees human beings as process in broader patterns. Just like the movement and pattern of bees visiting flowers become clear in time-lapse photography, the movement of people swarming and buzzing around the brightly colored red and yellow shop windows becomes clear from Orlando's motor car. Woolf is keenly aware that motion produces spacetime dilation. In such time-lapse dilation, hidden patterns beneath the cotton wool emerge to the fore.

The River of the Present

For Woolf, "Nothing is ever one thing" (O, 305). Old sounds mix with new places and transform them like rainbows or "many-coloured water" (O, 300). Old smells in new places can trigger a synesthesia in which one strongly feels and senses the immanence of the past inside the present. Thus, synesthesia, for Woolf, unveils the past inside the present.

Orlando, Woolf says, pulls up to a shop and is "enveloped" in the "shade and scent" of the store. Orlando feels time and space as a kind of *atmosphere*.[7] Lights and smells that were familiar in the past now take on a different mixture in the present. For Woolf, there is even a fluid-dynamics to the moment. "The present fell from her like drops of scalding water. Light swayed up and down like thin stuffs puffed out by a summer breeze" (O, 299–300). As Orlando speaks, Woolf says that the sounds drip out of her mouth and change into this new atmosphere. Orlando experiences the present as a blurry world like a river with icebergs floating in it. Woolf writes:

> She had a vision of innumerable coloured stuffs flaunting in a breeze from which came distinct, strange smells; and each time the lift stopped and flung its doors open, there was another slice of the world displayed with all the smells of that world clinging to it. She was reminded of the river off Wapping in the time of Elizabeth, where the treasure ships and the merchant ships used to anchor. How richly and curiously they had smelt!
>
> (O, 300)

Woolf's use of the image of icebergs floating down a river (O, 304) is a perfect image for a world in motion whose ordered crystallizations form the metastable objects we see around us. Matter flows and changes but also folds and crystallizes into relatively discrete things, which will, in turn, melt again in the river. Just then, "a whiff of scent … curved like a shell round a figure—was it a boy's or was it a girl's—furred, pearled, in Russian trousers—young, slender, seductive—a girl, by God! but faithless, faithless!" (O, 303). In other words, the conch-shaped swirl of wax candles and flowers turns into Orlando's Russian lover from the past, Sasha, but grown fat. The past surges up inside the present not through abstraction but through sensation. Something about present like a smell shapes how the past unfolds.

When Orlando goes back down the elevator Woolf says that the sound it makes as it hits the ground is the sound of a "pot broken against a river bank" when the Thames melted into icebergs (O, 304). Furthermore, the omnibuses on Oxford Street outside the store become the images of blocks of ice "tossed that day on the Thames" (O, 304). Where her car stood, Orlando sees one of the Irish rebels yelling from an iceberg. This is philosophically significant because it shows how Woolf's theory of time is deeply sensuous and performative. Bits of the past do not come out of nowhere but are brought into the present through smells, colors, motions, and sounds mixing in the present. This is one of the ways the past lives on folded up inside the present.

Here Woolf has a brilliant insight into the nature of sensation. Matter does not go away but recycles and returns. Why then should we be surprised if our sensations return, not just in memory, but in and through the world as atmospheres, colors, and textures? "Time has passed over me" (O, 304). Orlando says. For Woolf, time has passed *through* Orlando. Time is not a background grid on which things move, but rather passes through bodies as motion. Time, for Woolf, is merely a sensuous movement. Orlando continues:

> "I take up a handbag and I think of an old bumboat woman frozen in the ice. Someone lights a pink candle and I see a girl in Russian trousers. When I step out of doors—as I do now," here she stepped on to the pavement of Oxford

Street, "what is it that I taste? Little herbs. I hear goat bells. I see mountains. Turkey? India? Persia?" Her eyes filled with tears.

(O, 305)

For Woolf, memory is not just a mental association. It is a fully ecological and atmospheric event. Orlando's memory is the becoming-present of the past through taste, smell, and sight. Something from the mountains has left a trace in her that now unfolds. This is possible because the patterns of the present are iterations of the same matter of the past. Something material is shared for the affects to be passed on from world to mind.

Philosophically, Woolf's realism challenges us to rethink the nature of time and sensation. We tend to think of memories as representations or mental images of the past and sensations as representations of the present. But for Woolf, memories and sensations are not separate from one another and are not mental images. They are reality working itself out through us. Memories and sensations occur because the past is enfolded in the present and because they directly work on our bodies and brains. We only think our mental images are representational because we cannot see all the affective, sensuous, and atmospheric rhythms at work producing our experience of them. For example, Orlando knows that there are no goats on Oxford Street, yet she still hears the "same" sound—like a material reverberating echo in her body. In other words, memory, for Woolf, is not subjective but material, historical, and real as it weaves together our body with the world and the past inside the present.

Philosophical Biography

It follows, in Woolf's materialist philosophy of time, that there are many *times* and many *selves,* since the past lingers and leaves traces in the world and our bodies. The world, in other words, produces an archive of itself. All matter tells a story of its history through its material traces. The difficulty is synchronizing all these times and selves. Woolf writes:

> The most successful practitioners of the art of life, often unknown people by the way, somehow contrive to synchronise the sixty or seventy different times which beat simultaneously in every normal human system so that when eleven strikes, all the rest chime in unison, and the present is neither a violent disruption nor completely forgotten in the past. Of them we can justly say that they live precisely the sixty-eight or seventy-two years allotted them on the tombstone. Of the rest, some we know to be dead, though they walk among us; some are not yet born, though they go through the forms of life; others are hundreds of years old though they call themselves thirty-six.

(O, 305)

Here, Woolf gives us an interesting theory of subjectivity based on rhythm. Most of us say "I" as if we were a unified group of thoughts and actions, but for Woolf this is mostly not true. We are a flurry of different sensations, memories, and desires. Even where it seems most true, unity is an effect of a kind of difficult and rare synchrony of many different times and selves. For the rest of us, we are much more out of sync. The past like a turbulent river is constantly disturbing the smooth surface of the present. This is the strange sense in which *Orlando* is a realist novel. For Woolf, any biography is already filled with a multiplicity of sensations and connections as far back as we would want to go. A central question of biography then is how we can entirely separate "a life" from the vast material and historical processes that go into shaping and weaving it. Instead of isolating a single discrete life, which would be an abstraction, Woolf chooses to weave together all the temporal, geographical, gendered, and subjective lives into a "single" turbulent life.

This is yet another philosophical expression of her method of "saturation." Like poetry, biography typically reduces the world to a single concentrated life. However, history and what Woolf does not like about literary realism, expand life too broadly to include all the trivialities. By contrast, Woolf's method is to write a saturated biography that tells history through a manifolded life woven into the flux of the world.

In Woolf's view, every life *really is* saturated with historical and geographical relations beyond their directly perceptible everyday experience. We just don't experience our lives this way because we do not know or cannot sense the whole range of relations and affects that shape us. This is what Woolf tries to show us in *Orlando*. It only seems magical because our conscious awareness is like the tip of an iceberg. The lives of other people and material processes continue *through* us. For Woolf, again, this is a consequence of the philosophical belief that there is no hard separation between humans and the world. For instance, our everyday actions are not fully our own but built up by habits passed down by millions of years of evolution and thousands of culture history. Each generation iterates the previous ones without radical discontinuities or simple continuities. For Woolf, history and biography move through arabesque folds.

Woolf's philosophical realism thus results in a biographical method without autonomous individuals or depersonalized historical events. Each life lives the whole of history, and all of history flows through each individual—although we are mostly unaware of the full set of relations at work. The character of Orlando is the sensuous saturation of historical biography. Orlando's life is trans-geographical, trans-historical, trans-gendered, and trans-subjective. Orlando is history's material unconscious come to life.

As Woolf says, "The true length of a person's life … is always a matter of dispute" (O, 305–6) because one's life is not fully one's own. Material elements and patterns of motion precede the individual, condition their emergence, fold up inside them, and then dissipate through their bodies.

Indeed it is a difficult business—this time-keeping; nothing more quickly disorders it than contact with any of the arts; and it may have been her love of poetry that was to blame for making Orlando lose her shopping list and start home without the sardines, the bath salts, or the boots.

(O, 306)

For Woolf, art creates a rhythm of qualities that cannot be fully captured by discrete measurements. In particular, poetry, for Woolf, makes a meter or time that is not the time of the clock nor merely the time of subjective feeling. All artists, Woolf suspects, have probably had moments of being and that their art works try to express something of their moment (MB, 73). For Orlando, the instrumental logic of the shopping list of discrete items seems unimportant or small compared to the intense sensation of the past mixed up in the present.

The Material Transcendental Field

But what holds us and the world together? If everything is in flux, why does it feel relatively stable most of the time? As Orlando's experience of her self begins to unravel, Woolf considers what pulls them apart and weaves them together in more detail. In the novel, Orlando leaves the store without her bath salts and drives home through London. As she drives, the discrete measurement of time and the heterogeneity of city life seen at high speeds strike her. In motion again, Orlando's feels like a process. Her self loses its unity and feels more like a pool of water or little scraps of paper carried on the wind. Woolf writes:

Now as she stood with her hand on the door of her motor car, the present again struck her on the head. Eleven times she was violently assaulted. ... "Confound it all!" she cried, for it is a great shock to the nervous system, hearing a clock strike—so much so that for some time now there is nothing to be said of her save that she frowned slightly.

(O, 306)

The clock causes Orlando a "sudden violent shock" in the same way Woolf says moments of being grab her involuntarily (MB, 71). Orlando's whole nervous system responds to the shock and her senses widen. Woolf writes that there is nothing to be said about Orlando in this moment suggesting an ineffability of the moment of being. But once Orlando gets into her car and begins driving there is much to be said. As she drives by things in the city they become intense, singular, and blurred by motion.

Woolf writes that the color of meat Orlando sees in the street becomes intensely red and the events and people in the street become distinctly visible.

Orlando snatches fragments of signs and words quickly but incompletely: "Ra-Un," "Amor Vin" "Applejohn and Applebed, Undert—" (O, 307).

> Nothing could be seen whole or read from start to finish. What was seen begun—like two friends starting to meet each other across the street—was never seen ended. After twenty minutes the body and mind were like scraps of torn paper tumbling from a sack and, indeed, the process of motoring fast out of London so much resembles the chopping up small of body and mind, which precedes unconsciousness and perhaps death itself that it is an open question in what sense Orlando can be said to have existed at the present moment. Indeed we should have given her over for a person entirely disassembled were it not that here, at last, one green screen was held out on the right, against which the little bits of paper fell more slowly; and then another was held out on the left so that one could see the separate scraps now turning over by themselves in the air; and then green screens were held continuously on either side, so that her mind regained the illusion of holding things within itself and she saw a cottage, a farmyard and four cows, all precisely life size.
>
> (O, 307)

In motion, Orlando's consciousness becomes increasingly unconscious such that Woolf imagines death to be similar to this constant flow of matter. In this sense, Woolf compares motion to the unconscious activity of the brain and its power of imagination and association. Driving while in a moment of being gives Orlando a glimpse of a different temporality as things emerge and dissolve into one another. The faster Orlando drives, the more disparate her glimpses of the world become. "A woman looked out of a bedroom window, profoundly contemplative, and very still" (O, 307). For Orlando, words become letters; meat becomes redness; the countryside becomes "green screens." The world, body, and mind become scraps of torn paper "tumbling" and "turning" themselves over in currents of whirling eddies. Everything flows, but unevenly and turbulently. Matter, for Orlando, forms emergent and dissipative patterns like smoke rings in the air.

Woolf describes in these lines a process philosophy of subjectivity. For Woolf, the self is not a thing but a process of processes. The "art of life," according to Woolf, is to try and "synchronize" these turning or folding processes into a relatively stable pattern of circulation so the wind does not blow away the scapes of paper entirely. This is what art makes difficult by continually exposing the singular and nontotalizable nature of sensuous qualities.

For Woolf, Orlando *exists* not as a discrete or isolated individual but as a circulation of these little folding pedetic scraps. Existence, then, is not static or formal, but kinetic and practical. Existence, for Woolf, is a process. Being must persist to exist. When things begin to move, they lose their stability to some degree. They become more like dreams. Orlando's unified ego begins to dissolve back into its distributed processes. From there, unconscious brain processes can form new connections and associations.

For Woolf, this is not merely an internal cognitive process but is also ecological. The scraps of Orlando's selves mix with the world's scraps and are rewoven together on the wind. Orlando is not just affected by nature; she is also nature. Indeed, Woolf says that the pieces of paper are not geometrical shapes but "torn" "scraps." They are uneven, irregular, and jagged around the edges.

The scraps fly into the wind and almost dissolve Orlando. But then, Woolf says, the scraps began to move more slowly, turn, and float together until they turned into cottages and cows. This is how things come to attain stability for us. They slow down and move together relative to our own processes. The matters that flow together form together. Once the flows start forming objects distinct from one another and from her, then *and only then*, can Orlando imagine that her mind is the one holding the flows together. In this way, Woolf is critical of philosophical idealists who believe that reality is structured exclusively by our minds. For Woolf, however, it is the fields of grass and the movement of the car on the road that hold Orlando's body and mind together.

In Woolf's philosophy, the human mind is nested or woven into much larger ecological, atmospheric, and cosmic patterns. Only after the world weaves human minds into itself can a distinct human perception of the world emerge.

The Topological Self

In Woolf's theory, the subject has to be woven from the bottom up out of the stuff of the world. Once it is, Orlando "heaved a sigh of relief." There can be something comforting about the relative stability of being a particular body and brain. After this stability, one can move from this general field of embodied presence to the narrower field of synchronized subjectivity. Woolf writes:

> Then she called hesitatingly, as if the person she wanted might not be there, "Orlando?" For if there are (at a venture) seventy-six different times all ticking in the mind at once, how many different people are there not—Heaven help us—all having lodgment at one time or another in the human spirit? Some say two thousand and fifty-two. So that it is the most usual thing in the world for a person to say, directly they are alone, Orlando? (if that is one's name) meaning by that, Come, come! I'm sick to death of this particular self. I want another. Hence, the astonishing changes we see in our friends. But it is not altogether plain sailing, either, for though one may say, as Orlando said (being out in the country and needing another self presumably) Orlando?
>
> (O, 308)

For Woolf, it is not the "I" that speaks but the body that speaks and the plural selves that respond. This is an interesting inversion of how we typically think of language and subjectivity. We often think of the self as primary and of language as the attempt to communicate our self to others. Woolf inverts this. For her, the countryside is first, then the body, then the voice, then the self (among many selves) that may or may not come if called. Each self has its particular material and atmospheric conditions for emergence that will only come "if it is raining," or "in a room with green curtains," or "when Mrs. Jones is not there," or "if you can promise it a glass of wine" (O, 308). This is because, for Woolf, each self emerges from the bottom up in the unique field of circulation. Just as the tumbling scraps of paper on a gust of wind can come together in many ways so can selves.

> These selves of which we are built up, one on top of another, as plates are piled on a waiter's hand, have attachments elsewhere, sympathies, little constitutions and rights of their own.
>
> (O, 308)

First, for Woolf, there is a world filled with moving kinetic fields upon which reality orders itself into whirling and often hidden patterns. Then we have a body—something like the image of the walking waiter—walking around the restaurant carefully balancing a stack of plates (our many selves). Each of the plates is like a little ordered field of specific foods, colors, flavors, and smells. Our moving bodies are thus akin to the waiter's moving body, balancing our various subjective patterns. The body tries to serve the right self at the correct table in the right order. Thus, we have, in Woolf's philosophy, a fully relational and distributed self (or selves) tied not only to the body but also to a moving environment. The process and experience of subjectivity are not pre-organized or pre-unified, but it's a constant balancing act synching up multiple rhythms like a syncopated music.

For instance, as Orlando drives by a barn, she calls for "Orlando" again as if the environment itself might form an attachment with the self she wants to summon. But "Orlando" does not come. She then begins to talk out loud to herself. Then, all kinds of selves start to respond and communicate with one another (O, 309). "The one she needed most kept aloof, for she was, to hear her talk, changing her selves as quickly as she drove—there was a new one at every corner" (O, 310). As the countryside changes around her, different selves respond to each new topology. Every corner she turns brings a new dimension of the landscape and a new self into relation with the others.

For Woolf, the self we call the "true" self is no more or less true than the others but has a specific topological region or particular pattern that tries to synchronize the other selves and control them. She writes:

The conscious self, which is the uppermost, and has the power to desire, wishes to be nothing but one self. This is what some people call the true self, and it is, they say, compact of all the selves we have it in us to be; commanded and locked up by the Captain self, the Key self, which amalgamates and controls them all.

(O, 310)

Instead of a true self, Woolf says here that there are just more powerful selves.[8] Without its control, the other selves are free to play and talk to each other in a way that they usually cannot when the Captain self contains them.[9] In the absence of the Captain self, Woolf writes that Orlando's various selves begin to talk with one another and respond fluidly to the changing topology of landscape and speeds of the car. For instance, as the car slows down in the market, the voices slow down and become a song:

With my guineas I'll buy flowering trees, flowering trees, flowering trees and walk among my flowering trees and tell my sons what fame is ... And walk among my flowering trees, and see the moon rise low, the wagons go

(O, 312–13)

Orlando is a wealthy aristocratic writer and famous poet, but the real wealth in her life comes from her relationship with nature. Specifically, her award-winning poem, "Oak Tree," was inspired by various trees throughout her life from which she drew joy. Real fame for Orlando is walking and enjoying the trees and watching the moon. This is the knowledge she wants to pass on to her son. The song about walking comes amid a crowd of walkers at a market. The selves, therefore, respond to this slower pace of the world. Orlando's car is the wagon going on amid the walkers and alongside the sale of plants and flowers. Somehow this deeply unconscious song also expresses the material unconscious of the atmosphere and the context of her thought. In other words, Woolf shows here that Orlando's thought becomes what it is *doing* and is not a reflection or representation of something else.

"Here she stopped short, and looked ahead of her intently at the bonnet of the car in profound meditation. ... She gazed for ten minutes ahead of her, letting the car come almost to a standstill" (O, 313). Woolf describes here how the movement of the car directly is tied to Orlando's thought and sense of self. The slow but not quite stopped car is an expression of and has an effect on Orlando's subjective state. For Woolf, there is a feedback loop between the world and ourselves. One does not unilaterally cause the other in any mechanistic way.

In this moment, Orlando feels her deep entanglement with nature but also the inability to communicate it in language. Woolf says Orlando feels "haunted" by something like the flight of a wild bird or great fish that is always escaping language's net. Orlando then slams on the accelerator of the car to chase after the wild bird of reality.

> "I fling after it words like nets (here she flung her hand out) which shrivel as I've seen nets shrivel drawn on deck with only sea-weed in them. And sometimes there's an inch of silver—six words—in the bottom of the net. But never the great fish who lives in the coral groves." Here she bent her head, pondering deeply.
>
> (O, 312)

Words do not capture reality in Woolf's view. No speed of the car, grasping at air, or words are enough for reality. At most, they turn up scraps at the bottom of a net. Again, Orlando is lost in ponderous silence, *feeling* reality in its full immanence and the fluidity of her being without words to express it.

Her Mind Had Become a Fluid

Next, Woolf writes that the communicating selves are soon exhausted from their chase after the wild animal of reality. Simultaneously, Orlando's car begins to slow down. As the vehicle passes from the open road into the gates of her estate, the landscape topology begins to funnel Orlando's selves into the darkened and settled pool of her liquid mind walled in by the "true" Orlando. Woolf writes:

> The whole of her darkened and settled, as when some foil whose addition makes the round and solidity of a surface is added to it, and the shallow becomes deep and the near distant; and all is contained as water is contained by the sides of a well. So she was now darkened, stilled, and become, with the addition of this Orlando, what is called, rightly or wrongly, a single self, a real self. And she fell silent. For it is probable that when people talk aloud, the selves (of which there may be more than two thousand) are conscious of disseverment, and are trying to communicate but when communication is established there is nothing more to be said.
>
> (O, 314)

Woolf has been walking us through the dissolution, emergence, and temporal organization of the subjectivity. In the passage above, it comes into its more limited resting "single self" stage. Woolf describes the process atmospherically and ecologically. The park that Orlando drives through to get to her house is dark and full of oak and beach trees that contain and funnel her along the road's gentle curve slowly downward. As the landscape changes, so does her "ecological self." Entering the dark park, Orlando becomes settled, deepened, stilled, distant, silent, and contained like a fluid that is dripping downward toward the pool of her geographical and psychic "home." Her selves are brought back together through her movement across the landscape. Now, Woolf says, there is no longer anything for them to communicate. They have all gathered into a single dark and calm fluid.

> Masterfully, swiftly, she drove up the curving drive between the elms and oaks through the falling turf of the park whose fall was so gentle that had it been water it would have spread the beach with a smooth green tide.
>
> (O, 314)

Woolf now describes Orlando's driving as "masterful" as the Captain-self takes control. The turf slopes gently downward like water spreading smoothly on a green beach. The road curves as it falls—just as Lucretius describes the fall and swerves of matter. Orlando drives through a fully saturated fluid atmosphere and feels her mind becoming similarly fluid, Woolf says.

> All this, the trees, deer, and turf, she observed with the greatest satisfaction as if her mind had become a fluid that flowed round things and enclosed them completely.
>
> (O, 314)

In other words, as the landscape becomes fluid and the road curves like a winding river, so Orlando's mind becomes fluid and flows around and through things wrapping around them completely. For Woolf, this is how synchronized subjects are born. Our subjective states are not separate from the world but wholly entangled. The mind is made of moving fluids pushed and pulled in various patterns like landscape topologies.

The Beauty of Movement

After her drive, Woolf writes that Orlando feels the intense beauty and significance in every single thing and trivial phrase. There is something about the movement of things that is absolutely beautiful to Orlando.

> "Morning, James," she said, "there're some things in the car. Will you bring 'em in?" words of no beauty, interest, or significance in themselves, it will be conceded, but now so plumped out with meaning that they fell like ripe nuts from a tree, and proved that when the shriveled skin of the ordinary is stuffed out with meaning it satisfies the senses amazingly. This was true indeed of

every movement and action now, usual though they were; so that to see Orlando change her skirt for a pair of whipcord breeches, and leather jacket, which she did in less than three minutes, was to be ravished with the beauty of movement as if Madame Lopokova were using her highest art.

(O, 315)

Here we can see Woolf's philosophy of saturation at work. On their own, Orlando's words have no meaning or beauty. Yet, as entangled performances woven from the vast web of swerving and falling matter from her drive, they are charged and plumped out with meaning and beauty. In other words, for Woolf the meaning and beauty of things are in their relations and context not in what they represent or signify. Things treated in isolation are dead abstractions, but as processes continuous with the kinetic topology of the landscape, season, and cosmos become saturated with *relational significance*. We tend to treat ordinary things like shriveled skins because we consider only their surface appearance as if they were isolated from their kinetic relations. This allows us to be more instrumental effect but at the cost of their beauty.

In her moment of being, Orlando's intensified sensations allow her to see this vast network more intensely and thus be deeply satisfied with even the smallest things. Each expresses the arabesque pattern of the whole in its unique way. Orlando's amplified sensations allow her to see that everything is "stuffed," "plumped," and "saturated" with deeply woven patterns. Each thing takes up and continues what came before such that "every movement and action" is a singular continuation of the whole of nature. Everything is movement and action. There is nothing static, still, or isolated in the world.

Even the simple act of changing clothes, Woolf writes, becomes akin to the highest art of the great "Bloomsbury ballerina" Lydia Lopokoval.[10] In this moment, beauty saturates motion because each movement tells something about the whole situation. In this way, Orlando enacts Woolf's most significant philosophical insight about moments of being: "The whole world is a work of art; [and] we are parts of the work of art" (MB, 72).

In moments of being, Woolf's characters see every single ordinary movement as deeply *interwoven* with every other. Woolf writes of Orlando:

Memory runs her needle in and out, up and down, hither and thither. We know not what comes next, or what follows after. Thus, the most ordinary movement in the world, such as sitting down at a table and pulling the inkstand towards one, may agitate a thousand odd, disconnected fragments, now bright, now dim, hanging and bobbing and dipping and flaunting, like the underlinen of a family of fourteen on a line in a gale of wind. Instead of being a single, downright, bluff piece of work of which no man need feel ashamed, our commonest deeds are set about with a fluttering and flickering of wings, a rising and falling of lights.

(O, 78–9)

Woolf's poetic image of reality here is as striking as it is clear: matter weaves itself in and out through tiny ordinary motions. What makes them so worthy of awe is the indeterminacy of their movement: the fact that we know not what comes next. The world is not a cold dead place because it is deeply indeterminate down to the finest events. The world's memory, Woolf suggests, is woven from motions and held together by thousands of threads that vibrate the seemingly disconnected fragments they hold together.

However, we often see the world as composed of discrete objects like laundry on a clothesline. But the clothes are all held together relationally and blown around unpredictably by the wind. The wind fills them, folds them, and circulates them. All our movements are entangled, woven, and continuously supported by the flickering wings of the wind and the shimmering of light. This is what makes them awe-inspiring in moments of being.

But Orlando's moment of being does not end here. She hears a clock strike four and is pulled back in. In the final part of this long moment, Woolf gives us a process philosophy of nature, gender, and sexuality. Let's see how.

Moment 12: Everything Was Partly Something Else

After Orlando returns home, she strolls freely through the rooms of her enormous house in a state of ecstasy. Her "master self" orders and contains her selves like rooms in her house and she enjoys it. But soon her moment of being returns and she walks to the nearby forest where Woolf says she becomes the "bride of nature." Let's look more closely at this incredible moment and its philosophical implications for understanding perception, nature, gender, and sexuality.

A Microscope Stuck to Her Eye

Woolf writes that, after sitting for a bit in her house, thinking about the past, Orlando walks out to the stables. There, suddenly, the stable clock strikes four o'clock, and like an "earthquake," Woolf says, the clock makes Orlando "quiver and tingle." In the "light" of this sonic explosion, "everything near her showed with extreme distinctness" (O, 320).

In other words, the *sound* of the clock produces, Woolf says, a synesthetic *light,* which amplifies Orlando's sensations. The sound makes every singularity of color and texture extremely *distinct*. For instance, Orlando notices the uniquely blue sheen on the body of a fly, the singular knot on a piece of wood by her foot, the twitch of the dog's ear, a creaking bough in the garden, and a sheep coughing in the park (O, 320). Suddenly, as is part of Woolf's moments of being, the world of tiny movements and affects weave themselves together like a frosty wave against Orlando's quivering body.

With an "alertness of movement," Orlando then goes into the garden with the kind of acute perception typically associated with hypnotic, psychedelic, or altered states of consciousness.[11] Woolf writes:

> Here the shadows of the plants were miraculously distinct. She noticed the separate grains of earth in the flower beds as if she had a microscope stuck to her eye. She saw the intricacy of the twigs of every tree. Each blade of grass was distinct and the markings of veins and petals.
>
> (O, 320–1)

For Woolf, these are some of the hidden patterns beneath the cotton wool that one sees in moments of being. They are also all fractal patterns. The shadows of plants have a branching fractal pattern because most plants do, as do the twigs of trees and the veins of leaves and flower petals. Even the grain-size distribution of soils has a fractal pattern.[12] In her moment of being, Orlando sees the common and typically unnoticed patterns woven into nature (Figures 2.14.1, 2.14.2, and 2.14.3).

Figure 2.14.1 shows the branching veins in leaves in which the "branching pattern" is iterated across larger and smaller scales.

Figure 2.14.2 shows a roughly inverse proportion of large, medium, and small rocks on a mountain trail. There are a few large rocks, more medium ones, and many small ones in a roughly inverse fractal proportion

Figure 2.14.3 shows fractal branching patterns across scales of large, medium, and small branches of a tree.

In particular, these are the patterns that allow Orlando to see how all the singular and distinct intricacies of things nest together with one another. They are fractally related. Typically, we can only see things microscopically when we focus all our attention with great effort on a single aspect of something. But when we do this we cannot see all the other microscopic singularities around it simultaneously. However, Orlando, in her moment of being, does just this because she see that all the singularities follow an imperfect fractal pattern that weaves them together.

This is such a strange philosophical insight about the nature of order and form. How can a pattern emerge from heterogeneous *singularities*? If things are radically singular, then how can they resemble a "pattern" of any kind? Orlando's experience is Woolf's answer to the age-old philosophical question of whether being is one or many. For Woolf, being is neither one nor many, but fractal singularities. Particular things are not parts of the whole because nature is constantly changing what it is. Each singularity is not a part but a dimension, iteration, or tendril of everything else. Like a hologram, each part contains the whole. If one breaks a hologram into pieces, each piece will show the entire picture. This is the sense in which there is no unity or "same" stuff of the universe.

There are only processes or ways that iterate in their own way what everything else is *doing*. Only irregular fractal patterns emerge from singularities, not perfect forms. The universe tends to spread out from hot to cold and fractal patterns tend to optimize how well heat is dissipated. This is why we tend to see these patterns everywhere and feel that they get at something about the nature of things.

Immanent Perception

Woolf says that all these hidden patterns draw Orlando's eye to the blacksmith's exposed dendritic-veined skin where a fingernail used to be. But the sight is too much to bear, and Orlando flickers her eyes—feeling

> Faint for a moment, but in that moment's darkness when her eyelids flickered, she was relieved of the pressure of the present. There was something strange in the shadow that the flicker of her eyes cast, something which (as anyone can test for himself by looking now at the sky), is always absent from the present—whence its terror, its nondescript character—something one trembles to pin through the body with a name and call beauty, for it has no body, is as a shadow and without substance or quality of its own, yet has the power to change whatever it adds itself to. This shadow now while she flickered her eye in her faintness in the carpenter's shop stole out, and attaching itself to the innumerable sights she had been receiving, composed them into something tolerable, comprehensible.
>
> (O, 321–2)

What is this strange "shadow" that Orlando sees in the brief darkness of her eye flickering that we can also see in the sky? This is surely a philosophical provocation to think something that has no discrete body, substance, or quality of its own. Something about it is beyond philosophical or literary description. For Woolf, this shadow is the immanent process of fractal ordering that runs through things but is not itself a discrete thing. It is what makes and modulates the hidden patterns beneath the cotton wool. It is the indeterminate relational fluctuations that shape the world into beautiful and comprehensible things. If we look at the bright sky, we will flicker our eyes in its bright immensity and in that moment feel our being part of the world of processes. With eyes open we tend to think and act as if we were separate from the world. We see relatively discrete things in normal perception, but we do not see the non-discrete becoming of those things. Woolf is suggesting, however, that we can feel this process in the flicker of our eyes.

In Woolf's philosophy, this experience is also terrible and impersonal because it means that there is always something hidden supporting and organizing us and everything around us that does not directly appear in our perceptual frame as a thing. This is why Woolf says Orlando senses something with no discrete body. Process and movement are *immanent* to reality with no qualities of their own. They are the material flux of qualities. But what is material reality without substance or quality? As matter changes, it not only transforms the things we see but it transforms what it is too. For Woolf, the things of the world are the ripples or waves in a vast ocean of shadowy material flux that comprises all waves but is not reducible to any single wave.

Orlando catches a glimpse or feeling of the process that she is part of without identifying any substance, qualities, or discreteness. For Woolf, the "shadow" of process "composes" and weaves together all the "innumerable" singularities that Orlando sees through her micro-perceptual vision. This deep ocean of flux holds together and makes comprehensible and tolerable all the fluctuations, waves, and ripples on the surface.

However, Woolf also says that Orlando does not see this shadow without being changed by her act of seeing. Orlando gives "a deep sigh of relief. … I can begin to live again … the little boat is climbing through the white arch of a thousand deaths. I am about to understand. …" (O, 322). Orlando feels reborn by her experience of process and sees the world as if for the first time. She sees that it is not preordered but made by an emergent and imbricated ordering. In other words, Orlando sees that things are like waves in water. She can then live riding her boat through the waves' white-capped arches.

Everything Was Partly Something Else

In Woolf's thought, moments of being like this are not revelations of hidden propositional truths that can be reproduced. Orlando, Woolf says was a "very indifferent witness to the truth of what was before her" (O, 322). For Woolf, there is no message or particular meaning of reality that is distinct from reality itself. This is why it is so ineffable. It is also why Woolf says that Orlando misrecognizes things in her moment of being. She mistakes sheep for cows and an old man called Smith for Jones. This is why moments of being are not directly useful for anything else. If anything, they make instrumental and representational recognition more difficult. And so, Woolf says, the shadow moved to the "back of her brain" and "into a pool where things dwell in darkness so deep that what they are we scarcely know" (O, 323).

For Woolf, this pool is hidden but not inactive. Orlando even wonders if it is the deepest source of passion, art, and religion. "Indeed, some say that all our most violent passions, and art and religion are the reflections which we see in the dark hollow at the back of the head when the visible world is obscured for the time" (O, 323). The pool is dark because the immanent processes of nature do not yield entirely to scientific prediction, rational control, or even artistic representation. Something always escapes and thus provokes the ongoing search of various ways of knowing.

Furthermore, since this dark shadow of relational process is immanent to all things it tends to make everything look like everything else. This why Woolf writes that the present is partly past, things are partly other things, life is partly death, and truth mixes with falsity—and so on. Her philosophy is one of mixture, play, and experiment. As Orlando walks up a nearby hill, Woolf writes:

> The ferny path up the hill along which she was walking became not entirely a path, but partly the Serpentine; the hawthorn bushes were partly ladies and gentlemen sitting with card cases and gold-mounted canes; the sheep were partly tall Mayfair houses; everything was partly something else, and each gained an odd moving power from this union of itself and something not itself so that with this mixture of truth and falsehood her mind became like a forest in which things moved; lights and shadows changed, and one thing became another.
>
> (O, 323)

For Woolf, this is not just because Orlando's memory mixes with her perceptions. Her memory is triggered by the world because the past world is related immanently to the present one. Memory is only possible because the world can relate to itself in hidden patterns and orders. Our memories are so metamorphic and mixed because the world is. Our memories are not incomplete mental representations but move and work the same way the world does, by mixture and metamorphosis. For Woolf, Orlando's thoughts are neither true nor false because things in the world are neither true nor false. If the world is a changing process, then there is no such thing as a perfect form or fixed identity. No freeze-frame word or image will truly capture what is happening. In other words, for Woolf, thought and knowledge are more like metamorphoses than representations.

What the Land Has Given Me

When Orlando reaches the oak tree at the top of the hill, she throws herself on the forest ground. Her mind, Woolf writes, becomes like the forest, filled with the power of motion. Orlando feels her body and life not as living on the Earth but as an extension or expression of the Earth itself. Her brain continues the dendritic paths of the forest in her dendritic nervous system.

> Flinging herself on the ground, she felt the bones of the tree running out like ribs from a spine this way and that beneath her. She liked to think that she was riding the back of the world.
>
> (O, 324)

Many years ago, Orlando was first inspired to write her famous poem under an oak tree. Now she wants to reciprocate and give back to the tree something of what it gave to her. The paper of her poem is made of tree pulp, and the thoughts inside are about trees. And so, Orlando buries her book into the ground near the tree so that the tree will eat the book.

This is no mere symbolic gesture for Woolf, as we will see. Orlando buries the book so that the book will materially become the tree and the tree will become the book. Here, Woolf expands our idea of how books work. They are not just filled with symbols of human cultural meaning. Books are read by humans but also rely ecologically on forests and trees. By giving her book of poetry to a tree, Orlando is doing in her own way what the trees did for her. It is a kind of interspecies communication, but without representation. It also reveals Woolf's philosophy to be one of material mixture and metamorphosis and not one of mere human interiority.

Woolf even writes that Orlando planned to say a symbolic speech as she buried her book, "'I bury this as a tribute' she was going to have said, 'a return to the land of what the land has given me,'" but Lord! once one began mouthing words aloud, how silly they sounded" (O, 324). Again, for Woolf symbolism is ridiculous because it is not how the world works. Symbolism is a post hoc attempt to represent the nature of things. But symbolism is rather an emergent feature of nonsymbolic processes. This is a key consequence of Woolf's philosophy of moments of being: we cannot capture reality with philosophy, art, or words.

I Am Nature's Bride

For Woolf, the symbolic tribute and fame that Orlando considered offering sound so silly because they are so out of step with and irrelevant to the reality of the moment of being that inspired the poetic act. "What could have been more secret, she thought, more slow, and like the intercourse of lovers, than the stammering answer she had made all these years to the old crooning song of the woods" (O, 325). In this line, there is a key philosophical insight about the nature of art and sexuality. Woolf explicitly compares Orlando's stammering back to the song of the woods as a form of *sexual intercourse*. What are we to make of this? It completely changes the entire meaning of sex and sexuality to think of Orlando as having an explicitly sexual relationship with the forest and the oak tree in particular.

Of course, Orlando's gender and sexuality, as well as Woolf's, is the topic of much commentary.[13] However, commentators typically take an anthropocentric approach to understanding Woolf's idea of "androgyny." Here, however, we have a distinctly non-human description of art and sexuality. Orlando's sexuality, for Woolf, is just as much non-human as human. "I am nature's bride," Orlando says, "giving herself in rapture to the cold embraces of the grass as she lay folded in her cloak in the hollow by the pool" (O, 248). It is arbitrary and speciesist to define sex as something only discrete living beings can do with one another. Intercourse happens both reproductively and nonreproductively across species all the time.

For instance, ecosystems rely on trans-species sexuality like bees and flowers not only for biological reproduction among same-species relationships but for cross-species material reproduction. Think of the complex web of insect, plant, flower, wind, and animal movements that are required to sustain any ecosystem. Every forest overflows with sex in the broad sense of sensual acts of material production and reproduction. Given this, the real historical oddity is that humans think of their sex as separate from the larger web of non-human sexual relationships.

All sex is already multiple and composed of a vast web of material processes. Living bodies are filled with nonsexed cellular reproduction, trans-cellular viral reproduction, and traversed by all kinds of environmental processes (wind, water, soil fungi, etc.) needed for living bodies to persist and reproduce themselves. We are all born into queer ecologies with a thousand tiny sexes and nonsexes. Woolf's description of Orlando's intercourse with the earth suggests a much broader notion of sex that is not necessarily genital or even human.

Orlando, Woolf says, mounts the bones of the Earth and rides them. What we call the human intercourse of lovers is only a subset of a much more general material sexuality that traverses living and nonliving beings. Orlando is, therefore, for Woolf, not only a trans-sexual and trans-historical character. She is also a trans-species ecosexual character who feels passionately and sexually drawn to the Earth as much as, and perhaps more than, to humans.

Even when Orlando was a young man, he would fling himself on the Earth with "a passion in his movements which deserves the word." He would do, Woolf says, so with a "heart that seemed filled with spiced and amorous gales every evening about this time when he walked out …. as if all the fertility and amorous activity of a summer's evening were woven web-like about his body" (O, 19). The fertility of the dragonflies, swallows, and the whole summer forest ecosystem wrap around Orlando's body and mix with his own sexuality.

As Orlando lays by her oak tree on the hills she looks over each singularity of the whole landscape and is struck by a series of bell sounds similar to Mrs. Dalloway. Orlando loses count.[14] It is nighttime. But instead of closing her eyes, Orlando can see all the reflections from the "dark pool of the mind" (O, 327). The images surface and mix with the night landscape (the mountains, the goats, the memories). The present sensations all intertwine together into a vast darkened kinesthetic tapestry of sounds, sights, feelings, memories, and thoughts. Woolf writes:

> "Ecstasy!" she cried, "ecstasy!" And then the wind sank, the waters grew calm; and she saw the waves rippling peacefully in the moonlight.
>
> (O, 327)

Moments of being, for Woolf, do not abolish the self but rather show how the self is woven into the rest of the world. Orlando's ecstasy is not transcendent but ecological and dynamic as the literal meaning of the Greek word *ekstasis* as "out" of "stasis" suggests. As the wind and water move so Orlando feels their movement inside herself. When the world changes, Orlando's hypersensitive body and mind ripple and change with it.

After her intense moment of ecstasy, the wind calms and so does Orlando. She lays by the tree, looks up, and bares her breasts to the moon as "her pearls burnt like a phosphorescent flare in the darkness" (O, 329). Her moment of being ends as the book ends with the sound of a clock striking midnight and thus concluding the first day of the present.

By extending a main character's moment of being to over 7,500 words in *Orlando* Woolf gets closer to her next big idea to write *The Waves* as one long ebb and flow of moments of being. But another significant novelty of her next novel, *The Waves* was to combine the idea of one long modulated moment with her earlier attempts to describe how a moment of being could be shared simultaneously by several characters. So, before looking more closely at *The Waves,* I would like to briefly return in the next moment to *Mrs. Dalloway* where Woolf attempted her first "collective" moment of being.

Collective Moments

Moment 13: The World Wavered

The final kind of moment of being I want to look at in this book is what I call a "collective" moment of being. Woolf's first attempt to write this kind of moment first happens in *Mrs. Dalloway* when a mysterious royal motorcar breaks down on Bond Street while Clarissa is buying flowers for her party that night. Woolf describes how all the people on the street are temporarily shocked out of their daily routines by the political and historical character of the royal car after the First World War. Woolf does not go into great detail of how the individual people are affected in this moment, but she is clear that everyone is sharing some mysterious feeling of social, historical, geological, and affective interrelation.

In her later work, though, Woolf gets much more interested in how collective moments of being emerge and work. Her discovery from the Bond Street moment was that shared moments can be invoked by feelings of political and cultural becoming. As the moment on Bond Street progresses, it moves beyond narrow feelings of nationalism and toward more geological feelings of deeper interrelation. Woolf also experimented successfully with collective moments of being in her essay "A Moment: Summer's Night," and her novel *The Waves*. In the next three moments of being, I want to show some of the most significant philosophical implications that emerge in Woolf's uniquely collective "moments of becoming," including her unique theory of group affects and collective knowledge.

*

Mystery Had Brushed Them with Her Wing

As Mrs. Dalloway is gathering flowers for her party from the florist's shop on Bond Street, she hears an explosion in the street. Woolf writes that a "shock" rippled and wavered through everyone around and Mrs. Dalloway jumps when she hears the loud sound. "Passers-by who, of course, stopped and stared, had just time to see a face of the very greatest importance against the dove-grey upholstery, before a male hand drew the blind and there was nothing to be seen except a square of dove grey" (MD, 14). Slowly, Woolf writes, the whole street was transformed and affected in a "profound" way.

> Rumours were at once in circulation from the middle of Bond Street to Oxford Street on one side, to Atkinson's scent shop on the other, passing invisibly, inaudibly, like a cloud, swift, veil-like upon hills, falling indeed with something of a cloud's sudden sobriety and stillness upon faces which a second before had been utterly disorderly. But now mystery had brushed them with her wing; they had heard the voice of authority; the spirit of religion was abroad with her eyes bandaged tight and her lips gaping wide. But nobody knew whose face had been seen. Was it the Prince of Wales's, the Queen's, the Prime Minister's? Whose face was it? Nobody knew.
>
> (MD, 14)

What is so philosophically interesting here is the way Woolf describes *how* affects travel through the world. She describes in exquisite detail how our feelings and associative thoughts, although invisible to our eye, move and spread out in the world. The scene is also a mediation on how order and affective resonance emerge contextually from relative disorder. For instance, Woolf says that sounds and gestures (the rumors) began to "circulate" "inaudibly" and "invisibly" like a "cloud" or a "veil" upon hills.

The cloud, as we have seen in earlier moments, is a common hidden fractal pattern Woolf uses to describe how things work beneath the cotton wool of daily perception. Earlier in the novel, Woolf wrote that Mrs. Dalloway felt like she was "slicing through the world invisibly" and living between things like a "mist" held by trees (MD, 9). For Woolf, clouds are material structures with a strange ability to dampen the sound of everything they envelop. When clouds settle as fog, as they often do in London, they appear everywhere and nowhere at once. They create an atmosphere or weather that affects everyone around like a "luminous halo, a semi-transparent envelope" (E4, 160). Clouds also lack defined borders and are not discrete empirical objects. The events of the world are not only like clouds, but clouds themselves are also events. This is the sense in which Woolf is suggesting that human and natural events share a common material structure: the metastable cloud formation. Clouds emerge from relatively chaotic water vapor into quasi-forms with atmospheric power. Something similar happens in human events that gather individuals into a temporary collective or shared state of attention.

The loud noise on Bond Street is an empirical sensation, but on its own there is no reason it should mechanically cause a collective moment of being. What is philosophically interesting here is how Woolf describes how the nonempirical movement of shared affects. Passers-by do not merely hear a sound or see a motorcar; they suddenly *feel* themselves part of a much larger impersonal world-historical process. They suddenly realize that their motions are ripples on the crest of a much larger wave. All their individual preferences and preoccupations, buying flowers, drinking soda, and so on, are all suddenly and collectively gathered together or felt in what Woolf calls a "luminous halo," "envelope," "mist," "cloud," or "veil," of a field of "circulation."

In other words, for Woolf, the event is "invisible" and "inaudible" not because it is transcendent or immaterial but because it occurs as an *atmospheric process* that resists discrete conceptualization, mechanical explanation, and even conscious sensation. It is a process that slips through our fingers when we try and grab it. Moments of being include everything happening around and are highly contextual. For instance, in the cloud of the event, Woolf says everyone is *brushed* with mystery—"as a plant on the river-bed feels the shock of a passing oar and shivers: so she rocked: so she shivered" (MD, 30).

It's philosophically significant that Woolf says that the face of authority in the car does not appear directly. Instead, something like an affective shift emerges and starts to spread like clouds gather and spread with a source. God, the nation, and the state do not appear to our eyes because they are not things. They are impersonal collective habits that move through our bodies and brains and that can spread affectively. We do not see them but we help reproduce them in thousands of tiny ways in daily life.

Woolf does not merely reject God, nation, and state, just as Marx did not. In *Mrs. Dalloway*, Woolf is interested in what is happening to us when these things happen *through* us. What is it that we have already been caught up in without our directly knowing, intending, or agreeing consciously to? This, and not the empirical face in the car, is the source of the horror, suspense, and curiosity Woolf is interested in this shared moment of being.

The World Wavered and Quivered

This is also why moments of being can feel so involuntary and even frightening. Woolf writes:

> Everything had come to a standstill. The throb of the motor engines sounded like a pulse irregularly drumming through an entire body. The sun became extraordinarily hot because the motor car had stopped outside Mulberry's shop window; old ladies on the tops of omnibuses spread their black parasols; here a green, here a red parasol opened with a little pop. Mrs. Dalloway,

coming to the window with her arms full of sweet peas, looked out with her little pink face pursed in enquiry. Every one looked at the motor car. Septimus looked. Boys on bicycles sprang off. Traffic accumulated.

(MD, 14–5)

In the moment of being, for Woolf, the whole street begins to work like a single body. There is both a feeling of interrelation and indeterminacy.

And there the motorcar stood, with drawn blinds, and upon them a curious pattern like a tree, Septimus thought, and this gradual drawing together of everything to one centre before his eyes, as if some horror had come almost to the surface and was about to burst into flames, terrified him. The world wavered and quivered and threatened to burst into flames. It is I who am blocking the way, he thought. Was he not being looked at and pointed at; was he not weighted there, rooted to the pavement, for a purpose? But for what purpose?

(MD, 15)

Here again, Woolf evokes another one of her most common fractal patterns beneath the cotton wool, the tree. She does not say, however, that there was a tree on the drawn blinds, but that Septimus thinks the pattern he is seeing is "like a tree." This might be caused by branching crack patterns in older blinds or a woven design with branching patterns like a tree. Either way, the discovery of this pattern at the center of his vision suggests that something beneath the surface of the daily cotton wool reality was about to burst forth into flames.

For Woolf, this is partly, not only, because moments of being carry with them a hidden pattern but also because the patterns are indeterminate and unpredictable. When one sees how daily life is woven, it looks very different than the daily life that it weaves. The nonlinear structure of material emergence can be surprisingly beautiful and terrible at the same time. The horror of the moment is that some deeper process will entirely overthrow our collective conventions and social safeties.

In Woolf's philosophy, the "reality behind appearances" is not beyond appearances but behind them or beneath them supporting them like the reverse side of a piece of embroidery. The motorcar looks stable, solid, and protective like the nation-state, but suddenly the car gets a flat tire on Bond Street like the sound of an exploding bomb. The unstable reality beneath solid appearances comes through. The English state must act as if it is in control, but even the slightest contingencies and world war can bring it to its knees. Empire floats on a breeze and falters on a nail in the road.

In Woolf's description, Septimus, who stands watching this event, feels his actions no longer as his own but as regions or dimensions of a whole with an unknown purpose beyond his own. However, it is not only Septimus that is shell-shocked by the war. The world itself quivers as if it could all fall apart and burst back into war. There is no fundamental stability. The war has shattered the pretense of imperial stasis. Now, Woolf writes, there is only the pulse and throb and spasms of a giant global beast. This is the horror felt by Septimus when he says, "I will kill myself" to escape the danger of living even one day, as Mrs. Dalloway says.

When London Is a Grass-Grown Path

Now, Woolf says, as the car starts driving down Bond Street, the people around feel themselves part of a deeper history.

> The motor car with its blinds drawn and an air of inscrutable reserve proceeded towards Piccadilly, still gazed at, still ruffling the faces on both sides of the street with the same dark breath of veneration whether for Queen, Prince, or Prime Minister nobody knew. The face itself had been seen only once by three people for a few seconds. Even the sex was now in dispute. But there could be no doubt that greatness was seated within; greatness was passing, hidden, down Bond Street, removed only by a hand's-breadth from ordinary people who might now, for the first and last time, be within speaking distance of the majesty of England, of the enduring symbol of the state which will be known to curious antiquaries, sifting the ruins of time, when London is a grass-grown path and all those hurrying along the pavement this Wednesday morning are but bones with a few wedding rings mixed up in their dust and the gold stoppings of innumerable decayed teeth. The face in the motor car will then be known.
>
> (MD, 16)

Woolf describes the car's movement in fluid dynamic terms as an "air" or "dark breath" that "ruffles" people's faces on the street. This image of fluid history is consistent with her philosophy of time as a river discussed in previous moments. Over time, the contents in the river of history settle to the bottom and form a geological stratum. Woolf shifts her description in this moment of being to a collective future anterior, or "what will have been." Passers-by, in this moment, suddenly imagine what this moment will have meant to archeologists in the distant future. In this way, their experience of space and time dilates out into the impersonal and interconnected geological movement of material history.

The river of history will have ground the whole population of London to inconsequential dust. The daily tasks of the people on Bond Street, including buying and selling flowers, are suddenly reduced to the tiniest ripple in the enormous wave of global capitalism, imperialism, and geology. These passers-by will have been the blood and bones that made up the wave of the empire before it crashed on the shores of some distant time.

The passers-by feel that this moment will have been the only one where they came close to anything that a future antiquarian might record in the history books. Philosophically, the dilation of space and time puts human cultural activities and knowledges, including philosophy, in their broader and much more ephemeral material context. Woolf then says:

> The car had gone, but it had left a slight ripple which flowed through glove shops and hat shops and tailors' shops on both sides of Bond Street. For thirty seconds all heads were inclined the same way—to the window.
>
> (MD, 17)

Here, for Woolf, affects spread out like ripples diffracting with people and things in the world. By holding the gaze of so many different people a kind of affective resonance among them starts to happen. Even after the car passes, the affective sensations linger in the bodies of passers-by. They still feel wrapped in an affective mist. Everything that seemed so solid feels much less so after the flat tire and after the war. In time, London will be grass and the earth will flux and fold like waves. Everything is fluid on the geological scale. Woolf says:

> Choosing a pair of gloves—should they be to the elbow or above it, lemon or pale grey?—ladies stopped; when the sentence was finished something had happened. Something so trifling in single instances that no mathematical instrument, though capable of transmitting shocks in China, could register the vibration; yet in its fulness rather formidable and in its common appeal emotional; for in all the hat shops and tailors' shops strangers looked at each other and thought of the dead; of the flag; of Empire. In a public house in a back street a Colonial insulted the House of Windsor which led to words, broken beer glasses, and a general shindy, which echoed strangely across the way in the ears of girls buying white underlinen threaded with pure white ribbon for their weddings. For the surface agitation of the passing car as it sunk grazed something very profound.
>
> (MD, 18)

Like all moments of being in Woolf's philosophy, the transformation produced by the royal motor car is not something strictly empirical. It is something just below the level of normal perception, like a tiny vibration whose cumulative effects we feel but we are not sure from where. This collective moment of being on Bond Street is not just a widening of the senses but a widening of a feeling of human society as it lives and dies on the geological and unconscious scale.

Woolf describes the transmission of affects here in distinctly kinetic terms. Affects are "vibrations" or frequencies of light and sound running through the passers-by. Just as the apparent solidity of a misty cloud emerges slowly through the accumulation of unseen and unheard vapors, so the "trifling single instances" of everything affected by the passing motor car "transmitted shocks" or "vibrations" of "emotion" that produced a continuous transformation of the whole of reality. Everyone feels it simultaneously.

Shocks of Emotion

Woolf also frequently uses the phrase "transmit shocks of emotion" to describe her philosophy of moments of being (E3, 220; D3, 180; E5, 140; MB, 72). For her, these shocks are not immaterial, metaphysical, or metaphorical. Woolf uses the philosophical term "shocks" to describe a real material kinetic change in the world that happens without us being able to locate a single cause. For instance, as the motor car moves along the street in this singular context, it literally agitates the surface of reality. People stop what they are doing and feel something. This is not because of what the motorcar represents symbolically but because of how everyone moves together in response to its flat tire, drawn shade, and to one another's responses. The motor car does not just make people think of the empire as an idea. It makes them move, live, and feel the imbrication of singularities in the whole movement of the world on Bond Street as materially caught up in the larger projects of the war, the nation, religion, empire, and geology.

The empire moves because the people of Bond Street and London also move and circulate it every day. Future historians will not remember the lives and deaths of these passers-by with their little invisible vibrations, and shivers of feeling. Woolf, though, wishes to record the underside of reality in these patterns of collective affect. The moment of being shows the passers-by how their movements and affects together are weaving the world into the wave of a whip. The people and even the soda straws, Woolf says, seem to echo the moment in a "single voice expanded and made sonorous by the might of a whole cathedral" (MD, 18). This collective moment of being ends when the motor car turns down St. James street and "sinks" below the surface of reality to back to its profound depths. Life returns to "normal."

In the next moment, I would like to look at another short collective moment of being, this time more intimate among friends and less political, before moving on to the longer collective moment in *The Waves*.

Moment 14: "The Moment: Summer's Night"

Woolf wrote "The Moment: Summer's Night" as a fictional essay perhaps to experiment with a collective moment of being. She wrote in her diary in April 1938, "Last night I began making up again: Summers night: a complete whole: that's my idea." This idea was the beginning of what became Woolf's next book, *Between the Acts* (E, 514). This short piece is an attempt at writing a collective moment of being. I want to show here the two kinds of movements that sustain this moment and the philosophical implications of them. I will also include in brackets some early versions of the text relevant to our interpretation.

In this moment, Woolf shows how individuals can dissolve entirely into the larger turbulent flows of nature and one another and how they can fall apart into individuals again. Here, Woolf describes in detail how the metastable balance can shift between these two tendencies in a small group of people sitting outside on a summer evening. She describes how nature and humans flow together and form a knot of collective consciousness at a white table in a dark countryside. Here, Woolf also provides a philosophical description of collective subjectivity.

People Grew More Indistinct

Woolf begins her short essay with no introduction or narrative. She describes characters that are anonymous and relatively indistinct. She does not describe fixed forms but only indistinct shapes. It is also worth noting that this moment occurs in the evening like many of Woolf's moments of being. As the light fades, Woolf describes how the discreteness and individuality of the people sitting around the white table dissolve. She writes how the white table surrounded by the darkening forest seems to draw the characters together. Their subjective states begin to dissolve and merge together based on the space and color of the table. Woolf writes:

> The night was falling so that the table in the garden among the trees grew whiter and whiter; and the people round it more indistinct. An owl, blunt, obsolete looking, heavy weighted, crossed the fading sky with a black spot between its claws.
>
> (E6, 509)

Perhaps Woolf is making a jab here at philosophical knowledge, often represented with the owl of Minerva, the goddess of wisdom. To Woolf, the owl is obsolete-looking and heavily weighted compared to the light of the table that gathers people to the more "irrational" moment of being.

> The trees murmured. An aeroplane hummed like a piece of plucked wire. There was also, on the roads, the distant explosion of a motor cycle, shooting further and further away down the road.
>
> (E6, 509)

Now, Woolf begins to describe how the moment of being brings the sonic background into the foreground. The tiny murmuring of wind through trees and distant hum of an airplane become audible as the group's sensations are amplified. As they see things less distinctly in the dim light, they hear them more acutely. Woolf writes:

> Yet what composed the present moment? If you are young, the future lies upon the present, like a piece of glass, making it tremble and quiver. If you are old, the past lies upon the present, like a thick glass, making it waver, distorting it. All the same, everybody believes that the present is something, [here in this garden, seeking] seeks out the different elements in this situation in order to compose the truth of it, the whole of it.
>
> (E6, 509)

This is an important philosophical question about the nature of temporality and the search for the whole of a moment unbroken into discrete people and things. For Woolf, the truth of the situation is not in its pieces but in its interrelated whole. However, the way we know it does not seem to yield to merely passive or merely active knowledge. Woolf is explicit here and in her autobiography that she is active in making the whole but also passive in allowing it to work through her. Pure passivity led to her feeling attacked by the world and pure activity led to her trying to represent it in words or concepts. The truth is not something that can be entirely composed, but is shaped by the performance of the process of composition itself. The philosophical question then, for Woolf, is: what is it that makes these moments happen sometimes and not others? Is there some situation that prepares or opens one to having them?

The Surface of the Body Is Opened

With this in mind, Woolf begins to describe as best she can all the sensuous processes that run through the world in this summer moment. She writes:

> To begin with: it is largely composed of visual and of sense impressions. The day was very hot. After heat, the surface of the body is opened [extremely sensitive] as if all the pores were open and everything lay exposed, not sealed and contracted, as in cold weather. The air wafts cold on the skin under one's clothes. The soles of the feet expand in slippers after walking on hard roads. Then the sense of the light sinking back into darkness seems to be gently putting out with a damp sponge the colour in one's own eyes [One becomes aware that we are being all of us moved round the sun]. Then the leaves shiver now and again as if a ripple of irresistible sensation ran through them, as a horse suddenly ripples its skin.
>
> (E6, 510)

Knowledge, for Woolf, is not the abstraction of facts about the world formed into propositions. Prior to the generation of philosophical concepts and distinctions, there is a pre-philosophical situation that exposes us to the world in a unique way. We feel it in moments of being. It is everything that goes into our being in that situation, but it is also what we often forget or lose when we try to represent or conceptualize it. In the garden, at the same time as the heat opens our pores to the world, the dimming light reminds us that we are all moving around the sun. Synesthesia connects our bodies and minds to the world and to one another. Heat and light spread through leaves, horse skin, and human bodies on their path toward dissipation. In Woolf's description, each body is a relay in the movement of the world.

> But this moment is also composed of a sense that the legs of the chair are sinking through to the centre of the earth, passing through the rich garden earth; they seem weighted down. Then, the sky loses its colour perceptibly; and a star here and there makes a point of light. Then changes, unseen in the day, coming in succession seem to make an order evident. One becomes aware that we are spectators and also passive participants in a pageant. And as nothing can interfere with the order, we have nothing to do but accept; and watch.
>
> (E6, 510)

In moments of being, Woolf's characters, such as Septimus, often feel weighted down at the same time as they feel an amplification of movement. As their brains enter an altered state of noninstrumental activity, doing things becomes difficult, while feeling everything becomes easier. One's body feels exposed to the cosmos and the earth and weighed down by being such a small part of such vast processes. The emergence of stars and constellations reveals the patterns beneath the cotton wool of the daylight. Woolf says that "one becomes aware" of these things. This is philosophically interesting because the impersonal singular pronoun "one" suggests the fraying of an individual self and its absorption into the pageant of the universe. One is neither this nor that, neither he nor she.

Woolf also stresses that the visible order we see emerges from unseen "changes." These changes are the moving processes and patterns beneath the cotton wool discussed throughout this book. Here, order is an emergent property of process and change.

A Knot of Consciousness

Next, Woolf describes how the human bodies around the table are part of this emergent order. For Woolf, human consciousness is a "knot" or a pleat in the flow of matter. In *The Years*, she writes that "Perhaps there's 'I' at the middle of it, she thought; a knot" (Y, 366–7). Our self is not separate from the world but rather a "knot" in the world. As such, it can be knotted together with others. She continues:

> But that is the wider circumference of the moment. Here in the centre is a knot of consciousness; a nucleus divided up into four heads, eight legs, eight arms, and four separate bodies. They are not subject to the law of the sun and the owl and the lamp. They resist it. For sometimes a hand rests on the table; sometimes a leg is thrown over a leg. Now the moment becomes shot with the extraordinary arrow which people let fly from their mouths—when they speak.
>
> (E6, 510)

For Woolf, subjectivity can be shared in moments of becoming because people are not really entirely separate from one another to begin with. Rather, Woolf describes them "knotted" together; neither fully identical nor fully separate. Woolf imagines the table as the nucleus of a cell with human bodies as appendages. Humans are distinct from one another in the sense that they are different appendages of a common situation. The sun sets, the owl flies, but the little limbs keep moving around the table with one another.

Woolf then describes how her materialist theory of language works in this context. Words are not representations of the world but little arrows that fly and affect the world.

Woolf writes that "Words let fall this seed … now hit the mind with a wad, then explode like a scent suffusing the whole dome of the mind with its incense, flavour; let fall, from their ambiguous envelope." This is a rich description of language worth unpacking. Words, for Woolf, are like matter for Lucretius, they are seeds or sprouts. They are active and creative with a life of their own. Since they are material, they hit our minds and explode creating a synesthesia of associations in our brains and bodies. Their affects are not one-to-one correspondences with their "meanings" but are more like scents that spread out or flavors that diffuse across the palate. For Woolf, words are less like discrete objects than like envelopes of affect. Words can be just as vague as smoke. In another Lucretian turn of phrase, Woolf says that words make "the moment rock with laughter."[1]

> All this shoots through the moment, makes it quiver with malice and amusement; and the sense of watching and comparing; and the quiver meets the shore, when the owl flies out, and puts a stop to this judging, this overseeing, and with our wings spread, we too fly, take wing, with the owl, over the earth and survey the quietude of what sleeps, folded, slumbering, arm stretching in the vast dark and sucking its thumb too; the amorous and the innocent; and a sigh goes up.
>
> (E6, 511)

Woolf treats words as material waves with envelopes of smell, sound, and taste that make the moment quiver. For her, the moment is like a fractal wave that wraps up all the people and affects in the garden and crashes on the shore. For Woolf, moments of being are not moments of judgment. From the wider perspective of the earth, no word or person is better or worse than another. There is no fixed point in the universe from which to judge it. This is why Woolf says that the people around the table take flight and become part of the earth's processes.

> Could we not fly too, with broad wings and with softness; and be all one wing; all embracing, all gathering, and these boundaries, these pryings over hedges into hidden compartments of different colours be all swept into one colour by the brush of the wing; and so visit in splendour, augustly, peaks; and there lie exposed, bare, on the spine, high up, to the cold light of the moon rising, and when the moon rises, single, solitary, behold her, one, eminent over us?
>
> (E6, 511)

In their collective moment of being, the four people feel interwoven and interrelated like the imbricated and fractal feathers of a single bird wing. Their bodies do not merge into a single unity, but rather into a pied and pleated "unity" of a wing. This is an important feature of Woolf's philosophy. Reality is not one or many but fractal and interlaced like feathers. Singularities are neither identical nor different but rather iterations of a continual process of metamorphosis. For Woolf, each person is a fold or "hidden compartment" of the other. Inside and outside, self and other, are not opposites but enfolded regions in a "winged unity."

Although the four people are sitting at a table, Woolf says they feel part of a process that brings them to a "peak" of sensation as the moon rises above them. But the moon is not a static unity. Since ancient times, the moon has been viewed as a shape-shifting "unity." In other words, Woolf highlights the moon here, because it is a "one" of pure metamorphosis. The figures at the table are not united in a substance or god but in a changing process. Woolf writes:

> Issuing from a white arm, a long shape, lying back, in a film of black and white, under the tree, which, down sweeping, seems a part of that curving, that flowing, the voice, with its ridicule and its sense, reveals to the shaken terrier its own insignificance. No longer part of the snow; no part of the mountain; not in the least venerable to other human beings; but ridiculous; a little accident; a thing to be laughed at; discriminated out; seen clearly cut out, sneezing, sneezing, judged and compared. Thus into the moment steals self-assertion; ah, the sneeze again; the desire to sneeze with conviction; masterfully; making oneself heard; felt; if not pitied, then somebody of importance; perhaps to break away and go.
>
> (E6, 511)

For Woolf, each body may be collective but it is also distinct in the moment of being. When one body begins to sneeze, she says, it emphasizes its distinctness from the vague shapes that curve and flow continuously with the nearby tree. A body can be subject to unpredictable shaking like Lucretius' swerving matter. A body can be laughed at. But the sneezer sneezes with conviction, Woolf says, and affirms their place in the pageant of nature. However, they feel their passivity as an *active passivity*, just as Woolf says she was able to "blunt the sledge-hammer force of the blow" of her moments with an explanation (MB, 72). She feels her agency as part of the agency of nature moving through her.

The Moment Runs Like Quicksilver

Woolf asks, should the sneezing body leave the table and leave the collective moment? "But no; the other shape has sent from its arrow another fine binding thread" (E6, 511). This is an interesting materialist theory of language. For Woolf, words are threads that weave the moment of being together. Words do not signify anything but have a material meaning as actions, arrows, or threads that hold situations together or apart. They help make the moment "a complete whole" (E6, 514).

Within this woven whole, Woolf says that one of the figures at the table

> isolates cases from the mists of hugeness, sees what is there all the more definitely; refuses to be bamboozled; yet in this definite discrimination shows some amplitude. That is why the moment becomes harder, is intensified, diminished, begins to be stained by some expressed personal juice; with the desire to be loved, to be held close to the other shape; to put off the veil of darkness and see burning eyes.
>
> (E6, 512)

This is a wonderful account of how meaning-making works in Woolf's materialist philosophy. For Woolf, definite objects are cases isolated from the mists of interconnection. Words, meaning, and order do not precede the mist of the world but emerge and are woven from it. This means that moments of being can become solid and hardened and diminished the more one makes "definite discriminations" in them. Individual desires can emerge from the moment to see other individuals as discrete "burning eyes."

Then, the collective moment can unravel. Woolf writes, "The moment runs like quicksilver on a sloping board into the cottage parlour" (E6, 512). Just like that, the bodily shapes leave the dark table outside and go inside the parlor. There, the figures around the table hear a scene of rural domestic abuse and kids screaming. But, Woolf says, another match is lit in the dark, and their attention is dissolved into the dark again.

> The trees are growing heavier, blacker; no order is perceptible; there is no sequence in these cries, these movements; they come from no bodies; they are cries to the left and to the right. Nothing can be seen. We can only see ourselves as outlines, cadaverous, sculpturesque. And it is more difficult for the voice to carry through this dark. The dark has stripped the fledge from the arrow—the vibrations that rise red shiver as it passes through us.
>
> (E6, 512)

As things get darker, the figures feel that they will be swept into the void and be completely consumed. And so, Woolf says, there is a movement to go inside from the parlor. And yet at the same time, there is a desire to throw oneself into the darkness of the void rather than return to the relative discreteness of the individual self that the parlor lightning illuminates.

> Then comes the terror, the exultation; the power to rush out alone; unnoticed, to be consumed; to be swept away to become a rider on the random wind; the tossing wind; the trampling and neighing wind; the horse with the blown-back mane; the tumbling, the foraging; he who gallops for ever, now

hither traveling, indifferent; to be part of the eyeless dark, to be rippling and streaming, to feel the glory run molten up the spine, down the limbs, making the eyes glow, burning, bright, and penetrate the buffeting waves of the wind.

(E6, 513)

Right before the moment ends, Woolf says it reaches its peak of fluid intensity. The collective moment of being exists as a middle ground between discrete individuals and the total abolition of the individual. The moment of being is held together by threads but only for a limited time in the face of a world of rippling streams. If dissolution pushes too far, one overspills the moment and is lost entirely into the world.

In other words, for Woolf, the collective moment of being is like an eddy in a river. It is fragile. Winds and streams pummel the moment but it can be held together by threads. The bodies and minds of the figures, Woolf says, are like knots in the same fluid surface of the world. Nothing guarantees the moment, but nothing forbids it either. It is something that has to be held together. As the collective moment comes to an end, Woolf says, the shapes walk back to their houses, and they become circumscribed individuals again. The world looks like discrete objects again.

> "Everything's sopping wet. It's the dew off the grass. Time to go in." And then one shape heaves and surges and rises, and we pass, trailing coats, down the path towards the lighted windows, the dim glow behind the branches, and so enter the door, and the square draws its lines round us, and here is a chair, a table, glasses, knives, and thus we are boxed and housed, and will soon require a draught of soda-water and to find something to read in bed.
>
> (E6, 513)

Here, Woolf describes how the rectilinear angles of the house and its light help frame the world as discrete things. In contrast to the sky, owl, moon, and mountains outdoors, the house is filled with instrumental objects. Chairs, tables, and knives show us that the world is there to be used by individuals. Useful objects help ground us and limit us. They co-constitute us. However, as we will see in the next moment, the presence of chairs, tables, and knives, however, does not prohibit the moment of being. Collective moments of being are also possible in the middle of a restaurant. Let's see how.

Moment 15: Now the Current Flows

The final collective moment of being I want to look at is from Woolf's 1931 novel, *The Waves*. In *The Waves*, Woolf describes six childhood friends, now in their twenties living separate lives, meeting up for a farewell dinner for their school friend Percival. For the friends, the gathering stirs a mix of memories and emotions across time and space that put them into a moment of being together. They recall their childhood and relationship to one another. The character Percival also invokes a feeling of national identity since he is about to go to India as part of the English military. What unfolds during their friends' dinner with Percival is Woolf's most prolonged and most intimate collective moment of being with philosophically significant implications.

Woolf begins by describing how each of the six friends arrives at the restaurant in their unique way and waits for Percival (W, 122). Then, after Percival finally arrives at the restaurant, their shared world begins to change. The individuality of the friends begins to break down through their *transpersonal* "love" of Percival. This common love allows them to share stories, secrets, and feelings from their entire lives and see one another in a deeply candid, almost unconscious, new light (W, 123–34). Woolf writes, "Now let us issue from the darkness of solitude," Louis says. "Now let us say, brutally and directly, what is in our minds," Neville says. "Our isolation, our preparation, is over" (W, 123). The friends go from being individuals to becoming a knot in a collective moment of being.

The moment amplifies their senses, they start to feel the world flow together, and spacetime dilates (W, 135). The friends' moment of being continues until Percival leaves (W, 147). Many years later, the friends meet up for dinner again, but their moment is exceptionally brief and passes almost instantly (W, 229). Thus, their dinner with Percival is a unique moment unlike any of Woolf's other moments of being because it is shared among several people—although, importantly, not with Percival. This is a unique innovation of *The Waves* and opens up the possibility for shared aesthetic vision and ethics more broadly, which I will discuss in the conclusion of this book.

One Thing Melts into Another

Woolf describes how the six friends are drawn into their collective moment of being by the omnibuses racing by the window of the restaurant. As usual, movement prompts their moment of being.

> "Look," said Rhoda; "listen. Look how the light becomes richer, second by second, and bloom and ripeness lie everywhere; and our eyes, as they range

round this room with all its tables, seem to push through curtains of colour, red, orange, umber and queer ambiguous tints, which yield like veils and close behind them, and one thing melts into another."

(W, 135)

For Woolf, moments of being are not moments of unity but rather moments that amplify the singularities of colors and things. In this passage, Woolf describes how light suddenly reveals more and more subtleties of coloration, shadow, and texture. Everything becomes singular and interwoven together synesthetically. Rhoda then asks her friends to *listen* to this increasingly rich coloration with their *eyes*. Rhoda's eyes move and *palpate* the room. They "roam" responsively and interactively in a fractal pattern following veils of distributed color that are now visible to her.

In other words, for Rhoda, color and motion seem to palpate back on her eyes guiding them along the texture of things. These are the kinds of patterns beneath the cotton wool that Woolf believes really make up the world. For Woolf, color is not a homogeneous quality but something singular and woven into the world like a curtain or textile. Color cannot be abstracted from its singular textures in objects or from our other senses. This is why Rhoda feels all her senses interwoven and melted together—and yet each quality she sees remains distinct and singular.

"Yes," said Jinny, "our senses have widened. Membranes, webs of nerve that lay white and limp, have filled and spread themselves and float round us like filaments, making the air tangible and catching in them far-away sounds unheard before."

(W, 135)

Now, Jinny's senses begin to dilate wider and wider as web-like patterns that weave reality come to the foreground. Jinny's world increasingly becomes like the beautiful lines of Lucretius' *De Rerum Natura*—filled with woven [*texturas*] webs of filaments [*filo*] (4.88) "membranes," [*membranae*] (4.32) and simulacral images (4.155–8).

et quamvis subito quovis in tempore quamque
rem contra speculum ponas, apparet imago;
perpetuo fluere ut noscas e corpore summo
texturas rerum tenuis tenuisque figuras.

And however suddenly, at whatever time you place a mirror
in front of each thing, an image appears,
so that you may realize that constantly flowing from the outer surface
of things are thin woven webs and thin figures.

We can see from reading Woolf's marginal notes on this passage from Lucretius that she thought about this idea quite carefully. Both Lucretius and Woolf understood that our bodies' nervous system has the same branching fractal pattern as trees or spider webs. We are made of the same stuff of the world and woven together in much the same way. Philosophically, this is one of the reasons why Woolf believed that humans were not separate from nature but were the thing itself. The inside of our bodies is materially continuous with the outside. When we sense, the nerves in our organs are directly and physically vibrated and stroked by the world.

This is why Woolf writes that Jinny feels her body becoming what it is, that is, the world, web-like, stretched out, and woven together. All Jinny's senses and nerves are activated, and she feels that the world is full of a million tiny micro perceptions. Her body's nervous system stretches out to become a sensitive spider web that feels every single tiny ripple of motion, sound, light, and texture. Jinny says the air feels tangible because there is no empty space, only movement and process everywhere.

Neville says much the same thing, "I am immeasurable; a net whose fibres pass imperceptibly beneath the world. My net is almost indistinguishable from that which it surrounds" (W, 214). For Woolf, humans are not just embodied in the world, they are a region of the world "almost indistinguishable" from it. We tend to think about ourselves as much more distinct from the world than we are out of habit. Such a habit makes all kinds of instrumental activity possible, but there is no real absolute division. This is one of the important philosophical implications revealed in Woolf's moments of being and it does not occur conceptually but sensorily. One can know it only in the same way as someone who has never ridden a bicycle knows how it's done. Woolf's moments of being are about the feeling of being "immeasuable" not merely about *knowing* that there is no ontological division between human bodies and the rest of nature. This is why Rhoda, Jinny, and Neville all come to their philosophical realizations through the amplification of their senses.

Now, Woolf writes, the movement of traffic outside the restaurant continues to sweep up the diners into a feeling of collective motion. The traffic makes everything feel increasingly inter-related and kinetic.

"The roar of London," said Louis, "is round us. Motor-cars, vans, omnibuses pass and repass continuously. All are merged in one turning wheel of single sound. All separate sounds—wheels, bells, the cries of drunkards, of merrymakers—all churned into one sound, steel blue, circular. Then a siren hoots. At that shores slip away, chimneys flatten themselves, the ship makes for the open sea."

(W, 135)

What is interesting in this passage is that the continual roar of the traffic does not drown out the singular sounds within it. Somehow Louis can hear every tiny siren, bell, wheel, and drunkard all *distinctly woven* into the continuum of traffic. He hears the whole roar and the singular sounds that make up the roar simultaneously. This is a key feature of reality for Woolf. Smaller and faster sounds are woven into louder and longer ones without either drowning out the others. Sounds are nested with one another, creating a kind of music. This is how Louis hears the singular-woven-whole. Woolf is not describing a hallucination but a highly accurate description of what is *really* happening beneath the cotton wool of the restaurant scene. It only sounds strange to us because of our habit of focusing on only one or two sounds at a time, pulling them out of their web or nest.

We Undulate and Eddy Contentedly

For Woolf, the collective moment of being is a philosophical vision of reality that is woven by all the members. Reality, for Woolf, is not some objective state of patterns beneath daily appearances. When humans sense it, they also co-constitute it. Reality is not discovered by us but performed *through us*. This is how affect and rumor spread on Bond Street in *Mrs. Dalloway* and how the four figures in a "Summer's Evening" used words as threads. In *The Waves*, Woolf describes how each of the friends responds to the others by pointing out the minute lights, colors, textures, and sounds they can now see with their widened senses. The more each sees, the more they all see. Woolf writes:

> We sit here, surrounded, lit up, many coloured; all things—hands, curtains, knives and forks, other people dining—run into each other. We are walled in here. But India lies outside.
>
> (W, 135)

Woolf describes here how reality is relationally woven together. It is not like pieces in a puzzle, but like the fractal veined petals of the red carnation on the dinner table. "The flower," Bernard says, "the red carnation that stood in the vase on the table of the restaurant when we dined together with Percival is become a six-sided flower; made of six lives." "Marriage, death, travel, friendship," Bernard says, "town, and country; children and all that; a many-sided substance cut out of this dark; a many-faceted flower. Let us stop for a moment; let us behold what we have made. Let it blaze against the yew trees" (W, 229).

This is a beautiful image of Woolf's philosophical realism. Reality, like the flower, is not static but growing and dying. It is, like the flower, folded and unfolded out of itself without a prior plan, law, God, or eternal form. Reality, like the flower, is a fractal pattern that emerges from the dark soil of material indeterminacy. Order, for Woolf, emerges from indeterminate process. The collective moment of being does not dissolve six friends' lives into unity but reveals reality as a many-sided emergent and relational pattern. In this moment, all the seemingly discrete things in the restaurant run into each other as relational processes. The membranes and curtains of light bathe everything in a tangible air that holds and runs them all together and walls them.

Another interesting philosophical feature here is that the collective moment of being, for Woolf, is also one of increased suggestibility. In this altered state of consciousness, the friends become more receptive and responsive to the world and other people. Their words and sensations create a kind of feedback loop of feel and imagination around the idea of India.

> "I see India," said Bernard. "I see the low, long shore; I see the tortuous lanes of stamped mud that lead in and out among ramshackle pagodas. … Now one wheel sticks in the rut, and at once innumerable natives in loincloths swarm round it, chattering excitedly. But they do nothing. Time seems endless, ambition vain. Over all broods a sense of the uselessness of human exertion. There are strange sour smells. An old man in a ditch continues to chew betel and to contemplate his navel."
>
> (W, 136)

Percival's presence at the table suggests the thought of India and Bernard and the friends begin to imagine. In his daydream, Bernard feels the uselessness of instrumental action and the dilation of "endless" time. Bernard then imagines Percival riding upon his horse like an imperial and violent God to command the instrumental action of righting the stuck pagoda. Here, Woolf paints a complex image of British imperialism. Woolf condemned imperialism for many reasons, but to these reasons, we should add at least one more related to her philosophy of moments of being. Imperialism, for Woolf, is a paternalistic and theistic attempt to instrumentalize a vast natural and human world of indefinite space and time. In other words, there is something laughable and indeed tragic-ironic about Percival's accidental death caused by falling off his horse, which Woolf describes later in *The Waves*. This is the context in which Bernard's vision of India sets the stage for the absurdity and pointlessness of Percival's death later on.

And yet, for Woolf, Percival as a character, also seems to embody a natural and simple pre-reflective unity of mind and body that the other friends envy. He is a soldier and a man like so many others in England, forced to follow an absurd political destiny to kill and die for the British Empire in India. In this way, Percival brings together the six friends because of his almost naive biological courage in the face of his pointless destiny. But Woolf says nothing about Percival's thoughts on any of this. In this scene, he only has an occasion for a moment of being. Woolf writes:

> "Unknown, with or without a secret, it does not matter," said Rhoda, "he is like a stone fallen into a pond round which minnows swarm. Like minnows, we who had been shooting this way, that way, all shot round him when he came. Like minnows, conscious of the presence of a great stone, we undulate and eddy contentedly. Comfort steals over us. Gold runs in our blood. One, two; one, two; the heart beats in serenity, in confidence, in some trance of well-being.
>
> (W, 136)

For Rhoda, the point is that Percival, whoever he is, is a figure from their school days who expressed all the historical (male) human virtues that the friends would never attain—but which they were institutionally taught to respect. They were taught to admire him as their leader and gather around him like good British subjects. But in this moment of becoming, their gathering takes on a more general feeling of love, collective solidarity, and suggestive aesthetic vision. Their feelings toward Percival are not affirmations of empire, male potency, or any symbolic structures they learned to worship, yet they love Percival's presence in the restaurant as a dimension of their own.

Woolf's philosophical point here is not about what Percival symbolizes or represents for the friends but about what he *does* in the restaurant at this moment. Percival is a strange rock splashed down in the water of the friend's worlds for them to gather around and inspect like minnows would a fallen rock. They swim in the world that British imperialism made for them. But in Woolf's description, their gathering around him is performative with no more or less meaning than a fallen stone for some minnows. Their separate lives flow together now into a circulating eddy stimulated by the mere presence of Percival.

The friends feel the sun's warm golden color that rose in their childhood and hear the first rhythms of youth: the heart pumping and the waves crashing. In other words, for Woolf, Percival's effect is affective and material. He produces in them a shared vision, comfort, solidarity, and sonic coordination or group-trance that binds the past to the present and the far to the near. Percival is the affective point where space and time begin to dilate for the friends.

There Is a Chain Whirling Round

Woolf writes that Louis admires Percival's largely pre-reflective almost animal orientation to the world. Percival, unlike the friends, is not pricked continuously by doubt and uncertainty but sits silently on the Earth in the undulating grass like he was immediately and merely part of the Earth.

"It is Percival," said Louis, "sitting silent as he sat among the tickling grasses when the breeze parted the clouds and they formed again, who makes us aware that these attempts to say, 'I am this, I am that,' which we make, coming together, like separated parts of one body and soul, are false. Something has been left out from fear. Something has been altered, from vanity. We have tried to accentuate differences. From the desire to be separate we have laid stress upon our faults, and what is particular to us. But there is a chain whirling round, round, in a steel-blue circle beneath."

(W, 137)

This is a crucial formulation of Woolf's philosophy of subjectivity. We are "neither this, nor that," as Mrs. Dalloway said and so we can only form a unified "I" when we leave out the world because we are afraid. The "I," for Woolf, is, therefore, a protective mechanism. It is the source of our vanity and judgment of others. However, in this moment of being, Louis feels the world is much more like the relational emergence and dissipation of fractal clouds. Percival lets his body be part of the world. He allows himself to be a region of it just like grass or clouds. There is nothing for his body and mind to reflect on or contemplate because his being is already immediately that of the world's being.

In Woolf's thought, the mind and body are not two parts of a whole. There are no parts and no whole—only singular strands, filaments, or membranes that fold and curl like fractal eddies into one another. Each motion is a balancing act or a dance that responds back and forth with the world like a seedling groping and stretching into the light.

What has been "left out from fear" and "vanity," for Woolf, are the broader ecological and material conditions that run through us. Rigid individualism is an attempt to avoid fear but if we build our walls too high, individualism creates anxiety and alienation. We can see the consequences of this individualism at work in Woolf's description of how the friends try and differentiate and fault one another in the restaurant before Percival came in.

However, there is also something dangerous, exhilarating, and vertiginous about being swept up into a collective moment of being. Woolf writes:

"It is hate, it is love," said Susan. "That is the furious coal-black stream that makes us dizzy if we look down into it. We stand on a ledge here, but if we look down we turn giddy."

(W, 137)

The stream of reality brings the friends together (love) and simultaneously dissipates their individuality (hate/strife). These are the core ideas of the ancient Greek philosophical poet Empedocles, taken up explicitly in the opening proem of Lucretius' *De Rerum Natura*. For Empedocles, the universe is a vortex or eddy that begins with everything gathered together in a singularity (love) and then slowly dissipates outward into the periphery through strife. Afterward, it begins to contract again in a spiral toward the center through love, and so on, back and forth indefinitely.

For Woolf, the collective moment of being is like this. The friends are brought together in love for a moment and then spread out again. Woolf's image of the spiral, vortex, whirling chain, or eddy captures the way in which moments of being can arise atmospherically and kinetically and just as quickly dissipate. Just as Empedocles was said to have thrown himself into the volcano of Mt. Etna, so Woolf writes that Susan imagines the friends standing on a ledge looking down into a dizzying black spiral-stream.

It is exhilarating to be held together in the moving patterns of the world. Woolf is also personally aware that it is also a bit scary to be moved along by such impersonal forces.

"Yet these roaring waters," said Neville, "upon which we build our crazy platforms are more stable than the wild, the weak and inconsequent cries that we utter when, trying to speak, we rise; when we reason and jerk out these false sayings, "'I am this; I am that!'" Speech is false" (W, 138).

Here, Woolf explicitly describes the moment of being as a stability made of roaring waters. Upon these hidden patterns, we can build our crazy platforms of stability. But what is really wild, weak, and inconsequent to reality are our attempts at verbal representation and identification. Our conscious reason jerks out little noises from our mouth about our identity and individuality and Neville feels its failure to correspond with the reality of flux. This is not because the claims of reason are representationally false, but because representation itself falsely believes it can represent the world as something distinct from it. For Woolf, the speaker, speech, and things are caught up in the same stream of motion.

For example, Woolf says, as Neville eats, that he "gradually lose[s] all knowledge of particulars." He feels each mouthful in his mouth, throat, and stomach. He feels that his body has become stabilized and solid as his food becomes him, and he becomes his food. There are no particulars or wholes in this moment but only singular processes and flows of digestion.

> Now I can look steadily into the mill-race that foams beneath. By what particular name are we to call it?
>
> (W, 138)

Again, Woolf gives us a perfect image of reality as a foaming and turbulent stream of water. How can we possibly give a process a particular name as it continually changes in front of us? The stream is not identical to itself. As Neville eats, he feels continuous with the stream of matter that is making him. Now he can look down into the vortex of motion that holds together the friend's shared moment of being. It has no name.

The Whirlpool

Another important philosophical feature of the moment of becoming is its potential for dissolution. For instance, when Rhoda looks down into the "whirlpool" of the moment, she does not see love but sees beyond love into the roaring sea and the dark hollow at the center of the vortex (W, 139). The moment of being, just like a whirlpool, brings things together, but can also suck them down into the center and break them down completely. Rhoda does not feel giddy but rather sublime in the face of the dark center of the funnel that she feels she will never reach, but perhaps wants to.

At the center of the whirlpool, Woolf says, is a dark landscape with a white bubbling "fountain." The whirl of the moment holds the six friends together as if they were orbiting a black hole. Woolf was unaware that black holes existed, but her description is quite appropriate to one. Around the periphery of a black hole, space and time begin to warp as in her moments of being.

Woolf compares this collective moment of being to an ancient fertility ritual of the mother goddess Cybele.[2] She writes:

> "The flames of the festival rise high," said Rhoda. "The great procession passes, flinging green boughs and flowering branches. Their horns spill blue smoke; their skins are dappled red and yellow in the torch-light. They throw violets. They deck the beloved with garlands and with laurel leaves, there on the ring of turf where the steep-backed hills come down."
>
> (W, 140)

The use of green boughs, flowering branches, bull horns, laurel leaves, and thrown flowers was traditional in Dionysian ecstatic rituals, as Woolf would know from her close-friend and scholar of Greek religion, Jane Harrison. Thus, Woolf compares the altered states of consciousness in moments of being to the ecstatic states of drug-induced mountain revelers participating in Dionysian rituals.[3] Just like the ancient participants of the mysteries of Eleusis, Woolf's characters now enter the underworld.

> "We who are conspirators, withdrawn together to lean over some cold urn, note how the purple flame flows downwards." "Death is woven in with the violets," said Louis. "Death and again death."
>
> (W, 82)

Just as violets are tiny flowers with typically short blooms, so Louis and Rhoda anticipate the dissolution of things. Death, for Woolf, is woven in with life. In Woolf's philosophy, there is no vitalistic affirmation of life or enchanted matter.[4] Life is woven from death. The organic is woven from the inorganic. It is death that gives life. Woolf's characters rediscover this ancient ritual reenactment of creation, destruction, and recreation. Green branches produce flowers and "now," Woolf says, "the fruit is swollen beneath the leaf" (W, 141). Then the flowers fall and die, and the fruit rots. Woolf's moment of being sweeps up the friends into this cycle merging them and dissolving their individuality. Then it dissipates them back out in the world.

Susan suddenly notices all the world's tiny features that have become, along with the friends, swept up into the moment and help hold it together. Woolf writes:

"How strange," said Susan, "the little heaps of sugar look by the side of our plates. Also the mottled peelings of pears, and the plush rims to the looking-glasses. I had not seen them before. Everything is now set; everything is fixed. Bernard is engaged. Something irrevocable has happened. A circle has been cast on the waters; a chain is imposed. We shall never flow freely again."

(W, 142)

This is another interesting feature of the collective moment of being. The world feels timelessly interwoven as if it will be this way forever. For instance, Susan feels that things in the moment are perfectly fixed as if locked in by a circle. But, for Woolf, this fixed feeling is the byproduct of the edge of the moving whirlpool as one were held on the edge of two forces pulling one toward and away from the moment.

"For one moment only," said Louis. "Before the chain breaks, before disorder returns, see us fixed, see us displayed, see us held in a vice."

(W, 142)

It is as if the whirlpool swirls so fast that it forms a circle where the world moves so quickly it appears to be standing still and solid. It is just as if one swung a red ball on a string around so fast that the ball appeared to be a solid ring or loop. For a brief moment, overlapping processes seem to overlap into a single coherent object.

The Circle Breaks

Eventually, for Woolf, all moments of being come to an end. In this collective moment modeled on the whirlpool, it dissipates and flings its contents and eddies in all directions. The friends were swept up in an involuntary collective current and temporarily released from the demands of action, individuality, and instrumentality.

But now the circle breaks. Now the current flows. Now we rush faster than before. Now passions that lay in wait down there in the dark weeds which grow at the bottom rise and pound us with their waves. Pain and jealousy, envy and desire, and something deeper than they are, stronger than love and more subterranean. The voice of action speaks.

(W, 142)

It is as if, like Homer's Charybdis, the collective moment of being swallows everything up and then reverses course and spews it all back out again. Woolf describes how old habits and patterns of individuality (pain, jealousy, desire) return like waves. She writes, "An imperious brute possesses them. ... The circle is destroyed. We are thrown asunder" (W, 143).

But Louis savors the last bits of the moment, not wanting to be "cut" back into pieces by the restaurant's door as the friends leave the restaurant.

"Now once more," said Louis, "as we are about to part, having paid our bill, the circle in our blood, broken so often, so sharply, for we are so different, closes in a ring. Something is made. Yes, as we rise and fidget, a little nervously, we pray, holding in our hands this common feeling, 'Do not move, do not let the swing-door cut to pieces the thing that we have made, that globes itself here, among these lights, these peelings, this litter of bread crumbs and people passing. Do not move, do not go. Hold it for ever'."

(W, 145)

Here, Woolf likens the collective moment of being to the circulation of blood in the body. She uses a similar biological image in "A Moment: Summer's Evening." The friends feel that they are sharing not only a psychological moment but a bodily and atmospheric moment as well. Their altered states of consciousness simply make them aware of the way the moment is woven into the world. It is not merely a psychological state. Woolf continues:

"Let us hold it for one moment," said Jinny; "love, hatred, by whatever name we call it, this globe whose walls are made of Percival, of youth and beauty, and something so deep sunk within us that we shall perhaps never make this moment out of one man again."

(W, 145)

For Woolf, the collective moment is a revelation of an interwoven whole, but formed by a singular situation. In this case, Percival is like the flower that Woolf describes in her autobiography which reveals its connection to the whole earth. Hence, here too, Woolf's use of the "globe" image of the whole. The moment of being reveals a strangely "singular whole" without parts.

"Forests and far countries on the other side of the world," said Rhoda, "are in it; seas and jungles; the howlings of jackals and moonlight falling upon some high peak where the eagle soars."

"Happiness is in it," said Neville, "and the quiet of ordinary things. A table, a chair, a book with a paper-knife stuck between the pages. And the petal falling from the rose, and the light flickering as we sit silent, or, perhaps, bethinking us of some trifle, suddenly speak." "Week-days are in it," said Susan, "Monday, Tuesday."

(W, 145)

In this one singular moment of being, everything ordinary and extraordinary is "in it" because the moment reveals the process of interconnection, creation, and dissolution that is common to all things. For Woolf, the moment of being contains Monday and Tuesday like a whirlpool contains water or the ocean contains waves. One substance is not contained by the other like Russian dolls, but all are immanent within one another.

Woolf then has Bernard wrap everything up in a final moment of rapture.

"What is to come is in it," said Bernard. "That is the last drop and the brightest that we let fall like some supernal quicksilver into the swelling and splendid moment created by us from Percival. What is to come? I ask, brushing the crumbs from my waistcoat, what is outside? We have proved, sitting eating, sitting talking, that we can add to the treasury of moments. We are not slaves bound to suffer incessantly unrecorded petty blows on our bent backs. We are not sheep either, following a master. We are creators. We too have made something that will join the innumerable congregations of past time. We too, as we put on our hats and push open the door, stride not into chaos, but into a world that our own force can subjugate and make part of the illumined and everlasting road."

(W, 146)

Here, Woolf imagines a subterranean historical treasury of ineffable moments of being. It's a strange and paradoxical idea to say the least, but it is an important consequence of Woolf's philosophy. Moments of being, for Woolf, have been powerful motivators of creativity and thought through history. They lie at the source of great works of art, she says, and yet are impossible to accurately describe or represent in art or philosophy due to their profoundly singular features (MB, 73). By having these moments, the friends participate in this unwritten and unwritable history on par with the greatest and most ordinary people. The written histories we have of great artists and philosophers are tiny compared to the vast unrecorded history of moments of being.

The friends can now remember this moment when they are crushed by the petty instrumentality and individuality of daily cotton wool life. In this sense, the friends are no longer slaves to instrumental activity. For Woolf, their moment is also an ethical and political moment where they have realized the absurdity of all forms of authority and mastery in the face of the immensity of time and space. The friends have shared the ecstasy of reality without the approval or guidance from any master or law.

In Woolf's thought, reality is not random. In moments of being, the friends see how moving patterns weave everything and everyone together. They do not need to fear the world any longer because they are the world. The friends realize that they are not merely passive bodies. They are the thing itself. "The yellow canopy of our tremendous energy hangs like a burning cloth above our heads" (W, 146).

The moments end when Percival gets into his cab and drives away. As a conclusion to this book, let's continue to look more closely at the ethical, political, and social dimensions of moments of being in Woolf's philosophy.

Conclusion: Moments of Being Political

The central argument of this book is that Virginia Woolf's description of moments of being shows her to be a process philosopher of movement. Moments of being, for her, are amplified, pre-reflective, and synesthetic experiences that reveal the interconnection of reality through moving patterns. To my mind, Woolf's descriptions of these moments are some of the most beautiful and strange in the entire tradition of epiphanic, ecstatic, and philosophical writing. By looking closely at the philosophical assumptions and implications embedded in her descriptions of these moments, I have argued that they express a unique philosophical view.

Woolf shows how moments of what she calls "non-being" or "cotton wool" emerge and are maintained by immanent patterns of motion sensible only in moments of being. For her, there is no ontological dualism between being and non-being. The relatively discrete cotton wool objects of daily life are not false appearances but rather like the tips of enormous icebergs immanently woven from fractal patterns of motion.

Additionally, for Woolf, moments of being are not "better" than cotton wool appearances. Moments of being bring agony as well as ecstasy, as I have tried to show in this book. Movement and stability, for Woolf, are two sides of the same pool of water, one below and one above the surface. Daily instrumental activity and reason are required to get on with things, but moments of being remind us of the provisional, playful, and experimental world of interconnections that lives in them as well.

In Woolf's philosophy, moments of being reveal a wider range of a singular and situated reality, but not *all* of reality. Hers are not visions of unity, god, or unchanging forms outside space and time. Virginia Woolf was not a metaphysical philosopher speculating about the objective nature of reality. For her, there are no God, no sin, no lack, no great chain of being, no absolute judgment, and no reason to fear what happens after death. The philosophy contained in her descriptions of moments of being, as I have tried to show, is that reality is woven together in interrelated metastable patterns. In moments of being her characters feel her philosophical claim that "we are the thing itself."

What is more, Woolf's moments of being strongly impress upon her characters the falseness and absurdity of any ontological division in nature whatsoever, including many traditional philosophical divisions. In moments of being, Woolf's characters realize that treating the world as if it were made of discrete objects for human utility is limiting and even dangerous. In Woolf's view, nature is not discrete or divided up into fragments or kinds of things. Of course, this does not *necessarily* stop people from pretending that it is. Nor does such non-discreteness *necessarily* entail any absolute ethical imperative to act in a specific way. Indeed, moments of being do not necessarily change the outward behavior of Woolf's characters in any obvious way. Therefore, we should be careful, as she was, not to ascribe any universal normative consequences to moments of being.

That said, moments of being do seem to have an important *critical* function insofar as they reveal nature to be fundamentally mutable, mobile, and lacking in any ultimate or foundation or hierarchy. In this sense, they are, at the very least, *opportunities* to deeply reconsider past habits, world-views, or senses of self. But there is no guarantee of personal transformation, propositional knowledge, or artistic novelty as a result of moments of being. Moments are where something *different* seems more possible than before. This is an important social consequence of Woolf's realism. Nothing necessarily follows from a reality of process and movement, but much more feels possible, and fixed hierarchies are not foundational.

Indeed, the expanded sense of *real possibility* in a *moving reality* is why Woolf wanted moments of being to be socially protected and even encouraged. Social, economic, and physical safety temporarily frees people up from obligatory instrumental activity. However, this too does not guarantee that someone will have a moment of being or that such a moment will lead to new modes of aesthetic, social, or scientific activity. Though, it does make both more possible and likely. Woolf's political proposal, of course, in *A Room of One's Own*, is that we all get a room of our own and a guaranteed livable income. Even if nothing directly or indirectly comes from people's moments of being, for Woolf, such moments are important in themselves.

In addition to socially supporting moments of being, Woolf also wanted to depathologize and decriminalize people, like herself, who had them. Unless the moments of being are shared and understood, the individuals who have them will likely sound "mentally ill" when they report them. Woolf touches on this in *Mrs. Dalloway* in her description of Septimus.

> He did not want to die. Life was good. The sun hot. Only human beings—what did they want? Coming down the staircase opposite an old man stopped and stared at him. Holmes was at the door. "I'll give it you!" he cried, and flung himself vigorously, violently down on to Mrs. Filmer's area railings.
>
> (MD, 149)

Woolf no doubt felt similarly pathologized and medicalized by doctors and even well-meaning others. Woolf does not speculate about psychiatric alternatives but certainly draws our attention to the dangers of treating such moments as forms of illness.[1]

*

I want to argue in the conclusion to this book that moments of being have implications for Woolf's political philosophy, specifically her socialism and feminism. Woolf's socialism and feminism have many sources and consequences that I cannot cover in a single chapter. Instead, I want to focus here specifically on how they relate to her moments of being, which she described as "far more necessary than anything else" (MB, 73). In other words, for Woolf, it seems that politics is not an end in itself. Rather, politics secures the material conditions for moments of being and supports their consequences. If, as Woolf speculates, "all artists ... feel something like this (in moments of being)," then a radical politics of equality and liberty are needed to secure moments of being and to advance the arts (MB, 73). This, among other things, is what I would like to argue at the philosophical heart of Woolf's socialism and feminism. Let's begin with a brief and selective history of the connection between materialism, feminism, and socialism that informs Woolf's philosophy of moments of being.

Material Feminism and Philosophical Poetry

Many female European philosophers from the sixteenth through nineteenth centuries were attracted to the philosophical materialism of Epicurus and Lucretius because it rejected the God-given superiority of men over women.[2] For Lucretius, there was no God, no judgment, and *poetic imagination* was entwined with reason. Together, reason and imagination were capable of grasping the most profound aspects of reality. Indeed, of all classical Greek philosophers, Epicurus' school was the only one that allowed women to be members. Unlike Aristotle, who once described women as "mutilated men,"[3] Lucretius rejected all philosophical abstractions and hierarchical chains of being. He and Epicurus had an entirely material theory of the soul that did not grant men any natural superiority over women—or over anyone else. Of great importance too, for Lucretius, was that knowledge was not mental contemplation but a performative and aesthetic act involving moments of ecstasy, which women such as Hildegard of Bingen had used to claim unique and direct insight into reality.[4]

As I have shown elsewhere, *female desire* also played a widespread and crucial role throughout Lucretius' famous poem *De Rerum Natura*.[5] Against the patriarchal metaphysics of form and masculine reason, Lucretius developed perhaps the first non-mechanistic and non-deterministic materialism. In this way, knowledge, for Lucretius, was absolutely performative and practical. We might even say, as Emanuela Bianchi has, that Lucretius developed an "aleatory feminism."[6]

There remains a definite but understudied historical relationship between the emergence of feminist philosophy and women's interest and engagement with philosophical materialism in modern Europe.[7] This history was, and remains, actively hidden in favor of a mechanistic story about materialism. For instance, Bacon, Descartes, Gassendi, Boyle, Newton, and others deliberately excluded Venusian, feminine, sensuous, and ecstatic themes from their interpretations of *De Rerum Natura*. They tended, as most still do, to reduce Lucretius to philosophical propositions about discrete particles.

However, early women philosophers including Lucy Hutchinson, Margret Cavendish, Queen Kristina of Sweden, Anne Conway, Aphra Ben, and George Eliot often emphasized sensation and moments of ecstasy in their philosophical poetry.[8] Poetry, however, as is still often the case, was not considered philosophically equal to rationalism. This again is one of the historical reasons women were *allowed* to write poetry *and* why men dismissed women as philosophers.[9] The "relegation" of women's thinking to poetry is perhaps also one of the reasons why there are supposedly "so few" female "philosophers."

Another relevant example of the gendering of poetry and philosophy in the nineteenth century was the way that Lucretius' work was interpretively split up into its aesthetic dimensions and philosophical propositions. As Samuel Coleridge wrote to William Wordsworth, in 1815, "Whatever in Lucretius is Poetry is not Philosophical, whatever is Philosophical is not Poetry."[10] This is a typical example of the age-old divisions between poetry and philosophy, sensation and reason, matter and form, female and male, that have plagued the Western tradition.

I offer this brief history only to remind readers that many male philosophers did not treat women as philosophers because of a historical belief that women and poetry were fundamentally non-philosophical. I am suggesting here that we think of Woolf's use of moments of being in her work as part of a longer historical path of ecstatic, mystical, and poetic materialism invoked by other women writers against the dominant male and mechanistic traditions of their time. In my view, Woolf's work is part of a larger effort to overcome the opposition between poetry and philosophy. By not treating Woolf as a philosopher in her own right, many have unwittingly contributed to this larger history of the gendered division and hierarchy of thought. Woolf instead offers us a fluid dynamic materialism against the static one championed by the masculine sciences of mechanism.[11]

Socialism

Much has also been written on Woolf's socialism.[12] My aim is not to survey it all here but to focus on its connection with her moments of being. As I said above, one of the consequences of moments of being, for Woolf, is that her characters experience the interwoven nature of reality without God or an ontological hierarchy among things. For Woolf, humans make up hierarchies and they can unmake them, although this is easier said than done.

Woolf, I believe, would have agreed with Karl Marx's statement that communism was "the emancipation of the senses." "Naturalism," as Marx wrote in his *1844 Manuscripts* "is humanism, is communism."[13] This is roughly what Woolf's friend Roger Fry wrote in his essay "Art and Socialism":

> As I understand it, art is one of the chief organs of what, for want of a better word, I must call the spiritual life. It both stimulates and controls those indefinable overtones of the material life of man which all of us at moments feel to have a quality of permanence and reality that does not belong to the rest of our experience. Nature demands with no uncertain voice that the physical needs of the body shall be satisfied first; but we feel that our real human life only begins at the point where that is accomplished, that the man who works at some uncreative and uncongenial toil merely to earn enough food to enable him to continue to work has not, properly speaking, a human life at all.[14]

Humans, nature, freedom, reality, and art are all connected for Fry, as they were for Woolf.[15] It was not enough for the materially privileged to enjoy art, nature, and the ecstasy of reality. Reality, for Woolf, was naturally for everyone and everything. I believe that this was the philosophical core of what initially drew Woolf to join the Fabian Society, a political movement in favor of democratic socialism. The Fabian Society believed that material security and collective ownership of the means of production were the conditions by which individuals could express their full freedom and unique being. For Woolf, this of course would have included moments of being.

In Woolf's political philosophy, aesthetic creativity has to be supported with at least basic material conditions. "The imagination is largely the child of the flesh," Woolf wrote (E5, 179). Without the natural and material flourishing of the flesh and body, the imagination cannot flourish either. For "one cannot think well, love well, sleep well, if one has not dined well" (RO, 18). It follows that moments of being, for Woolf, are also entirely material and also require a good meal.

For Woolf, intellectual and creative freedom was perhaps one of the most important aspects of human existence. "Intellectual freedom depends upon material things. Poetry depends upon intellectual freedom. And women have always been poor, not for two hundred years merely, but from the beginning of time. Women have had less intellectual freedom than the sons of Athenian slaves" (RO, 108). This is what makes Mrs. Ramsey's moment of being at the end of a busy day so powerful in *To the Lighthouse.*

In Woolf's thought, there is nothing essential or inherent in women's biology that makes them spiritually or materially inferior to men. Nor are poor people inferior to wealthy ones from a materialist perspective.[16] Unfortunately, however, social, economic, and political disenfranchisement have made women and the laboring classes unfree, and uneducated. As a consequence, Woolf made a radical vow to oppose "any domination of one over another; any leadership, any imposition of the will" (D1, 256). This vow is a strong political declaration that may align her more with *anarchism* than with *socialism*.[17] Especially after the emergence of fascism across Europe, Woolf rejected all forms of "the patriarchal state" completely. She wrote:

> They were fighting the tyranny of the patriarchal state as you are fighting the tyranny of the Fascist state …. Now you are being shut out, you are being shut up, because you are Jews, because you are democrats, because of race, because of religion …. But now we are fighting together. The daughters and sons of educated men are fighting side by side.
>
> (TG, 102–3)

These lines and others suggest that Woolf rejected borders, states, and all forms of social domination and hierarchy. "No more towers and no more classes," she wrote, we will "stand, without hedges between us, on the common ground" (E6, 274). Indeed, most famously, Woolf aligned herself not with any country but with the entire world. "As a woman, I have no country. As a woman, I want no country. As a woman, my country is the whole world" (TG, 109).

This political stance is not just an affirmation of global solidarity with women worldwide as a subordinated sex-class but with all subordinated people of all kinds everywhere. As an oppressed person, Woolf's allegiance was not just to her identity group of women struggling for rights but to *all* groups struggling against of all forms of social domination. Woolf's political position thus overlaps with variations of socialism, anarchism, and feminism. It is, also, and this is what I am trying to show here, in her eyes, part of her own philosophical commitment to process materialism, naturalism, and moments of being.

She supported an end to all forms of domination so that everyone could be free to enjoy reality. Moments of being, for Woolf, do not tell us what to do or guarantee utopia, but they help us see that much more is possible. Domination, by contrast, restricts moments of being.

In *Three Guineas*, Woolf explicitly directs her political critique to the state more broadly, referring three times to race or color and one time to religion as bases of oppression within the nation-state (TG, 80, 103, 184–5). This broader political philosophy is also why she was critical of suffragist feminism, narrowly understood. Woolf even went as far as to suggest that we burn an "old word, a vicious and corrupt word that has done much harm in its day and is now obsolete," namely, the word "feminist" (TG, 101). Woolf did not want to abandon feminism, of course, but to expand it into a much broader anarcho-feminist critique of the state, war, patriarchy, racism, fascism, imperialism,[18] and *all forms of social domination*. She felt that the term "feminist" had become too narrow and wanted to expand its aspirations beyond liberal and economic equality to the liberation from all forms of oppression. This brings us to Woolf's feminism.

Feminism

Much has also been written on Woolf's feminism.[19] My focus here again, though, is strictly on its relationship to her moments of being. The aim of Woolf's feminism in its broadest and most empirical sense was first and foremost solidarity with all oppressed groups everywhere, as described above. In particular, she argued brilliantly that waged slavery, poverty, patriarchy, and the exclusion of women from legal, political, artistic, educational, and other spheres had a devastating effect on women's minds and bodies. If women are going to contribute to fiction, Woolf famously proposed, they will need the material conditions to do so: money, time, a room, and freedom from the domestic tyranny of hetero-patriarchy. This is the part of her feminism that overlaps with her socialism.[20]

However, at another level beneath the cotton wool of solid objects, classes, rooms, sexes, and identities, Woolf also valued women's moments of being which "prove that one's life is not confined to one's body and what one says and does" (MB, 73). What shall women and oppressed peoples do with their daily liberation from authority? Woolf's demand for women's emancipation (and others) does not contradict her simultaneous hope and encouragement that free women will also experience, create, and write about the deeper processes of reality discovered in their exceptional moments of being. Indeed, this is what Lily Briscoe explicitly aimed for in *To the Lighthouse*.

Woolf's feminism was also about giving everyone access to "the common life which is the real life," viewed by "human beings not always in their relation to each other but in relation to reality; and the sky, too, and the trees or whatever it may be in themselves; [...] our relation is to the world of reality and not only to the world of men and women" (RO, 114). Again, there is a political battle to be fought to secure the possibility of moments of being but there is also the vision of reality in which men and women are also "part of the nature of things" (TL, 188).

For Woolf, feminism means more than women's political and even economic equality with men. It is the practice of discovering the real, material, and relational patterns of the world that we are, including the sky, trees, waves, and mountains. In other words, Woolf's feminism does not reject politics but adds aesthetic and ontological dimensions to it. Woolf deepens and broadens feminism. Indeed, Woolf questions the entire masculine philosophical framework that we are unified and rational "I"s. As we have seen throughout this book, in Woolf's philosophy of moments of being, people are neither this nor that. "I" is just the term we use to designate an intricate pattern of material processes (RO, 4). It is never really isolated. In Woolf's philosophy, the "I" is a cork on the surface of a wave. Below this surface, however, Woolf says, "there was scarcely anything left of body or mind by which one could say 'This is he' or 'This is she'" (TL, 126). Woolf's theory of the subject is spread out everywhere; not "here, here, here" ... but everywhere. Our apparitions, the part of us which appears, are so momentary compared with the other, the unseen part of us, which spreads wide (MD, 152–3).

Indeed, Woolf bemoaned the inadequacy of thinking about people in terms of two sexes. "Two sexes are quite inadequate. For we have too much likeness as it is, and if an explorer should come back and bring word of other sexes looking through the branches of other trees at other skies, nothing would be of greater service to humanity" (RO, 88). For Woolf's time, this idea would not have been easy to fit into the term "feminism."

For Woolf, sex and sexuality, like any identity, are metastable states—things that spread wide through trees, skies, and through other people. Just as no "I" is fully isolatable, for Woolf, no sex is strictly identical to itself either. "One has only to go into any room in any street for the whole of that extremely complex force of femininity to fly in one's face. How should it be otherwise?" (RO, 87). In Woolf's feminism, each sex is itself a complex network of singular relations such that the category "woman" has no strict essence one could apply across all women.[21]

Part of Woolf's feminism is also aesthetic. She hopes women will not write "as a woman, but as a woman who has forgotten that she is a woman, so that her pages were full of that curious sexual quality which comes only when sex is unconscious of itself" (RO, 93).

There is certainly a place for overtly political writing in the struggle for social justice, but Woolf also hoped women's "unconscious" writing might "grow in the minds of others" (RO, 104) and occasion *new* forms of subjectivity. This is how Woolf describes Lily Briscoe's moment of being in *To the Lighthouse*. Woolf says, Lily "subdu[ed] all her impressions as a woman to something much more general; becoming once more under the power of that vision which she had seen clearly once and must now grope for among hedges and houses and mothers and children—her picture" (TL, 53).

In Woolf's philosophy, the sexes are different *from* one another *and within* themselves.[22] In a sense, Woolf's feminism is two-sided without being contradictory. At one level, everyone must fight for the material security of all identity groups. But at another level, everyone should be free to explore and feel the patterns and processes that situate their singular existence in the world even if these feelings are not reducible to one's sex or gender.

In my view, the key to making sense of Woolf's feminism is holding together these two sides of her political-aesthetic-ontological feminism, just as Woolf herself navigated her transition between moments of being and non-being.

Some Limitations

No book can do everything. This book has several limits I would like to acknowledge explicitly. It has not attempted to include all the moments of being in Woolf's work but to look closely at several key selections from five kinds of moments. My goal was not to exhaust every example of Woolf's philosophy in her work, but to introduce the reader to enough moments of being to identify their key philosophical features and consequences. I also did not attempt here a total understanding of Woolf's novels, their meaning, history, plot, literary techniques, or Woolf's biography and influences while she wrote them. For this, I defer to the robust scholarship already published by Woolf scholars. My focus here was just on moments of being and the philosophy they express.

Directions for Future Work

When we look intensely and synesthetically at the world through Woolf's moments, we discover a real but strange world of motion and flux. The world of cotton wool objects may help us survive and get things done, but what is the purpose of survival if we cannot catch a glimpse of the rapturous beauty going on beneath it all? In these moments, we are vessels opened up to a metastable world of flows, folds, and eddies. These are not Platonic forms but the woven patterns and relations that singularly orient us in the world.

Future research building on this book might begin by tracking down and developing other moments of becoming found throughout Woolf's work. Ultimately though, this book has provoked me to ask some broader questions leading beyond Woolf's oeuvre. For instance, why have other epiphanic authors not found the same thing Woolf did beneath the cotton wool? Why do some writers find God, demons, mind, forms, vital spirit, life, and so on, and Woolf found the interrelation and indeterminacy of matter in motion? Are these merely different names given to a similar visionary experience, or are they genuinely different revelations of the world, or are they perhaps something else altogether?

There is also something philosophically provocative about the experience of altered states of consciousness that can lead to moments of being. The precise sources and historical context including madness, drugs, religion, mediation, hypnosis, and dreams vary significantly and yet some common themes also emerge.

What are the material-kinetic patterns and structures of various mystical moments of being in history? What is the broader role of these moments in human beings' material evolution, the Earth, and the cosmos? These kinds of questions are beyond the scope of this book to answer of course, but I hope to continue working on them.

Finally, I must say that my questions after writing this book have surprised me. They have led me in the end toward a book project on the history of human consciousness written from a material-kinetic perspective: *Pink Noise*.

Appendix

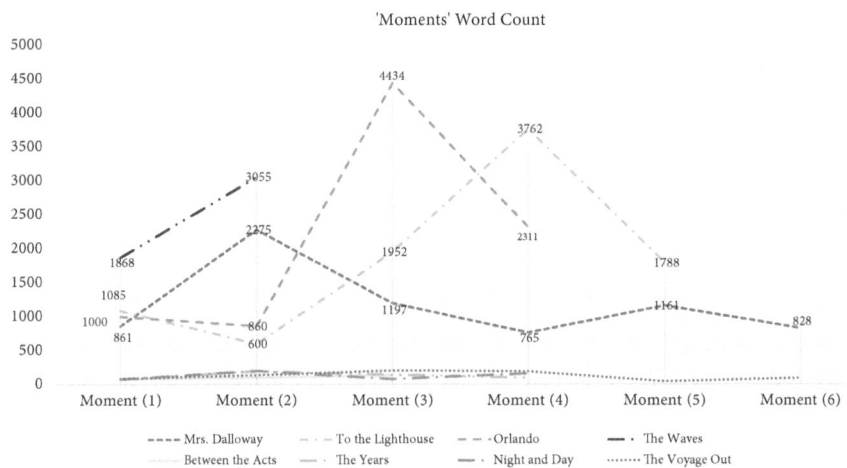

Mrs. Dalloway

    Moment 1: Neither This nor That (MD, 8-9)-861
    Moment 2: The World Wavered (MD, 13-22)-2775
    Moment 3: The Death of the Soul (MD, 57-58)-1197
    Moment 4: Time Split Its Husk (MD, 68-69)-765
    Moment 5: The Knotted Roots of Infinite Ages (MD, 80-82)-1161
    Moment 6: She Felt Herself Everywhere (MD, 151-153)-828

To the Lighthouse

    Moment 7: The Lake of Being (TL, 62-65)-1085
    Moment 8: A Sense of Movement (TL, 112-113)-600
    Moment 9: Part I, A Glimpse Only (TL, 125-131)-1952
    Moment 9: Part II, Stars Flashing in Their Hearts (TL, 131-145)-3762
    Moment 10: The Fluidity of Life (TL, 156-161)-1788

Orlando

    Moment 11: The Odds and Ends of the Universe (O, 97-101)-1000
    Moment 12: Hail! Natural Desire! (O, 292-295)-860
    Moment 13: The Beauty of Movement (O, 298-315)4434
    Moment 14: Everything Was Partly Something Else (O, 321-329)-2311

The Waves

    Moment 15: There Is No Stability in This World (W, 111-118)-1868
    Moment 16: Now the Current Flows (W, 135–147) -3055

Between the Acts

    1st Moment-(215) 79
    2nd Moment-(98) 100
    3rd Moment-(183-184) 133

The Years

    1st Moment-(110) 74
    2nd Moment-(132-133) 194
    3rd Moment-(277-278) 141
    4th Moment-(390) 94

Night and Day

    1st Moment-(259) 78
    2nd Moment-(260) 198
    3rd Moment-(261) 78
    4th Moment (439) 159

The Voyage Out

    1st Moment-(72) 84
    2nd Moment-(127) 137
    3rd Moment-(174) 204
    4th Moment-(314) 190
    5th Moment-(314-315) 42
    6th Moment-(315) 94

Notes

Preface

1 The paragraph above is a synthetic paraphrase of a number of features Woolf describes in various moments of being.

2 See Woolf's discussion of Thomas Hardy's "*Moments of Vision*." "His own word, '*Moments of Vision*,' exactly describes those passages of astonishing beauty and force which are to be found in every book that he wrote. With a sudden quickening of power which we cannot foretell, nor he, it seems, control, a single scene breaks off from the rest … Vivid to the eye, but not to the eye alone, for every sense participates, such scenes dawn upon us and their splendor remains. But the power goes as it comes. The moment of vision is succeeded by long stretches of plain daylight." (E4: 509–10). See also, Emma Simone, *Virginia Woolf and Being-in-the-World: A Heideggerian Study* (Edinburgh: Edinburgh University Press, 2017).

3 For a full account of this point, see Naomi Toth, "Disturbing Epiphany: Rereading Virginia Woolf's 'Moments of Being'/Perturber l'épiphanie: Une Relecture Des « moments d'être » de Virginia Woolf," *Etudes Britanniques Contemporaines: Revue de La Société d'Etudes Anglaises Contemporaines* 46 (June 2014).

4 I am not the first to make the connection of the "Moments of Being" in sketches of the past to her fiction. See Meg Jensen, "Tradition and Revelation: Moments of Being in Virginia Woolf's Major Novels," in *The Cambridge Companion to the Modernist Novel*, ed. Morag Shiach and Suzanne Hobson (Cambridge: Cambridge University Press, 2007), 112–25. See also, Adriana Varga, "Music, Language, and Moments of Being: From the Voyage Out to between the Acts," in *Virginia Woolf and Music*, ed. Adriana Varga and Mihály Szegedy-Maszák (Bloomington, IN: Indiana University Press, 2014), 75–109. These are both wonderful essays and I would like to build on their idea of reading Woolf's fiction in terms of moments of being.

5 For studies of Woolf's autobiographical moments of being, see Christopher C. Dahl, "Virginia Woolf's Moments of Being and the Autobiographical Tradition in the Stephen Family," *Journal of Modern Literature* 10, no. 2 (June 1983): 175–96; Frank Baldanza, "Virginia Woolf's 'Moments of Being'," *Modern Fiction Studies* 2, no. 2 (1956); Nicolas Boileau,"Virginia Woolf's Auto-Reading in Moments of Being," in *Woolf as Reader/Woolf as Critic, or The Art of Reading in the Present*, ed. Catherine Bernard (Montpellier: Presses universitaires de la Méditerranée, 2011), 127–37; Nóra Séllei, "The First Memory: Or, Why Is Virginia Woolf's Moments of Being Unfinished?" *BAS: British and American Studies/Revista de Studii Britanice Şi Americane* 2, no. 1 (1997): 106–14; Carla Locatelli,"Figures of Displacement

and Displacements of Figures: The Play of Autobiography in Moments of Being," in *La Tipografia Nel Salotto: Saggi Su Virginia Woolf*, ed. Oriana Palusci (Pisa, Italy: Tirrenia, 1999), 11–22; and Josephine Donovan, "Everyday Use and Moments of Being: Toward a Nondominative Aesthetic," in *Aesthetics in Feminist Perspective*, ed. Hilde Hein and Carolyn Korsmeyer (Bloomington, IN: Indiana University Press, 1993), 53–67.

6   Harvena Richter was one of the first to emphasize the process-nature of Woolf's philosophy in connection with the French philosopher Henri Bergson. See Harvena Richter, *Virginia Woolf: The Inward Voyage* (Princeton, NJ: Princeton University Press, 1970), 40. Jon Hughes also emphasized the importance of movement in Woolf's philosophy. See Jon Hughes, *Lines of Flight: Reading Deleuze with Hardy, Gissing, Conrad, Woolf* (Sheffield: Sheffield Academic Press, 1997), chapter six.

7   For the psychedelic state, see Fernanda Palhano-Fontes, Katia C. Andrade, Luis F. Tofoli, Antonio C. Santos, Jose Alexandre S. Crippa, Jaime E. C. Hallak, Sidarta Ribeiro, and Draulio B. de Araujo, "The Psychedelic State Induced by Ayahuasca Modulates the Activity and Connectivity of the Default Mode Network," *PLoS One* 10, no. 2 (2015): e0118143. For the dream state, see Silvina G. Horovitz, Allen R. Braun, Walter S. Carr, Dante Picchioni, Thomas J. Balkin, Masaki Fukunaga, and Jeff H. Duyn, "Decoupling of the Brain's Default Mode Network during Deep Sleep," *Proceedings of the National Academy of Sciences of the United States of America* 106, no. 27 (July 2009): 11376–81. For the sedative state, see Michael D. Greicius, Vesa Kiviniemi, Osmo Tervonen, Vilho Vainionpaa, Seppo Alahuhta, Allan L. Reiss, and Vinod Menon, "Persistent Default-Mode Network Connectivity during Light Sedation," *Human Brain Mapping* 29, no. 7 (January 2008): 839–47. For the meditative state see Joon Hwan Jang, Wi Hoon Jung, Do-Hyung Kang, Min Soo Byun, Soo Jin Kwon, Chi-Hoon Choi, and Jun Soo Kwon, "Increased Default Mode Network Connectivity Associated with Meditation," *Neuroscience Letters* 487, no. 3 (January 2011): 358–62. For the hypnotic state see William J. McGeown, Giuliana Mazzoni, Annalena Venneri, and Irving Kirsch, "Hypnotic Induction Decreases Anterior Default Mode Activity," *Consciousness and Cognition* 18, no. 4 (December 2009): 848–55. On the connection between mania and the psychedelic state, see:

> Because manic delusions and hallucinations create and/or accompany ideas of sometimes cosmic proportions, they are frequently interpreted as religious experiences, especially by those who have been raised in a religion. The patient may believe that she has been chosen by God-why else would she suddenly feel so captivated? When euthymic (not ill), John Custance recognized that his religious delusions and visions were similar to the pseudo-revelations induced by nitrous oxide and other drugs, but when manic, he fervently believed that "depth beyond depth of truth" had been revealed to him, that the mystery of the universe had been "unveiled" and become "certain beyond the possibility of a doubt." Such mystical experiences of universal communion can also be induced by mescaline, LSD, and other hallucinogenic substances that alter the biochemistry of the brain.

Thomas C. Caramagno, *The Flight of the Mind: Virginia Woolf's Art and Manic-Depressive Illness* (Berkeley and Los Angeles, CA: University of California Press, 1992), 45. Caramagno acknowledges the feeling of the revelation of truth. But Caramagno also pathologies mania and LSD as delusions. He treats them as anti-realist disorders of the mind; mental illness. But can mania and LSD also give us unique insight into reality? This is where Woolf's insight comes from in part. See also, Frederick K. Goodwin and Kay Redfield Jamison, *Manic-Depressive Illness* (New York: Oxford University Press, 1990).

8   See Caramagno, *The Flight of the Mind*.

9   "… & these curious intervals in life—I've had many—are the most fruitful artistically-one becomes fertilized-think of my madness at Hogarth-& all the little illnesses …" (D3: 254). "I've had some very curious visions in this room too, lying in bed, mad, & seeing the sunlight quivering like gold water, on the wall. I've heard the voices of the dead here. And felt, through it all, exquisitely happy." (D2: 283). "And yet both mania and depression, as I will argue in Chapter six, taught her valuable lessons about what this moment of being was." See Caramagno, *The Flight of the Mind*, 51.

10 The following works focus on drawing comparisons of Woolf's work to other philosophers. Simone, *Virginia Woolf and Being-in-the-World*; Derek Ryan and Laci Mattison, "Deleuze, Virginia Woolf, and Modernism," *Deleuze Studies* 7, no. 4 (November 2013): 421–6; Ian Buchanan and John Marks, eds., *Deleuze and Literature* (Edinburgh: Edinburgh University Press, 2001); and Ian Buchanan and Claire Colebrook, eds., *Deleuze and Feminist Theory* (Edinburgh: Edinburgh University Press, 2005).

11 Veronika Krajickova, *Virginia Woolf as a Process-Oriented Thinker: Parallels between Woolf's Fiction and Process Philosophy* (New York: Lexington Books, 2023).

12 Woolf's "*Moment of Being*" is equivalent to Bollas's "*Aesthetic Moment*," when "the subject feels held in symmetry and solitude by the spirit of the object," a wordless occasion, "notable for the density of the subject's feeling and the fundamentally non-representational knowledge of being embraced by the aesthetic object …. [S]elf and object feel reciprocally enhancing and mutually informative." "To the perceiver, 'uncanny moments' seem to be 'partially sponsored by the object' itself, as if it were 'the hand of fate' leading us to some unspecified involvement." See Christopher Bollas, *The Shadow of the Object: Psychoanalysis of the Unthought Known* (New York: Columbia University Press, 1987), 31.

13 Bilge Ebiri, "'I Wanted to Create a Prophet': The Rebirth of 'Jodorowsky's Dune,'" *Rolling Stone*, March 19, 2014, https://www.rollingstone.com/movies/movie-news/i-wanted-to-create-a-prophet-the-rebirth-of-jodorowskys-dune-242168/.

Introduction

1   Paul Valéry, *Cahiers/Notebooks 5*, trans. and ed. Brian Stimpson, Paul Gifford, Robert Pickering, and Norma Rinsler (Frankfurt am Main: Peter Lang, 2010), 174.

2   There have been a number of non-book-length studies on Woolf's moments of being. I have read them all and I briefly survey some of their shared conclusions in the next section of this chapter. Naomi Toth, "Disturbing Epiphany; Josephine Donovan, "Everyday Use and Moments of Being: Toward a Nondominative Aesthetic," 53–67; Benjamin D. Hagen, "Feeling Shadows: Virginia Woolf's Sensuous Pedagogy," *PMLA: Publications of the Modern Language Association of America* 132, no. 2 (March 2017): 266–80; Carla Locatelli, "Figures of Displacement

and Displacements of Figures: The Play of Autobiography in Moments of Being," in *La Tipografia Nel Salotto: Saggi Su Virginia Woolf*, ed. Oriana Palusci (Pisa, Italy: Tirrenia, 1999), 11–22; Becky Tipper, "Moments of Being and Ordinary Human-Animal Encounters," *Virginia Woolf Miscellany* 84 (2013): 14–16; Adriana Varga, "Music, Language, and Moments of Being: From the Voyage Out to between the Acts," 75–109; Nóra Séllei, "The First Memory," 106–14; Louise A. DeSalvo, "The Importance of Moments of Being," *Virginia Woolf Miscellany* 5 (1976): 1–3; Meg Jensen, "Tradition and Revelation: Moments of Being in Virginia Woolf's Major Novels," 112–25; Emma Simone, *Virginia Woolf and Being-in-the-World*; Nicolas Boileau, "Virginia Woolf's Auto-Reading in Moments of Being," 127–37; Frank Baldanza, "Virginia Woolf's 'Moments of Being,'" 78; and Christopher C. Dahl, "Virginia Woolf's Moments of Being and the Autobiographical Tradition in the Stephen Family," 175–96.

3   As Naomi Toth argues against the epiphany theory of Morris Beja and formalist philosophy of Ann Banfield. See Toth, "Disturbing Epiphany." "'Moments of Being' cannot therefore be considered as arresting time, nor as a homogenous, transcendent present detached from all other temporalities. This view of Woolf's work is widespread. It is one of the modalities of 'Moments of Being' Beja identifies. Morris Beja, *Epiphany in the Modern Novel* (Seattle, WA: University of Washington Press, 1971), 119–20. See also, for example, Ann Banfield, "Time Passes: Virginia Woolf, Post Impressionism and Cambridge Time," *Poetics Today* 24, no. 3 (2003): 471–516; 492.

4   Toth, "Disturbing Epiphany."

5   Michelle Pridmore-Brown, "1939–40: Of Virginia Woolf, Gramophones, and Fascism," *PMLA* 113 (May 1998): 408–21; 411.

6   Tipper, "Moments of Being," 15.

7   Ibid.

8   Simone, *Virginia Woolf and Being-in-the-World*, 190.

9   Varga, "Music, Language, and Moments of Being," 75.

10 DeSalvo, "The Importance of Moments of Being," 3.

11 My italics.

12 Jensen, "Tradition and Revelation," 112.

13 Simone, *Virginia Woolf and Being-in-the-World*, 140.

14 Ibid., 142.

15 Ibid., 190–1.

16 See Gillian Beer, "Virginia Woolf and Prehistory," in *Virginia Woolf: The Common Ground* (Edinburgh: Edinburgh University Press, 1996), 6–28.

17 Louise Westling, "Virginia Woolf and the Flesh of the World," *New Literary History* 30, no. 4 (Autumn 1999): 855–75; 856.

18 Ibid., 859.

19 Virginia Woolf, *A Passionate Apprentice: The Early Journals 1897–1909*, ed. Mitchell A. Leaska (New York: Mariner Books Classics, 1990), 192.

20 For a lovely survey of these recent approach, one can read Chantal Delourme, "Virginia Woolf among the Philosophers," *Le Tour Critique* 2 (2013): 1–9.

21. Ann Banfield, *The Phantom Table: Woolf, Fry, Russell and the Epistemology of Modernism* (Cambridge: Cambridge University Press, 2000), 66.
22. Banfield, "Time Passes," 471.
23. Katelynn Carver, "'Behind the Cotton Wool': Process Philosophy in the Works of Virginia Woolf," *The Graduate Journal of Harvard Divinity School* (Spring 2013), accessed December 12, 2020, https://projects.iq.harvard.edu/hdsjournal/book/behind-cotton-wool.
24. Gabriel Franks, "Virginia Woolf and the Philosophy of G. E. Moore," *Personalist: An International Review of Philosophy* 50, no. 2 (1969): 222–40.
25. Timothy Mackin, "Private Worlds, Public Minds: Woolf, Russell and Photographic Vision," *Journal of Modern Literature* 33, no. 3 (2010): 118; and Erin Greer, "'A Many-Sided Substance': The Philosophy of Conversation in Woolf, Russell, and Kant," *Journal of Modern Literature* 40, no. 3 (2017): 1–17.
26. Justin W. Keena, "David Hume in *To the Lighthouse*," *Philosophy and Literature* 42, no. 2 (October 2018): 376–93.
27. S. P. Rosenbaum, "Virginia Woolf among the Apostles," *Le Tour Critique* 2 (2013), accessed December 12, 2020, http://letourcritique.u-paris10.fr/index.php/letourcritique/article/view/27/html; S. P. Rosenbaum, *Georgian Bloomsbury: Volume 3: An Early Literary History of the Bloomsbury Group, 1910–1914* (Toronto: Palgrave Macmillan, 2004); S. P. Rosenbaum, "Preface to a Literary History of the Bloomsbury Group," *New Literary History* 12, no. 2 (1981): 329–44.
28. Richard Shusterman, "*The Phantom Table: Woolf, Fry, Russell and the Epistemology of Modernism* (review)," *Common Knowledge* 8, no. 3 (Fall 2002): 551.
29. For a more detailed evaluation of Whitehead and Bergson's process philosophies, please see Thomas Nail, *Being and Motion* (Oxford: Oxford University Press, 2018), chapter three.
30. Harvena Richter, *Virginia Woolf: The Inward Voyage*; John Hughes, *Lines of Flight*.
31. Mark Hussey, *The Singing of the Real World: The Philosophy of Virginia Woolf's Fiction* (Columbus, OH: Ohio State UP, 1986).
32. Jean-Michel Rabaté, "A Constellation of Modernist Historiography: Woolf with Benjamin," *Journal of Modern Literature* 36, no. 1 (2012): 163–5; Sanja Bahun, "The Burden of the Past, the Dialectics of the Present: Notes on Virginia Woolf's and Walter Benjamin's Philosophies of History," *Modernist Cultures* 3, no. 2 (2008): 100–15.
33. Suzette A. Henke, "Virginia Woolf's *The Waves*: A Phenomenological Reading," *Neophilologus* 73 (1989): 461–72; Genevieve Lloyd, *Being in Time: Selves and Narrators in Philosophy and Literature* (New York: Routledge, 1993); Heidi Storl, "Heidegger in Woolf's clothing," *Philosophy and Literature* 32, no. 2 (2008): 303–14; Simone, *Virginia Woolf and Being-in-the-World*; and Lucio Ruotolo, *Six Existential Heroes: The Politics of Faith* (Cambridge, MA: Harvard University Press, 1973).
34. A. O. Frank, *The Philosophy of Virginia Woolf: A Philosophical Reading of the Mature Novels* (Budapest: Akadémiai Kiadó, 2001).
35. Ralph Strehle, "A Risky Business: Internal Time and Objective Time in Husserl and Woolf," in *Literature and Philosophy: A Guide to Contemporary Debates*, ed. David Rudrum (London: Palgrave Macmillan, 2006), 81–91.

36. Michael Lackey, "Modernist Anti-Philosophicalism and Virginia Woolf's Critique of Philosophy," *Journal of Modern Literature* 29, no. 4 (2006): 94.
37. Ibid., 95.
38. Erwin R. Steinberg, "G. E. Moore's Table and Chair in *To the Lighthouse*," *Journal of Modern Literature* 15, no. 1 (1988): 161–8; 161.
39. Rohini Shukla, "Feeling Moral Obligation and Living in an Organic Unity: Virginia Woolf's Response to G. E. Moore," *Transnational Literature* 8, no. 1 (November 2015): 1–10; 1.
40. "Her crucial philosophical intervention lies in conceptualising this new materialism as at once logically continuous with Moore's realism and critical of the subject–object dichotomy he upholds." Ibid., 2.
41. Martin Ŝtelf and Rohini Shukla are both correct to identify Woolf's philosophy of "states of heightened perceptive intensity" as consistent with new materialism. See Martin Ŝtelf, "'A Very Remarkable Piece of Iron': Towards a Theory of Material Imagination in Virginia Woolf's 'Solid Objects,'" *Prague Journal of English Studies* 3, no. 1 (2014): 19. "Woolf's new materialism, if not mystic, does seem antithetical to Moore's philosophy." Shukla, "Feeling Moral Obligation," 7.
42. Daniel Ferrer, *Virginia Woolf and the Madness of Language*, trans. Geoffrey Bennington and Rachel Bowlby (London and New York: Routledge/Taylor & Francis Group, 1990).
43. Frank, *The Philosophy of Virginia Woolf*, 21.
44. For a wonderful set of quotes from Woolf about the limits of description, see Dora Zhang, "Naming the Indescribable: Woolf, Russell, James, and the Limits of Description," *New Literary History: A Journal of Theory and Interpretation* 45, no. 1 (2014): 51–70.

Chapter 1

1. Paul Valéry, *Cahiers/Notebooks 5*, 122.
2. See Derek Ryan, *Virginia Woolf Miscellany* 85 (Spring 2014). https://virginiawoolfmiscellany.files.wordpress.com/2014/06/vwm85spring2014.pdf.
3. See Derek Ryan, *Virginia Woolf and the Materiality of Theory: Sex, Animal, Life* (Edinburgh: Edinburgh University Press, 2013), chapter one.
4. Ibid., 3.
5. Lucretius, *De Rerum Natura*, trans. W. H. D. Rouse and Martin Smith as *On the Nature of Things* (Cambridge, MA: Harvard University Press, 1992), my translation.
6. Matter [*corpora*] (4.55) pours out of things [*diffusa solute*] (4.55) and weaves [*contexta*] (4.57) figures together like fabric, clothing [*tunicas*] (4.58), or armour [*vestem*] (4.61).
7. Christina Alt, *Virginia Woolf and the Study of Nature* (Cambridge and New York: Cambridge University Press, 2010).
8. Holly Henry, *Virginia Woolf and the Discourse of Science: The Aesthetics of Astronomy* (Cambridge and New York: Cambridge University Press, 2003).

9   Ryan, *Virginia Woolf and the Materiality of Theory*; and Pam Morris, *Jane Austen, Virginia Woolf, and Worldly Realism* (Edinburgh: Edinburgh University Press, 2017).

10 See footnote 19 for a list of the literature on Woolf and new materialism.

11 Stacy Alaimo and Susan Hekman, eds., *Material Feminisms* (Bloomington, IN: Indiana University Press, 2008). See also, Rosi Braidotti's interview in *New Materialism: Interviews & Cartographies*, ed. Rick Dolphijn and Iris van der Tuin (London: Open Humanities Press, 2012).

12 See Alaimo and Hekman, "Introduction: Emerging Models of Materiality in Feminist Theory," in *Material Feminisms*, ed. Stacy Alaimo and Susan Hekman, (Bloomington, IN: Indiana University Press, 2007), 1–19.

13 Mel Y. Chen, *Animacies: Biopolitics, Racial Mattering, and Queer Affect* (Durham, NC: Duke University Press, 2014).

14 "Reflecting on these poststructuralist and postmodernist approaches to Woolf and to feminism, and acknowledging that self-identifying as either is now considered to be unfashionable (indeed, according to Moi's own recent comments, 'the poststructuralist paradigm is now exhausted' and postmodern feminism is 'an intellectual tradition that has been fully explored.')" Ryan, *Virginia Woolf and the Materiality of Theory*, 8. Cited within: Toril Moi, "'I Am Not a Feminist, but …': How Feminism Became the F-Word," *PMLA* 121, no. 5 (October 2006): 1735–1741; 1735, 1740.

15 For a list of precursors, see Thomas Nail, *Matter and Motion: A Brief History of Kinetic Materialism* (Edinburgh: Edinburgh University Press, 2024); Thomas Nail, *Marx in Motion: A New Materialist Marxism* (Oxford: Oxford University Press, 2020); Thomas Nail, *Lucretius I: An Ontology of Motion* (Edinburgh: Edinburgh University Press, 2018); and Thomas Nail, *Lucretius II: An Ethics of Motion* (Edinburgh: Edinburgh University Press, 2020). See also, Sarah Ellenzweig and John H. Zammito, *The New Politics of Materialism: History, Philosophy, Science* (New York: Routledge, 2017).

16 Jerry L. Rosiek, Jimmy Snyder, and Scott L. Pratt, "The New Materialisms and Indigenous Theories of Non-Human Agency: Making the Case for Respectful Anti-Colonial Engagement," *Qualitative Inquiry* 26, no. 3–4 (2019): 331–46. See also, Zoe Todd, "An Indigenous Feminist's Take on the Ontological Turn: 'Ontology' Is Just Another Word for Colonialism," *Journal of Historical Sociology* 29, no. 1 (March 2016): 4–22; Bronwyn Davies, "Ethics and the New Materialism: A Brief Genealogy of the 'Post' Philosophies in the Social Sciences," *Discourse: Studies in the Cultural Politics of Education* 39, no. 1 (2018): 113–27; Vanessa Watts, "Indigenous Place-Thought and Agency amongst Humans and Non-Humans (First Woman and Sky Woman Go on a European World Tour!)," *Decolonization: Indigeneity, Education, & Society* 2, no. 1 (2013): 20–34; James Maffie, *Aztec Philosophy: Understanding a World in Motion* (Boulder, CO: University Press of Colorado, 2014).

17 For a wonderful critique and gesture of commonality between new materialism and indigenous philosophy, see Rosiek, Snyder, and Pratt, "The New Materialisms and Indigenous Theories of Non-Human Agency."

18 Ryan, *Virginia Woolf and the Materiality of Theory*.

19 See Leanna Lostoski, "'Imaginations of the Strangest Kind': The Vital Materialism of Virginia Woolf," *Journal of the Midwest Modern Language Association* 49, no. 1 (Spring 2016): 53–74; Iris Van Der Tuin, "Signals Falling: Reading Woolf and

Guattari Diffractively for a New Materialist Epistemology," *Minnesota Review* 88, no. 1 (2017): 112–15; Madeline Thatcher, "'Life Is a Solid Substance': Materialism and the Use of Objects in Virginia Woolf's *The Waves*," *Criterion: A Journal of Literary Criticism* 9, no. 1 (2016): 61–74; Claire Colebrook, *Death of the Posthuman: Essays on Extinction, Volume 1* (Ann Arbor, MI: Open Humanities Press with Michigan Publishing, 2014); Rosi Braidotti, *The Posthuman* (Cambridge: Polity Press, 2013); Ryan, *Virginia Woolf and the Materiality of Theory*; Ian Buchanan and Clare Colebrook, eds., *Deleuze and Feminist Theory* (Edinburgh: Edinburgh University Press, 2005); Derek Ryan and Laci Mattison, "Deleuze, Virginia Woolf and Modernism," *Deleuze Studies* 7, no. 4 (November 2013): 421–6; Astrida Neimanis, *Bodies of Water: Posthuman Feminist Phenomenology* (London: Bloomsbury Academic, 2017), 2; and Rosi Braidotti and Ruth Clemens, "The Shimmering Intensity of Virginia Woolf: An Interview with Rosi Braidotti," *The Modernist Review*, October 10, 2018, accessed December 12, 2020, https://modernistreviewcouk.wordpress.com/2018/10/10/the-shimmering-intensity-of-virginia-woolf-an-interview-with-rosi-braidotti/.

20 Lostoski, "Imaginations of the Strangest Kind," 53–74; Van Der Tuin, "Signals Falling," 112–15; Thatcher, "Life Is a Solid Substance," 61–74; Graham Fraser, "Solid Objects/Ghosts of Chairs: Virginia Woolf and the Afterlife of Things," *Journal of Modern Literature* 43, no. 2 (Winter 2020): 80–97; and Ryan, *Virginia Woolf and the Materiality of Theory*.

21 For a survey of the literature on Woolf and philosophy please, see Chantal Delourme, "Virginia Woolf among the Philosophers," 1–9. See also Ryan, *Virginia Woolf and the Materiality of Theory*.

22 Thomas Nail, "What Is the Philosophy of Movement?" *Mobilities Humanities* 1, no. 1 (January 2022): 9–25.

23 Thomas Nail, *Being and Motion*.

24 I cannot possibly defend this claim here, but curious readers can follow up with my books on *Lucretius*, *Marx*, and *Being and Motion* where I argue it at length.

25 See Susanna Rich, "*De Undarum Natura*: Lucretius and Woolf in *The Waves*," *Journal of Modern Literature* 23, no. 2 (Winter 1999–2000): 249–57; and James Morland, "The Influence of Lucretius on Unity in *The Waves*," *Virginia Woolf Bulletin* 38 (2011): 23–6.

26 Nail, *Lucretius I* and *Lucretius II*.

27 Woolf records "stumbling through Lucretius" in early 1907 (L1, 280; see also 284), and was reading him again in September 1918 (D1, 192). There are a number of translations of Lucretius in Woolf's library, now in Washington State University Library.

28 "We might say that Bloomsbury first entered the public sphere on a battleship, then on a rocking horse, tilting at naturalism (for which also read Woolf's 'materialism'):" Andrew McNeillie, "Bloomsbury," in *The Cambridge Companion to Virginia Woolf*, ed. Susan Sellers (Cambridge: Cambridge University Press, 2000), 16. "Elsewhere Lucretius, a favorite Bloomsbury author, is praised in an essay [by Leonard Woolf] as a great poet, thinker, scientist and satirist." S. P. Rosenbaum, *Victorian Bloomsbury: Volume 1: The Early Literary History of the Bloomsbury Group* (London: Palgrave Macmillan Limited, 2016), 131.

29 Robert Calverley Trevelyan and Titus Lucretius Carus, *Lucretius on Death: Being a Translation of Book III, Lines 830 to 1094 of the De Rerum Natura* (London: Omega Workshops, 1917). Woodcut title page designed by Roger Fry and Dora Carrington.
30 Alt, *Virginia Woolf and the Study of Nature*.
31 Bonnie Kime Scott, *In the Hollow of the Wave: Virginia Woolf and Modernist Uses of Nature* (Charlottesville, VA: University of Virginia Press, 2012). Woolf was invoked by some of the earliest ecofeminists. See Irene Diamond and Gloria Orenstein, eds., *Reweaving the World: The Emergence of Ecofeminism* (San Francisco, CA: Sierra Club Books, 1990); Alt, *Virginia Woolf and the Study of Nature;* Ryan, *Virginia Woolf and the Materiality of Theory*; Kristin Czarnecki and Carrie Rohman, eds., *Virginia Woolf and the Natural World: Selected Papers from the Twentieth Annual International Conference on Virginia Woolf* (Clemson, SC: Clemson University Digital Press, 2011); Diana L. Swanson, "Woolf's Copernican Shift: Nonhuman Nature in Virginia Woolf's Short Fiction," *Woolf Studies Annual* 18 (2012): 53–74; and Kelly Sultzbach, *Ecocriticism in the Modernist Imagination: Forster, Woolf, and Auden* (New York: Cambridge University Press, 2016).
32 Simone Beauvoir, *The Second Sex*, trans. Constance Borde and Shelia Malovany-Chevallier (London: Vintage Books, 2011), 669.
33 Ibid.
34 Daniel Albright, *Quantum Poetics: Yeats, Pound, Eliot, and the Science of Modernism* (Cambridge: Cambridge University Press, 1997).
35 Michael H. Whitworth, "Virginia Woolf, Modernism and Modernity," in *The Cambridge Companion to Virginia Woolf*, ed. Susan Sellers (Cambridge: Cambridge University Press, 2010), 107–23.
36 See Gillian Beer, "Physics, Sound, and Substance: Later Woolf," in *Virginia Woolf: The Common Ground* (Ann Arbor, MI: University of Michigan Press, 1996), 112–24. See also, Mark Hussey, "*To the Lighthouse* and Physics: The Cosmology of David Bohm and Virginia Woolf," in *New Essays on Virginia Woolf*, ed. Helen Wussow (Dallas: Contemporary Research Associates, 1995), 79–98; Hermione Lee, *Virginia Woolf* (London: Chatto & Windus, 1996), 554; and Michelle Pridmore-Brown, "1939–40: Of Virginia Woolf, Gramophones, and Fascism," 408–21.
37 Arthur Stanley Eddington, *The Nature of the Physical World: The Gifford Lectures, 1927* (Cambridge: Cambridge University Press, 1928), 1.
38 On this point, see also, Linden Peach, "Virginia Woolf and Realist Aesthetics," in *The Edinburgh Companion to Virginia Woolf and the Arts*, ed. Maggie Humm (Edinburgh: Edinburgh University Press, 2010), 104–17.
39 For an account of Moore's realism in relation to Woolf's writing see S. P. Rosenbaum, "The Philosophical Realism of Virginia Woolf," in *English Literature and British Philosophy: A Collection of Essays*, ed. S. P. Rosenbaum (Chicago, IL: University of Chicago Press, 1971), 316–56. I agree with Shukla that Woolf moves beyond Moore's subject object dualism though. Rohini Shukla, "Feeling Moral Obligation and Living in an Organic Unity: Virginia Woolf's Response to G. E. Moore," *Transnational Literature* 8, no. 1 (November 2015): 1–10.
40 Mark Hussey, *The Singing of the Real World*, 96.
41 Morris, *Jane Austen, Virginia Woolf and Worldly Realism*, 117.

42 Ibid., 114.
43 Ibid., 130. "Lucretius' arguments against idealism, along with his atomic theory of matter, in which chance collisions 'heedless, without aim, without intention', produce the entire universe had renewed relevance for Woolf's generation in the wake of Einstein's atomic theory (DRN, p. 177). In 1918, for example, H. Woods published a defence of materialism with the Lucretian title *On the Nature of Things*." Cited in Morris, *Jane Austen*, 116.
44 Linden Peach, *Virginia Woolf*, 169. See, for example, Jean Guiguet, *Virginia Woolf and Her Works* (San Diego, CA: Harcourt, Brace & World, 1965); James Hafley, *The Glass Roof: Virginia Woolf as Novelist* (Berkeley, CA: University of California Press, 1954); and Shiv K. Kumar, *Bergson and the Stream of Consciousness Novel* (New York: New York University Press, 1963).
45 Alex Zwerdling, *Virginia Woolf and the Real World* (Berkeley, CA: University of California Press, 1986); Rosenbaum, "The Philosophical Realism of Virginia Woolf,"; and Ann Banfield, "Time Passes: Virginia Woolf, Post-Impressionism, and Cambridge Time," 471–516.
46 Morris, *Jane Austen*, 57–8. See also Ryan, *Virginia Woolf and the Materiality of Theory*, 49–50.
47 Morris, *Jane Austen*, 57. "She does, undoubtedly, express strong dissatisfaction with the novelistic aims of Bennett and his contemporaries to 'embalm' probability within a mass of factual detail, but this constitutes a criticism of what I suggest is actualist writing rather than realist. Indeed, in both essays she explicitly praises realists like Austen, Thackeray, Hardy, Chekov and Tolstoy."
48 "In her recent work on Woolf and realism, Pam Morris has argued that Woolf's 'representations of public world, individual consciousness and interpersonal discourse retain a realist underpinning in conjunction with experimental form.'" "And she therefore favors a 'metonymic realism' that is symptomatic of a contiguous materialism, rather than metaphoric or symbolic, where 'symbolism and metaphoric idealisation function to impose totality and universality upon diversity, to deny a troublesome material heterogeneity by merging' together. Keen to move away from an inflated and dominant subjectivity, Morris insists that Woolf seeks 'outwardness as much as inwardness'." Pam Morris, "Virginia Woolf's Metonymic Realism in Mrs Dalloway," English Literature Visiting Speaker Series, University of Glasgow, 2008. Quoted in Ryan, *Virginia Woolf and the Materiality of Theory*, 50.
49 Fry, like Bernard from *The Waves*, also describes the daily reality of "dressing and eating and talking and going to bed" as a sham—at "any moment the surface may dissolve and the reality appear, whatever that reality may be" (RF, 58).

Chapter 2

1 Jane Goldman, "Modernist Studies," in *Palgrave Advances in Virginia Woolf Studies*, ed. Anna Snaith (New York: Palgrave Macmillan, 2007), 39.
2 See Kelly Sultzbach, "The Phenomenological Whole: Virginia Woolf," *Ecocriticism in the Modernist Imagination: Forester, Woolf, and Auden* (New York: Cambridge University Press, 2016), 82–145.

3   Caroline J. Tully and Sam Crooks, "Dropping Ecstasy? Minoan Cult and the Tropes of Shamanism," *Time and Mind* 8, no. 2 (2015): 129–58; Nanno Marinatos, "The Character of Minoan Epiphanies," *Illinois Classical Studies* 29 (2004): 25–42. See also Aldous Huxley, *The Perennial Philosophy* (New York: Harper & Brothers, 1945) and Thomas Rickert, "Rhetorical Prehistory and the Paleolithic," *Review of Communication* 16, no. 4 (2016): 352–73.

4   See also, Woolf's annotated translations in her copy of Homer's *Illiad* in the Washington State Library.

5   Brian C. Muraresku has recently uncovered definitive archeo-chemcial evidence of ergot, the fungus from which the Swiss chemist Albert Hoffman derived LSD, inside a drinking vessel used during the mystery rites of Eleusis. See Brian C. Muraresku, *The Immortality Key: The Secret History of the Religion with No Name* (New York: St. Martin's Press, 2020). See also, Robert G. Wasson, Albert Hofmann, Carl A. P. Ruck, Robert Forte, Huston Smith, and Blaise D. Staples, *The Road to Eleusis: Unveiling the Secret of the Mysteries* (Berkeley, CA: North Atlantic Books, 2008). For the original archeological evidence, see Jordi Juan-Tresserras, "La arqueología de las drogas en la Península Ibérica: una síntesis de las recientes investigaciones arqueobotánicas," *Complutum,* no. 11 (2000): 261–74.

6   For a full account of this connection between Harrison, Woolf, ancient ritual, and modern art, see Martha C. Carpentier, "Jane Ellen Harrison and the Ritual Theory," *Journal of Ritual Studies* 8, no. 1 (Winter 1994): 11–26. On the connection between Woolf and Harrison more broadly, see Jane Marcus, *Virginia Woolf and the Languages of Patriarchy* (Bloomington, IN: Indiana University Press, 1987).

7   My transcription of Woolf's annotations/translations from her copy of Lucretius' *De Rerum Natura,* Book I, lines 919–28. Woolf's translations in parentheses.

> *"fiet uti risu tremulo concussa cachinnent*
> *et lacrimis* (INSPIRING WIND) *salsis umectent ora genasque.*
> *Nunc age, quod super est, cognosce etclarius audi.*
> *nec me animi fallit quam sint obscura; sed acri*
> *percussit thyrso laudis spes magnameum cor*
> *et simul incussit suavem mi in pectus amorem* (SMITTEN DEEP)
> *925 Musarum, quo nunc instinctus mente vigenti* (PRICKED HEART)
> *avia Pieridum peragro loca nullius ante* (roam trackless wilds)
> *trita solo. iuvat integros* (VIRGIN) *accedere fontis*
> *atque haurire iuvatque novos decerpere flores"*

8   My transcription of Woolf's annotations/translations from her copy of Lucretius' *De Rerum Natura,* Book III, lines 28–9. Woolf's translations in parentheses.

> *"his ibi me rebus quaedam* (THRILLING AWE) *divina voluptas*
> *percipit atque horror* (RAPTURE)*, quod sic naturatua vi"*

9   My transcription of Woolf's annotations/translations from her copy of Lucretius' *De Rerum Natura.* Woolf's translations in parentheses.

> *"nam sua cuique, locis ex omnibus, omnia plagis"* (SHOCKS) (2.1112)
> *"Denique si vocem rerum natura repente."* (SHOCKS) (3.931)
> *"vim subitam* (SHOCK) *tolerare: ita magno turbidus* (IN TURMOIL) *imbri* (SEETHING)" (1.286)
> *"impetibus* (SHOCKS) *crebris, inter dum vertice torto"* (CURLING EDDY) (1.293)
> *"denique per maria ac montis fluviosque rapacis"* (WHIRLING). (1.7)
> *"verrunt ac subito vexantia turbine* (WHIRL) *raptant,"* (1.279)

10 My transcription of Woolf's annotations/translations from her copy of Lucretius' *De Rerum Natura,* Book III, lines 28–9. Woolf's translations in parentheses.
> *"his ibi me rebus quaedam* (THRILLING AWE) *divina voluptas percipit atque horror* (RAPTURE)*, quod sic naturatua vi"*

11 See Lucretius' description of his Bacchanalian wandering movement through the mountains of the Muses (1.921–30). "The DRN opens with a religious vision, an epiphany, of Venus, diverted to Epicurean ends." Philip Hardie, "Lucretius and Later Latin Literature in Antiquity," in *The Cambridge Companion to Lucretius*, ed. Stuart Gillespie and Philip Hardie (Cambridge: Cambridge University Press, 2007), 119. "For Lucretius poetic vision serves the purposes of philosophical insight." Cambridge companion," Hardie, "Lucretius and later Latin literature," 118. On the acuity of Lucretian visualisation, see Richard Jenkyns, *Virgil's Experience: Nature and History; Times, Names, and Places* (Oxford and New York: Oxford University Press, 1998), 275–8.

12 My italics.

13 Perry Meisel, *The Absent Father: Virginia Woolf and Walter Pater* (New Haven, CT: Yale University Press, 1980), 52.

14 Woolf states that such writing reflects Conrad's propensity to experience "a 'moment of vision' in which he sees people as if he had never seen them before; he expounds his vision, and we see it, too. These visions are the best things in his books." (E2, 142). Quoted in Emma Simone, *Virginia Woolf and Being-in-the-World*, 187. See also, Jay B. Losey, "Pater's Epiphanies and the Open Forum," *South Central Review* 6, no. 4 (Winter 1989): 48.

15 Woolf states that such writing reflects Conrad's propensity to experience "a 'moment of vision' in which he sees people as if he had never seen them before; he expounds his vision, and we see it, too. These visions are the best things in his books" (E2, 142). Conrad writes:

> Nothing could have been more commonplace than this remark; but its utterance coincided for me with a moment of vision. It's extraordinary how we go through life with eyes half shut, with dull ears, with dormant thoughts. Perhaps it's just as well; and it may be that it is this very dullness that makes life to the incalculable majority so support-able and so welcome. Nevertheless, there can be but few of us who had never known one of these rare moments of awakening when we see, hear, understand ever so much—everything—in a flash—before we fall back again into our agreeable somnolence. I raised my eyes when he spoke, and I saw him as though I had never seen him before.

Joseph Conrad, *Lord Jim* (New York: Oxford University Press, 2008), 104. Quoted in Simone, *Virginia Woolf and Being-in-the-World*, 187.

16 See Simone, *Virginia Woolf and Being-in-the-World*, chapter five. See also, Jane de Gay, *Virginia Woolf's Novels and the Literary Past* (Edinburgh: Edinburgh University Press, 2007); Ashton Nichols, *The Poetics of Epiphany: Nineteenth-Century Origins of the Modern Literary Moment* (Tuscaloosa, AL: University of Alabama Press, 1987); Morris Beja, *Epiphany in the Modern Novel* (London: Peter Owen Press, 1971); Wim Tigges, ed., *Moments of Moment: Aspects of the Literary Epiphany* (Amsterdam: Rodopi, 1999), 43; and Verity J. Platt, *Facing the Gods: Epiphany and Representation in Graeco-Roman Art, Literature, and Religion* (Cambridge: Cambridge University Press, 2011).

17 See Thomas C. Caramagno, *The Flight of the Mind: Virginia Woolf's Art and Manic-Depressive Illness* (Berkeley, CA: University of California Press, 1992). "I believe these illnesses are in my case-how shall I express it?—partly mystical." (D3, 287) "As an experience, madness is terrific I can assure you, and not to be sniffed at; and in its lava I still find most of the things I write about. It shoots out of one everything shaped, final, not in mere driblets, as sanity does" (L4, 180). And contemporary research into manic depression, Woolf's particular mental disability, backs her up on that point. In *The Flight of the Mind*, Thomas Caramagno explains that the manic stage of the illness is associated with "torrents of ideas and words connected by complex webs of associations," delusions, hallucinations, a heightened sense of the meaning of life, a sensation of being able to "read" one's environment, even auras and halos around things. Victims are prone to interpret such episodes as "religious experiences." Caramagno, *The Flight of the Mind*, 40–2. "Yet I am now & then haunted by some semi-mystic very profound life of a woman, which shall all be told on one occasion; & time shall be utterly obliterated; future shall somehow blossom out of the past. One incident-say the fall of a flower-might contain it. My theory being that the event practically does not exist—nor time either." (D3, 118).

18 Caramagno, *The Flight of the Mind*.

19 See Julie Kane, "Varieties of Mystical Experience in the Writings of Virginia Woolf," *Twentieth Century Literature* 41, no. 4 (Winter 1995): 328–49.

20 Miriam M. Clark, "Consciousness, Stream and Quanta, in *To the Lighthouse*," *Studies in the Novel* 21, no. 4 (Winter 1989): 413–23; Ian Ettinger, "Relativity and Quantum Theory in Virginia Woolf's *The Waves*," *Zeteo: The Journal of Interdisciplinary Writing* 3 (Spring 2012): 1–19; and Paul Tolliver Brown, "Relativity, Quantum Physics, and Consciousness in Virginia Woolf's *To the Lighthouse*," *Journal of Modern Literature* 32, no. 3 (Spring, 2009): 39–62.

21 See "Gas at Abbotsford" (E6, 213).

22 Derek Ryan, "Woolf and Contemporary Philosophy," in *Virginia Woolf in Context*, ed. Bryony Randall and Jane Goldman (Cambridge: Cambridge University Press, 2013), chapter 30.

23 See Aldous Huxley, *The Doors of Perception* (London: Chatto and Windus, 1968).

24 The heightened perception of patterns or pareidolia is also something characteristic of both mania and psychedelic states.

25 For an excellent review of the literature on fractals and evidence of their effects on human psychology, see R. P. Taylor "The Potential of Biophilic Fractal Designs to Promote Health and Performance: A Review of Experiments and Applications," *Sustainability* 13 (2021): 823.

26 Lucretius says in lines 4.136–42 of *De Rerum Natura* that

> sometimes majestic mountains and rocks ripped from
> mountains seem to go ahead and pass before the sun,
> then a monster seems to drag and pull in other clouds.
> They never stop dissolving, changing their shapes,
> and turning into the outlines of shapes of every kind.

27 Klaus Linkenkaer-Hansen et al., "Long-Range Temporal Correlations and Scaling Behavior in Human Brain Oscillations," *The Journal of Neuroscience* 21, no. 4 (February 15, 2001): 1370–77.

28 See Thomas Nail, *Pink Noise: A History of Consciousness*, forthcoming.

29 B. B. Mandelbrot, *The Fractal Geometry of Nature* (New York: WH Freedman, 1982.

30 On the connection between poikilos and fractals, see Amy Lather, *Materiality and Aesthetics in Archaic and Classical Greek Poetry* (Edinburgh: Edinburgh University Press, 2021), 34. See also, Nikolaus Dietrich, "Order and Contingency in Archaic Greek Ornament and Figure," in *Ornament and Figure in Graeco-Roman Art*, ed. Nikolaus Dietrich and Michael Squire (Rethinking Visual Ontologies in Classical Antiquity, Berlin-New York: De Gruyter, 2018), 167–201.

31 Paul Lake, "The Shape of Poetry," in *The Measured Word: On Poetry and Science,* ed. Kurt Brown (Athens, GA: University of Georgia Press, 2005), 156–80.

32 Hopkins did not directly use the word *poikila* in his writing. However, he likely knew of the Greek word *poikila* from Walter Pater or John Ruskin. For a survey of the evidence of this transmission, see Lisa Dowling, "Ruskin's Pied Beauty and the Constitution of a 'Homosexual' Code," *Victorian Newsletter* (The), no. 75 (1989): 1–8.

33 See Dwight Lindley, "Woolf and Hopkins on the Revelatory Particular," in *Religion, Secularism, and the Spiritual Paths of Virginia Woolf,* ed. Kristina K. Groover (New York: Palgrave, 2019), 87–107.

34 Stanisław Drożdż, Paweł Oświę cimka, Andrzej Kulig, Jarosław Kwapień, Katarzyna Bazarnik, Iwona Grabska-Gradzińska, Jan Rybicki, and Marek Stanuszek, "Quantifying Origin and Character of Long-Range Correlations in Narrative Texts," *Information Sciences* 331 (2016): 32–44.

35 See Susanna Rich, "*De Undarum Natura*: Lucretius and Woolf in *The Waves*," *Journal of Modern Literature* 23, no. 2 (Winter, 1999–2000): 249–57 and James Morland, "The Influence of Lucretius on Unity in *The Waves*," *Virginia Woolf Bulletin* 38 (2011): 23–6.

36 For a full commentary and analysis of this, see Thomas Nail, *Lucretius I* and *Lucretius II*.

37 See Rich, "De Undarum Natura," and Morland, "The Influence of Lucretius."

38 Nail, *Lucretius II,* 147–69.

39 Meisel, *The Absent Father*, 52.
40 Walter Pater, *The Renaissance: Studies in Art and Poetry*, ed. Donald L. Hill (Berkeley, CA: University of California Press, 1980), 186–7.
41 Walter Pater, *Marius the Epicurean*, ed. Michael Levey (Harmondsworth: Penguin, 1985), 113.
42 Walter Pater, *Marius the Epicurean: His Sensations and Ideas, volume 1* (London: Macmillan, 1908), 113.
43 Ibid., 98–9.
44 See Irena Ksiezopolska, *The Web of Sense: Patterns of Involution in Selected Works of Virginia Woolf and Vladimir Nabokov*, New Americanists in Poland Series (Frankfurt am Main: Peter Lang, 2012).
45 Henry R. Harrington, "The Central Line Down the Middle of *To the Lighthouse*," *Contemporary Literature* 21, no. 3 (Summer 1980): 363–82.
46 Sue Roe, "The Art of Making Memories," *Virginia Woolf Bulletin* 20 (2005): 22.
47 See also, Stephen Ullmann, *The Image in the Modern French Novel: Gide, Alain-Fournier, Proust, Camus* (Cambridge: Cambridge University Press, 1960), viii.
48 Nail, *Lucretius II*, 175.

Brief Moments

1 Miriam M. Clark, "Consciousness, Stream and Quanta, in *To the Lighthouse*," 413–23; Ian Ettinger, "Relativity and Quantum Theory in Virginia Woolf's *The Waves*," 1–19; and Paul Tolliver Brown, "Relativity, Quantum Physics, and Consciousness in Virginia Woolf's *To the Lighthouse*," 39–62.
2 Thomas Nail, "Why Is Walking So Good for the Brain? Blame It on the 'Spontaneous Fluctuations'," *Salon Magazine*, August 28, 2021. https://www.salon.com/2021/08/28/walking-and-spontaneous-fluctuations-brain/.
3 Thomas C. Caramagno, *The Flight of the Mind: Virginia Woolf's Art and Manic-Depressive Illness* (Berkeley, CA: University of California Press, 1992), 209.
4 Nicole L. Urquhart, "Moments of Being in Virginia Woolf's Fiction," *Writing@CSU*, accessed December 12, 2020, https://writing.colostate.edu/gallery/matrix/urquhart.htm.

Individual Moments

1 Walter Pater, *The Renaissance* (New York: Modern Library, 1873), 195.
2 For wonderful new materialist account of ASMR and its similarities to musique concrète, see Joanna Łapińska, "Vibrations of Worldly Matter: ASMR as Contemporary Musique Concrète," *The Polish Journal of Aesthetics* 57, no. 2 (2020): 21–35.

3   Emma L. Barratt, Charles Spence, and Nick J. Davis, "Sensory Determinants of the Autonomous Sensory Meridian Response (ASMR): Understanding the Triggers," *PeerJ* 5 (2017): e3846.

4   On Virginia Woolf and ASMR, see Clemens Setz, "High durch sich räuspernde Menschen," *Süddeutsche Zeitung*, April 6, 2015, https://www.sueddeutsche.de/kultur/gastbeitrag-das-namenlose-gefuehl-1.2423469 and Hannah Maslen and Rebecca Roache, "ASMR and Absurdity," *Practical Ethics*, July 30, 2015, http://blog.practicalethics.ox.ac.uk/2015/07/asmr-and-absurdity/.

5   Christoph Cox, "Beyond Representation and Signification: Toward a Sonic Materialism," *Journal of Visual Culture* 10, no. 2 (2011): 145–61.

6   Davide Albertini, Marco Lanzilotto, Monica Maranesi, and Luca Bonini. "Largely Shared Neural Codes for Biological and Nonbiological Observed Movements but Not for Executed Actions in Monkey Premotor Areas," *Journal of Neurophysiology* 126, no. 3 (2021): 906–12.

7   Urban soundscapes are very commonly fractal in their frequency ranges. B. D. Coensel, D. Botteldooren, and T. D. Muer. "Scientific Papers—Environmental Acoustics—1/f Noise in Rural and Urban Soundscapes." Acustica United with Acta Acustica: The *Journal of the European Acoustics Association* (eeig) 89, no. 2 (2003): 287.

8   Aldous Huxley, *The Perennial Philosophy* (New York: Harper & Brothers, 1945); and Gordon Wasson, Albert Hoffman, and Carl A. P. Ruck, *The Road to Eleusis: Unveiling the Secret of the Mysteries* (New York: Harcourt, 1978).

9   Paul Valéry calls this "mysticism without god." See Paul Valéry, *Cahiers/Notebooks* 5, 544.

10 "… and since fog and smoke disperse outward into the air, understand that the soul too is poured out and perishes much more quickly and is dissolved more rapidly into its first bodies" (3.436–8).

11 "Yes you, just as you are now asleep in death, so you will be for what remains of time, freed from all bitter sorrows." (3.904–5).

12 According to Lucretius, we sleep because our minds, bodies, and souls are, following Book 3, metastable processes that require them to "work" or "labor" [*opera*] (4.920) to sustain the habitual patterns of motion (electrical, chemical, etc.) that reproduce and form us. Just like simulacra, human and animal bodies are diffractive patterns iterated over and over again. They are formed through figuration. We sleep when the metastable labors that sustain us become too disordered, entropic, or turbulent [*conturbantur*] (4.943). We sleep not because we are out of energy but because the mind and body need time to organize the iterative patterns of motion in the body and mind.

13 " … 'spectral presences,' all the more so as cannot but evoke the fatal Sisters and the inexorable flow of time (already su rings of smoke wobbling into 'hour-glass shapes'). Yet in the vision proper, time comes to a standstill, or partakes of another dimension signaled by the shifting from preterite tense to the general present: 'spectral presences … rise,' 'the traveler sees.'" André Viola, "'Buds on a Tree of Life': A Recurrent Mythological Image in Virginia Woolf's 'Mrs. Dalloway,'" *Journal of Modern Literature* 20, no. 2 (Winter 1996): 241.

14 Carlo Rovelli, *The Order of Time*, trans. Erica Segre and Simon Carnell (New York: Riverhead Books, 2018).
15 See Thomas Nail, *Lucretius I* and *Lucretius II*.
16 DRN (4.963–5).
17 See Robert P. Harrison, *Forests: The Shadow of Civilization* (Chicago, IL: University of Chicago Press, 2014).
18 See Nail, *Lucretius II*.
19 Ibid.
20 Lucretius, *De Rerum Natura*, Book 1, Lines 1–25.
21 Ibid., Lines 66–71.
22 Animals tend to hunt and evade one another in fractal patterns of motion. J. M. Kembro, M. A. Perillo, P. A. Pury, D. G. Satterlee, and R. H. Marin. "Fractal Analysis of the Ambulation Pattern of Japanese Quail," *British Poultry Science*. 50, no. 2 (2009): 161–70. G. M. Viswanathan, V. Afanasyev, S. V. Buldyrev, E. J. Murphy, P. A. Prince, and H. E. Stanley "Lévy Flight Search Patterns of Wandering Albatrosses," *Nature* 381 (1996): 413–5. S. C. Le Comber, E. W. Seabloom, and S. S. Romañach, "Burrow Fractal Dimension and Foraging Success in Subterranean Rodents: A Simulation," *Behavioral Ecology* 17, no. 2 (March/April 2006): 188–95, https://doi.org/10.1093/beheco/arj011.
23 Lucretius, *De Rerum Natura*, Book 2, Lines 216–93.
24 Ibid., Line 6.
25 For a kinetic theory of time, see Thomas Nail, *Being and Motion*, Part IV. See also Thomas Nail, *Theory of the Object* (Oxford: Oxford University Press, under review).
26 P. Szendro, G. Vincze, and A. Szasz, "Pink-Noise Behaviour of Biosystems," *European Biophysics Journal* 30, no. 3 (July 1, 2001): 227–31, https://doi.org/10.1007/s002490100143.
27 Pink noise tends to slow down brain wave frequencies aiding relaxation and sleep. J. Zhou, D. Liu, X. Li, J. Ma, J. Zhang, and J. Fang. "Pink Noise: Effect on Complexity Synchronization of Brain Activity and Sleep Consolidation," *Journal of Theoretical Biology* 306 (August 7, 2012): 68–72.
28 Bernice Rogowitz and Richard Voss, "Shape Perception and Low-Dimension Fractal Boundaries," *Proceedings of SPIE—The International Society for Optical Engineering*, January 1990, https://www.researchgate.net/profile/Bernice-Rogowitz-2/publication/247506403_Shape_perception_and_low-dimension_fractal_boundaries/links/5f6bbf78458515b7cf496658/Shape-perception-and-low-dimension-fractal-boundaries.pdf.
29 Viola, "Buds on a Tree of Life," 239–47.
30 Friedrich Nietzsche, *Philosophy and Truth: Selections from Nietzsche's Notebooks of the Early 1870's*, trans. Daniel Breazeale (Amherst, NY: Humanity Books, 1999), 79.
31 See Arne Naess, "Gestalt Ontology and Gestalt Thinking," in *The Selected Works of Arne Naess*, ed. Alan Drengson (Dordrecht, Netherlands: Springer, 2005), 2727–33.

32   See Nikolaus Dietrich, "Order and Contingency in Archaic Greek Ornament and Figure," in *Ornament and Figure in Graeco-Roman Art*, ed. Nikolaus Dietrich and Michael Squire (Rethinking Visual Ontologies in Classical Antiquity, Berlin-New York: De Gruyter, 2018), 167–201.

33   Gerard Manley Hopkins, Lesley Higgins, and Michael F. Suarez, *The Collected Works of Gerard Manley Hopkins / Volume III, Diaries, Journals, and Notebooks / Edited by Lesley Higgins* (Oxford: Oxford University Press, 2015), 504.

34   Lucretius, *De Rerum Natura*, Book 1, Lines, 144–8.

35   See Mark A. S. McMenamin and Dianna L. S. McMenamin, *Hypersea: Life on Land* (New York: Columbia University Press, 1996) and Thomas Nail, *Theory of the Earth* (Stanford, CA: Stanford University Press, 2021).

36   Marily Oppezzo and Daniel L. Schwartz, "Give Your Ideas Some Legs: The Positive Effect of Walking on Creative Thinking," *Journal of Experimental Psychology. Learning, Memory, and Cognition* 40, no. 4 (2014): 1142–52.

37   Gregory Bateson, *Mind and Nature: A Necessary Unity* (Cresskill, NJ: Hampton Press, 2002), 11.

38   Aldous Huxley, *The Doors of Perception* (New York: Harper & Row, 1954).

39   Henri Bergson, *Matter and Memory* (New York: Zone Books, 1991), 38–9.

40   See Derek Ryan, "Queering *Orlando* and Nonhuman Desire," *Virginia Woolf and the Materiality of Theory: Sex, Animal, Life* (Edinburgh: Edinburgh University Press, 2013), 101–31.

41   "That which is directly transmitted, without the 'detour' or the 'boredom' of a story to tell," Paul Valéry quoted by Gilles Deleuze in *Francis Bacon: The Logic of Sensation*, trans. Daniel W. Smith (London: Continuum, 2010), 36.

42   For a study of fractal sound spectrums in urban environments, see Coensel, Botteldooren, and Muer. "Scientific Papers—Environmental Acoustics—1/f Noise in Rural and Urban Soundscapes," 294.

43   Sean Carroll, *Something Deeply Hidden: Quantum Worlds and the Emergence of Spacetime* (New York: Dutton, 2019).

44   Albert Newen, Leon De Bruin, and Shaun Gallagher, eds., *The Oxford Handbook of 4E Cognition* (Oxford: Oxford University Press, 2018).

Non-Human Moments

1   See Carlo Rovelli, *Reality Is Not What It Seems: The Journey to Quantum Gravity*, trans. Simon Carnell and Erica Segre (New York: Riverhead Books, 2017).

2   Lucretius, *De Rerum Natura*, trans. W. H. D. Rouse and Martin Smith as *On the Nature of Things* (Cambridge, MA: Harvard University Press, 1992) (1.249).

3   Carlo Rovelli, *The Order of Time*, trans. Erica Segre and Simon Carnell (New York: Riverhead Books, 2018).

4   See James Frazer, *The Golden Bough: A Study in Magic and Religion* (Oxford: Oxford University Press, 1998 [1890]); and Jane E. Harrison, Gilbert Murray, and

Francis M. Cornford, *Themis: A Study of the Social Origins of Greek Religion* (Cambridge: Cambridge University Press, 2010).

5   See Kelly Sultzbach, *Ecocriticism in the Modernist Imagination: Forster, Woolf, and Auden* (Cambridge: Cambridge University Press, 2016), chapter 2.
6   See Thomas Nail, *Theory of the Earth*.
7   See Ibid.
8   Again, it is hard to ignore the clear similarity between this description and Lucretius' in Book IV. See Thomas Nail, *Lucretius II*.
9   See Gaston Bachelard, *The Poetics of Space*, trans. Maria Jolas (New York: Orion Press, 1964), chapter two.
10 See Thomas Nail, *Being and Motion*, chapter 15.
11 See Thomas Nail, *Theory of the Object*.
12 Just as Lucretius describes in the opening lines of *De Rerum Natura*.
13 This is the inverse of Maurice Merleau-Ponty's idea of the flesh. See Maurice Merleau-Ponty, *The Visible and the Invisible: Followed by Working Notes*, ed. Claude Lefort (Evanston, IL: Northwestern University Press, 2000).
14 Percy B. Shelley, "Triumph of Life," in *The Complete Poems of Percy Bysshe Shelley* (New York: Modern Library, 1994).
15 Vojislav V. Mitic, Hans-Jorg Fecht, Markus Mohr, Goran Lazovic, and Ljubisa Kocic. "Exploring Fractality of Microcrystalline Diamond Films," *Aip Advances* 8, no. 7 (2018).
16 Pollan describes a similar reduced fear of death in: Michael Pollan, "Psychedelics in Psychotherapy: Dying, Addiction, Depression," *How to Change Your Mind: What the New Science of Psychedelics Teaches Us about Consciousness, Dying, Addiction, Depression, and Transcendence* (New York: Penguin Press, 2018), 331–89.
17 "They constitute the material content of wealth, whatever its social form may be. In the form of society to be considered here they are also the material bearers [*Trager*] of … exchange-value." Karl Marx, *Capital: A Critique of Political Economy*, trans. Ben Fowkes (New York: Penguin, 1976), 126.

Extended Moments

1   Turbulent smoke has a fractal pattern. See K. Sreenivasan and C. Meneveau, "The Fractal Facets of Turbulence," *Journal of Fluid Mechanics* 173 (1986): 357–86. doi:10.1017/S0022112086001209.
2   "Evolution does but sunder, in order to develop them to the end, elements which, at their origin, interpenetrated each other." Henri Bergson, *Creative Evolution*, trans. Arthur Mitchell (New York: Henry Holt and Co., 1911), 175.
3   Keith Ansell-Pearson, "Bergson and Philosophy as a Way of Life," in *Interpreting Bergson: Critical Essays*, ed. Alexandre Lefebvre and Nils F. Schott (Cambridge: Cambridge University Press, 2019), 121–38.

4   See Thomas Nail, *Lucretius I* and Thomas Nail, *Lucretius II*. The subject of what is now called quantum entanglement was only just beginning to be theorized in physics when Woolf wrote *Orlando* in 1928, but as a close reader of Lucretius, the basic idea had already been formulated long ago.
5   Alt, *Virginia Woolf and the Study of Nature*.
6   Mark McMenamin and Dianna McMenamin, *Hypersea: Life on Land*.
7   See Gernot Böhme, "Atmosphere as the Fundamental Concept of a New Aesthetics," *Thesis Eleven* 36, no. 1 (August 1993): 113–26 and Mădălina Diaconu, "Patina—Atmosphere—Aroma: Towards an Aesthetics of Fine Differences," in *Logos of Phenomenology and Phenomenology of the Logos. Book Five: The Creative Logos: Aesthetic Ciphering in Fine Arts, Literature and Aesthetics*, ed. Anna-Teresa Tymieniecka (Dordrecht, Netherlands: Springer, 2006), 131–48.
8   Frederic Nietzsche, *The Will to Power*, trans. Walter Kaufmann (New York: Vintage, 1968), 358–9.
9   For interesting neuro-scientific theory of how this might work see Robin L. Carhart-Harris, "The Entropic Brain—Revisited," *Neuropharmacology* 142 (2018): 167–78.
10 Judith Mackrell, *Bloomsbury Ballerina: Lydia Lopokova, Imperial Dancer and Mrs John Maynard Keynes* (London: Phoenix, 2008).
11 Richard Doyle, *Darwin's Pharmacy: Sex, Plants, and the Evolution of the Noösphere* (Seattle, WA: University of Washington Press, 2011).
12 Y. F. Xu, H. Matsuoka, and D. A. Sun, "Fractal Model for Grain-Size Distribution of Soils," in *Powder and Grains*, ed. Y. Kishino (Milton: Taylor & Francis Group, 2001), 3–6.
13 See Toril Moi, *Sexual/Textual Politics: Feminist Literary Theory* (London and New York: Routledge, 2002) and Derek Ryan, *Virginia Woolf and the Materiality of Theory: Sex, Animal, Life*.
14 See Friedrich Nietzsche and Walter A. Kaufmann, *On the Genealogy of Morals*. (New York: Vintage Books, 2011), 15.

Collective Moments

1   Lucretius, *De Rerum Natura*, Book 1, Line 919.
2   Anne Baring and Jules Cashford, *The Myth of the Goddess: Evolution of an Image* (London: Penguin, 1991). See also Thomas Nail, *Lucretius I*, chapter 10.
3   See Karl Kerenyi, *Dionysos: Archetypal Image of Indestructible Life* (Princeton, NJ: Princeton University Press, 1996) and Carl A. P. Ruck, *Sacred Mushrooms: Secrets of Eleusis* (Berkeley, CA: Ronin, 2016).
4   See Jane Bennett, *Vibrant Matter: A Political Ecology of Things* (Durham, NC: Duke University Press, 2010) and Derek Ryan, *Virginia Woolf and the Materiality of Theory: Sex, Animal, Life* (Edinburgh: Edinburgh University Press, 2013), 12–4, 106–7, 184–6.

Conclusion

1. David Nutt, "Psychedelic Drugs—A New Era in Psychiatry?" *Dialogues Clin Neurosci* 21, no. 2 (June 2019): 139–47.

2. See Margaret Atherton, ed., *Women Philosophers of the Early Modern Period* (Indianapolis, IN: Hackett Pub., 1994); Catherine Wilson, *Epicureanism at the Origins of Modernity* (Oxford: Oxford University Press, 2008); Emanuela Bianchi, *The Feminine Symptom: Aleatory Matter in the Aristotelian Cosmos* (New York: Fordham University Press, 2014), 232. For a full commentary, see Thomas Nail, *Lucretius I* and Thomas Nail, *Lucretius II*. Not everyone agrees about how to interpret Lucretius' description of women but elsewhere I have tried to show that he does not essentialize women to maternal wombs, fertility, or objects of male desire, but quite the opposite. For discussion, see Georgia S. Nugent, "'Mater' Matters: The Female in Lucretius' *De Rerum Natura*," *Colby Quarterly* 30, no. 3 (September 1994): 179–205. Nugent shows convincingly that while Lucretian matter certainly has positive, generative feminine qualities, the feminine is also associated in the poem with decay, stench, stifling romantic love, mortality, and void and is therefore thoroughly ambivalent: both celebrated *and* repudiated. See also Elizabeth Asmis, "Lucretius' Venus and Stoic Zeus," *Hermes* 110, no. 4 (1982): 458–70; and for positions seeking to reclaim Lucretius for feminism, see Don Fowler, "The Feminine Principle: Gender in the *De Rerum Natura*," *Lucretius on Atomic Motion: A Commentary on "De Rerum Natura", Book Two, Lines 1–332* (Oxford: Oxford University Press, 2002), 444–52; and Barbara Clayton, "Lucretius' Erotic Mother: Maternity as a Poetic Construct in *De Rerum Natura*," *Helios* 26, no. 1 (1999): 69–84. I thank Brooke Holmes for alerting me to these lively debates.

3. "The female is, as it were, a mutilated male" Aristotle, *The Works of Aristotle*, ed. W. D. Ross (Oxford: Clarendon Press, 1908–1931), *The Generation of Animals* 2.3.737a27–8.

4. See Thomas Nail, *Lucretius III: A History of Motion* (Edinburgh: Edinburgh University Press, 2022). See also Hildegard Von Bingen, *Hildegard Von Bingen's Mystical Visions*. Translated from Scivias by Bruce Hozeski (Santa Fe, NM: Bear & Company, 1995).

5. Nail, *Lucretius II*.

6. Bianchi, *Feminine Symptom*, 232.

7. Wilson, *Epicureanism at the Origins of Modernity*.

8. See Warren Chernaik, "My Masculine Part: Aphra Behn and the Androgynous Imagination," *Sexual Freedom in Restoration Literatures* (Cambridge: Cambridge University Press, 1995), 160–213. See also Sophie Tomlinson, "'A Woman's Reason': Aphra Behn Read Lucretius," *Intellectual History Review* 22, no. 3 (September 2012): 359; Elizabeth Potter, "Modeling the Gender Politics in Science," *Hypatia* 3, no. 1 (1988): 19–33; Atherton, ed., *Women Philosophers*; Mark Allison, "Utopian Socialism, Women's Emancipation, and the Origins of 'Middlemarch,'" *ELH* 78, no. 3 (Fall 2011): 715–39; George Eliot, *George Eliot's Middlemarch Notebooks: A Transcription*, eds. John Clark Pratt and Victor A. Neufeldt (Berkeley, CA: University of California Press, 1979), 41; and Emanuela Bianchi, "Matter," in

The Bloomsbury Handbook of 21st Century Feminist Theory, ed. Robin Truth Goodman (London: Bloomsbury Academic, 2019), 383–98.

9 Moira Gatens, "Feminist Methods in the History of Philosophy, or Escape from Coventry," in *The Routledge Companion to Feminist Philosophy*, ed. Ann Garry, Serene J. Khader, and Alison Stone (New York: Routledge, 2017), 13–22.

10 William Wordsworth, *The Poetical Works of William Wordsworth, Volume 10*, ed. William Angus Knight (Edinburgh: W. Paterson, 1889), 258.

11 On feminine fluid dynamics and masculine statics, see Luce Irigari, *This Sex Which Is Not One*, trans. Catherine Porter and Carolyn Burke (Ithaca, NY: Cornell University Press, 1985), 106–118.

12 Jane Marcus, "Britannia Rules *The Waves*," *Hearts of Darkness: White Women Write Race* (New Brunswick, NJ: Rutgers University Press, 1992), 59–85; and Kathy J. Phillips, *Virginia Woolf against Empire* (Knoxville, TN: University of Tennessee Press, 1994).

13 "The supersession of private property is therefore the complete emancipation of all human senses and attributes; but it is this emancipation precisely because these senses and attributes have become human, subjectively as well as objectively." Karl Marx, *Early Writings of Karl Marx*, trans. Rodney Livingstone and Gregor Benton (Harmondsworth: Penguin, 1992), 352.

14 Roger Fry, "Art and Socialism," *Vision and Design* (London: Chatto and Windus, 1921), 36.

15 Ruth Livesey, "Socialism in Bloomsbury: Virginia Woolf and the Political Aesthetics of the 1880s," *The Yearbook of English Studies* 37, no. 1 (2007): 126–44.

16 See Nail, *Lucretius II*.

17 Susan Stanford Friedman, "Wartime Cosmopolitanism: Cosmofeminism in Virginia Woolf's 'Three Guineas' and Marjane Satrapi's 'Persepolis,'" *Tulsa Studies in Women's Literature* 32, no. 1 (Spring 2013): 23–52.

18 "Jane Marcus's essay 'Britannia Rules The Waves' (1992) and Kathy J. Phillips's book Virginia Woolf Against Empire (1994) were critical broadsides pointing to the undeniable presence of a critique of Empire in Woolf's writing, and were highly significant interventions in Woolf studies." Helen Carr, "Virginia Woolf, Empire, and Race," in *The Cambridge Companion to Virginia Woolf*, ed. Susan Sellers (Cambridge: Cambridge University Press, 2010), 201.

19 For some wonderful introductory and survey works on Woolf's feminism, see Eileen Barrett and Patricia Cramer, eds., *Virginia Woolf: Lesbian Readings* (New York: New York University Press, 1997) and Jane Marcus, ed., *Virginia Woolf: A Feminist Slant* (Lincoln, NE: University of Nebraska Press, 1983).

20 See Anne E. Fernald, *Virginia Woolf: Feminism and the Reader* (Basingstoke: Palgrave Macmillan, 2007); Jane Marcus, *New Feminist Essays on Virginia Woolf* (Lincoln, NE: University of Nebraska Press, 1991); Leila B. Jamili and Ziba Roshanzamir, "Postmodern Feminism: Cultural Trauma in Construction of Female Identities in Virginia Woolf's *The Waves*," *Advances in Language and Literary Studies* 8, no. 4 (2017): 114–21; and Sam See, "The Comedy of Nature: Darwinian Feminism in Virginia Woolf's *Between the Acts*," *Modernism/Modernity* 17, no. 3 (2010): 639–67.

21 "As Catherine Driscoll notes, androgyny is an example of where 'for Woolf, as for Deleuze […] woman is an infinitive, a process or event, a speaking position perhaps but not an identity'." Catherine Driscoll, "The Woman in Process: Deleuze, Kristeva and Feminism," in *Deleuze and Feminist Theory*, ed. Ian Buchanan and Claire Colebrook (Edinburgh: Edinburgh University Press, 2000), 80. Quoted in Derek Ryan, *Virginia Woolf and the Materiality of Theory*, 72.

22 For feminist and political aspects of the moment of being, see Josephine Donovan,"Everyday Use and Moments of Being, 53–67.

Index

aesthetic(s)
   of chaos 133–5
   creativity 108, 239
   emotion 22, 34
   involuntarism 125–7
   materialism 39–40
   patterns 36, 39
   of saturation 98–9
   susceptibilities 34, 107–9
Alt, Christina 18
Aristotle 41, 237
art of life 186, 189
automatic art 127
autonomous sensory meridian response (ASMR) 73–4

Banfield, Ann 6, 250 n.3
Barad, Karen 16
Bateson, Gregory 127
Beauvoir, Simone de, *The Second Sex* 18
Beja, Morris 250 n.3
Bell, Clive 6
Benjamin, Walter 7
Bennett, Arnold 13, 22, 256 n.47
Bergson, Henri 6–7, 248 n.6
   Matter and Memory 128
Between the Acts (Woolf) 50, 58, 214, 246
   Miss La Trobe (fictional character) 61–2
Bianchi, Emanuela 238
The Birth of Venus (Botticelli) 165
Bond Street moment 91, 207–8, 213, 225
brief moments xi, 47–50, 63, 115, 149, 173
   Between the Acts 50, 58, 61–3
   Jacob's Room 50, 57–8
   Night and Day xi, 50, 54–7
   The Voyage Out xi, 47, 50–4

The Waves 136
The Years 50, 58–61
British imperialism 226–7
Brontë, Emily 18

Caramagno, Thomas, *The Flight of the Mind* 57–8, 248 n.7, 259 n.17
Christopher, Bollas, "Aesthetic Moment" 249 n.12
civilization 106–7, 155
Coleridge, Samuel 238
collective moments xi, 5, 48, 61, 205, 221
   discreteness and individuality of people 214–15, 219
   human consciousness (knot) 217–19
   "A Moment: Summer's Night" 207, 214–21, 232
   Mrs. Dalloway 207
      Bond Street moment 207–8, 212–13, 225
      nonempirical movement 209
      Septimus 210–11
   quicksilver, moments 219–21
   The Waves 62, 207, 213, 222–34
Conrad, Joseph, moments of vision 34, 258 nn.14–15
cotton wool, patterns xii, 1, 4, 9, 21, 23, 35–6, 47–8, 50, 63, 72, 110, 116, 118, 125, 127, 155–9, 174, 179, 208, 210, 216–17
   discrete people and things 139, 144, 156
   fractal entropy 104, 210
   hidden patterns 74, 144, 158, 160, 184, 197, 200
   of non-being 29, 235
culture and nature 15, 29, 57, 60, 154–5, 163

Index

Deleuze, Gilles xiii, 16
DeSalvo, Louise 4
desire, theory of 176–7
discordant harmonies 27, 96, 170–1
disharmony, theory of 171
Dostoevsky, Fyodor 27
Driscoll, Catherine 269 n.21

Eddington, Arthur 19
Einstein, Albert
   atomic theory 256 n.43
   theory of relativity 18
Eliot, T. S., "Fisher King" 176–7
emotions, theory of 109
Empedocles 228–9
empirical realism 20–2
English Downs 5
Epicurus 93, 237
epiphany tradition 33–6, 235
exceptional moments 1, 68, 241
extended moments xi, 47–9, 149, 173
   Orlando (see *Orlando* (Woolf))

Fabian Society 239
feminism 237, 241–3
   aleatory 238
   moments of being 241
   and philosophical poetry, material 237–8
   political-aesthetic-ontological 243
   postmodern 253 n.14
   women philosophers 238
fractal patterns 100, 104, 127–8, 164, 197, 199, 208, 223, 235, 263 n.22
Frank, A. O. 8
Fry, Roger 6, 40
   aesthetic anarchism 178
   "Art and Socialism" 239
   Omega Workshops Press 18
   theory of aesthetic emotion 22, 34

Garnett, David 21
Glastonbury, John 13

Hardy, Thomas 19
   "*Moments of Vision*" 34, 247 n.2
Harrison, Jane 34, 84, 230
Heidegger, Martin 3, 7

Heraclitus 104
Hoffman, Albert 257 n.5
Homer 33, 84
   Charybdis 232
   Illiad 257 n.4
Hopkins, Gerard Manley 119, 260 n.32
   inscape idea 37
human consciousness 20, 26, 95, 117, 129, 217–19, 244
humans and non-humans 15, 19, 147, 204
Hume, David 6, 121
Husserl, Edmund 7
Hussey, Mark, *The Singing of the Real World: The Philosophy of Virginia Woolf's Fiction* 20–1
Huxley, Aldous, reducing valve of consciousness 35, 128

individual moments xi, 47–8, 63, 65, 147, 149, 168, 173
   To the Lighthouse 65, 115–35
   Mrs. Dalloway 65–114 (see also *Mrs. Dalloway* (Woolf))
   Orlando 65, 67, 76, 145, 147
   The Waves 65, 136–47
intellectual and creative freedom 239
interrelation xii, 2, 10, 13, 25, 43, 47–8, 63, 65, 147, 173
   humans and natural world 17, 57
   and indeterminacy 210, 243
   kinetic xiii, 2, 48
   life and death 3, 55
   material 20, 22–3, 49, 57, 60, 74
   movement and stability 4, 51
   senses (synesthesia) 3, 50, 74
   subject and object 3
   textual 49
   time and space 5, 52–3, 63
irrational moment of being 215

Jeans, James 19
Jensen, Meg 4
Jodorowsky, Alejandro xiv–xv
Joyce, James, *Finnegans Wake* 37

kinesthesia 111
kinetic interrelation xiii, 2, 48

kinetic patterns 4, 25, 36–7, 43, 91, 101, 103, 105, 139
  aesthetic materialism 39–40
  material 39, 55, 91, 244
  plot and 40–2
  susceptibility 40
  words as processes 42–3
kinetic realism 20–2, 139

Lackey, Michael 7
literary techniques 48–9
Lucretius 16–17, 21, 37, 51, 80–2, 84, 87, 95, 121, 133, 144, 150, 176, 217–19, 254 n.27, 256 n.43
  Bacchanalian wandering movement 258 n.11
  De Rerum Natura/On The Nature of Things 14, 18, 34, 38, 93–4, 223–4, 228, 237–8, 257–8 nn.7–10, 260 n.26
  description of women 267 n.2
  dying material universe 103
  flows of matter 38, 151–2
  indeterminate process materialism 14–15
  materialist philosophy 119
  materialist theory of form 43
  simulacra 38, 223, 262 n.12
  theory of pores (*foramina*) 19

Mandelbrot, Benoit 37
Mansfield, Katherine 6, 18
Marcus, Jane, 'Britannia Rules The Waves' 268 n.18
Marx, Karl 16–17, 170
  1844 Manuscripts 239
material feminism and philosophical poetry 237–8
material interrelation 20, 22–3, 49, 57, 60, 74
materialism 13–15, 50, 238
  aesthetic 39–40
  passive and indeterminate 20
materialist theory of language 72, 217, 219
material unconscious xiii, 81, 113, 158–60, 178, 187, 192
McMenamin, Dianna 180

McMenamin, Mark 180
Merleau-Ponty, Maurice 7, 265 n.13
metaphysics 7
metastable patterns 4, 19–20, 26, 134, 235
metis 84, 117–18
metonymic realism 256 n.48
mirror-touch synesthesia 75
moment of extraordinary exaltation 82
moments of becoming xi, 1, 25, 28–33, 109, 124, 143, 156, 164, 176, 217, 227, 230, 243
moments of being ix–xi, xiii–xiv, 1–2, 4, 8–9, 22–3, 25, 43, 63, 68, 82, 88–9, 91, 94, 96–8, 103, 105, 111, 119, 123, 125, 128, 130, 135, 140, 147, 149, 157, 179, 197, 201, 205, 214, 219, 222, 224, 228–9, 231, 235, 243, 249 n.2. *See also specific moments*
  and art-making 124
  autobiographical 247 n.5
  cosmic naturalism 164–5
  critical function 236
  emotions 110
  ineffability 161, 188
  music 174
  opportunities 236
  real possibility 236
  singular 232–3
  state of consciousness 55, 76, 95, 99, 117, 123, 135, 141, 174–5, 226
moments of emergency 140
moments of nakedness 128–30
moments of non-being 29, 68, 235, 243
moments of vision 34–5, 62, 85, 108, 247 n.2, 258 nn.14–15
Moore, George Edward 7, 20, 27
  Principia Ethica 6
  realism 252 n.40, 255 n.39
Morris, Pam 21, 256 n.48
movement xii, 47, 153, 183
  beauty of 194–6
  and chaos, patterns 134
  philosophy of 17, 25, 32, 35–6, 43
  and stability 4, 51, 235

Index

Mrs. Dalloway (Woolf) xiv, 3, 47, 50, 58, 65, 105, 136, 142, 145, 179, 205, 245
  aesthetics of saturation 98–9
  aesthetic susceptibility 107–9
  atmosphere of affect 109–10
  beauty 93–5
  Bond Street moment 207–8, 212–13, 225
  civilization 106–7
  Clarissa Dalloway (fictional character) 28, 68–9, 78, 105–6, 108, 207
    haunting 113
    moment of philosophical clarity 112
    moment of susceptibility 111
    theory of knowledge 112
    time dilating 66–7
    transcendental materiality of the soul 112–14
    "unseen" and "unknown" 70–1
  death of soul 78
  Elizabeth (fictional character) 78–9
  Fraulein Daniels (fictional character) 68
  hydrology of time 104–5
  kinesthetic perception 110–11
  material unconscious 81
  "The Moment: Summer's Night" xi
  music 92–3, 102–4
  myriads of things 85–7
  nonempirical movement 209
  ordinary things 87–8, 91, 94
  Peter Walsh (fictional character) 3, 78–81, 87–9, 94–7, 105–8
  process epistemology 111–12
  Richard Dalloway (fictional character) 70
  Septimus' moment 28, 32–4, 72–3, 88, 210–11, 236
    ASMR experience 73–4
    earth thrilled beneath him 91–2
    material interrelation 73–4
    mirror-touch synesthesia 75
    Regent's Park 89, 97
    religious experiences 76–7
    sonic pareidolia 76
    veil of fibers 90–1
  solitary traveler 82–3, 86
  supreme flavour to existence 97–8
  time split 89–90
  visions 83–5

Muraresku, Brian C. 257 n.5
mystical religious experiences 161

natural mysticism 34
nature/naturalism 15, 17–20, 120, 157
  culture and 15, 29, 57, 60, 154–5, 163
  divine goodness 155–6
  as fluid process 25–8, 43
  hora and 165
  humans and 166–9, 214
  immanent divinity of 177
  of knowledge 112
  material processes 14
  Möbius strip 166
  radical 84, 88
  of reality x, 9, 26, 32, 49, 66, 68, 176, 235
  of temporality 215
  truth 89, 156
new materialism 8, 13, 17, 252 nn.40–1
  in Western tradition 15–16
Nietzsche, Friedrich 7, 103, 178
Night and Day (Woolf) 50, 246
  Katharine Hilbery (fictional character) 56–8, 66
  Mary Datchet (fictional character) 54–6, 58, 61, 66
  Ralph (fictional character) 57
non-anthropocentric philosophical realism 15–16
non-human moments xi, 5, 47, 115, 147, 168, 173
To the Lighthouse 149–72

Odysseus 180
  Penelope 84, 118
Orlando (Woolf) xi, 19, 47, 50, 67, 76, 145, 147, 172, 246, 266 n.4
  amplification of senses 182–3
  beauty of movement 194–6
  branching fractal patterns 197–200
  consciousness and unconsciousness 180–1, 189–90
  desire and happiness 177–8
  ecological self 193
  gender and sexuality 204
  immanent perception 200–1
  life in motion 183–4

material transcendental field 188–90
memory 202
moment of becoming 180
natural desire 175–6
nature's bride 197, 203–5
"Oak Tree" 192, 202–3, 205
philosophical biography 186–8
sensuous movement 185–6
topological self 190–3
waves of thought 173–5
whole of nature 178–9

Pater, Clara 39–40
Pater, Walter 39
   aesthetic susceptibilities 34
   The Renaissance 70
performative knowledge 123
Phillips, Kathy J., *Virginia Woolf Against Empire* 268 n.18
philosophical amplification xiv
philosophical concept 48–9
philosophical realism 187, 225
philosophy xi–xv, 13, 23, 167, 218, 243
   of irrational feeling 8
   of movement 17, 25, 32, 35–6, 43
   philosophical influences 6
   poetry and 237–8
   reality behind appearances 210
   rejecting Woolf as philosopher 7, 9
   of saturation at work 195
   states of heightened perceptive intensity 252 n.41
   of subjectivity 187, 189, 228
   work alongside or among philosophers 6–7
philosophy of time 152, 168, 182, 211
   materialist 150, 186
pink noise patterns 100
Plato 79, 178
poikilos 37
political moments
   directions for future work 243–4
   feminism 237, 241–3
   limitations 243
   material feminism and philosophical poetry 237–8
   socialism 237, 239–41
political philosophy 237, 239, 241

Pollan, Michael 265 n.16
Pridmore-Brown, Michelle 3
processes of interrelated movement. *See* interrelation
process materialism. *See* materialism
process-nature of knowledge xiii

Rachel Vinrace (fictional character, *The Voyage Out*) 3, 14–15, 50–4, 58, 63
realism (reality) 6, 20, 94, 99, 119, 144, 154–5, 179, 186, 190, 252 n.40, 255 n.39, 256 n.48
   empirical and kinetic 20–2, 91, 139
   as möbius strip 163
   non-anthropocentric philosophical 15–16
   objective nature of 235
   philosophical vision of 225
   reality of nature x, 9, 26, 32, 49, 66, 68, 176, 235
   saturated 130
   theory of desire and 176
   through sensation 20
   undulating 127–8
Richter, Harvena 248 n.6
Roe, Susan 41
Russell, Bertrand 6, 20, 27
Rutherford, Ernest 19
Ryan, Derek 14, 16

saturation, aesthetics of 98–9
   literary method of 99
sex and sexuality 204, 242
shock-receiving capacity 29, 108
Shukla, Rohini 7, 252 n.41, 255 n.39
Simone, Emma 3, 5
socialism 237, 239–41
Steinberg, Erwin 7
Ŝtelf, Martin 252 n.41
Stephen, Leslie 7, 18
symbolism 203, 256 n.48
sympathetic resonance 142–3
synesthesia of associations 218

Telphusa 101
textual interrelation 49
Thoby 154

"Time Passes" moment (*To the Lighthouse,* Woolf) 47, 149, 172–3
  autumn 152–5
  certain airs 151–2
  hora of nature 165
  indeterminacy 150, 152
  life and death 162–4
  nature 157
  seasonal change 154
  spring and summer 162–7
  time, darkness, and water 150–1
  winter 155–61
  years
    birth and death of form 168–70
    pedesis of nature 167–8
    rebirth 171–2
time, theory of 81, 104, 152, 182, 185
Tipper, Becky 3
To the Lighthouse (Woolf) xi, 7, 19, 28, 40–1, 43, 47, 50, 58, 75, 136, 147, 172, 245. *See also* "Time Passes" moment (*To the Lighthouse,* Woolf)
  aesthetic involuntarism 125–7
  aesthetics of chaos 133–5
  Augustus Carmichael (fictional character) 117, 131, 135
  currents of sensation 130–2
  ecological imagination 124–5
  ecological self 120–1
  fluidity of life 124–35
  Lily Briscoe (fictional character) 28, 62, 123–7, 140, 172, 241–2
    moment of becoming 124, 129
    moments of being 128, 130, 132–3, 135
    work of art 130–2, 134
  moment of one's own 115–16
  moments of nakedness 128–30
  Ramsey (fictional character) 7, 115, 120, 130, 150, 152, 157–8, 240
    transcendence 119
    waves of pure delight 121–3
    weaving self 116–18
  undulating realism 127–8
  work of art and meaning of life 132–3
Toth, Naomi 3, 250 n.3

universal knowledge 146
Urquhart, Nicole L. 62

Valéry, Paul 1, 13
Varga, Adriana 4

The Waves (Woolf) xi, 26, 37, 40–1, 48, 50, 62, 130, 136, 179, 205, 222, 245
  Bernard (fictional character) xiv, 28, 30, 136–7, 225–6, 256 n.49
    individuality 138–9
    majestic animality 137
    mystical experience 144
    pavements 140–1
    philosophical abstractions 140
    totality of the world 142
    vision of India 226
  community of desire 137–8
  general impulse 139–40
  Jinny (fictional character) 223–4, 232
  Louis (fictional character) 225, 227–8, 230–2
  Neville (fictional character) 32, 224, 229, 233
  Percival (fictional character) 21, 222, 226–7, 232, 234
  Rhoda (fictional character) 32, 222–3, 227, 230, 233
  sounds and patterns 141–4
  sunless territory of non-identity 144–5
  Susan (fictional character) 228–9, 231
  sympathetic resonance 143
  unknown quantities 146–7
  whirlpool of moment 230–1
Webb, Mary 18
Wells, Herbert George 13
Westling, Louise 5
Whitehead, Alfred North 6, 27
Wiener, Norbert 25
Woolf, Leonard 18, 118
Woolf, Virginia ix–xi, xv, 1, 3, 17–18, 50, 56, 81–2, 95, 229, 235, 243, 258 n.14. *See also* works of Woolf
  androgyny 204, 269 n.21
  car's movement in fluid dynamic 211

fluid dynamic ontology 170
material unconscious 81, 113, 158–60, 178
onto-epistemology 133, 161, 166
walker's thoughts 71
Wordsworth, William 238
works of art 1, 8–9, 17, 36–7, 49, 60, 95, 99, 123, 127, 130, 132, 134, 141, 176, 195
   and meaning of life 132–3
   moth wing patterns 179
   and natural desire 179
works of Woolf
   Between the Acts 50, 58, 61–3, 214, 246
   Jacob's Room 50, 57–8
   To the Lighthouse (see *To the Lighthouse* (Woolf))
   "Modern Fiction" 13–14, 37, 39
   Moments of Becoming xi, 28–33
   Moments of Being 2, 4, 6, 249 n.12
   "The Moment: Summer's Night" xi, 48, 207, 214–21
   The Moths 179
   Mrs. Dalloway (see *Mrs. Dalloway* (Woolf))
   Night and Day xi, 50, 54–8, 61, 66, 246
   Orlando (see *Orlando* (Woolf))
   A Passionate Apprentice 92
   A Room of One's Own 116, 236
   "A Sketch of the Past" 2, 39, 125
   Three Guineas 240
   The Voyage Out xi, 3, 14, 47, 50–4, 246
   The Waves (see *The Waves* (Woolf))
   The Years (see *The Years* (Woolf))

The Years (Woolf) 19, 50, 217, 246
   Colonel Abel Pargiter (fictional character) 58
   Eleanor Pargiter (fictional character) 58, 60
   Kitty Malone (fictional character) 60
   Peggy (fictional character) 61
   Sally (fictional character) 58–60, 83
   Sir Digby Pargiter (fictional character) 58